Britain and Ireland, 900–1300

Insular Responses to Medieval European Change

There is a growing interest in the history of relations between the English, Scottish, Welsh and Irish as the United Kingdom and Ireland begin to construct new political arrangements and become more fully integrated into Europe. This book brings together the newest work on how these relations developed between 900 and 1300, a period crucial for the history of the formation of national identities.

The conquest of England by the Normans and the subsequent growth of English power required the inhabitants of Britain and Ireland to reassess their dealings with each other in the face of self-confident and expansionist francophone culture. Old ties were broken and new ones formed. Economic change, the influence of chivalry, the transmission of literary motifs and questions of aristocratic identity are among the topics tackled here by leading scholars from Britain, Ireland and North America. Little has been published hitherto on this subject, and the book marks a major contribution to a topic of lasting interest.

BRENDAN SMITH is Lecturer in History, University of Bristol. His publications include *Colonisation and Conquest in Medieval Ireland: The English in Louth, 1170–1330* (1999).

Britain and Ireland 900–1300

Insular Responses to Medieval European Change

Edited by
Brendan Smith

PUBLISHED BY THE PRESS SYNDICATE OF THE UNIVERSITY OF CAMBRIDGE
The Pitt Building, Trumpington Street, Cambridge CB2 1RP, United Kingdom

CAMBRIDGE UNIVERSITY PRESS
The Edinburgh Building, Cambridge, CB2 2RU, UK http://www.cup.cam.ac.uk
40 West 20th Street, New York, NY 10011–4211, USA http://www.cup.org
10 Stamford Road, Oakleigh, Melbourne 3166, Australia

© Cambridge University Press 1999

This book is in copyright. Subject to statutory exception and to the provisions of relevant collective licensing agreements, no reproduction of any part may take place without the written permission of Cambridge University Press

First published 1999

Printed in the United Kingdom at the University Press, Cambridge

Typeset in Plantin 10/12 pt   [CE]

A catalogue record for this book is available from the British Library

Library of Congress cataloguing in publication data

Britain and Ireland, 900–1300: insular responses to medieval European change / edited by Brendan Smith.
  p. cm.
Includes bibliographical references and index.
ISBN 0 521 57319 X
1. Great Britain – Civilization – 1066–1485.
2. Great Britain – Civilization – European influences.
3. Ireland – Civilization – European influences.
4. Great Britain – Civilization – To 1066.
5. Culture diffusion – History – To 1500.
6. Social change – History – To 1500.
7. Civilization, Medieval.   I. Smith, Brendan, 1963–
DA185.B75   1999
941 – dc21 98–42845 CIP

ISBN 0 521 57319 X hardback

Contents

Contributors	*page*	vii
Preface		ix
List of abbreviations		xii

1 The effect of Scandinavian raiders on the English and Irish churches: a preliminary reassessment   1
ALFRED P. SMYTH

2 The changing economy of the Irish Sea province   39
BENJAMIN T. HUDSON

3 Cults of Irish, Scottish and Welsh saints in twelfth-century England   67
ROBERT BARTLETT

4 Sea-divided Gaels? Constructing relationships between Irish and Scots *c.* 800–1169   87
MÁIRE HERBERT

5 The 1169 invasion as a turning-point in Irish–Welsh relations   98
SEÁN DUFFY

6 Killing and mutilating political enemies in the British Isles from the late twelfth to the early fourteenth century: a comparative study   114
JOHN GILLINGHAM

7 Anglo-French acculturation and the Irish element in Scottish identity   135
DAUVIT BROUN

8 John de Courcy, the first Ulster plantation and Irish church men   154
MARIE THERESE FLANAGAN

9 Coming in from the margins: the descendants of Somerled
   and cultural accommodation in the Hebrides, 1164–1317   179
   R. ANDREW McDONALD

10 Nobility and identity in medieval Britain and Ireland: The
   de Vescy family, c. 1120–1314   199
   KEITH J. STRINGER

Bibliography   240
Index   264

Contributors

ROBERT BARTLETT is Professor of Medieval History at the University of St Andrews

DAUVIT BROUN is Lecturer in Scottish History at the University of Glasgow

SEÁN DUFFY is Lecturer in Medieval History at Trinity College Dublin

MARIE THERESE FLANAGAN is Senior Lecturer in Modern History at The Queen's University of Belfast

JOHN GILLINGHAM is Professor of History at the London School of Economics

MÁIRE HERBERT is Associate Professor in the Department of Early and Medieval Irish, University College Cork

BENJAMIN T. HUDSON is Associate Professor of History at the Pennsylvania State University

R. ANDREW McDONALD is Assistant Professor in Medieval British and World History at the University of Alberta at Edmonton

BRENDAN SMITH is Lecturer in Medieval History at the University of Bristol

ALFRED P. SMYTH is Professor of Medieval History and Master of Keynes College at the University of Kent, and Warden of St George's House, Windsor Castle.

KEITH J. STRINGER is Reader in Medieval British History at the University of Lancaster

Preface

> ... it is well to remember that the unity of our civilisation does not rest entirely on the secular culture and the material progress of the last four centuries. There are deeper traditions in Europe than these, and we must go back behind Humanism and behind the superficial triumphs of modern civilisation, if we wish to discover the fundamental social and spiritual forces that have gone to the making of Europe.
> (Christopher Dawson, *The Making of Europe: An Introduction to the History of European Unity 400-1000 A.D.* (London, 1932))

Asked to identify the fundamental forces which made Europe in the centuries between 900 and 1300 most historians would mention population expansion and urban growth; the dominance of French aristocratic culture and the chivalric code it spawned; the renewal of religious fervour which found expression in the rise of papal power, the spread of new religious orders, and the crusading movement; the appearance of new institutions such as universities and representative assemblies; and an increased sense of national identity among some of Europe's peoples. Britain and Ireland constitute a particularly interesting region in which to examine these developments, since here was to be found a remarkable variety of reactions to European change.

In mainland Europe the tenth century saw the end of the era of defeat at the hands of Slav, Magyar and Arab attackers from the east and south, but Britain and Ireland remained at the mercy of enemies from the north. The depredations of the pagan Vikings disrupted older patterns of communication within the British Isles, and between the British Isles and the mainland, but also served to strengthen the shared Christian identity of those who endured and survived. The commercial element in Viking involvement also resulted in the creation of new trading links in the region and encouraged its rise to unprecedented levels of economic prosperity in the eleventh and twelfth centuries. Furthermore, the continued involvement of Christianized Scandinavian rulers in the Irish Sea zone to the end of the thirteenth century shaped the politics of the region in decisive ways. It is easy to overlook the extent to which the character of Norman conquest in England, and the subsequent expansion of Norman-English power throughout the British Isles, was conditioned by this sustained Scandinavian influence.

Norman-English culture was born in military conquest and thrived because of the willingness of victor and vanquished thereafter to compromise and adapt. It is not surprising that in its dealings with its neighbours in Britain and Ireland this culture demonstrated both the violent intolerance and the deep respect of which it was itself a product. The cults of Celtic saints could be vigorously promoted in England at the same time as the Christian aristocracies of Wales and Ireland were treated with the barbarity reserved for those excluded from the ranks of the chivalric. English control of the southern reaches of the Irish Sea from the 1170s quickly eliminated previous types of contact between Wales and Ireland, but further north the situation was more complex. The history of the Isle of Man, ruled at different times in the three centuries after 1000 not only by its own kings but also by kings of Ireland, Norway, Scotland and England, encapsulates the tumultuous nature of politics in this area. The career of John de Courcy at the end of the twelfth century, with its northern English, Scottish, Manx and Ulster dimensions addresses many of the same themes and brings into focus the central importance of the shared religious identity of all those concerned in the politics of this region.

It was Scotland which benefited most from the fast-changing conditions of the north Irish Sea zone. In seeking to fulfil their ambitions to join the Anglo-French culture-club while retaining political independence from England, the kings of Scotland found it useful to draw upon their country's historical associations with Ireland. The incorporation of the Norse-Gaelic dynasties of the Western Isles into the mainstream of Scottish political life in the course of the thirteenth century was greatly facilitated by this acknowledgement of the Irish element of the country's identity. Scotland's resilience in turn provided opportunities for aristocratic English Border families such as the de Vescys to pursue regional ambitions in the North which at times threatened the stability of England as a whole. The fortunes of the de Vescys were eclipsed in the reign of Edward I, and his reign saw the dismantling of many other features of the history of the British Isles constructed in the previous four centuries.

In approaching the medieval history of Britain and Ireland in a way which transcends traditional boundaries of chronology, geography and historiography, this collection has been inspired by a number of volumes which have appeared in the last fifteen years. *The English in Medieval Ireland,* ed J. F. Lydon (Dublin, 1984) contained the proceedings of the first joint meeting of the British Academy and the Royal Irish Academy, held in Dublin in 1982. Not the least significant feature of this volume lay in the fact that it brought together in print for the first time the two historians who were subsequently to do most to encourage new ways of thinking about the medieval history of Britain and Ireland: Rees Davies and Robin Frame. Lydon's volume was followed by *The British Isles 1100-1500: Comparisons, Contrasts and Connections*, ed. R. R. Davies (Edinburgh, 1988). This resulted from a conference held at Gregynog in 1986 and was crucial in widening the focus of discussion to include Wales and Scotland as well as Ireland and England. It also served to prepare the way for two single-author volumes of utmost importance, both published in 1990. R. R. Davies', *Domination and Conquest: The Experience of Ireland, Scotland and Wales 1100-1300* (Cambridge, 1990) contained his Wiles lectures, delivered at The Queen's University of Belfast in 1988, while Robin Frame's, *The Political Development of the British Isles 1100-1400* (Oxford, 1990) provided, at last, a general survey on which undergraduate teaching of medieval 'British Isles history' could be based.

This volume also originated in a conference, held at the University of Bristol in September 1996, and it is a pleasure to thank the various bodies and individuals whose support made this project possible. Within Bristol University, the Centre for Medieval Studies, the Arts Faculty Research Fund and the Alumni Foundation all gave generous financial support, while outside funding was also gratefully received from the Economic History Society, the Royal Historical Society, and the Royal Irish Academy. The advice of Professor Bernard Alford and Dr Kieran Flanagan in arranging the conference is gratefully acknowledged, as are the efforts of the Warden of Clifton Hill House, Mrs Annie Burnside, and her staff. Finally, it remains to express my sincere thanks for their assistance to Professor James Lydon, Professor Rees Davies, and Professor Robin Frame.

Brendan Smith

Abbreviations

AC	*Annála Connacht, The Annals of Connacht (A.D. 1224–1544)*, ed. A. Martin Freeman (Dublin, 1944)
Acta Sanctorum	*Acta Sanctorum Quotquot Toto Orbe Coluntur*, ed. J. Bolland *et al.* (Antwerp, Tongerloo, Paris, Brussels, 1643–in progress)
AFM	*Annála Ríoghachta Éireann; Annals of the Kingdom of Ireland by the Four Masters from the Earliest Period to the Year 1616*, ed. and trans. J. O' Donovan, 7 vols. (Dublin, 1851, reprint, New York, 1966)
AI	*The Annals of Inisfallen (MS Rawlinson B 503)*, ed. and trans. S. Mac Airt (Dublin, 1951, reprint 1977)
ALC	*The Annals of Loch Cé: A Chronicle of Irish Affairs, 1014–1690*, ed. W. M. Hennessy, 2 vols. (RS, London, 1871)
Anderson, *Early Sources*	*Early Sources of Scottish History 500–1286*, ed. A. O. Anderson, 2 vols. (Edinburgh, 1922; reprint Stamford, 1990)
AT	'The Annals of Tigernach', ed. W. Stokes in *Revue Celtique* 16–18 (1895–7); (reprinted in 2 vols., Felinfach, 1993)
AU	*The Annals of Ulster (to AD 1131* ed. S. Mac Airt and G. Mac Niocaill (Dublin, 1983). *Annála Uladh: Annals of Ulster*, ed. W. M. Hennessy and B. MacCarthy, 4 vols. (Dublin, 1887–1901) [Unless otherwise stated, references to entries in *AU* dating from before 1132 are to the Mac Airt and Mac Niocaill edition.]

BBCS	*Bulletin of the Board of Celtic Studies*
Bk Leinster	*The Book of Leinster, Formerly Lebar na Núachongbála*, ed. R. I. Best, O. Bergin, M. A. O'Brien and A. O'Sullivan, 6 vols. (Dublin, 1954–83)
BL	British Library
Brut	*Brut y Tywysogyon or the Chronicle of the Princes. Peniarth MS. 20 Version*, ed. and trans. T. Jones (Cardiff, 1952)
Brut (RHB)	*Brut y Tywysogyon or the Chronicle of the Princes. Red Book of Hergest Version*, ed. and trans. T. Jones (Cardiff, 1955)
Cal. Doc. Ire.	*Calendar of Documents Relating to Ireland*, ed. H. S. Sweetman, 5 vols. (London, 1875–86)
Cal. Papal Letters	*Calendar of Entries in the Papal Registers Relating to Great Britain and Ireland: Papal Letters* (London, 1893–)
CCR	*Calendar of the Close Rolls* (London, 1900–)
CDS	*Calendar of Documents Relating to Scotland*, ed. J. Bain et al., 5 vols. (Edinburgh, 1881–1986)
CGH	*Corpus Genealogiarum Hiberniae*, ed. M. A. O'Brien (Dublin, 1962, reprinted 1976)
CGS	Johannis de Fordun, *Chronica Gentis Scotorum*, ed. W. F. Skene, Historians of Scotland, vol. i (Edinburgh, 1871)
Cl. R.	*Close Rolls of the Reign of Henry III*, 14 vols. (London, 1902–38)
CPR	*Calendar of Patent Rolls* (London, 1906–)
CS	*Chronicon Scotorum*, ed. W. M. Hennessy (RS, London, 1866)
Econ. Hist. Rev.	*Economic History Review* (London, 1927–)
EETS	Early English Text Society
EHD	*English Historical Documents*
EHR	*English Historical Review* (London, 1886–)
EYC	*Early Yorkshire Charters*, ed. W. Farrer (vols. i–iii: Edinburgh, 1914–16) and C. T. Clay (vols. iv–xii: Yorkshire Archaeological Society, Record Series, extra series, 1935–65)
Foedera	*Foedera, Conventiones, Litterae et Cuiuscunque Generis Acta Publica*, ed. T. Rymer, 4 vols. in 7 parts (London, 1816–69)

Giraldus Cambrensis, Opera	*Giraldus Cambrensis, Opera*, ed. J. S. Brewer, J. F. Dimock and G. F. Warner, 8 vols., RS (London 1861–91)
Giraldus, *Expugnatio*	Giraldus Cambrensis, *Expugnatio Hibernica: The Conquest of Ireland*, ed. A. B. Scott and F. X. Martin (Dublin, 1978)
Giraldus, *Topographia*	Giraldus Cambrensis, *The History and Topography of Ireland*, ed. J. J. O'Meara (Mountrath and Harmondsworth, 1982)
Hist. & Mun. Doc. Ire.	*Historic and Municipal Documents of Ireland, 1172–1320*, ed. J. T. Gilbert, RS (London, 1870)
IHS	*Irish Historical Studies: The Joint Journal of the Irish Historical Society and the Ulster Society for Irish Historical Studies* (Dublin, 1938–)
ITS	Irish Texts Society
MGH	*Monumenta Germaniae Historica*
Misc. Ir. Annals	*Miscellaneous Irish Annals (AD 1114–1437)*, ed. S. Ó hInnse (Dublin, 1947)
MPL	*Patrologiae Cursus Completus. Series Latina*, ed. J. P. Migne (Paris, 1841–64)
NHI	*A New History of Ireland, under the auspices of the Royal Irish Academy*, 9 vols. (Oxford, 1976–)
NUI	National Universtiy of Ireland
PRO	Public Record Office, London
PRS	Pipe Roll Society, 38 vols. (1884–1925), new series, 41 vols. (1925–67)
RIA Proc.	*Royal Irish Academy Proceedings*
RLC	*Rotuli Litterarum Clausarum in Turri Londinensi Asservati*, ed. T. D. Hardy, 2 vols. (London, 1833–4)
RRS	*Regestra Regum Scottorum*, ed. G. W. S. Barrow et al. (Edinburgh, 1960–)
RS	Rolls Series
RSAI Jn	*Journal of the Royal Society of Antiquaries of Ireland* (Dublin, 1892–)
s.a.	*sub anno / sub annis*
Scotichronicon	*Scotichronicon by Walter Bower in Latin and English*, gen. ed. D. E. R. Watt, 9 vols. (Aberdeen/Edinburgh, 1987–98)
SHR	*Scottish Historical Review*

STS	Scottish Text Society
Song of Dermot	*The Song of Dermot and the Earl*, ed. G. H. Orpen (Dublin, 1892)
TRHS	*Transactions of the Royal Historical Society*
ZCP	*Zeitschrift für celtische Philologie* (Halle, 1896–1943, 23 vols.; Tubingen, 1953–)

1 The effect of Scandinavian raiders on the English and Irish churches: a preliminary reassessment

Alfred P. Smyth

Assessments of the effects of Scandinavian raiders in the ninth and tenth centuries have focused for over three decades on an agenda set by revisionist historians – an agenda which has obscured and sometimes trivialized many of the complex issues involved in an analysis of annalistic and other records. An over-zealous approach, driven by a desire to show that Scandinavian raiders were not numerous and that they were no more destructive to church property and personnel than were the native Christian opposition, has too often led to conclusions which fly in the face of historical evidence and common sense. Revisionists must also take responsibility for polarizing historical arguments in relation to the destructive power of the Northmen. In their zeal to promote an image of Scandinavian raiders as yet one more political, cultural and religious grouping in Western Europe – little different from their Christian neighbours in most respects – they either minimized evidence which did not fit their preconceptions or else they distracted historians' attention away from those negative effects which Vikings wrought on Western society, to concentrate on the economic and material benefits which later Scandinavian colonists supposedly brought to a conquered people. At best, the books in 'Viking' studies fail to balance: at worst they are intellectually cooked.

The self-congratulatory mood of post-revisionists in medieval Irish studies gives cause for concern, not least because of serious shortcomings in the intellectual debate.[1] There is little disagreement over the fact that in all parts of the Christian West, indigenous violent elements existed long before Northmen arrived in the ninth century, and I have long ago shown how several aspects of Norse kingship and warrior cults

---

[1] See P. Holm, 'Between apathy and antipathy: the Vikings in Irish and Scandinavian history', *Peritia*, 8 (1994), p. 168, for an uncritical and embarrassing appraisal of an Irish historian who in that writer's opinion had 'introduced the essential historical methodology of source criticism (*sic*) in this and later valuable revisionist work'.

appealed to elements within the native Christian aristocracies.² This rapport between warriors led, in turn, to military alliances and intermarriage from the earliest stages of the Norse invasions. It is also possible to contrast the hostility which the churches in Wessex and Ireland showed against the Northmen, with the very definite evidence for cooperation between the churches of York and Chester-le-Street (Lindisfarne) with Danish rulers in Northumbria. Different political circumstances dictated different approaches, but whenever a native Christian aristocracy survived to resist Scandinavian attack, the church invariably backed its own kings – even to the point of Frankish, West Saxon and Irish churchmen personally going into battle against the pagans. In Northumbria, on the other hand, where native Anglian Christian kings had been annihilated by the Northmen, the archbishops of York were left with no choice but to do business with the invaders, just as Christian bishops in Francia had been forced to come to terms with earlier Germanic barbarians in the fifth century.³ As for the intermonastic violence for which there is definite evidence in Ireland prior to the Viking age, this is a subject which has not been properly evaluated by historians on any side of the debate. By the eighth century some Irish monasteries had not only become very rich, but they had also grown to fill a vacuum in Irish economic and social life – a life which had hitherto been exclusively agrarian. The monks had inadvertently triggered the growth of monastic townships from the seventh century onwards, thereby giving monasticism a monopoly on urban development – with all the economic and political advantages that implied. Monasteries had attracted communities of craftsmen, agrarian tenants and serfs, and of course, merchants. This must have created a conflict of interest *vis-à-vis* the warrior aristocracy, which unlike their counterparts in England, for instance, had no coinage to control and no traditional rights over markets in these novel and burgeoning monastic townships. When, therefore, we read of battles between Irish monasteries and of Irish kings attacking monasteries, it would be naïve to conclude that professed monks or ordained clergy had begun to slay each other out of personal spite. However unedifying such violent engagements may have been, they were unquestionably the result of dynastic rivalry and economic tension at a *secular* level within the church and in society at large. The situation was unquestionably aggravated by the fact that senior church

---

² A. P. Smyth, *Scandinavian Kings in the British Isles 850–880* (Oxford, 1977), pp. 128–33, 149–53; Smyth, *Scandinavian York and Dublin: the History and Archaeology of Two Related Viking Kingdoms*, 2 vols. (repr., Dublin, 1987), i, pp. 49–53.
³ Smyth, *Scandinavian York and Dublin*, i, pp. 41–6; ii, pp. 91–4; J. M. Wallace-Hadrill, *Early Germanic Kingship in England and on the Continent* (Oxford, 1971), pp. 18–20.

offices within monastic 'cities' or *civitates* had become hereditary and were no doubt largely controlled by the lay aristocracy.[4] We are reminded of Carolingian and later Capetian control of certain key monasteries in Francia. But none of this evidence can be used to suggest that *all* monks had become corrupt politicians or that all monks had abandoned their celibacy. The rise of the Céli Dé movement of monastic reformers and ascetics had already established itself in the Irish midlands prior to the Scandinavian onslaught, which clearly shows that however decadent monastic culture had become, there was an influential element within monasticism which still strove after the ideals of the Desert. Iona is a good example of a most powerful and wealthy monastery whose leaders, although drawn from the leading Uí Néill dynasty, maintained their celibacy and high spiritual standards right up to the time of Norse inroads, and Iona was also a centre which like so many others on the Irish mainland, had developed *dísert* sites where anchorites and lay penitents could get on with the business of praying, at one remove from the high politics of the monastic *civitas* itself. To imply, therefore, that *all* monastic communities in pre-Viking Ireland had become degenerate and violent places, or to misuse the already flawed statistics of pre-Viking monastic 'burnings' and raidings as presented in the raw figures of a much misquoted paper by Lucas in 1967, is to present a grotesque distortion of the historical evidence.[5]

Discussions on the extent of Norse destructiveness on Western society have been obfuscated by the parading of economic benefits which accrued from the growth of Norse towns and from the injection of money into the Western economy through payments of Danegeld. No one would deny the impressive contribution which the Scandinavians made to town life in the English Danelaw and in Ireland.[6] But those settlements were founded initially at the cost of native lives and livelihoods. Clergy who had been terrorized by Norse raiders, or those landowners who had been driven off their lands in the Vale of York, may have benefited as much from trading in the markets of York as the Plains Indians benefited from the opening up of the American West by European colonists in the nineteenth century. As for the notion that Danegeld prised money and other frozen assets out of monasteries and into general circulation, we need only remind ourselves that Northmen did not operate charities for the benefit of their victims. Danegeld went

---

[4] Smyth, *Scandinavian York and Dublin*, ii, pp. 134–40.
[5] A. T. Lucas, 'The plundering and burning of churches in Ireland: 7th to 16th century', in *North Munster Studies: Essays in Commemoration of Monsignor Michael Moloney*, ed. E. Rynne (Limerick, 1967), pp. 172–229.
[6] Smyth, *Scandinavian York and Dublin*, pp. 191–258.

into the Scandinavian economy, as the multitude of pennies from the reign of Æthelraed the Unready found in Scandinavian hoards demonstrates.[7] As for the undoubted Norse contribution to the growth of towns in tenth-century England and Ireland, that was part of a colonization process which was scarcely a boon to those who lost their lives or were dispossessed in the earlier era of piracy, slave-raiding, and violent confrontation.

Arguments relating to Norse destructiveness have tended to hinge on technical matters such as the size of each Norse ship and the numbers of men in each ship. The technical approach has its uses in sanitizing Norse violence and taking attention away from the effects of the more barbarous levels of ninth-century Scandinavian society on the culture of the Christian West. It took the crews of only sixty-seven ships to bring about the notorious sack of Nantes on the Feast of John the Baptist (24 June) in 843.[8] The 'numbers approach' does not take account of the devastating effect of even smaller bands of Northmen – well armed and with surprise and mobility on their side – attacking an unarmed population. We are reminded of the *Chronicle*'s statement that in 896 only six enemy ships were involved in a raid on the Isle of Wight where they 'did great harm there, both in Devon and everywhere along the coast'.[9] It only took one Northman – with a different and more regressive set of cultural values – to torch an undefended monastic library which had taken two and a half centuries to accumulate, or to slay a monastic scholar who carried that accumulated wisdom in his or her head. The debate regarding numbers cannot be side-stepped since it has an obvious bearing on levels of destructiveness, as has the more intangible issue of relative levels of violent behaviour *vis-à-vis* different cultural groups in the early middle ages. If, for instance, we were to accept all Sawyer's arguments regarding the smallness of scale of the Scandinavian invading force described as the 'Great Army' (*micel here*) in the *Anglo-Saxon Chronicle* between the years 865 and 878,[10] we would find it difficult to account for the phenomenal military successes enjoyed by the Danes during that thirteen-year period. It is one thing to acknowl-

---

[7] P. H. Sawyer, *The Age of the Vikings* (2nd edn, London, 1971), pp. 117–19. Sawyer pointed to the fact that there were 1,000 Frankish coins in the Cuerdale hoard (dating to c. 900; *ibid.*, p. 101). It also needs stressing that there were close on 1,000 coins of Alfred the Great in that same hoard – many of which may have been collected as loot and Danegeld. See C. S. S. Lyon and B. H. I. H. Stewart, 'The Northumbrian Viking coins in the Cuerdale hoard', in *Anglo-Saxon Coins: Studies presented to F. M. Stenton*, ed. R. H. M. Dolley (London, 1961), p. 96.

[8] *The Annals of St-Bertin*, ed. J. N. Nelson (Manchester, 1991), s.a. 843, p. 55, and n. 2.

[9] *The Anglo-Saxon Chronicle*, trans. D. Whitelock, *EHD*, i, s.a. 896, p. 189.

[10] Sawyer, *Age of the Vikings*, p. 123; Sawyer, *Kings and Vikings: Scandinavia and Europe AD 700–1100* (London and New York, 1982), pp. 93–4.

edge Danish successes by stating that they conquered the English kingdoms of Northumbria, East Anglia and Mercia and that they brought Alfredian Wessex to the very brink of defeat. It is another thing to view that phenomenal success in the context of what had gone before.

Because pre-conquest English history is conveniently compartmentalized between pre-Viking, Viking and post-Viking periods, we encounter strange anomalies in Anglo-Saxon studies when we choose to move freely back and forth across the historiographical air-locks which divide these 'periods' off, one from another. Seventh- and eighth-century English history has been viewed as a relentless struggle between leading contestants in a 'Heptarchy' which curiously consisted of only three major players – Northumbria, Mercia and Wessex. That struggle was once viewed by Stenton and by others as promoting the evolution of a unified English polity. Yet during that era when England was ruled by its native kings, Northumbria, Mercia and Wessex were rarely, if ever, capable of imposing their rule over each other or over their neighbours to the extent of permanently replacing tributary kingships and indigenous aristocracies with puppets and colonists of their own choosing. Mercian rulers in the eighth century might require subject-kings of Kent, for instance, to seek ratification for land-grants, or Mercia might likewise install the West Saxon Beorhtric as their client-king in Wessex (*c.* 800), but there never came a point in the Mercian supremacy when even after military victory Wessex could ever be viewed as being fully annexed – not to say colonized – by its more powerful Midland neighbour. So in spite of constant jockeying for military advantage, an old-style *Brytenwealda* or 'Wide Ruler' had to confront the political realities of dealing with two or three other potentially rival overlords whose armies were intact and whose magnates were in control of patronage throughout their own shires and lesser territories. How then, we may well ask, did a 'Great Army' of Danes succeed in accomplishing in eleven or thirteen years what the most able native English warlords had failed to accomplish in over three centuries? This simple but grim reminder of overwhelming Danish military superiority has rarely if ever been acknowledged by historians. It was the Danish kings, Ivar and Halfdan, and later on, Olaf Gothfrithsson – rather than their English predecessors – who first came close to qualifying for that elusive title of *Bretwalda* or 'Ruler of Britain'. The Danes not only annihilated three leading English royal dynasties, but in the case of the Mercians, their war-machine – which had been the glory of Penda, Æthelbald and Offa – surrendered to the invaders without apparently offering a single battle. The Northumbrians and East Angles were each brought separately to their knees and their dynasties destroyed after only one battle – an extraordinary ordering of events when we recall how obdurate the relatively small Kentish kingdom had been in defending its independence against the might of Offa. Yet if we were to accept revisionist interpretations of ninth-century history, we would have to conclude that a force made up of hundreds rather than thousands of Scandinavian 'travelling warriors' redrew the political map of the whole island of Britain (including all of what is now Scotland and its Isles)[11] in that short period from 866 to 880.

We cannot argue that English armies were a spent force by the time the Great Heathen Army landed in 865. Kirby reminds us that although Mercia had experienced dynastic discord in the early ninth century, it was still a force to be reckoned with in the 820s.[12] Although Mercian power had been eclipsed by Ecgberht of Wessex temporarily in 825, even Stenton conceded that when Wiglaf returned to the Mercian kingship in 830, Mercia again got the upper hand, controlling most of Berkshire and perhaps also Essex and London.[13] We have definite evidence for Mercian control of parts of Berkshire in the reign of Wiglaf's Mercian successor, Brihtwulf, in 843–4.[14] And by the middle of the century, although the balance of power between Mercia and Wessex had by then tilted marginally in favour of Wessex, nevertheless, Æthelwulf, the West Saxon king, went on a joint expedition with Burgred of Mercia against the Welsh in 853, and Æthelwulf married off his daughter, Æthelswith, to that same Burgred later in the same year. Wessex was compelled to deal with its Mercian neighbour through diplomacy rather than brute force. And even if we were to argue, in the face of good evidence to the contrary, that Wessex alone possessed the only credible warband to resist Viking attack in the mid-ninth century, we would still have to explain the remarkable Danish successes in that kingdom – successes which but for a great element of luck would eventually have toppled the West Saxon leadership as they had toppled that in other Anglo-Saxon kingdoms.

Ecgberht of Wessex is seen by Anglo-Saxon historians as laying the foundations for later Alfredian expansion through his subjugation of the Cornishmen and his casting off the Mercian yoke in 825 and 829. Yet that same successful king who had supposedly 'conquered the kingdom of the Mercians' according to the partisan *Anglo-Saxon*

---

[11] A. P. Smyth, *Warlords and Holy Men: Scotland A.D. 80–1000* (London, 1984), pp. 141–74.
[12] D. P. Kirby, *The Earliest English Kings* (London, 1991), pp. 188–9.
[13] F. M. Stenton, *Anglo-Saxon England* (2nd edn, repr., Oxford, 1967), p. 233; Kirby, *Earliest English Kings*, pp. 191–2.
[14] Kirby, *The Earliest English Kings*, p. 192; A. P. Smyth, *King Alfred the Great* (Oxford, 1995), p. 4.

Chronicle,[15] was defeated by as few as twenty-five or thirty-five ships' crews of Viking raiders at Carhampton in 836. The *Chronicle* – never keen to elaborate on a West Saxon defeat – laconically records that battle as though it were some isolated skirmish. But Carhampton was almost certainly a royal estate (it was so in Alfred's time) and there is evidence to suggest that Scandinavian invaders, bent on conquest or on obtaining significant loot, massed their armies around such key centres.[16] It may be no coincidence that in 843 the invaders attacked Carhampton yet again, and again they won a victory – this time against Ecgberht's son, King Æthelwulf. In 843, the laconic reporting of the Chronicle is supplemented by the Annals of St-Bertin, which source may be referring to the Viking victory at Carhampton when it tells us that: 'The Northmen launched a major attack on the island of Britain, in that part which is largely inhabited by the Anglo-Saxons. After a battle lasting three days, the Northmen emerged the winners: plundering looting, slaughtering everywhere, they wielded power over the land at will.'[17]

Sawyer argued for a scaling down in our assessment of the size of Viking fleets and the consequent numbers of warriors which they carried. While he was willing to accept the many references in the *Anglo-Saxon Chronicle* to small fleets of under forty ships, he dismissed the round figures of 200 or 250 ships which invaded Kent in 892 'as [no] more than an attempt by the Chronicler to indicate large fleets'.[18] Sawyer dismissed an estimate of 350 ships given by the *Chronicle* under 851 as 'likely to be exaggerated' because it was not strictly contemporary,[19] yet the numbers given for the 892 fleets were indeed a contemporary estimate and included, incidentally, an additional fleet of eighty ships led by Hæsten at Milton Regis in Kent. Sawyer's approach was in truth both selective and subjective, and failed to take into account that Anglo-Saxon, Irish and Frankish annalists offer consistent contemporary estimates for fleet sizes ranging from a few ships to as many as 200 and above, for larger fleets. If we agree with Sawyer that Anglo-Saxon, Frankish and Irish annalists could accurately count and report on fleets of four, six, sixteen, thirty-two, forty, sixty and eighty ships,[20] how then can we deny that even if reports of 100 or 200 ships are estimated in round figures, that they are none the less accurate

---

[15] *Anglo-Saxon Chronicle*, EHD, i, *s.a.* 829, p. 171.
[16] Smyth, *King Alfred the Great*, p. 38.
[17] Nelson (ed.), *Annals of St-Bertin*, *s.a.* 844, p. 59. Sawyer suggested that the record of the 843 raid on Carhampton was a duplication of the annal for 836. Sawyer, *Age of the Vikings*, p. 125.
[18] Sawyer, *Age of the Vikings*, p. 126. [19] *Ibid.*, p. 17.
[20] Smyth, *King Alfred the Great*, p. 21.

estimates in relation to those reliable numbers for smaller fleets? When we use contemporary annals from different countries to exercise a control over estimates for Norse fleet sizes, and when we do this over a sufficiently wide time-span, we find a remarkable consistency in reporting.[21] An account in the *Anglo-Saxon Chronicle*, for instance, which describes a Danish pincer-movement in Devon and the Cornish peninsula in 893, reports that a fleet of forty ships 'went north around the coast and besieged a fortress on the north coast of Devon'. The other part of that pincer – a fleet on the south coast at Exeter, consisted initially of 100 ships, but may have been reduced to 60 if the northern contingent were included in the chronicler's total figure.[22] The number of ships involved in this operation together with the pincer tactic was replicated earlier in Ireland in 837 when two fleets, each of 60 ships, had swept across the territories between the Boyne and the Liffey.[23] In Francia in 861, Weland's crews of 200 ships on the Seine acted in unison with another Norse fleet of 60 ships on the river Tellas.[24] The numbers of ships for large and medium-sized war parties in Anglo-Saxon England tally well with figures found in Frankish, Irish and Iberian annals. The Northman, Weland, whose fleet almost certainly attacked Winchester in 860, commanded 200 ships on the Seine in 861, while Ivar, according to the Annals of Ulster, led 200 ships back to Dublin from Dumbarton in Strathclyde in 871. Guthrum lost 150 ships off Swanage in a storm in 877 and he still had enough men to capture Exeter immediately afterwards, and to overrun parts of western Wessex in 878. The Islamic chronicler, Ibn Adhari put the number of Viking ships which attacked Seville in 843–4 at eighty. He reported that four Norse ships were captured and that later thirty ships were burnt by the Moslems and 500 Norsemen were slain.[25] The burning or breaking up of captured ships – a sure indication of the menace they posed even when bereft of their Norse crews – is vouched for in Spanish, Frankish, English and Irish annals.[26] Ibn Adhari quoted a letter from the governor of Lisbon to the ruler at Cordoba in 843–4 'that *madjus* ("Heathens" or Northmen) had been seen on the coast of his province in fifty-four ships

---

[21] I have argued elsewhere for accepting the existence of large fleets of up to 200 ships and above. Smyth, *Scandinavian York and Dublin*, ii, pp. 197–8, 218 n. 33.

[22] *Ibid.*, i, pp. 32–3.

[23] *AU*, s.a. 836 (*recte* 837), pp. 294–5. (Unless otherwise stated all *AU* references to years before 1132 are to the 1983 edition of the *Annals of Ulster* edited by Mac Airt and Mac Niocaill.)

[24] Smyth, *King Alfred the Great*, p. 124.

[25] J. Stefánsson, 'The Vikings in Spain from Arabic (Moorish) and Spanish sources', *Saga-Book of the Viking Club: Society for Northern Research*, 6 (1909), pp. 35–6.

[26] Smyth, *King Alfred the Great*, p. 134; Smyth, *Scandinavian York and Dublin*, ii, pp. 197, 251.

Scandinavian raiders

and in the same number of smaller vessels'.[27] He also reported a Norse expedition of sixty-two ships off the western coast of Iberia in 859–60, while twenty-eight ships were sighted in 966.[28] If we accept that each ship carried, say, 30 men then the army which attacked Carhampton in 836 and 843 may have been 1,000 strong while the invaders of Kent who began King Alfred's Last War, could have been as many as 5,000 or 6,000 men.

The West Saxon armies which Æthelwulf bequeathed to his sons, King Æthelraed and his younger brother Alfred, were hammered time after time by the Great Army which took Reading in 871. There is an inescapable conclusion that the Great Army, which had already well-nigh conquered the whole of Anglo-Saxon England by 876, consisted of a massed force of warriors, the like of which had never been seen in England before. Even in distant heroic days when the English had themselves come as invaders they, unlike the Danes, had edged forward much more cautiously and much more slowly along the river valleys and across the lowlands of Britain. Alcuin, writing home from the Carolingian court to his native Northumbria at the very beginning of the Scandinavian migrations, was the first English writer to see that Northmen were no ordinary raiders, but rather a force which could undo everything which the English had accomplished in Britain over three centuries. Alcuin's knowledge of Danish military capability must have been considerable due to his Frankish connections. For too long, this scholar has been dismissed as an elderly monk whinging about the restoration of discipline and the need for decent behaviour in monasteries and between English kings. Already in his letter to Bishop Higbald of Lindisfarne, written soon after 793, Alcuin was aware that the Norse attack – 'the calamity of your tribulation'[29] – could be merely 'the beginning of greater tribulation'. He subjected King Æthelred of Northumbria to a history lesson, which showed how clearly he grasped the threat posed even by that first piratical raid back in 793:

Lo, it is nearly 350 years that we and our fathers have inhabited this lovely land, and never before has such terror appeared in Britain as we have now suffered from a pagan race, nor was it thought that such an inroad from the sea could be made. Behold the church of St Cuthbert spattered with the blood of the priests of God, despoiled of all its ornaments; a place more venerable than all in Britain is given as a prey to pagan peoples. And where first after the departure of St

---

[27] Stefánsson, 'Vikings in Spain', p. 35.   [28] *Ibid.*, pp. 40, 42.
[29] *Councils and Ecclesiastical Documents Relating to Great Britain and Ireland*, ed. A. W. Haddan and W. Stubbs (Oxford, 1869–71: repr. 1964), iii, pp. 472–3; *EHD*, i, p. 778. A detailed discussion of Alcuin's letters written back to Northumbria in the wake of the Scandinavian attack in 793 will be found in D. A. Bullough, 'What has Ingeld to do with Lindisfarne?', *Anglo-Saxon England*, 22 (1993), pp. 95–115.

Paulinus from York [in c. AD 634] the Christian religion in our race took its rise, there misery and calamity have begun. Who does not fear this? Who does not lament this as if his country were captured?[30]

These were prophetic words. Seventy-three years and numerous devastations later, Alcuin's 'country (*patria*)' – the land of the Northumbrian Angles – collapsed in the face of the onslaught of the Great Army, and York was to become the centre of power for a Scandinavian dynasty for almost a century afterwards.[31] Alcuin's comment conveys the sense of disbelief regarding the sudden and unexpected capability of Northmen to cross the North Sea, but he also provides clear evidence for the slaughter of monks (*sanguine aspersa*) and the despoliation of an immensely rich monastery. In his letter to Bishop Higbald he mentions that the raiders 'poured out the blood of saints around the altar' and he refers to the survivors as 'you who are left'.[32] He reveals, too, that in addition to the slaying of monks, 'youths' – perhaps the inmates of the monastic school – had been taken captive by the pagans, and there is a hint that they might be ransomed through the influence of Charlemagne.[33] Sawyer's use of a later account of this Lindisfarne attack written some 'three hundred years later', to reduce the evidence for the catastrophe which befell Lindisfarne in 873 to the level of a tale 'which grew with the telling' and which was full of fanciful 'elaborations',[34] failed to take seriously repeated contemporary comments by a scholar of Alcuin's standing. Sawyer failed, too, to give due weight to the account in northern versions of the *Anglo-Saxon Chronicle* regarding the 'ravages of heathen men [who] miserably destroyed God's church on Lindisfarne, with plunder and slaughter'.[35] This notice of the destruction of a particular English church by Scandinavian raiders is almost unique in any version of the *Chronicle* reporting on ninth-century events and the reference to *man sleht* ('murder' or 'slaughter') supports Alcuin's references to loss of life. Alcuin's account has all the ingredients associated with Norse terror which reappear in accurate and contemporary accounts of subsequent raids – the element of surprise, loss of life, looting and slave-raiding with the possibility of ransom. Even Page, in an uncritical and speculative mood, conceded that while the Lindisfarne raiders may have been viewed by their own

---

[30] Haddan and Stubbs (eds.), *Councils and Ecclesiastical Documents*, iii, p. 493; *EHD*, i, p. 776.
[31] Smyth, *Scandinavian York and Dublin*.
[32] Haddan and Stubbs (eds.), *Councils and Ecclesiastical Documents*, iii, p. 472.
[33] *Ibid.*, iii, p. 473; *EHD*, i, pp. 778–9.   [34] Sawyer, *Kings and Vikings*, pp. 94–5.
[35] Anglo-Saxon Chronicle (Version E) *s.a.* 793, in *Two of the Saxon Chronicles Parallel*, ed. C. Plummer and J. Earle, 2 vols. (Oxford, 1892–9, repr. 1965), i, pp. 55–7.

kind as 'young men of good family', they might nevertheless have been 'hired killers'.³⁶

Sawyer likewise played down the effects of dislocation endured by monastic communities which were forced to flee before the Northmen. He cited Wallace-Hadrill's views on the flight of people from Périgord and Limousin to Turenne in the Haut-Limousin as being based on a sermon of Adhemar of Chabannes – 'a most unreliable source'.³⁷ But we do not have to depend on Adhemar of Chabannes for evidence of dislocation of monastic communities. We know from near-contemporary sources such as Odo of Cluny's Life of Count Gerald of Aurillac, for instance, that the relics of St Martial were moved out of the way of Norse raiders from Limoges to Turenne.³⁸ And since the relics and treasures of a monastery were at the core of its spiritual *raison d'être* we can be certain that in some instances the monastic community as a whole followed in the wake of their founders' relics. The classic Frankish example of this is provided by a series of moves up the Loire made by the monks of St Philibert between 836 and 875 when they were displaced by Northmen from their island home on Noirmoutier.³⁹ But other instances of long-term and more temporary dislocation abound, as in the case of the canons and nuns of Cologne and Bonn who fled from the Northmen with their relics and treasures to Mainz in 881.⁴⁰ In Northumbria the monks of Lindisfarne were eventually forced from their home with the relics of St Cuthbert in 876. The wanderings of the Lindisfarne community and their eventual settlement at Chester-le-Street provide evidence both for the resilience as well as the long-term dislocation and permanent rehousing of monastic personnel in the Viking age.⁴¹ Important monasteries on offshore locations such as Lindisfarne and Iona found themselves in the front line of Viking attack. Iona was first attacked – probably by raiders connected with the Lindisfarne assault – in 795. The Hebrides were again raided in 798 and in 802 Iona was again attacked and burnt by heathen raiders. The *coup de grâce* was delivered in 806, when sixty-eight members of Iona's monastic community (*familia*)

---

36 R. I. Page, *Chronicles of the Vikings: Records, Memorials and Myths* (London, 1995), p. 79.
37 Sawyer, *Kings and Vikings*, p. 97.
38 *Vita Sancti Geraldi Auriliacensis comitis*, in *MPL*, 133 (Paris, 1853), p. 666; *St Odo of Cluny: Being the Life of St Odo of Cluny by John of Salerno and the Life of St Gerald of Aurillac by St Odo*, ed. G. Sitwell (London and New York, 1958), p. 128.
39 R. H. C. Davis, *A History of Medieval Europe from Constantine to Saint Louis* (London, 1970), p. 169.
40 *The Annals of Fulda*, ed. T. Reuter (Manchester and New York, 1992), s.a. 881, pp. 90–1.
41 Smyth, *Scandinavian York and Dublin*, i, pp. 42–4.

were slain.[42] The fact that a 'new monastic city' (*noue civitatis*) was laid out for construction in the following year at Kells in Ireland shows that a community decision had been taken by then to abandon Iona as the headquarters of the community. And when Kells was completed in 814, Cellach resigned the office of superior (*principatus*) and Diarmait was appointed in his place.[43] Cellach's death on Iona in 815 shows that the mother house was not abandoned altogether, but henceforth in the Viking Age, Iona would constitute a *disert* or 'desert' site where anchorites risked their lives to maintain a physical association with the saints of their church.[44] Sawyer's conclusion regarding Frankish monasteries, that 'although many houses were destroyed by Viking raiders, losing their libraries and treasures, many recovered in a remarkable way',[45] does not help the discussion. It is indeed true that the monks of Tours were back in business in August 854,[46] in spite of an attack by Northmen in the previous year, and communities too numerous to mention all across the Christian West drifted back to sites hallowed by the lives of holy founders as soon as the Northmen had disappeared. But that is a fact of doubtful significance in relation to the relative violence of any one raid. It was already clear to visitors brave enough to filter back to the pavement cafés in Sarajevo in 1996 that the city had begun its painful recovery after four years of bombardment and siege. Such a recovery speaks only of the resilience of the human spirit, and will, one hopes, never be used by historians of a later age to deny the genocidal nature of total war in the Balkans between 1992 and 1996. The Life of Odo of Cluny written by John of Salerno *c.* 943, yields much incidental information on the dislocation of monastic communities during the Viking wars in Francia. We are told that monks abandoned their monasteries to return to live with their relatives during the Scandinavian invasions;[47] that the Northmen 'were cruelly laying waste' the countryside around Poitiers and Tours at a time when two monks of the Fleury community happened to have been captured and bound by Norse raiders;[48] and that Odo's nephew

---

[42] Smyth, *Warlords and Holy Men*, pp. 145–7.   [43] *AU, s.a.* 813, pp. 270–1.
[44] I cannot agree with conclusions reached by Professor M. Herbert (*Iona, Kells and Derry: the History and Hagiography of the Monastic Familia of Columba*, Oxford, 1988 p. 68) on the status of Iona in the years immediately after 814. She argued 'that initially Kells was to function as a place of safety for personnel and precious objects from Iona, and was not designed to replace its mother-house'. But a place of refuge for personnel and their all-important relics would suggest that Iona survived at best with a token community made up of zealots like the unfortunate Blathmac.
[45] Sawyer, *Kings and Vikings*, p. 97.   [46] Nelson (ed.), *Annals of St-Bertin*, p. 77, n. 12.
[47] *Vita Sancti Odonis abbatis Cluniacensis secundi*, in *MPL*, 133, p. 76; Sitwell (ed.), *St Odo of Cluny*, p. 72.
[48] Sitwell (ed.), *St Odo of Cluny*, pp. 54–5; *Vita Odonis*, p. 67.

and nurse were taken captive during another devastating Norse raid around Tours and carried off on an eight-day journey to the far side of a deep river.[49] The Life of Odo also tells us of the removal of relics out of the path of Norse raiders[50] and more crucially that the monks of Fleury – one of the leading Benedictine houses of Francia – were scattered 'through fear of the enemy'.[51]

The debate surrounding the temporary or permanent abandonment of monastic centres has often been narrowly focused on the lives of professed monks and has seldom taken account of the wider implications for monastic tenants. Sawyer did address this issue in passing and drew the following conclusions:

> It is likely that the raiders also forced many laymen, especially landowners, into exile, but there is nothing to suggest that there was any significant displacement of whole populations. Bishops and their households, monastic communities and secular lords naturally took to flight, but that does not mean that the peasantry abandoned their lands.[52]

There are several gratuitous assumptions here which do not stand up to scrutiny, and it can be misleading to discuss higher clergy in isolation from the ecclesiastical and monastic economy as a whole. Early medieval monasteries and bishoprics lay at the centre of great estates which depended on church lords and their entourage for their administration. By driving off a bishop and his household from his see, or an abbot and his monks from a monastery, the Northmen had dealt a serious blow to agrarian organization, and since we now know that Scandinavian raiders were interested in seizing corn and livestock, ecclesiastical estates were easy targets. We also now know that from the very beginnings of Norse piracy contemporary sources constantly refer to the taking of captives. The idea therefore of 'the peasantry' remaining on estates which had been stripped bare of produce; which were lacking in farm managers; and where they would have been easy targets for slave-raiders, simply does not hold up. We learn from a charter issued by Bishop Wærferth of Worcester that the bishop was forced to lease off church lands at Nuthurst in Warwickshire 'because of the very pressing affliction and immense tribute of the barbarians' in 872.[53] Later on, Bishop Denewulf of Winchester remonstrated with King Edward the Elder (c. 900) not to force the Winchester clergy to lease their estate at Beddington in Surrey because it had once been 'quite without stock and stripped bare by heathen men'. The stock which the bishop had managed to restore to the lands at Beddington included – in addition to 9 oxen, 114 pigs and

---

[49] *Vita Odonis*, pp. 69–70; *St Odo of Cluny*, pp. 59–60.
[50] *St Odo of Cluny*, p. 84 and n. 1.   [51] *Ibid.*, p. 79; *Vita Sancti Odonis*, p. 80.
[52] Sawyer, *Kings and Vikings*, p. 97.   [53] *Ibid.*, p. 41.

160 sheep – 7 bondsmen who, as in the case of the livestock, had replaced predecessors presumably carried off by Northmen.[54] It was no doubt such monastic tenants – servile and free – who went to make up the 3,000 captives taken by the Dublin Northmen from monasteries in Meath (Brega) in eastern Ireland in 957 together with 'a great spoil of cattle and horses'.[55] Ealhburg, a female landowner in Kent, was unable to pay her food-rents to St Augustine's in Canterbury (c. 850–60) 'because of the ravages of the heathen army' which had stripped her lands bare of produce and very probably also of its workforce.

It is clear from a wide range of contemporary sources from across the Christian West that a major objective of the Northmen was to acquire loot by way of monastic treasure or from the ransom of high-status captives or of high-status ecclesiastical cult objects such as Gospel Books and reliquaries. Those archaeologists who purvey the 'benign Viking' theory sometimes argue that parts of Christian shrines found their way back to graves in the Scandinavian homeland by way of trade with monastic communities. Such ideas fail to take into account that cult objects 'under worship' and at the heart of a particular saint's pilgrimage centre were never negotiable to believers, much less to non-believers. Indeed, one of the reasons why monasteries may have served as banks offering a 'safe deposit' facility to local lay lords was that their strong-rooms enjoyed immunity from attack and theft within an otherwise violent Christian society in the early Middle Ages. Lucas was correct in attributing this 'banking' role in regard to frozen assets to early Irish monasteries.[56] It is clear from the Life of St Dunstan, for instance, that in tenth-century England it was considered normal for King Eadred (946–55) to deposit part of his treasure for safe-keeping in Glastonbury.[57] 'All the best' of King Eadred's 'goods' included, incidentally, not only 'the ancient treasures of preceding kings as well as various precious things he [Eadred] had acquired himself' but also 'many title-deeds (*cartulas*)' from the royal archive. The whole point of placing treasure and all-important charters from secular lords in a monastery was to ensure they enjoyed the same 'off-limits' status as church reliquaries and other cult objects. This point is made clear in the reporting of the ravages of Lothar, son of Louis the Pious, in the Annals of St-Bertin. Lothar invaded the territory of his brother, Charles the Bald, in 841 and ravaged the Le Mans region with 'rape, sacrilege and blasphemy': 'He lost no time in carrying off whatever treasures he could

---

[54] *Ibid.*, pp. 45–6.   [55] *AU, s.a.* 950.
[56] Lucas, 'Plundering and burning of churches', pp. 199–200.
[57] *Sancti Dunstani Vita Auctore B* in *Memorials of St Dunstan*, ed. W. Stubbs, RS (London, 1874), p. 29; *EHD*, i, 829.

find deposited in churches or their strong rooms for safe-keeping – and this, even though the priests and clergy of other ranks were bound by oath to preserve those things.'[58] Writers who would use evidence such as this to highlight the violent nature of ninth-century Christian society would do well to consider that the incident is reported as a remarkable event; that it is condemned in the strongest terms; and that it demonstrates the otherwise sacrosanct nature of treasure placed under monastic protection and under monastic oath. Lucas could find no early references to the physical desecration of shrines or relics by the Irish prior to the Norse invasions, and rightly surmised that early references to 'profanation' of shrines referred to the breaking of oaths taken on reliquaries rather than to physical damage.[59] Furthermore, severe ecclesiastical sanctions, laid down in Penitentials and the *Cáin Adamnáin*, operated against any would-be thief or vandal who dared to purloin an Irish Gospel Book or shrine.[60]

Ó Corráin, following Lucas, pointed to the fact that 'the bullion value of the great bulk of the Irish metalwork of the time [of the Northmen] was very small',[61] as though an art dealer might value a painting because of the price paid for its once blank canvas and for its paint, or a pot for the value of its clay. Reliquaries made of gilt bronze or containing gold filigree on a gilt bronze field must have seemed to any raider as though they were made of solid gold and silver. But the key point regarding looted reliquaries and other cult objects was that Northmen were well aware that their monastic custodians would pay any ransom to have the bones of their patrons and holy founders returned to them. In 859, the monks of St Denis – the richest monastery in Francia – had 'the bones of the blessed martyrs Denis, Rusticus and Eleutherius removed to Nogent, one of the *villae* belonging to St Denis in the Morvois district. There on 21 September the bones were reverently placed in reliquaries.'[62] Why would the monks of St Denis move the bones of their patron saints out of the path of the Northmen if they had not feared for their safety? As for reliquaries, their exquisite craftsmanship rendered them valuable in their own right, but they acquired added value through their association with the bones of holy men and women in churches where they became sanctified by association. Even secular objects of intricate workmanship could also fetch high prices in the early Middle Ages regardless of their crude bullion value. A ninth-century West

---

[58] Nelson (ed.), *Annals of St-Bertin*, s.a. 841, p. 52.
[59] Lucas, 'Plundering and burning of churches', pp. 180–1.   [60] *Ibid.*, p. 180.
[61] D. Ó Corráin, *Ireland before the Normans* (Dublin, 1972), p. 89; Lucas, 'Plundering and burning of churches', p. 212.
[62] Nelson (ed.), *Annals of St-Bertin*, s.a. 859, p. 91.

Saxon belt, whose owner was close to the Alfredian dynasty, was valued at the price of a West Saxon estate,[63] and a reliquary executed in the style and quality of say, the Tara Brooch, would have been instantly recognizable even to the most uncouth Northman as a treasure beyond price. In short, Northmen were quick to learn that regardless of 'bullion value', an ecclesiastical cult object was worth whatever a monastic community might be willing to pay to get it back. Ealdorman Alfred has left us his own record of how he and his wife, Wærburh, ransomed the Golden Gospels (now in Stockholm) 'from the heathen army for pure gold', probably in 871–2, and then presented that codex to Canterbury Cathedral.[64] Those Gospels may well have been encased within a sumptuous metalwork shrine which would have excited the greed of its looters in the first instance, but for Ealdorman Alfred and the clergy of Canterbury it was the early Gospel text which they wished to retrieve and the Northmen were well aware of that. Earlier in Ireland in 824, Heathens plundered Bangor in Co. Down 'and destroyed the oratory and shook the relics of Comgall from their shrine'. It may have been the precious reliquary, inlaid with gold, silver and enamel, which the Northmen were after on that particular early raid. Eight years later we read of the shrine of Adomnán (abbot of Iona and biographer of St Colum Cille) which was seized from Donaghmoyne (Co. Monaghan).

The monks of St Martin's moved the body of their saint from Tours to Cormery and moved other treasures to Orleans in 853, having had advance warning of an impending Viking attack.[65] That attack, which the Northmen had launched from Nantes on 8 November, was 'known about beforehand with complete certainty' because no doubt, as in Ireland, the Northmen had become well known for raiding churches on or close to patronal festivals, and St Martin's feast fell on 11 November. The Lindisfarne community managed to preserve the relics of St Cuthbert in 793,[66] and Iona clearly managed to save the relics of Colum Cille in spite of sustaining heavy casualties among its monks in 806. Scandinavian raiders did not shrink from extracting information as to the whereabouts of monastic treasure by torturing captured monks. This evidence was played down by revisionist historians in the face of early accounts by distinguished writers such as Walafrid Strabo. Walafrid's Life of Blathmac shows that this Irish monk had wilfully returned to Iona with his companions in 825 in the knowledge that he would face martyrdom at the hands of Northmen – 'a pagan horde armed with

---

[63] Smyth, *King Alfred the Great*, p. 398. [64] *Ibid.*, p. 47. [65] *Ibid.*, p. 43.
[66] The fact that the Lindisfarne monks managed to save some of their church treasures is not an argument against contemporary accounts of loss of life on that raid. (Sawyer, *Kings and Vikings*, p. 94.)

malignant greed'. Blathmac and his companions – like the monks of Tours – had prior warning of an attack and some among them fled 'by a footpath through regions known to them'. When the raiders arrived

> they came rushing through the open buildings ... and after slaying with mad savagery the rest of the associates, they approached the holy father to compel him to give up the precious metals wherein lie the holy bones of St Columba. But [the monks] had lifted the shrine from its pediments, and had placed it in the earth, in a hollowed barrow, under a thick layer of turf; because they knew then of the wicked destruction [to come]. This booty the Danes desired, but the saint remained with unarmed hand and with unshaken purpose of mind.[67]

It may be that by 825, the relics of Colum Cille (i.e. his physical remains as distinct from the reliquary) had already been divided out between the community of Kells and others in Scotland. It seems from this early account, however, that some at least of Colum Cille's bones had been reinterred under the turf of Iona after the first Scandinavian onslaught. The Northmen would have rightly surmised that Colum Cille's reliquary must have been one of the most dazzling cult objects in the entire repertoire of early Irish monastic metalwork. That reliquary – whatever its eventual fate – would seem to have survived at Kells in the charge of the new abbot, Diarmait, who took Colum Cille's relics (*minna*) from Ireland to Scotland, and back to Ireland again, in 829. Blathmac refused to yield to the Northmen's threats and 'therefore the pious sacrifice was torn limb from limb'.[68] Whatever the condition and exact whereabouts of the relics and reliquary in 825, and whatever the precise details of Blathmac's ordeal, he was tortured to death. From Francia we have an account of the torture of four monks at St-Bertin of whom only one survived.[69] We are reminded of Blathmac's suffering in the account by Abbo of Fleury (*c.* 986) of the slaying of King Edmund of East Anglia by the Danes in November 869: 'His ribs were laid bare by numberless gashes, as if he had been put to the torture of the rack, or had been torn by savage claws.'[70] Frank argued that Abbo's reference to 'rack' (*eculeus*) and 'claw' (*ungula*) as instruments of torture used on the unfortunate Edmund was nothing more than part of a stock motif and vocabulary drawn from late antique and early medieval writers and hagiographers.[71] But if that were so it is curious that Abbo first attributed a form of death

---

[67] *Walafridus Strabo: Vita Sancti Blaithmaic Martyris*, ed. E. Dümmler in *M.G.H Poetae Latini Aevi Carolini*, ii (1884, repr. 1978), pp. 299–301; Anderson, *Early Sources*, i, p. 264.
[68] *Ibid.*, p. 265.
[69] J. M. Wallace-Hadrill, *The Vikings in Francia*, Stenton Lecture (Reading, 1975), p. 10.
[70] Smyth, *Scandinavian Kings*, p. 211.
[71] R. Frank, 'Viking atrocity and Skaldic verse: the rite of the blood-eagle', *EHR*, 99 (1984), pp. 341–3.

to Edmund which is borrowed from the Life of St Sebastian and then felt it necessary to add in a different form of torure and death altogether. And because writers borrow motifs from a late antique repertoire does not in itself invalidate the message which those borrowed motifs may contain. Revisionists who hold that allusions to Norse brutality and to human sacrifice in Old Icelandic literature belong to the realm of literary motif in a heroic genre, argue in the face of evidence from Icelandic sources themselves as well as from much earlier accounts of Norse behaviour in the written records of their victims and their enemies. The concentration by Frank on evidence for and against the practice of 'blood-eagling' rituals in the ninth century – to the exclusion of evidence for other forms of ritual slaying – was as flawed methodologically as it was intellectually disingenuous.[72] The key passage is a stanza from *Knútsdrápa*, composed c. 1030–38, the conventional translation of which runs:

> And Ivar
> who dwelt at York
> Carved the eagle
> on Ælla's back.

If this translation is accepted, then this poem shows that by the early eleventh century the tradition that Ivar (one of the leaders of the Great Heathen Army in England), had slain King Ælla of Northumbria (in AD 867) by scoring an eagle's image on his back, was in wide circulation at that time. Frank argued, however, that mistranslation of this stanza in the twelfth century led to a 'chain of guesses' in the thirteenth which resulted in the invention of more embroidered Norse accounts of this ghoulish rite, such as the following passage from *Orkneyinga Saga*: 'Einar carved the bloody-eagle on his [Halfdan's] back by laying his sword in the hollow at the backbone and hacking all the ribs from the backbone down to the loins, and drawing out the lungs; and he gave him to Odin as an offering for his victory.'[73]

Frank offered her own alternative translation of the stanza in *Knútsdrápa* with an interpretation which supposedly had eluded Icelandic writers and scholars of the twelfth century. She would have us believe that through a judicious rejigging of Old Icelandic syntax, we ought to read: 'And Ivar who dwelt at York, had Ælla's back cut by an eagle',[74] so in her interpretation, it was the eagle that did the carving, and what we really have here is an allusion to the slaying of King Ælla in battle and the subsequent eating of his corpse by the bird of battle. Deprived of the

---

[72] *Ibid.*, pp. 332–43.   [73] Smyth, *Scandinavian Kings*, p. 191.
[74] Frank, 'Viking atrocity and Skaldic verse', p. 337.

evidence from this crucial early stanza from *Knútsdrápa*, the case for believing any longer in 'blood-eagling' might collapse. Frank's interpretation of the key stanza was but the opinion of one linguist, and in her own words, her conclusions boiled down to this: 'Ella's back may have been incised with the picture of an eagle, but it could also have been lacerated by a real one.'[75] Her analysis of Norse references to *blóðörn* or the 'blood eagle' quickly ran into the sands of antiquarian debate on how eagles may or may not devour their prey, and she was challenged relentlessly in her interpretation of the textual evidence by Einarsson.[76] Furthermore, her concentration on textual evidence for one particular rite of human sacrifice in Old Norse culture to the exclusion of all others, and her parading of linguistic detail, created a false impression that her conclusions had more wide-ranging significance for historians than they actually had. I have never at any point suggested that Archbishop Ælfheah of Canterbury, who was murdered by Northmen in 1012, was subjected to the blood-eagle ritual by his Scandinavian captors,[77] but I have suggested, given that human sacrifice was practised throughout Scandinavia before its conversion to Christianity, that the murder of captives such as Ælfheah may well have had a ritual significance. Furthermore, in relation to the 'blood-eagle' rite itself, it was clearly Frank and her self-proclaimed 'pro-viking opposition' who had become obsessed with the demonic aspects of Norse paganism.[78] We have only to turn to the pages of Adam of Bremen (d. 1076) to appreciate that the ritual slaughter of human beings was still a regular and bloody spectacle at Old Uppsala as late as his time.[79] My own views are best summed up by Einarsson, who reiterated in 1990 what I first stated back in 1977:

---

[75] *Ibid.*, p. 337.
[76] 'With this [i.e. Frank's interpretation of the 'blood-eagle' stanza in *Knútsdrápa*] I am convinced that no experienced Icelandic reader of skaldic poetry could possibly agree', B. Einarsson, '*De Normannorum Atrocitate*, or on the execution of royalty by the aquiline method', *Saga-Book*, 22, i (1986), pp. 79–82, and p. 80. To which Frank modestly replied: 'It, is of course, an undeniable advantage [for Bjarni Einarsson] to have Icelandic as mother tongue' (R. Frank, 'The blood-eagle again', *Saga-Book*, 22, v (1988), p. 288). The debate strayed ever further off the point with Frank denying any need to discover an 'ornithological reality' in skaldic verse (R. Frank, 'Ornithology and interpretation of Skaldic verse', *Saga-Book*, 23, ii (1990), pp. 81–3), but with Einarsson sticking to his scholarly guns (B. Einarsson, 'The blood-eagle once more: two notes', *Saga-Book*, 23, ii (1990), pp. 80–1).
[77] Smyth, *Scandinavian Kings in the British Isles*, p. 214.
[78] Frank, 'Viking atrocity and Skaldic verse', p. 332.
[79] *Magistri Adam Bremensis: Gesta Hammaburgensis Ecclesiae Pontificum* (IV, 27), ed. R. Buchner in *Ausgewählte Quellen zur deutschen Geschichte des Mittelalters*, ix (Darmstadt, 1968), pp. 470–2.

It goes without saying that Sighvatr's verse is not proof that King Ella [of Northumbria] was in fact executed by the aquiline method [in 867] some 150 years and more before the lines were composed. But it must be counted evidence showing that there was a Scandinavian tradition about it already in the first third of the eleventh century, as there probably also was about the killing of Hálfdan, son of Haraldr hárfagri [king of Norway, c. AD 930], by the same method.[80]

No historian who seeks a genuine understanding of pre-Christian Norse society can ignore the inherent brutality in Norse accounts of ritual slayings, even if they do date from the thirteenth century, when there is at least the possibility that they are accurately interpreting earlier eleventh-century texts. And whether or not Irish, English or Frankish victims of Norse savagery were subjected to 'blood-eagling' matters less than the realization that Northmen practised rites of human sacrifice on their captives until late into the eleventh century if not beyond. What was that 'bloody spectacle' (*visum cruentum*) which the Northmen put on for the benefit of the besieged Frankish garrison at Paris in 885?[81] That is impossible to say, but we need at least to be aware of the probable rites involved – the same Norse 'rites' perhaps which Pippin II of Aquitane embraced in 864 in place of his Christianity, and which he paid for with his life before a Frankish tribunal at Pîtres. And when we read in the Annals of Ulster that in 833 'Lough Brickland (Co. Down) was plundered to the detriment of Congalach son of Echaid, and he was killed afterwards at the ships'[82] we need no longer concur with commentators such as Ó Corráin or Nelson, and assume that captives were either 'not much the worse of their experience'[83] or that they were killed in custody because they might have offended their hosts by offering 'some resistance' – for which there is no evidence.[84]

Not all Northmen were hostile to Christianity *per se*, but however violently the native aristocracy may have behaved towards Christian cult-centres, it is the exception rather than the rule to find Christian rulers perpetrating acts of sacrilege against the persons of individual churchmen, and equally exceptional to find evidence for the desecration of sacred relics. Attacks against monastic townships and inter-monastic feuding were another matter, involving, as they did, secular power struggles and infiltration and interference by rival segments of the warrior aristocracy in church politics. It was largely Norse greed, rather

[80] Einarsson, '*De Normannorum Atrocitate*', p. 80; Smyth, *Scandinavian Kings*, pp. 190–4.
[81] Wallace-Hadrill, *Vikings in Francia*, p. 10.   [82] *AU*, s.a. 832, pp. 290–1.
[83] Ó Corráin, *Ireland before the Normans*, p. 90.
[84] Nelson (ed.), *Annals of St-Bertin*, p. 91, n. 10, where that writer suggests Bishop Immo of Noyon was slain in 859 by Northmen as a captive on the march because he may have offered them resistance. There is no evidence to support such an idea. Besides, any resistance would have been extremely difficult if not impossible for captives who had been surprised in a night attack.

than any well-thought-out hostility to Christianity, which prompted the capture of churchmen and the looting of reliquaries and torture of monastic personnel in the quest to locate treasure. The taking of human captives held out a two-fold promise of gain – the possibility of ransom by kinsmen and institutions or the prospect of selling on through the slave markets of Scandinavia. We have already seen that the earliest Lindisfarne raid involved the capture of youths – by far the more profitable type of captive. Young women as well as young men were especially desirable and the Annals of Ulster record that when Northmen attacked Howth (Co. Dublin) in 821 'they carried off a great number of women into captivity'. We read in 836 of 'the first prey taken by the heathen from southern Brega (Co. Meath) i.e. from *Telach Dromain* and *Dermag of the Britons* and they carried off many prisoners and killed many and led away very many captive'.[85] Four years later, nearby Louth was plundered by heathens from Lough Neagh 'and they led away captive bishops and priests and scholars and put others to death'.

Revisionists have largely ignored the record of slave-trading among Northmen although it pervades the records of Francia, England, and Ireland down to the early eleventh century. Many accounts of the taking of captives reveal that church centres were a primary target, since people would have instinctively flocked there for sanctuary in the face of attack, and on other occasions there is evidence for captives being taken from monastic and church centres on major church festivals when many unarmed worshippers would be expected to be there. When Olaf attacked Armagh in 869 and 'a thousand were carried off or slain', it was almost certainly on the Feast of St Patrick (17 March).[86] Armagh was raided by Olaf Gothfrithsson on its second greatest Feast Day – St Martin's Eve (10 November), 933, while Halfdan Gothfrithsson was defeated when raiding close to Armagh during the days of Christmas (28 December) in 926. Kildare was plundered by Gothfrith on its patronal feast of St Brigit (1 February), 929; the monks of Clonmore (Co. Carlow) were massacred on Christmas Night, 836; and Roscrea was attacked on the Feast of Saints Peter and Paul (29 June), 845, 'when the fair had begun'.[87] York was captured by the Danes on All Saints' Day (1 November) 866, while Nantes was sacked on the Feast of John the Baptist (24 June), 843. The list goes on. There is also extensive evidence for the killing of some captives and the enslaving of others during raids on church centres. The old and infirm were useless to slave-raiders and in the conditions of total war which the Northmen practised against those who were of no use to them the elderly and infants were

[85] *AU, s.a.* 820 and 835, pp. 276–7, 294–5. [86] Smyth, *Scandinavian Kings*, p. 148.
[87] *Ibid.*, pp. 154–5; Smyth, *Scandinavian York and Dublin*, ii, pp. 130–1.

extremely vulnerable. In other cases, captives might be slaughtered either because no ransom was paid (as in the case of Archbishop Ælfheah) or because they may have slowed down a Norse war-party anxious to make its escape. So, we read of a Norse attack on Noyon in 859 when the raiders 'took captive Bishop Immo along with other nobles, both clerics and laymen, and after laying waste the *civitas* [they] carried the prisoners off with them and slew them on the march'.[88] Contemporary Irish records not only record the 'martyrdom' of individual Christians at the hands of Northmen in 825 and 828, and of the capturing of named magnates in 831, 832, 842 and 845,[89] but we are also told of captives who died later at the hands of their enemies. We read of an anchorite from Skellig who 'was carried off by the heathen [in 824] and died shortly afterwards of hunger and thirst'; of Congalach son of Echaid who 'was slain afterwards at the ships' in 832; of the abbot of Clogher who 'was taken prisoner by the Foreigners of Anagassan (Co. Louth) and later died among them' in 842; and of the abbot of Anagassan who in the same year 'was fatally wounded and burned by heathens and [renegade] Irish'.[90]

High status captives offered rich rewards for ransom. When in 858 Abbot Louis of St Denis was captured by Northmen from the Seine along with his brother Gauzlin, they

demanded a very heavy fine for their ransom. In order to pay this, many church treasuries in Charles's realm were drained dry, at the king's command. But even all this was far from being enough: to bring it up to the required amount, large sums were eagerly contributed also by the king, and by all the bishops, abbots, counts and other powerful men.[91]

As a grandson of Charlemagne and abbot of Francia's leading monastery, Louis was a rich prize for the Northmen to have captured. He fetched 686 lb of gold and 3250 lb of silver on the ransom market.[92] When an army of Northmen from Brittany captured Cyfeiliog, bishop of Archenfield in 914, King Edward the Elder ransomed him for 40 pounds.[93] The captive Cyfeiliog had been 'taken with them to the ships'. In his will, King Edward's father, Alfred the Great, had left 100 pounds each, to his wife and three daughters. Alfred left 12.50 pounds to each of his earldormen, to his nephews and to his archbishop of Canterbury.[94] Judged by the scale of these royal legacies to the close relatives and intimates of a ninth-century West Saxon king, the ransom

---

[88] Nelson (ed.), *Annals of St-Bertin*, s.a. 859, p. 91.
[89] *AU* (see under relevant years).   [90] *AU* (see under relevant years).
[91] Nelson (ed.), *Annals of St-Bertin*, s.a. 858, p. 86.   [92] *Ibid.*, p. 86 and n. 5.
[93] *Anglo-Saxon Chronicle*, s.a. 914, *EHD*, i, p. 194.
[94] Smyth, *King Alfred the Great*, p. 420.

paid for a bishop on a remote Welsh frontier was a considerable sum of money. In 845 Forannán, abbot of Armagh, was taken prisoner by the heathens in *Cluain Comarda* 'with his relics and his companions', and like the unfortunate Cyfeiliog and so many others, he 'was brought to the ships' at Limerick.[95] In the following year he was released 'with the relics of Patrick'. Ó Corráin, who conceded that a ransom was 'doubtless' paid for Abbot Forannán, commented that he returned to freedom 'not much the worse for his experience'.[96] Such a trite and unsubstantiated comment was inspired by revisionist zeal rather than by any genuine understanding of contemporary accounts of Scandinavian society in the ninth century. Why should we assume that Forannán's release implied any act of clemency on the part of his captors? Or why might we assume that such a captive suffered no physical or psychological damage when all the evidence points the other way? Only twelve years later, on 12 June 858, Flotbald, bishop of Chartres, fled from his *civitas* as it was being attacked by Northmen. We are told that the bishop 'fled on foot and tried to swim across the river Eure but he was overwhelmed by the waters and drowned'.[97] Later in Ireland in 940, Coibdenach, abbot of Killeigh (Co. Offaly) was 'drowned in the sea off Dalkey while fleeing from the Foreigners'.[98] Coibdenach had clearly been sold on, and was being held captive on that off-shore island near Norse Dublin after his capture by the Irish Munster king, Cellachán, in the year before. If for high-status churchmen being a 'guest of the Northmen' were no different from being under house-arrest at the hands of some Christian trouble-maker or being caught up in violent disputes between Christian warriors, then why did bishops and magnates in Francia and Ireland throw themselves into the raging torrent in their desperate attempts to escape? In 882, when Rheims lay undefended in the face of an impending attack by Northmen, Archbishop Hincmar, by then old and sick, 'only just managed to escape by night, taking with him the body of Remigius, and the treasures of the church of Rheims'.[99] Hincmar, who assures us that he himself was aware of what the Northmen had in mind, knew these enemies better than revisionist historians of the twentieth century. No one will ever know what humiliation or terror Forannán may or may not have endured at the hands of his captors. We do know from Thietmar of Merseburg that when the Danes captured Archbishop Ælfheah of Canterbury and his companions as late as 1011 they 'ill-treated them with chains and hunger and

---

[95] *AU, s.a.* 844, pp. 302–3. [96] Ó Corráin, *Ireland before the Normans*, p. 90.
[97] Nelson (ed.), *Annals of St-Bertin, s.a.* 857, p. 85.
[98] Smyth, *Scandinavian York and Dublin*, ii, p. 133.
[99] Nelson (ed.), *Annals of St-Bertin, s.a.* 882, p. 226.

indescribable torments after their abominable fashion'.[100] Florence (alias John) of Worcester put the ransom demanded for Ælfheah at 3,000 pounds[101] – in addition to a staggering Danegeld of 48,000 pounds which we know from the *Anglo-Saxon Chronicle* was paid independently by way of a general levy from the English to the Danes, in London after Easter 1012. We also know that when Ælfheah's ransom was not paid he was done to death by an enraged army which pelted him with bones and ox heads until he was finally dispatched with a blow from the blunt end of an axe.[102] The 3,000 pounds which Florence claimed was demanded for Ælfheah was not too far out of line with the sums demanded in the ninth century for the Carolingian Abbot of St Denis, and was in keeping with Ælfheah's high status. Forannán, the leading churchman in ninth-century Ireland, was captured with the relics of Ireland's greatest saint, and we can be certain that a commensurate price was put on the head of this abbot of Armagh. As such its payment would have put as great a strain on Armagh's resources and on those of its Uí Néill royal patrons as the burden endured by the Carolingian church and its protecting dynasty at almost the same time in Francia.

Thietmar's mention of cruel treatment of prisoners by the Northmen 'after their abominable custom' prompts the question as to whether there was something about Norse paganism which was conspicuously shocking and cruel in the eyes of contemporary observers in the Christian West. Sawyer came close to the heart of the matter when he commented: 'The significant question is not whether the Vikings were more violent and brutal than others, which seems unlikely, but rather what effect their violence had, directed as it was to somewhat different ends than that of their Christian contemporaries.'[103] The crucial ingredient in this statement was the notion of violence 'directed ... to different ends'. The fact that Norse society in its earliest piratical – and therefore most brutal – form was untouched by Christianity, meant that Northmen were not only playing by different rules from their Christian victims, but that they were uninhibited by Christian taboos against abuse of the human person. They were clearly ignorant of and therefore unmoved by Christian teaching on the inherent dignity of every human being regardless of social status. Arguments that native Christian rulers

---

[100] *Thietmari Merseburgensis Episcopi Chronicon*, ed. R. Holzmann in *MGH, Rerum Germanicarum Nova Series*, ix, 2nd edn (Berlin, 955), pp. 449–50; *EHD*, i, p. 320.

[101] *Florentii Wigorniensis Monachi Chronicon ex Chronicis*, ed. B. Thorpe, 2 vols. (London, 1848–9), i, p. 165.

[102] *Anglo-Saxon Chronicle*, s.a. 1012; *EHD*, i, p. 222. Cf. the account of Archbishop Ælfheah's killing is preserved in the *Chronicle of Thietmar of Merseburg*, ibid., p. 321.

[103] Sawyer, *Kings and Vikings*, p. 95.

did themselves not live up to those standards may be misplaced. Christian society did, at the very least, hold up such ideals to be honoured by its rulers, while to Northmen the notion of every individual's unique value in the sight of God was either unknown or ridiculed by warriors who pursued a heroic lifestyle which gloried in unbridled violence. For a pagan Northman the only promise of an acceptable afterlife depended on acquiring a heroic reputation for slaughter and pillage in this. We do not need to argue that Northmen were hostile to Christianity *per se*. For many invaders it was yet another religion with its own pantheon of supernatural beings. And because monks and nuns were sitting targets, located in undefended treasure-houses, they found themselves in the front line of a conflict motivated as much by greed as by any hatred for their religious calling. That in itself must have triggered a major crisis in Western culture, for although revisionists never fail to point out rivalries which occasionally erupted into violence between religious houses, such conduct was never tolerated – from the standpoint of canon law at least – as the norm.[104] Even in the teeth of the Norse menace, Archbishop Hincmar of Rheims had serious misgivings about allowing churchmen to take part in battles against the very Northmen who were inflicting such injuries on his church.[105] So, even if the Scandinavian invaders had not been conspicuous for violence, their military capability when married to their ignorance of Christianity (or of any other more developed religion such as Islam or Judaism) spelt ruin for much of what had been achieved in the religious culture of the West over the previous three centuries. The crisis was compounded by the fact that Northmen constituted roving armies of male predators locked into a state of Iron Age cultural regression and operating with a belief system and a set of values appropriate to Celtic or Germanic peoples from a distant pre-Christian past. No one denies that violence is a part of the human condition and that institutionalized violence remains embedded in that condition. But to point to the survival of hanging, drawing and quartering on the English legal statute books into the nineteenth century is to confuse archaic legal survivals – which could be

---

[104] I have dealt with spiritual decline and inter-monastic feuding and warfare in Ireland elsewhere. Smyth, *Scandinavian York and Dublin*, ii, pp. 134–7, 140–1, 145, 150–1; Smyth, *Celtic Leinster: Towards an Historical Geography of Early Irish Civilisation* (Dublin, 1982), p. 89.

[105] Frankish bishops did personally lead armies, and even fleets, against the Northmen (Nelson (ed.), *Annals of St-Bertin*, *s.a.* 854, p. 79). Even though Hincmar's diocese had its own force of fighting men to resist Northmen (*ibid.*, p. 226), Hincmar disapproved of bishops taking part in battle. Elsewhere he accused Bishop Wala of Metz of 'bearing arms and fighting, contrary to sacred authority and the episcopal office' (*ibid.*, *s.a.* 882, p. 224).

and indeed were invoked in times of extreme political crisis – with a culture where extreme violence was a way of everyday life.[106]

The key to understanding the impact which the Northmen had upon their victims in the Christian West lies in the recognition that a cultural time-lag existed between the two societies. Early medieval Christendom had benefited from the ameliorating effects of late antique culture as transmitted through several centuries of Christianity. No one is suggesting that individual rulers in Anglo-Saxon England or Ireland might not have equalled their opposite numbers in Scandinavia for cruelty and bloodshed or for otherwise transgressing moral precepts. We need only point to King Æthelbald of Mercia (716–57) who was reproached by St Boniface for fornicating with nuns, or to King Feidlimid of Munster (820–47) who, although a bishop and a supposed reformer, waged constant wars against his enemies and plundered their monasteries at will. But Northmen had never known evangelists such as Patrick, Colum Cille or Augustine. They had never been touched by the spiritual passion of a Cuthbert, the scholarship of an Adomnán or Bede, or the aesthetic sensibility of the calligrapher of the *Book of Kells*. Illiterate barbarians that they were, they could only come to impede and destroy the Carolingian Renaissance – not to foster it. And while they remained pagan and in a state of armed migration, their religious needs were served by the bloody rites of their war-god, Odin. To point, as some revisionists do, to the alacrity with which Northmen eventually turned to Christianity, is somewhat akin to minimizing the persecutions under Diocletian by pointing to the promotion of Christianity under Constantine. Besides, it is not at all clear to what extent Norsemen embraced the spirit of Christian teaching in tenth-century England or Normandy. It was not until the early eleventh century that Christianity took hold in colonies such as Dublin or the Orkneys, while parts of the Scandinavian homeland remained impervious to Christian beliefs for much longer. Norse paganism and especially Norse war-cults showed remarkable resilience in the face of more advanced Christian cultures in the south and west of Europe.

Thietmar's comment in the early eleventh century about 'abominable customs' regarding cruel treatment of prisoners by Northmen could be dismissed as naked prejudice were it not that references to such distinctive practices are found all across the Christian West. When the Frankish magnate, Imino, was castigated by the annalist 'for causing widespread devastation' in 878 and consequently for 'behaving the way the Northmen do (*more Nortmanico*)', the annalist was pointing to a

[106] Sawyer, *Kings and Vikings*, p. 95.

destructiveness in Norse activity which had taken on a distinctive quality in late ninth-century Francia. The Irish Uí Néill over-king, Máel Sechnaill I, attacked a band of native Irish renegade warriors in 847 who were holding out on an island in Lough Ramor (Co. Cavan), because as 'Sons of Death' they 'had been plundering territories in the manner of the heathen (*more gentilium*)'.[107] It was men such as these who had aided Northmen in the wounding and burning of the abbot of Anagassan in 842, and such collaborators were to be found in most Christian societies across the medieval West. But here in these two completely independent and contemporary observations, we have it spelt out that Norse culture – and therefore Norse paganism – lent a peculiarly vicious edge to Norse raiding. Nor can it be argued that here we have monks whinging yet again at the destruction of church property. The Irish king took action against raiders who were attacking territories (*na tuath*) or society at large. What is remarkable also is that the very earliest observers of Scandinavian armies in Francia, England, Ireland, and Islamic Spain were all aware of the pagan character of these warbands long before any of their individual leaders or country of origin were identified in the records. The Franks regularly applied the term *pagani* to their Norse enemies, and they frequently refer to the native defenders as 'Christian men'. Such terminology is not surprising in the Carolingian empire whose rulers had a special Christian mandate. There is some evidence, too, on the part of Frankish writers for the development of an ideological conflict between Norse paganism and the Christian way of life. A monk who had gone over to the Northmen on the Loire and 'had abandoned Christendom' was executed by his Frankish captors in 869 because he 'had been extremely dangerous to Christians'.[108] Pippin II of Aquitane, another apostate monk, was indicted at Pîtres in 865 for having 'joined company with the Northmen and served their rituals'. He was condemned as a traitor 'to his fatherland and to Christianity'.[109] The Old Irish annalist whose record survives within the Annals of Ulster consistently applied the term *gentiles* and *gennti* to the earliest raiders of the late eighth and early ninth centuries. So, too, in the *Anglo-Saxon Chronicle*, the West Saxon compiler invariably reported on 'heathen men' in a 'heathen army', led by 'heathen kings'.[110] Even though English observers soon became aware of the Danish origin of the raiders, their 'heathen' attributes continued to be used as an identifying tag into the second half of the ninth century and beyond. The attitude of

---

[107] *AU*, s.a. 846, pp. 306–7.   [108] Nelson (ed.), *Annals of St-Bertin*, p. 163.
[109] Smyth, *King Alfred the Great*, p. 81, and see note 67 (pp. 617–18), where I offer a different interpretation of this annal from that of Professor Nelson.
[110] *Ibid.*, pp. 80–1.

the West Saxon chronicler is important, because however much the origin of the *Chronicle* is debated, there can be no doubt as to its secular tone in contrast to Frankish and Irish annals which were clearly monastic in character. Islamic writers, too, referred to the Northmen as *madjus* – 'heathen', 'magician' – and were struck by the ferocity with which they threw themselves against Islamic cult centres in Seville and elsewhere.[111] Modern commentators are not always aware of the embattled nature of ninth-century Western Christianity, surrounded as it was by pagan Scandinavians, Slavs and Magyars to the North, East and South-east, while it felt menaced by Islamic rulers on its south flank in the Mediterranean. This siege mentality is well exemplified in Alcuin's letter to his English colleague, Speratus, where he reveals that pagan kings – even in literary fiction – occupy a separate world from Christians in this life and the next: 'The Heavenly King does not wish to have communion with pagan and forgotten kings listed name by name: for the eternal King reigns in Heaven, while the forgotten pagan king wails in Hell.'[112]

Labels identifying Northmen as 'pagan' are not in themselves indicative of extraordinarily violent behaviour, but because those labels were used from the earliest encounters, it does suggest that there was something conspicuously 'heathen' about the appearance or behaviour of Norse raiding parties in the earliest piratical phase of Norse attacks. We have seen, too, how those who raided 'in the manner of Northmen' were described as 'Sons of Death' – the opposite to one who is saved, a 'Son of Life' (*Mac Bethad* or Macbeth). There is additional evidence to show how Norse paganism manifested itself in practice when raiders assailed whole communities. I have already referred to accounts of slaughtering prisoners who were of no commercial use, and to the torture and mistreatment of captives. There are other references to Norse raiding which suggests that Northmen practised total war against certain target populations with a view, perhaps, to land-clearance and colonization. The Frankish account of a dawn raid by Northmen on Quentovic in 842 tells us that: 'They plundered it and laid it waste, capturing or massacring the inhabitants of both sexes. They left nothing in it except for those buildings which they were paid to spare.'[113] The reference to the slaying of 'people of both sexes' during the 842 raid on Quentovic points to that element of total war in Norse raiding which was peculiarly shocking to Christian writers. Ecclesiastical legislation of the later tenth century in Francia would strive to protect non-combatants from the

[111] Stefánsson, 'Vikings in Spain', pp. 31–46.
[112] Bullough, 'What has Ingeld to do with Lindisfarne?', p. 124.
[113] Nelson (ed.), *Annals of St-Bertin*, s.a. 842, p. 53.

horrors of warfare, and in Ireland as early as the late seventh century, the *Cáin* or *Law* of Adomnán provided the same safeguards. And while atrocities did occur among Christian warriors, there were ideals to be formally proclaimed by clergy, and there were sanctions against those who over-stepped the bounds of acceptable behaviour. Repeated contemporary references to the slaying of women and children by Northmen show how raiders playing by a different set of social rules could terrorize an entire population. When Northmen sacked the town of Nantes in 843, 'lay people of both sexes were slaughtered' as well as the bishop and many clergy.[114] Ten years later Danish raiders went on a rampage on the Seine from October to March: 'They ravaged burnt and took captives all the more savagely for being completely unrestrained.'[115] When Charles the Bald eventually awoke to the seriousness of the Norse threat in the 860s he built forts and bridges and fortified the towns of West Francia on the Seine and Marne and on the middle Loire. This left coastal areas of Francia along the English Channel at the mercy of invaders, and also the region between the Somme and the Rhine.[116] There is evidence to show that Northmen made a serious and concerted attempt to conquer that north-eastern region of Francia in the 880s and they would probably have succeeded were it not for their defeat in battle on the banks of the river Dyle near Louvain in 891, and even more importantly perhaps because of an outbreak of famine and disease in their own ranks.[117] The Annals of St Vaast record the activities of Hæsten's army in that region in 884 in a way which suggests the Northmen were bent on wiping out the native inhabitants – ethnic cleansing, Norse style:

> The Northmen did not desist from the slaying and taking captive of Christians, tearing down churches, razing fortifications to the ground and burning settlements. On all the streets lay the corpses of clerics, of nobles and of other lay people, of women, young people, and sucklings. There was no street or place where the dead did not lie, and it was for everyone a torment and a pain to see how Christian people had been brought to the point of extermination.[118]

This account mirrors Abbo's description of the siege of Paris only one year before, when he tells us that the Northmen roamed through the countryside on horseback and on foot indulging in an orgy of destruction, slaying 'infants, children, young men, old men, fathers, sons and mothers'.[119] One year earlier yet again, in 882, Regino of Prüm described a raid on that monastery on Twelfth Night (6 January) when

---

[114] *Ibid.*, p. 55.   [115] *Ibid.*, pp. 75–6.
[116] Sawyer, *Kings and Vikings*, pp. 89–92.   [117] Smyth, *King Alfred the Great*, p. 119.
[118] *Ibid.*, p. 129.
[119] Abbo, *Le Siège de Paris par les Normands*, ed. H. Waquet (Paris, 1942), pp. 28–30.

Northmen slaughtered an unarmed population and 'fell upon them with a great cry and struck them down with such carnage that it seemed as though brute beasts (*bruta animalia*) were being slaughtered rather than people'.[120] The Annals of Ulster, in a relentless contemporary catalogue of Norse raiding throughout Ireland in the 830s, note 'a most cruel devastation (*Uastatio crudelissima*) of all the lands of Connacht by the heathen' in 836, and in 837 two separate fleets of Northmen, each of sixty ships swept the lands between the Boyne and Liffey 'plundering churches, fortifications and dwellings' suggestive of a campaign against an entire population. That same sense of mass devastation is reiterated by the Annals of St-Bertin in the account of a Danish raid on Rouen in 841: 'Danish pirates plundered the town with pillage, fire and sword, slaughtered or took captive monks and the rest of the population, and laid waste all the monasteries and other places along the banks of the Seine, or else took large payments and left them thoroughly terrified.'[121] The 'large payments' cannot be seen as a humanitarian alternative to violence. It was good hard-headed business. When Gothfrith, the pagan king of Dublin, attacked Armagh on the Saturday before the Feast of St Martin in 921, he did so in the knowledge that the place would be preparing for that festival and would most likely provide a rich booty of food-renders. We are told that 'he spared from destruction the prayer-houses with their communities of Céli Dé (reformist ascetics) and the houses of the sick, and also the monastery except for a few dwellings which were burnt through carelessness'.[122] Gothfrith grandson of Ivar was no humanitarian. He was described in the same annals at his death in 934 as 'a most cruel king of the Northmen (*rí crudelissimus Nordmannorum*)' and his sparing of buildings in Armagh was probably prompted by a desire to preserve the heart of a monastery which provided such rich pickings from routine Norse raiding. Gothfrith almost certainly extracted his price from the Armagh monks as the account of the raid on Quentovic in 842 – when buildings were spared at a price – amply demonstrates.[123] We also read of 'a great ransom' being paid to Vikings from the Seine to save a few important Paris churches from being burnt in 857, while other churches in that town were given up to the flames.[124]

Sawyer believed that while 'there is no reason to doubt the general reliability of [these] accounts of the movements of groups of Vikings,

---

[120] *Reginonis Chronica*, s.a. 882, ed. R. Rau, in *Ausgewählte Quellen zur deutschen Geschichte des Mittelalters*, VII, ii (c. 1960), pp. 260–2.
[121] Nelson (ed.), *Annals of St-Bertin*, p. 50.   [122] *AU*, s.a. 920, pp. 372–3.
[123] Nelson (ed.), *Annals of St-Bertin*, s.a. 842, p. 53.   [124] *Ibid.*, s.a. 857, p. 85.

there is every reason to suspect exaggeration in their descriptions of the size and destructiveness of the raiding bands'.[125] Ó Corráin, writing ten years after Sawyer had tried to rehabilitate his Vikings in England, attempted to do a similar service for Norse raiders in Ireland:

One thing is clear: they [the Vikings] made little or no impact on secular society. In the first quarter century of Viking attack, only twenty-six plunderings, or other acts of violence to be attributed to the Vikings are recorded in the Irish annals. In the same period the annals record some eighty-seven acts of violence which occur amongst the Irish themselves. In twenty-five years the raids average out at a fraction of over one per year, a rate which if the annals are at all representative, can have caused no widespread disorder or great distress in Irish society even if we multiply it by a factor of five. Many historians, forgetting the timespan of these events, telescope them, and produce a picture of widespread ravaging and plundering, made even more lurid by the lack of any attempt to take into account and allow for the bias of the monastic annalists.[126]

Ó Corráin's analysis was statistically flawed and lamentably lacking in historical judgement. He chose to attach sweeping generalizations regarding the impact of Scandinavian raiders on Irish society on to his manipulation of statistics relating only to the first twenty-five years of raiding. Yet on his own admission – epitomized by his headline *Intensification of Raids and Settlements*[127] – Norse raiding in Ireland escalated to alarming proportions from 830 onwards, culminating in the foundation of a settlement at Dublin in 841. Ó Corráin conceded that by 845 'it appeared that the country was about to be overrun'.[128] Even in distant Francia – itself hard-pressed by Scandinavian marauders – alarm bells were set off in 847 regarding Norse successes in Ireland: 'The Irish who had been attacked by the Northmen for a number of years, were made into regular tribute-payers. The Northmen also got control of the islands all around Ireland and stayed there without encountering any resistance from anyone.'[129]

Did that also make 'little or no impact on secular society'? And is such an account of a Norse maritime stranglehold on the whole of Irish society – which must have been building up since c. 800 – suggestive of small numbers of ships and small numbers of fighting men? And even if the same Frankish annals reported that in the following year (848) the Irish had regained ground, it would have been impossible for a land-based people to have shaken off the Norse stranglehold on the off-shore islands. By overrunning those islands, the Northmen destroyed the monastic culture which centred on major island sanctuaries around the Irish coast – places such as Rathlin, Tory, Inismurray, Inisglora, Iniskea

---

[125] Sawyer, *Age of the Vikings*, p. 120.
[126] Ó Corráin, *Ireland before the Normans*, p. 83.   [127] *Ibid.*, p. 89.
[128] *Ibid.*, p. 90.   [129] Nelson (ed.), *Annals of St-Bertin*, s.a. 847, p. 65.

North, Caher, Inisboffin, St MacDara's Island, Aran, Bishop's Island, Scattery (in the mouth of the Shannon), Skellig Michael, Begerin and Lambay. All these islands either still contain important architectural early Christian remains – some have several monastic sites – from the pre-Norse era, or else they are documented in early medieval sources as centres of asceticism and learning. The catalogue does not contain a list of major coastal monasteries – mainland houses which lay near the Irish coast and which were just as vulnerable to Norse attack. Such places included Lusk, Tallaght or Clondalkin, on or near the east coast; Lismore and Cloyne in the south; Ardfert in the south-west; and Fahan, Derry, Raphoe and Bangor in the north. Many of these houses did survive the Viking Age, but Byrne's comment that the confederation of Céli Dé houses had 'suffered disastrously from Viking raids and particularly from the Norse settlement at Dublin' may be applied to the Irish monastic scene as a whole.[130] Nor will we ever know the full number of lesser, isolated, early Christian foundations which, lacking the protection of powerful dynasties, quickly disappeared forever. Such ecclesiastical outposts as those on Omey Island (near Cleggan in Connemara) or at Illaunloughan (in the Portmagee Channel between Valentia and the Kerry mainland) only come to light through chance discovery and the excavational skills of the archaeologist.[131] These and other countless exposed coastal cult-centres and lesser places of local pilgrimage had no place in a world infested by Northmen, and their demise as communities must have damaged the infrastructure of early Irish civilization. A poem written in the margin of the St Gall Priscian conveys an Irish monk's obsessive but well-founded fear of Norse attack:

> Rough is the wind tonight
> tossing the white-combed ocean;
> I need not dread fierce Northmen
> crossing the Irish Sea.[132]

Using the waterways of the Shannon, Erne, Boyne, Liffey and Lough Neagh, the Northmen penetrated the very heartlands of Irish civilization from the 830s onwards, and given their element of surprise, brutality and mobility, it is clear that they shook Irish society to its foundations – transforming the nature of kingship and arresting the progress of monastic learning and achievements in the arts. From the 840s onwards

---

[130] F. J. Byrne, *Irish Kings and High-Kings* (London, 1973), pp. 157–8.
[131] T. O'Keefe, 'Omey and the sands of time', *Archaeology Ireland*, 8, no. 2 (1994), pp. 14–17; J. W. Marshall and C. Walsh, 'Illaunloughan: life and death on a small early monastic site', *Archaeology Ireland*, 8, no. 4 (1994), pp. 25–8.
[132] Translation after L. de Paor, 'The age of the Viking wars', in *The Course of Irish History*, ed. T. W. Moody and F. X. Martin (Cork, 1967), p. 93.

no major inland monastery was out of range of Norse attack and storehouses of learning and the arts such as Clonmacnoise and Clonfert, together with all the island sanctuaries in the Shannon, found themselves in the front line of Norse aggression.

It is a futile exercise to count numbers of raids and divide that total by the number of years involved. Historians who examine the impact of enemy action over Kent in the Second World War do not focus on the total number of bombing raids or on the number of bombs that were dropped. Nor do they hope to reach any valid conclusions by dividing the total number of air-raids by the five years of war. The location chosen for raids, the intensity of individual attacks, and the social anxiety generated by the fear of impending attack, are surely what count for modern as well as for early medieval students of warfare. A single Baedeker raid on Canterbury on a night in June 1942 wrought more havoc than hundreds of doodle-bugs dropped on country lanes.[133] It is more important to observe that Armagh was involved in no less than five violent encounters with Northmen in the nine years between 831 and 840 than to embark with Ó Corráin on a dubious exercise in elementary sums without any reference to specific locations. In 831 Armagh fielded an army against pagan Northmen and was defeated. In the following year, Armagh was plundered no less than three times in one month, and in 840 its oratory and stone church were burnt. If that were not enough, Armagh's abbot, Forannán, was taken captive by Northmen, as we have seen, in 845. It is a nonsense to suppose that this intense targeting of Ireland's chief ecclesiastical centre by Scandinavian invaders did not have the most profound effect on 'secular society' as well as on ecclesiastical and cultural life.

Conclusions reached by revisionists on the Viking Age do not stand up to scrutiny when we compare like with like across the period, and when we disentangle accounts of earliest piratical activity (795–c. 885) from later accounts of settlement and colonization. When we examine sources from widely different societies – the Carolingian empire, Anglo-Saxon England, Iona and Ireland – we are faced with a catalogue of atrocities carried out by an invading people who did not share the belief systems of their victims. It was naive if not mischievous of revisionists to differentiate between contemporary attitudes of 'church' and 'state' to Norse raiders, as though these were two separate institutions as in a

---

[133] For those who have a need for statistics, Canterbury was the recipient during the War of 445 high explosives and 10,000 incendiaries. The town lost 115 of its inhabitants and some 800 of its buildings. In spite of all that, and its 2,477 alerts, the great mass of damage to Canterbury was accomplished in a brief but intensive June blitz of 1942. J. Boyle, *Portrait of Canterbury* (London, 1974), p. 128.

modern state. That approach – which essentially imposed a set of post-Christian 'detached' values on the thought world of the Middle Ages – conveniently marginalized the testimony of contemporary annalists as the exaggerations of hysterical monks. It is the failure of historians on all sides of this debate to comprehend the psychological and cultural consequences of Norse paganism on the thinking of the all-inclusive Christian establishment in the ninth and tenth centuries which has led to such grotesque weakness in the intellectual debate. Sawyer informed us that Charles the Bald probably postponed a decision to fortify his towns on the upper Seine until as late as 862 because 'perhaps even at that stage the Franks thought the Vikings were a judgement from God to be met by prayer and reform rather than stone walls'.[134] 'Perhaps' indeed, but revisionists cannot have the argument both ways. Sawyer's conclusion only serves to underline the devastating effect which invaders with a different belief system and a different world view could have on a Christian society where 'church' and 'state' were almost one. If Charles were indeed so imbued with such sentiments of Christian piety that his clerical aristocracy could influence military decisions in favour of prayer and fasting rather than direct military action, then his Franklish realm was even more vulnerable to the depredations of pagan Northmen than any historians have hitherto believed possible. Ó Corráin, setting up a straw target, strove to show that Irish monasteries were worldly and wealthy places long before Northmen arrived to attack or subvert them. While playing down the devastating effects of Norse raiders, he argued from the record of 3,000 captives taken from Kells in 951, that the place was a rich ecclesiastical centre.[135] But that is only half the story. The captives in 951 cannot all have been monks in any strict sense, and many may have been fugitives from the surrounding countryside. What Ó Corráin failed to tell his readers was that the Kells raid was carried out by Northmen; was led by Gothfrith Sytryggsson of Dublin; and that the 3,000 captives were made up of victims not only from Kells but from Kells, Donaghpatrick, Arbracken, Tulane and Kilskyre.[136]

When the historian of the late ninth and tenth centuries is left to do the book-keeping in the aftermath of the Viking catastrophe, there are some formidable entries on the debit side. The catalogue of slayings of individual bishops to be found in the Frankish annals in the mid-ninth century resulted in the abandonment of Bordeaux by its prelate who eventually moved to Bourges in 876, having found Poitiers as unsafe as the capital of Aquitane. The bishop of Nantes, not surprisingly, fled further up the Loire in 868 (his predecessor had been slain in the raid of

---

[134] Sawyer, *Kings and Vikings*, p. 89.
[135] Ó Corráin, *Ireland before the Normans*, p. 88.   [136] *AU*, s.a. 950, pp. 396–7.

843), while the bishop of Coutances moved to Rouen. And although Norman historians of the eleventh and twelfth centuries could trumpet the promotion of church building and church reform, the truth is that their Viking ancestors were responsible for the disruption of episcopal succession right across Normandy in the late ninth century – at Avranches, Bayeux, Evreux and Liseux.[137] It is also the case that Scandinavian inroads into Francia exacerbated the political divisions which were already a fact of life in the later Carolingian empire, and the Northmen played no small part in hastening the break up of the Carolingian world. It is also the case that pagan aspects of Scandinavian aggression against the West accelerated the militarization of Christianity in Germany, Francia and the British Isles, resulting in the active participation of churchmen on the battlefield and in the militarization of Christian ideology *vis-à-vis* non-Christian neighbours.

In late tenth-century England, there would not have been need for monastic reconstruction under St Oswald had not the Danes wiped out monasticism – if not indeed organized Christianity altogether – throughout the Southern Danelaw. The founding of Ramsey and the reconstruction of houses such as Ely, Peterborough and Thorney, testify to the devastations of the century before.[138] The burden of proof still rests with those who would attempt to argue that monasticism was a spent force in England before the Vikings arrived. Decline in monastic fervour and true monastic principles is one thing. The obliteration of entire monasteries and monastic culture is quite another. Episcopal successions at Lindsey, Leicester, Dunwich and Elham were disrupted or destroyed, with the obvious implications that had for the ordination of clergy and pastoral care of the native English population. While some English bishoprics reemerged, others such as Hexham and Whithorn in Northumbria never recovered. As Stenton put it: 'throughout England the Danish raids meant, if not the destruction, at least the grievous impoverishment of civilization'.[139] Just as cultural power-houses such as Whitby never regained their former standing, so too in Ireland spiritual, scholarly and artistic achievements never returned to pre-Viking levels of excellence. The process of secularization of Irish monasteries among those communities which managed to survive, and levels of violent participation on the part of monasteries in the politics of the warrior aristocracy, were accelerated by the Viking wars. In Sawyer's words: 'Viking attacks certainly made matters worse.'[140] The difficulties of the

---

[137] The list is taken from Sawyer, *Kings and Vikings*, p. 90.
[138] C. [R.] Hart, *The Danelaw* (London, 1992), pp. 598–623; Stenton, *Anglo-Saxon England*, pp. 444–62.
[139] Stenton, *Anglo-Saxon England*, p. 427.   [140] Sawyer, *Kings and Vikings*, p. 96.

Irish terrain, combined with the cellular nature of Irish society ensured, first of all, the survival of many native Christian dynasties. The survival of native Irish royal protection and patronage ensured in their turn the preservation of larger Irish monastic houses, but in a greatly diminished form. It must surely have been because of diminished resources that the churches of Armagh and Iona were united under the same abbot, Máel Brígte mac Tornáin, in the early tenth century. And although Iona recovered to become a cult centre for the Norsemen of the Hebrides in the late tenth century,[141] the age of exquisite calligraphy as exemplified in the earlier Gospel Books, or of the scholarship of Adomnán or Dicuil, were gone forever. On the Irish mainland, centres such as Bangor, Tallaght or Terryglass were also past their golden days by the later tenth century, and even at Clonmacnoise, which enjoyed the patronage of the richest of kings, scholarly output seems to have shied away from Latin and biblical scholarship and to have reverted to antiquarian studies in the vernacular. A land denuded of libraries, and with its monastic communities concentrating on sheer survival, could not hope to produce another Eriugena or Sedulius Scotus in the later tenth century. While Northmen – for political reasons – began to turn to Christianity in England and Francia in the early tenth century, that process was delayed in Ireland by another hundred years.[142] By misreading an entry in the Annals of Ulster under the year 872 (*recte* 873), Ó Corráin wrongly concluded that the notorious Ivar of Dublin had died a Christian,[143] and he equally wrongly assumed that Northmen in Ireland were embracing Christianity by the 860s. Unlike the York Danes, their Irish Scandinavian counterparts remained heathen, nor is there any evidence to suggest that Irish clergy mounted any serious or successful attempt to evangelize their Norse enemies in the ninth century or indeed before the last quarter of the tenth. Tenth-century records show a continuous catalogue of raiding, burning and looting of Irish monasteries by the Northmen of Dublin and other new coastal strongholds. When Christianity did percolate to the Hiberno-Norsemen, it seems to have done

---

[141] Smyth, *Warlords and Holy Men*, pp. 210–14.

[142] Smyth, *Scandinavian York and Dublin*, ii, 309–12.

[143] Ó Corráin, *Ireland before the Normans*, p. 96. Ó Corráin followed a later reading (*in Christo quieuit*) of the text of *The Annals of Ulster* for the notice of Ivar's death in 873 – a reading clearly marked as less reliable in W. M. Hennessy's edition (*Annála Uladh: Annals of Ulster* ed. W. M. Hennessy and B. MacCarthy, 4 vols. (Dublin, 1887–1901), i, n. 6, p. 387). The oldest manuscript reading has *uitam finiuit* (S. Mac Airt and G. Mac Niocaill (eds.), *Annals of Ulster* (to AD1131) (Dublin, 1983), p. 328). This egregious handling of the text of the *Annals of Ulster* was put right by B. Jaski, 'The Vikings and the kingship of Tara', *Peritia*, 9 (1995), p. 320, n. 40.

so largely via their contacts with England and the Hebrides in the late tenth and early eleventh centuries.[144]

When we look back across the length and breadth of the Viking Age from Spain to Iona and from Inisboffin to Saxony, monastic communities and other church centres can be clearly identified as major victims in the conflict. Night raids, dawn raids, mid-winter raids across frozen lakes and rivers,[145] raids on Christmas Night, Twelfth Night, the Feast of All Saints, St Martin, Sts Peter and Paul, St John the Baptist, St Patrick and St Brigit – all of these were part of the course for Norse marauders. No advantage was too mean for a Northman to resist taking, and no atrocity seemed too great. The undefended ritual sites of the Christian West were ransacked for loot, and the Christian calendar was exploited with profit to catch a community when it was most likely to be off guard. Monks and nuns as well as secular clergy were tortured, slain, captured, held for ransom or driven off their lands. Their shrines were broken up and melted down: their books burnt or held for ransom. Since in other contexts and in less emotive historical debates scholars are agreed that Christianity formed a major pillar of early medieval civilization, it is difficult not to conclude that the impact of the Northmen was nothing less than catastrophic. As for the 'pro-Viking opposition' – the very phrase[146] reveals a misplaced partisan approach that has no place in historical methodology. We do not have to conclude that 'Vikings' or their civilization were 'good' or 'bad', nor does the recognition of culture-lag in relation to north Germanic barbarism preclude us from recognizing Norse expertise in ship-building and town-building as well as acknowledging skills in wood-carving and story-telling. The fact that Norse warriors like all their Iron Age Indo-European cousins may well have been regarded as an élite within their own societies who had leisure to perfect skills in sport, hunting, rhyming or in chess, should not beguile us into following Page's naïve description of these barbarians as 'accomplished gentlemen' of 'good family'.[147] We need to be aware of relative states of cultural progression and to appreciate that ninth-century Scandinavian society was still languishing in a pre-literate warrior Iron Age, while its victims in the West had moved on into a sub-Roman world heavily influenced by an advanced religion and the rudiments of Graeco-Roman philosophical thought.

[144] Smyth, *Warlords and Holy Men*, pp. 210–14.
[145] See Smyth, *Scandinavian York and Dublin*, ii, pp. 130–1, for Irish and other evidence. The *Annals of St-Bertin* record a dawn raid on Quentovic in 842; and night attacks on Noyon (859), Bordeaux (848) and Chartres (858). Such tactics are amply supported by contemporary Irish accounts of Norse raiding.
[146] Frank, 'Viking atrocity and Skaldic verse', p. 330.
[147] Page, *Chronicles of the Vikings*, pp. 79, 167–8.

And for those who persevere in the cynical belief that human kind never advances morally or culturally, I offer this challenge based on evidence from two different cultural scenarios in the Early Middle Ages – one from Old Uppsala in the late eleventh century and another from Anglo-Saxon England and Celtic Ireland in the ninth and tenth. The evidence from Uppsala refers to a time so late in the Middle Ages that the Anglo-Saxon Age was already past and when by then a Norman king had come to rule over Winchester, Westminster and York. Yet at Old Uppsala in the third quarter of the eleventh century, the bodies of human sacrificial victims to Odin, Frey and Thor, were reported by Adam of Bremen to have hung in a sacred grove alongside the putrefying carcasses of hung horses and dogs.[148] And down a nearby well, other sacrificial victims were propelled to their deaths.[149] While Adam can be shown to be shaky on detail, he was nevertheless in a position to hear eye-witness accounts of the pagan rites at Old Uppsala and he cites a Christian witness who saw the corpses hanging in the sacred grove. The iconoclastic Page conceded that 'even the sceptical must accept there could be truth behind some of it [i.e. the account of the pagan temple and the nearby grove]'.[150] The challenge facing the 'pro-Viking' lobby is this: do they accept such a society to have been on a par with those in the British Isles which several centuries earlier had already produced the outstanding library used by Alcuin at York, or the hospital for the sick which was maintained by monks at Armagh at a time when its abbot, mac Tornáin, produced his celebrated Gospels? And will they not accept that those early Christian societies which had achieved such cultural gains were seriously damaged by the incursions of warriors erupting out of the prehistory of the North, whose descendants more than two centuries later were still languishing in a state of bloody barbarism at Old Uppsala?

---

[148] *Magister Adam Bremensis*, pp. 470–2.
[149] *Ibid.*, the account of the well at Uppsala is found in one of the scholia to Adam's text, p. 470.
[150] Page, *Chronicles of the Vikings*, p. 220.

2 The changing economy of the Irish Sea province: AD 900–1300

Benjamin T. Hudson

The beginning of a survey about the trade and economy of the Irish Sea province should note that there has been much general acknowledgement of its importance, but little specific study of it. The wealth and economic vitality of the Irish Sea are frequently mentioned in discussions of insular history during the high Middle Ages, but there has been little scholarly study of its commercial history as a whole. This neglect is not unexpected, especially since the materials customary for economic history begin to appear only late and sparsely in the period. Irish Sea commerce, moreover, is intertwined with other considerations such as the spread of saintly cults – the veneration of St Wulfstan of Worcester at Dublin was due as much to maritime contacts with southeast England as to his patronage of clergy from the town – or the composition of literature; the Irish locations found in the tales of the Mabinogion suggest the avenues of Hiberno-Welsh trade. The following discussion does not propose to remedy the defect, for a comprehensive study would be a book in itself. Merely a few comments will be made concerning some interesting aspects of trade and economy in the Irish Sea province from the tenth to thirteenth centuries, a period of change throughout Europe.

The beginning of the tenth century is a useful starting point for a study of the economy of the Irish Sea province. Late in the ninth century the West Saxon king, Alfred the Great, was visited by a Norse traveller named Othere, who told the king much about commerce from the Arctic Circle to the English Channel; but other than knowledge of the sailing route from Norway to Ireland, he had nothing to say of trade in the Irish Sea region.[1] Moving forward almost three centuries, in the late twelfth century a monk named Lucian wrote a somewhat overenthusiastic praise poem on the great trading port of Chester; there he

---

[1] *Bright's Old English Grammar and Reader*, ed. F. G. Cassidy and R. N. Ringler, 3rd edn (New York, 1971), pp. 184–95; *King Alfred's Orosius*, ed. H. Sweet (London, 1883); J. Bosworth, *King Alfred's Anglo-Saxon Version of the Compendious History of the World by Orosius* (London, 1859).

noted that ships from as far north as Norway and as far south as Aquitaine sailed to the Irish Sea and called at Chester.[2] The centuries between Alfred and Lucian saw the development of the Irish Sea province into one of the great trading areas of northern Atlantic Europe. Not only were fortunes made for those who controlled that trade, but the region's commercial activity had an influence throughout northwestern Europe. Ships from the Baltic and Arctic Circle brought their cargoes of furs, hawks and amber to trade for the grain of Britain and Ireland and wine of Aquitaine.

What constituted the Irish Sea province?[3] The region extended beyond the shores of the Irish Sea as defined geographically. The Irish Sea province included the southern Hebrides, then south through the North Channel separating Ireland and Galloway as far as the southern limit of St George's Channel, which linked Waterford and Wexford in the west and Bristol in the east. Three main routes crossed the Irish Sea province. The first was across St George's Channel, which linked the Bristol Channel, the Severn and south Wales with southeast Ireland, especially the rivers Nore, Suir and Barrow and the Slaney; this connected the ports of Bristol and St David's with those at Waterford and Wexford. The second route was parallel to the first, but it linked the river Dee, the north Welsh coast and the Isle of Man with the rivers Liffey and Boyne; on that route were found the important ports of Chester, Holyhead, Dublin and Drogheda. The third route was a north–south passage extending southwards to the Bay of Biscay and Galicia while the northern extension carried along the western coast of Scotland to Iceland, due north, and turning east past the Orkneys and Shetlands to Norway and the Baltic.

The Irish Sea is a relatively shallow extension of the Atlantic. The climate is fairly benign, although dangerous storms and unsettled weather make shipwreck a constant threat. The Irish Sea province also is relatively small in extent; in the late eleventh century the Welsh prince, Gruffudd ap Cynan, rowed himself from Wales to Ireland.[4] Sailing times could be correspondingly brief. When Henry II sailed from Wexford to St Davids the voyage took about six hours.[5] Heavily laden merchant ships travelled more slowly, and in the fifteenth century William of Worcester was informed by Bartholomew

---

[2] *Liber Luciani de Laude Cestrie*, ed. M. V. Taylor, Lancashire and Cheshire Record Society, vol. 64 (Edinburgh and London, 1912).

[3] For a discussion of this problem in a different context see L. Alcock, 'Was there an Irish Sea culture-province in the Dark Ages?', in *The Irish Sea Province in Archaeology and History*, ed. D. Moore (Cardiff, 1970), pp. 55–65.

[4] *Hanes Gruffydd ap Cynan*, ed. A. Jones (Manchester, 1910), p. 134.

[5] Giraldus, *Expugnatio*, p. 104.

Rossynell, a Dublin merchant, that a cargo ship could sail from Dublin to the Isle of Man in a day and a night.[6] Such times were not constant because of the dependence on the wind by sailing ships, which could be forced to remain in harbour for weeks while waiting for favourable breezes.

The sea routes communicated with Ireland and Britain by way of the great natural lowland gaps that furnished the avenues for travel into the interior. By the high Middle Ages control of those avenues became crucial, both politically and ecclesiastically, which brought them into the notice of the written records. A useful example is the Solway Firth, which is noticed in the English records in 1092 when the king of the English, William Rufus, took direct control of Carlisle and colonized the region with settlers from the south of England.[7] To the south, the river Dee gave access to the English midlands; its importance for control of traffic from the Irish Sea had been recognized by the Romans who there built their great northwestern garrisons at Chester and, well to the west of the Dee, another one at the Isle of Anglesey. The commercial relationship of the Isle of Anglesey to Chester is a problem which could bear more study, for it has been suggested that the docks and weirs built at Holyhead in the tenth century were servicing the traffic between northwest England and eastern Ireland.[8] The important region of the Bristol Channel – South Wales did not receive mention in the medieval chronicles as early as Chester, although the prominence of St Davids and the ties between the early Welsh and Irish churches may have been partly responsible for the traffic between western Wales and eastern Ireland. In Ireland the gaps furnished by the Slaney and the Liffey had opened the interior to travellers and traders since the earliest days of sailing. By this period the towns in Ireland which grew up in those gaps – Dublin, Waterford and Wexford – connected the Scandinavian world with the Celtic.

Trade had an ancient lineage in the Irish Sea, and at the beginning of the Middle Ages there is visible an international dimension. A passage in Adomnán's Life of Columba notes that the truth of a saintly prophecy was revealed when a ship arrived in the Irish Sea from Gaul.[9] The *Vita* of Philibert of Jumièges (composed in the eighth century and reworked in the ninth) mentions a merchant ship from Ireland arriving in the Loire

---

[6] William Worcestre, *Itineraries*, ed. J. H. Harvey (Oxford, 1969), p. 171, after T. O'Neill, *Merchants and Mariners in Medieval Ireland* (Dublin, 1987), p. 118.
[7] Plummer and Earle (eds.), *Two of the Saxon Chronicles Parallel*, i, p. 227.
[8] H. R. Loyn, *The Vikings in Wales* (London, 1976).
[9] Adomnán, *Life of Columba*, ed. A. O. Anderson and M. O. Anderson (Oxford, 1991), p. 54.

with a cargo of shoes and clothes.[10] The cargo in the ship from Gaul or the commodity to be collected by the Irish ship was probably wine, the earliest pan-European commodity. The Irish ships might also have carried home the type of pottery known as E-ware, which was produced in western and northwestern Gaul in the sixth to eighth centuries; shards of E-ware have been found in the western and northern Irish Sea region.[11] Trade was valued by the rulers of the lands. The Old Irish tract *Tecosca Cormaic* ('Instructions of Cormac'), attributed to the high-king Cormac mac Airt, states that ships putting into harbour are signs of a good king.[12] Those ships carry foreign goods, such as wine and fine cloth.

The beginning of the tenth century saw the revival of economic life throughout Europe, a prosperity in which the Irish Sea region shared. In the Irish Sea province there was a precocious development; by the end of the century the economic structure here had features more commonly expected to be found in the Mediterranean. Commerce was controlled largely by a few ports/market-towns which often had mints and fleets; their mixed economic and political interests can be difficult to disentangle. After the year 1000, the Irish Sea region was part of an Atlantic trading zone extending as far as North America. According to the *Hauksbók* version of the saga of Eirik the Red, one of the first ports to receive news of lands beyond Greenland was Dublin; the same text suggests that the indigenous inhabitants of Markland knew of Ireland, surely reflecting confusion on someone's part.[13] The precocity did not endure, and by the end of the eleventh century the rapid commercial development throughout the rest of north Atlantic Europe had caught up to the Irish Sea province, which then developed within the general rate of economic change found elsewhere in Europe. Even though this economic expansion is credited to the great Italian cities of the Mediterranean, the northern European aspect should not be dismissed. In 1027 the English and Danish king Cnut the Great made his famous journey to Rome to attend the coronation of the Emperor Conrad II; he sent to England an oft-quoted letter which specifically mentions his success in ending the tolls charged on the journey to Rome.[14] There was a commercial benefit to Cnut's actions. A treatise on the imperial customs

---

[10] *MGH*, SS rer. Merov. V, 568–604 (p. 603), after J. Kenney, *The Sources for the Early History of Ireland: Ecclesiastical*, ed. L. Bieler (Dublin, repr. 1979), p. 495.
[11] N. Edwards, *The Archaeology of Early Medieval Ireland* (Philadelphia, 1990), p. 70.
[12] F. Kelly, *A Guide to Early Irish Law* (Dublin, 1988), p. 7.
[13] *Eiríks saga Rauda* in *Eyrbyggja Saga*, ed. Einar Ól. Sweinsson and Matthías Pórdarson (Reykjavík, 1935), pp. 234–5.
[14] The letter is preserved by William of Malmesbury, *De Gestis Regum Anglorum Libri Quinque*, ed. W. Stubbs, 2 vols., RS (London, 1887–89), i, p. 222.

stations of the eleventh century notes that the fights between the English merchants and the imperial officials ended after the tolls had been paid off by the English king.[15] The Irish Sea benefited directly from the opening of those routes, as silver was coming into the Irish Sea region from the Holy Roman Empire by way of England.[16]

At times during the tenth and eleventh centuries the Irish Sea province could resemble a Scandinavian lake. The Viking heritage of towns such as Dublin, Wexford and Waterford is well known, as is the Viking presence on the Isle of Man. Less well known is the Viking connection with Wales on the Isle of Anglesey, where there were fortified harbours at Holyhead from the tenth century, or at Moel-Y-Don Ferry where a colony from Dublin had flourished in the eleventh century.[17] Economic ties had a long duration and influenced literary remembrances, such as the saga of the Icelander named Gunnlaug 'Serpent's tongue', which tells much about trade. The saga is interesting because it was written down after the main Scandinavian economic presence had ended. Gunnlaug sails from Norway to England to Dublin and then on to the Orkneys before returning home.[18] At each place the saga preserves incidental material about trade goods. The young king of Dublin named Sitriuc 'Silkenbeard' is so gratified to be honoured by Gunnlaug's poem that he wants to reward the poet with a ship before being advised that clothing and ornaments are the customary gifts. Early in the twelfth century William of Malmesbury noted that ships from Ireland continued to be among those calling at York. That could explain why it is known that among the places whose devastation by fires was recorded in the *Anglo-Saxon Chronicle* in 1032 was the town of York, because it is named specifically only in the report in the Irish Annals of Tigernach.[19]

Not only do the Vikings deserve much of the credit for the deliberate creation of an Irish Sea trading zone from Dublin, Waterford and Wexford, but they were also responsible for the renewal of one of the most important commercial centres on the Irish Sea, the town of Chester. In 893 Viking forces campaigning in Mercia were being

---

[15] R. S. Lopez and I. W. Raymond, *Medieval Trade in the Mediterranean World* (New York, 1990), pp. 57–8.

[16] P. H. Sawyer, 'The wealth of England in the eleventh century', *TRHS*, 5th series, 15 (1965), pp. 145–64.

[17] Loyn, *The Vikings in Wales*, p. 10; *History of Gruffydd ap Cynan (1054–1107)*, ed. and trans. A. Jones (Manchester, 1910), p. 105; B. Hudson, 'Knútr and Viking Dublin', *Scandinavian Studies*, 66 (1994), pp. 319–35 (pp. 328–9).

[18] *Gunnlaugs Saga Ormstungu*, ed. P. G. Foote and trans. R. Quirk (London, 1953), pp. 14–20.

[19] William of Malmesbury, *De Gestis Pontificum*, ed. N.E.S.A. Hamilton, RS (London, 1870), p. p. 208.

pursued and took refuge in the ruins of the old Roman legionary garrison by the river Dee. The Vikings eventually departed, but within a decade the ruined settlement had been repaired by the Mercians who saw its possibilities for trade. Commercial wealth attracted raiders, and the townspeople subsequently held off an assault by Vikings by hurling boiling beer and bee-hives onto the heads of the attackers.[20] The town prospered and at the end of the century Chester was not only one of the leading ports of northern Europe, but also had a mint and was a centre for the famous changes in coinage carried out by the Anglo-Saxon kings. Chester's economic vitality allowed it to survive disasters such as William the Conqueror's devastation of northern England in the winter of 1070, and sixteen years later Domesday Book provides a picture of a flourishing port where tolls were collected by royal representatives on a variety of goods.

This leads to another aspect of Irish Sea economic history that could repay study: the exploitation of the Vikings by the natives. The popular view of unrelieved hostility between the newcomers and the established populations is reinforced by reading the contemporary records. However, after the mid-tenth century in England and after the mid-eleventh century in Ireland, the Viking market towns were under the control of native princes. A century later, when Gerald of Wales commented on the domination of the Irish Sea by the Scandinavians and their importance for the town life of the region, he stated that their settlement in Ireland had been part of a deliberate action on the part of the Irish kings, possibly a reflection of the very real manipulation of the colonists by the natives.[21] Little attention has been given to the question of who was buying the wares being traded by the Vikings. Such exchange was possible only if the native princes saw in it an advantage for themselves. Apparently they did, as Irish and Anglo-Saxon kings both appreciated the usefulness of thriving commercial centres and tried to encourage them. Legislation from the reign of King Edgar regulated the cattle trade between the English and the Scandinavians; while a poem on the fair of Carmen, in Leinster, mentions the presence there of screeching foreigners with their wares, made possible only by permission of the provincial king of Leinster who presided over the gathering.[22] Dublin in the ninth century appears to have been little more than a garrison, but at the end of the tenth century it was a storehouse of

---

[20] *Fragmentary Annals of Ireland*, ed. J. Radnor (Dublin, 1978), p. 172.
[21] Giraldus, *Topographia*, p. 112.
[22] The regulation of the cattle trade is printed by W. de Gray Birch in *Cartularium Saxonicum*, 3 vols. (London, 1885–93), iii, 389–91. The verses on the fair of Carman are edited by Edward Gwynn, *The Metrical Dindshenchas*, 5 vols. (Dublin, 1903–35), iii, 2ff.

treasures and goods.²³ This commercial aspect to Dublin appears to reflect an increasing market for imported and luxury wares within Ireland, which was being paid for in foodstuffs and raw materials. When Brian Bóruma, the future high-king of Ireland, captured the fortress of Dublin on New Year's Day in the year 1000 he found brightly coloured clothes, gold and silver, harnesses and weapons.²⁴ After his troops had gathered sufficient loot from Dublin to compensate themselves and their king, Brian gave strict orders not to destroy the town; he knew better than to kill the goose that would continue to lay golden eggs. Most of the goods would have used raw materials available in Ireland, although the origin of the precious metals is not certain. Irish gold was famous in antiquity, but in the twelfth century Gerald of Wales claimed that gold was brought into Ireland by traders.²⁵ Some of the silver might have come from the mines of northern Wales, which seem to have supplied the mint at Chester, or it might have come from Irish mines; the Old Irish law tracts specifically mention silver mines in the section on trespass.²⁶

The rise of Irish Sea mercantilism was matched by the expansion of urban centres during the tenth and eleventh centuries. When Bristol first appears in the *Anglo-Saxon Chronicle* it is a fully functioning port with ships departing to Ireland. Within the Roman bounds of Gloucester, which communicated with the Irish Sea by way of the river Severn, there was cultivation of crops in the tenth century; by the early eleventh century the town had expanded beyond its ancient limits. Chester was physically expanding in the tenth century, and the Viking raid on Cheshire in 980 was particularly devastating round the area of the Castle Esplanade.²⁷ In 1015 a raid on Dublin led by the high-king Máel Sechnaill II burned the suburbs round the fortress proper. These towns were not only supplying other urban centres, but also serviced the fortresses which were being constructed in the tenth century and provided ready markets for goods. When the West Saxon king Edward the Elder and his sister Æthelflaed of Mercia built fortresses in northern England to meet the threat from the Scandinavians in Northumbria, those garrisons ensured that there would be buyers of essential

---

[23] A survey is by P. F. Wallace, 'The economy and commerce of Viking age Dublin', in K. Düwel *et al.*, *Untersuchungen zu Handel und Verkehr der vor- und frühgeschichtlichen Zeit in Mittel- und Nordeuropa IV* (Göttingen, 1987), pp. 200–45.
[24] *Cogadh Gaedhel re Gallaibh*, ed. J. Todd, RS (London, 1866), pp. 114–17.
[25] Giraldus, *Topographia*, p. 102.
[26] Kelly, *Early Irish Law*, p. 105.
[27] G. Webster *et al.*, 'A Saxon treasure horde found at Chester', *Antiquities Journal*, 33 (1953), pp. 26–9.

commodities; the troops stationed there had to be fed and clothed.[28] This was true also in Ireland. The princes of the relatively minor southern kingdom of Dál Cais, whence came the high-king Brian Bóruma, built fortresses to maintain their control in southern Ireland. They captured Viking ports, and part of the attraction must have been their ability to provide the means to maintain those fortresses.[29] Whether in Ireland or Britain those troops required vast amounts of foodstuffs. The Welsh poem *Armes Prydein* ('Prophecy of Britain') complains about the collection of tribute (paid in livestock) by the stewards of the 'Great King' Æthelstan.[30] Although one does not need to subscribe to the figure of 25,000 head of cattle which William of Malmesbury claims was paid in tribute by the Welsh to Æthelstan, it is clear that the trade in livestock was flourishing.[31] The legislation from the reign of King Edgar for the buying and selling of cattle has been noted. A similar concern is apparent in Ireland where the claimant to the high-kingship, the son of Brian Bóruma named Donnchad, issued an edict attempting to end what seems to have been widespread cattle-rustling on the part of small farmers.[32]

Rulers of the lands around the Irish Sea tried to control and manipulate trade, with varying degrees of success. The laws of the Anglo-Saxon kings demonstrate how, beginning early in the tenth century, they were trying to legislate and profit from maritime commerce. The law code attributed to Edward the Elder states that all buying and selling was to be done in a port with a port-reeve witnessing the transaction.[33] In the code 'II Æthelstan' this provision is modified to the extent that no one should buy goods worth more than 20 pence outside a port.[34] Clearly the king was determined to have his share of the profits of trade, and the designation of ports as the appropriate area for exchange gives a good idea of the location of much of the commercial activity. This law was almost impossible to enforce and in 'IV Æthelstan' the restriction of trading to towns was revoked.[35] One of the reasons why restriction of

---

[28] S. R. H. Jones, 'Transaction costs, institutional change, and the emergence of a market economy in later Anglo-Saxon England', *Econ. Hist. Rev.*, 2nd series, 46 (1993), pp. 658–78.
[29] B. Hudson, *Prophecy of Berchán* (Westport, CT, 1996), p. 178.
[30] *Armes Prydein*, ed. Sir Ifor Williams, trans. R. Bromwich (Dublin, 1972), p. 3.
[31] William of Malmesbury, *De Gestis Regum Anglorum*, i, p. 148.
[32] This edict, described as *cáin [ocus] rechtge*, 'law and ordinance', was proclaimed by Donnchad in 1040 with four prohibitions: against theft; against fighting on Sunday; against labouring on a Sunday; and against the enclosure of cattle within doors; *AI*, p. 204. A second decree, described as a *cáin mór*, 'great law', was made in 1050 by Donnchad, but no specific information has survived.
[33] F. L. Attenborough, *The Laws of the English Kings* (New York, 1963), p. 114 (1).
[34] Ibid., p. 134 (12). [35] Ibid., p. 146 (2).

trade to towns or ports was so difficult to enforce was the ease with which that trade could be conducted outside a town. The law code 'II Æthelraed', composed *c.* 991, describes how a merchant would draw up his ship and build a hut or set up a tent.[36] Later there is evidence that merchants might not land their entire cargo, but would bring ashore only samples, while the bulk of the merchandise remained on board ship. The Domesday account of Chester states that the reeve was to be allowed on board ship in order to make his selection of goods for the payment of the toll. Occasionally these foreign merchants provided a more immediate service, and the future King John's charter of liberties to Bristol in 1188 states that foreign merchants may not set up a tavern in the town, although they could have one on board their ship.[37] Occasionally commerce and piracy were combined, as in the early twelfth century when the canons of St Mary's, Laon, were travelling through England on a fund-raising tour. At Bristol they wanted to buy new clothes, but were warned by the local merchants not to go out to the Irish ships, because the sailors might cast off and hold them for ransom.[38]

Together with efforts to control commerce went efforts to protect it. Foreign merchants were understandably worried about their safety and that of their wares, so the law code 'VIII Æthelraed', written *c.* 1014, states that the king would act as the kinsman and protector of any stranger and his goods.[39] Along the same line of thought is the regulation in 'II Cnut' which states that there will be no interference with any bargain successfully concluded, obviously an effort to protect merchants from disgruntled customers.[40] The military disasters of the reign of Æthelraed were believed to be divine retribution for the sins of the people and new legislation was enacted to end impieties such as trading on a Sunday, which was a ban periodically renewed.[41] In addition to legislation there were more direct efforts to control commerce by princes. When the Leinster king Diarmait mac Máel na mBó captured Dublin in 1052, he installed his son Murchad in the town; when Toirrdelbach ua Briain took direct control of the town in 1075, he set up his son Muirchertach to rule it on his behalf. The use of the Irish Sea region as a training ground for young royals continued in the twelfth and thirteenth centuries. The future King John of England was not only

---

[36] A. J. Robertson, *Laws of the Kings of England from Edmund to Henry I* (Cambridge, 1925), p. 56 (3.2).
[37] *Bristol Charters 1155–1373*, ed. N. D. Hardinge, Bristol Record Society, vol. 1 (Bristol, 1930), p. 10.
[38] *MPL*, 156, cols. 985–6.
[39] Robertson, *Laws of the Kings of England*, p. 126 (33).
[40] *Ibid.*, p. 216 (81).   [41] *Ibid.*, p. 122 (17).

set up in Ireland by his father but was also given estates in western England. Two generations later his grandson, the future King Edward I, would have his financial office placed at Bristol in 1254 in addition to receiving the lordships of Chester, Montgomery, Builth, Upper Gwent, Cardigan and Carmarthen and Ceredigion north of Cardigan. While there were sound political and military reasons for these actions, there were also sound economic reasons. Princes had a very real and direct reason for wishing to control the merchants in their harbours, who might work against their interests. When Maurice de Prendergast attempted to leave the service of Diarmait Mac Murchada *c.* 1170, Diarmait prevented his departure by sending instructions to all merchants at Wexford forbidding them to carry Maurice and his men.

Royal profit from trade was tied to some extent to coins, and the coin-hoard evidence can provide a useful indication of the wealth of the Irish Sea region. While there is a tendency to treat all such finds as loot from raiding it is quite possible that some represent the moveable assets of merchants. At the end of the tenth century there were mints on both the western and eastern shores of the Irish Sea; by the eleventh century there was a mint right in the middle, on the Isle of Man. These coins were used to pay tolls and settle payment in the towns as well as provide a currency of account. The persistent metallurgical imbalance in coins from the mints of Ireland and England, such as the production at Dublin of reduced-weight imitations of English issues, might have been practised deliberately as an incentive for English merchants with heavier coins to trade in Ireland.[42] English merchants would be familiar with the style of the coinage and their heavier weight coins would allow them to receive a favourable exchange rate. No doubt there could be disagreement about the exchange rate as well as the proper size or volume of weights; such disputes could be the basis for the exhortation in 'II Cnut' for correct measures and weights, as well as the prohibition for the circulation of reduced-weight coins.[43] Fair payment was not a worry solely with coins; the Irish law tract *Gúbretha Caratniad*, 'False Judgements of Caratnia' notes that a contract is invalid if the price is paid in defective silver.[44] The international circulation of coinage confirms the contacts of the Irish Sea merchants with other areas of the north Atlantic. Irish coins produced in the eleventh century imitated English issues, and Norwegian coins copied the Irish imitations.[45] At the same

---

[42] For a time in the eleventh century the ratio was consistently 3:2; see B. Hudson, 'William the Conqueror and Ireland', *IHS*, 29 (1994), pp. 145–58 (pp. 153–4).
[43] Robertson, *Laws of the Kings of England*, p. 178 (9).
[44] Kelly, *Early Irish Law*, p. 160.
[45] M. Dolley, *The Hiberno-Norse Coins in the British Museum* (London, 1966), pp. 146–8.

time, some stylistic features of Danish coins were being copied at Dublin.⁴⁶ There might have been a contraband trade in old coins between English mints and Dublin, in which Irish moneyers purchased coins of supplanted issues from their English counterparts as a convenient and cheap method of acquiring silver bullion.⁴⁷

Early in this period the goods traded round the Irish Sea were foodstuffs and luxury items. When Muirchertach mac Néill of the Cenél nEógain, the famous Muirchertach of the Leather Cloaks, was paid so that he would not plunder Dublin, among the goods he received were bacon, meat, cheese and flour; these are essentially ship's stores.⁴⁸ Within the following twenty-five years, shoe-making became an important industry at Dublin, together with comb-making and fashioning of game pieces. In Ireland the Vikings seem to have taken over the manufacture of commodities which had a low social status. The leather workers and comb makers whose products are so abundant at Dublin were at the bottom of the social scale among Irish craftsmen. The Old Irish law tracts claim that a wright who could build a church or mill might have an honour-price as high as 15 séts, while a leather worker or comb maker had an honour-price of $\frac{1}{2}$ sét.⁴⁹ The comb-maker was a particular object of derision as he rooted through rubbish heaps looking for bones and horns. The antiquity of the Irish clothing trade has been noted. Clothes made at Dublin were widely known and considered luxuries; they were considered a suitable reward for a poet in the saga of Gunnlaug, 'Serpent's tongue'. The merchants from Ireland who were selling clothes at Cambridge during the reign of Edgar probably were from Dublin, travelling in an area where communications with the local population would not be difficult.⁵⁰ Clothing from the Irish Sea province was exported to Scandinavia and Iceland. One of the most widely selling articles was a woollen cloak in which the fibres were pulled through into tufts on the outside; this type of material was known in Old Norse as 'rögg'. There was also a trade from east to west in metal goods. The *Vita* of the Welsh saint Cadog tells of a bell manufactured in Ireland which was brought to Wales. An interesting aspect to this story is that the person who brought the bell is described as a *callidus artifex*, 'skilled craftsman', which suggest that artisans were deliberately seeking out models for their own wares.⁵¹

Of all the commodities shipped round the Irish Sea region in the early

⁴⁶ *Ibid.*, p. 137.   ⁴⁷ *Ibid.*, p. 136.
⁴⁸ Cormacán Eigeas, *The Circuit of Ireland*, ed. J. O'Donovan (Dublin, 1841), pp. 32, 34.
⁴⁹ Kelly, *Early Irish Law*, pp. 62–3. *Sét* means 'treasure' or 'valuable' and appears to be a currency of account rather than a currency of exchange.
⁵⁰ *Liber Eliensis*, ed. E. O. Blake, Camden Society, vol. 92 (London, 1962), p. 107.
⁵¹ *Vita Sanctorum Britanniae et Genealogiae*, ed. A. Wade-Evans (Cardiff, 1944), p. 84.

high Middle Ages, the traffic in slaves was one of the most profitable. A small example from the tenth century illustrates how this trade connected the Irish Sea region with the continent: the travels of an Irishman named Moriuht.[52] His journey began when he and his wife were captured in a slave raid. Moriuht escaped from servitude after some adventures and then went in search of his wife, which led him to a place near Rouen. He finally found her and they were given sanctuary there and so remained. Legislation by Anglo-Saxon kings attempted to end the international aspect to the trade. The code known as 'VII Æthelraed', composed c.1009, expressly forbids selling anyone out of the country; a prohibition repeated in a legal code attributed to William the Conqueror.[53] The laws of Cnut forbid the selling of Christians out of the country, especially to heathens.[54] Despite the prohibition the trade remained lucrative. William of Malmesbury claims that the noblewoman Gytha, mother of the future Anglo-Saxon king Harold Godwinsson, was engaged in the trade in a particularly revolting fashion; she purchased pregnant women and resold them into slavery.[55] In the second half of the eleventh century the great Bishop Wulfstan II of Worcester travelled to Bristol to denounce the slave trade that was carried on with Ireland.[56] Despite the abolition of slavery at the Council of London in 1102, the twelfth-century legal tract called 'the Laws of King William' again forbids the selling of Christians out of the country.[57] In Ireland a ready market for slaves continued, and in 1172 Gerald of Wales claims that a council of churchmen held at Armagh decided that the success of the Anglo-Normans in Ireland was divine punishment of the Irish for their purchase of English slaves.[58]

Slaves were not the only lucrative, and restricted, commodity; another was the trade in horses. British (i.e. Welsh) horses are mentioned in the Old Irish law tracts.[59] The late eleventh-century tract known as the *Book of Rights* includes horses from Scotland among the proper goods for a king. In 1028 a prince of Dublin named Olaf Sigtryggsson was captured and his ransom included 120 Welsh ponies. Efforts to restrict the export of horses began in the tenth century when the law code 'II Æthelstan' declared that no one would send a horse across the sea unless he wishes

[52] H. Ormont, 'Satire de Garnier de Rouen contre le poète Moriuht', *Annuaire bulletin de la Soc. de l'hist. de France*, 31 (1894), pp. 193–210.
[53] Robertson, *Laws of the English Kings*, pp. 112 (5) and 242 (9)
[54] *Ibid.*, p. 176 (3).
[55] William of Malmesbury, *De Gestis Regum Anglorum*, i, p. 245.
[56] *Vita Wulfstani*, ed. A. Campbell, Camden Society, vol. 40 (London, 1928), pp. 42–4.
[57] Robertson, *Laws of the English Kings*, p. 270.
[58] Giraldus, *Expugnatio*, pp. 68, 70.
[59] Kelly, *Early Irish Law*, p. 7 (*Corpus Iuris Hibernici*, ed. D. A. Binchy, 6 vols. (Dublin, 1978), p. 1507.34).

to make a gift of it.⁶⁰ Again, the trade was too profitable to be ended by mere legislation, so the emphasis turned to controlling it, and an edict of William the Conqueror forbade the buying and selling of livestock outside of a town.⁶¹

The economic prosperity of the Irish Sea region had its drawbacks, one of which was the way in which trade became a pawn in political machinations. The battle of Clontarf may have had an economic aspect, which could explain the presence there of Jarl Sigurd of the Orkneys. Two reasons are presented in Icelandic materials such as *Orkneyinga Saga* and *Njal's Saga*; the first, that he had been offered the hand of Sitriuc Silkenbeard's mother, can be set aside as a romantic elaboration. The second reason is more interesting, that he was offered the kingship of the town. There are hints from other, admittedly late, sagas that the lords of the Orkneys had been extending their domain into the Irish Sea since the late tenth century. If the forces of the high-king Brian Bóruma had been defeated at Clontarf, Sigurd would have controlled the Viking towns of eastern Ireland, allowing him to profit from the Irish Sea trade. The wealth of Dublin continued to make the town a magnet for claimants for the Irish high-kingship, and after 1052 the town was only occasionally independent. During the overlordship of Diarmait of Leinster the town must have prospered as Diarmait effectively ruled the Irish Sea after his conquest of the Isle of Man in 1061 and maintained good relations with Harold Godwinsson. Dublin was not alone in seeing its prosperity attract unwelcome attention. In 1068 the sons of Harold Godwinsson sailed from Dublin and raided Bristol in an effort to secure a base of operations for their efforts to lead an Anglo-Saxon uprising in England.⁶² The choice of Bristol as a target could be as much a reflection of Dublin's interest in securing control of a trade rival as a sign of its strategic importance. When the lordship of Dublin was taken by Diarmait's protégé Toirrdelbach ua Briain, the town continued to benefit from the good relations Toirrdelbach and his son Muirchertach fostered with William the Conqueror and his sons William Rufus and Henry.⁶³ But political change could lead to economic disaster, and the temporary conquest of Dublin by the Manx king Godred Crovan in 1091 saw the beginning of the debasement of the town's coinage.⁶⁴

Other Irish Sea ports saw their commercial position involving them in

---

[60] Attenborough, *Laws of the English Kings*, p. 136 (18).
[61] Robertson, *Laws of the Kings of England*, p. 238 (5).
[62] B. Hudson, 'The family of Harold Godwinsson and the Irish Sea Province', *RSAI Jn.*, 109 (1979), pp. 92–100 (p. 95).
[63] Hudson, 'William the Conqueror and Ireland', pp. 145–58.
[64] Dolley notes that the year 1095, so far as the coinage series is concerned, is the beginning of the end, *Hiberno-Norse Coins*, p. 135.

political affairs. When Harold Godwinsson fled England in 1051 for Ireland, he went to Bristol to take ship. After Harold was slain at Hastings, his mother fled to Exeter, on account of the number of ships from Ireland that called there, according to Orderic Vitalis.[65] When Diarmait Mac Murchada, the bad man of Irish history, wanted to appeal for troops from Henry II, he sailed to Bristol and stayed with a local merchant named Robert fitz Harding.[66] Trade embargoes were used then, as now, as a tool to achieve political settlement without military intervention. William of Malmesbury tells the well-known story of an English embargo on Irish goods when Muirchertach Ua Briain had angered Henry I, and how this swiftly brought Muirchertach to reconcile with the English prince.[67] The embargo probably was connected with Muirchertach's support for the Montgomery rebellion in 1102 because he was the father-in-law of Arnulf de Montgomery, who recruited troops from Ireland; after the failure of the rebellion Archbishop Anselm of Canterbury was able to reconcile Henry with Arnulf, and Muirchertach wrote a letter to Anselm thanking him for his good offices.[68] The fear of Henry II that efforts were afoot to create an independent Anglo-Norman kingdom in Ireland led him to place an embargo on trade with Ireland in an attempt to bring Strongbow to heel.[69]

In keeping with the medieval fascination with division and category, the history of the Irish Sea economy of the High Middle Ages can be separated into two periods with the change coming in the twelfth century. The successes of the Norwegian king Magnus Barefoot between 1098 and 1103 meant that the Kingdom of the Isles, encompassing the Isle of Man and the Hebrides, came to be formally recognized as a Norwegian colony. At the time of Norwegian lordship in the region, trade between Norway and the Irish Sea appears to have steadily decreased, and by the thirteenth century there seems to have been little trade directly from Norway into the Irish Sea. The dominant economic force was England, and the Irish sea began to assume some of the attributes of an English lake. This aspect has been overstated in the past, largely because of William of Malmesbury's famous question, what would happen to the Irish without the imports from England? The sharp retort is that the Irish were doing quite well with or without English

---

[65] Orderic Vitalis, *Ecclesiastical History*, ed. M. Chibnall, 6 vols. (Oxford, 1969–80), ii, p. 225.
[66] *Song of Dermot*, p. 232.
[67] William of Malmesbury, *De Gestis Regum Anglorum*, ii, pp. 484–5.
[68] James Ussher, *The Whole Works of the Most Reverend James Ussher, D.D.*, ed. C. R. Elrington and J. H. Todd, 17 vols. (Dublin, 1847–64), iv, pp. 526–7.
[69] Giraldus, *Expugnatio*, p. 70.

goods. Until the twelfth century Ireland was the wealthy section of the Irish Sea and our, admittedly meagre, records show the Irish as the main buyers of luxury goods: slaves, horses and wine. Even in the thirteenth century the Chester historian Ranulph Higden, certainly no Hibernophile, remarked that the only raw materials sent in any quantity to Ireland were salt and iron. Those commodities reflect the increased demands of certain industries rather than any deficiency in the land. The Old Irish law tracts mention the operation of iron mines. Ireland, the Isles and Wales found that their raw materials were eagerly sought. Much of the salt imported into the Irish Sea region came from the continent, especially from Bourgneuf Bay, known as 'The Bay', near the estuary of the Loire, and the need to import salt is a reflection of the expansion of trade in preserved goods. This included bacon, beef, hides and, very importantly, fish. The Irish Sea fish trade was not limited just to the commonplace herring destined for Bristol or Chester, but included luxury fish such as salmon, destined for Bordeaux. The increasing domination of Irish Sea trade by the English in the twelfth century was due to ports on the eastern shore, especially Bristol. They were able to take advantage of the growing trade with the continent. There had long been an important trade between England and Flanders, but the ascension to the English throne of Henry II in 1154 brought the Bay of Biscay into the orb of Irish Sea trade, and began the economic supremacy of Bristol. Access to goods throughout the Irish Sea was crucial, however, and the English ports began to insist on written evidence of their rights to trade with other ports, especially in Ireland. The grants made by Henry to Chester and Bristol concerning their right to the Dublin trade reflects the economic rivalry between them.

Also in the twelfth century the church became actively involved in encouraging Irish Sea trade. The spread of the reformed monastic orders throughout England, Ireland, the Isle of Man, Scotland and Wales led to economic changes. These orders – Savigny, Citeaux and Tiron to name three – were an important avenue through which continental personnel and techniques entered the Irish Sea region. The Cistercians call for special mention because they were the great agricultural pioneers of the age and were responsible for advances in wool production, livestock selection, land reclamation and soil improvement. These new houses were also notable for the extent of their economic interests. The great monastery at Furness, initially a Savigniac house, had its own harbour in Lancashire. A daughter house was founded at Rushen on the Isle of Man, and the lords of Man granted to Furness economic benefits as well as the right of providing the bishop of the Isles. To other houses of the reformed monastic orders, the lords of the

Isles granted commercial privileges such as grazing of livestock, freedom from tolls and fishing rights.[70] Farther across the Irish Sea Furness had another daughter house at Inch or Inchcourcy, in Co. Down; south along the coast there was a warehouse at Drogheda. The Cistercian (initially Savigniac) abbey of St Mary's Dublin had a harbour on the Liffey, somewhere in the vicinity of the Four Courts, and another at Dalkey. The establishment of these new houses and their influence on the Irish Sea economy was rapid. In addition to the houses of the reformed monastic orders already mentioned, the half century before the Anglo-Norman expeditions to Ireland saw the establishment of Holm Cultrom on the Solway, Dundrennan in Galloway, Newry near Carlingford Lough, Flaxly at the mouth of the Severn, Margam, Neath and Basingwerk on the Dee. Often these houses were wealthy, and the plundering of the abbey of St Dogmaels (a house of the order of Tiron) was the reward for the mercenaries employed in Wales in 1138. One can add to this list the contemporary bishops' seats which were located on the coasts of the Irish Sea: Whithorn, Carlisle, St Davids, Rushen, Downpatrick, Dublin and Ferns.

From the end of the eleventh century exports of manufactured goods from Ireland and Wales or the Isle of Man began to decline in comparison with the exports of raw materials from those lands. Part of the reason is simply stated: fashions changed, and the goods made according to local designs in Ireland or Scotland were considered old-fashioned and naïve. The biographer of St Margaret of Scotland, writing for her daughter Matilda, the queen of Henry I of England, praised her for bringing in new styles and encouraging merchants from the continent.[71] When Margaret's son King David I died, his friend Aelred of Rievaulx noted that among the good works of his reign was the introduction of the latest continental fashions among his subjects: 'He enriched your ports with foreign wares and exchanged your shaggy cloak for precious raiment.'[72] This shaggy cloak has already been mentioned and it was one of the main trade items made in Ireland, the Isle of Man and Iceland; it was made by weaving short lengths of wool into the cloth which gave the appearance of a fur cloak. Gerald of Wales noted that the woollen cloth of Ireland was almost always black because of the dark fleeces of the sheep.[73] Aelred's oration marks the end of a trade that had enriched the Irish Sea region for two centuries; from then on the tufted cloak was fit only for peasants while the new masters of the land,

---

[70] B. Hudson, 'Economy and trade', in *A New History of the Isle of Man*, ed. S. Duffy, vol. iii (forthcoming).
[71] R. L. G. Ritchie, *The Normans in Scotland* (Edinburgh, 1954), pp. 79, 80.
[72] *Ibid.*, p. 302.   [73] Giraldus, *Topographia*, p. 101.

regardless of their origins, followed the fashions of the continent. This prejudice against native fashions continued throughout the Middle Ages, and a frieze-type weave of coarse manufacture that was popular among the humble folk of southwest England was known as 'Welsh cloth', even though it was produced in Wiltshire. Together with changes in fashion were new grading systems that penalized the coarse wools. According to the drapery regulations of Bruges in 1282 the finest wool was English, followed by Scottish wool and lastly Irish wool.[74] Local manufactures received a new appreciation, however, in literature and they were introduced to give a suitable exotic quality to a setting, or antiquity to an era. In the late twelfth century, Chrétien de Troyes writes in *Erc* that a fair lady lying under a bower wore a gown made in the stripped cloth of Scotland.[75] In Eyrbyggja Saga a woman named Thora comes to Iceland with merchants from Dublin and the Isles who are carrying a cargo of cloaks; Thora's clothes and room furnishings, designed in Irish style, excite the envy of the Icelandic ladies.[76]

In the eleventh and twelfth centuries the Irish Sea province can best be compared with the wild west of North America, with speculators and settlers rushing in to make their fortunes. One of the most desired commodities was land. The hunger for land was not limited to impoverished nobles, or younger sons of the powerful aristocrats. Promise of a small farm could lure the peasants-turned-soldiers who manned the castles and fought for the great nobles. In the rush to acquire land the secular and ecclesiastical interests found common ground, so to say. The church needed donations of land on which to plant monasteries and chapels, and such donations also provided the means to pay for an expanding administration. This land frenzy was fuelled by writers such as Gerald of Wales, who was not alone in commenting on the fertility of the land of Ireland or the useful grazing to be found in Wales. The Irish Sea economy prospered and at the same time new peoples were introduced into the region. The late eleventh century saw the successful Norman penetration of south Wales, and the less successful efforts in the north. The Normans were followed by the Flemish, who were greatly responsible for the economic boom in south Wales. In northwest England, Rufus' military conquest of Carlisle was followed by the establishment of new settlers from the south. When the future King David I of Scotland, as prince of Cumbria, granted lands to his friends to the north of the Solway, they were followed by settlers looking for

[74] O'Neill, *Merchants and Mariners*, p. 59.
[75] Chrétien de Troyes, *Erc and Enide*, ed. C. W. Carroll (New York, 1987), line 5185; Ritchie, *Normans in Scotland*, p. 360.
[76] Sweinsson and Pórdarson (eds.) *Eyrbyggja Saga*, pp. 137–45.

new lands. The greatest prize was the last major area, the eastern coasts of Ireland. Over and over again, land is the bait used to lure noble and commoner alike. Diarmait Mac Murchada enticed Strongbow and his followers to Leinster with the promise of estates, and a generation later King John would use Irish land to recompense his supporters who had lost their lands in Normandy.[77] This did not pass without comment from the natives, as over and over again is heard the demand, 'get rid of the foreigners'. When Duncan II of Scotland survived a coup attempt in 1094, he was allowed to keep the kingship (for a brief time as it happened) only if he banished the French and English surrounding him. Almost a century later the Irish high-king, Ruaidrí Ua Conchobair, offered similar terms to Diarmait Mac Murchada: Diarmait could remain, but not his followers from Britain. Among the newcomers were Jewish merchants who had settled in the towns of the Irish Sea region. What seems to have been the earliest Jewish settlement in Britain was made at London after the conquest of William I; the emigrants came from Rouen. According to the Annals of Inisfallen, in 1079 a delegation visited the Irish king Toirrdelbach ua Briain. They seem not to have been given permission to settle in Ireland, for they were sent home, but by the end of the twelfth century there are the names of several Jewish merchants among the freemen of Dublin. Their names, such as Solomon of Cardiff, indicate that they came primarily from south Wales, although one, Abram of Cardigan, came from farther north.[78]

Why were people so eager to acquire farms in strange lands? Part of the reason was the very real fact that one could become quite wealthy as a farmer during this period. The land which provided social status and privilege also provided a more material reward: ready cash. Although only English records give specific information about prices in this early period, they seem to be an accurate reflection of prices throughout the Irish Sea province. So far as the admittedly sparse records can tell us, prior to the mid-twelfth century grain prices had either remained stable or fallen. But in the half century between 1160 and 1210 the price of grain doubled in England and the value of livestock trebled.[79] There were also periods during which prices fluctuated wildly, as from 1200 to 1205 when a series of disastrous harvests saw wheat prices soar, and a quarter of wheat which cost 4 shillings in 1199 cost 14 shillings in

---

[77] W. L. Warren, 'The interpretation of twelfth-century Irish history', in *Historical Studies*, 7, ed. J. C. Beckett (New York, 1969), pp. 1–19 (p. 17).

[78] *Hist. & Mun. Doc. Ire.*, pp. 2ff., 136ff., after E. A. Lewis, 'Industry and commerce in medieval Wales', *TRHS*, new series, 17 (1903), pp. 121–74 (p. 129 n. 5).

[79] D. L. Farmer, 'Some price fluctuations in Angevin England', *Econ. Hist. Rev.*, 2nd series, 9 (1956), pp. 34–43 (p. 43).

1205.⁸⁰ Such astonishing rises did not endure, and subsequent good harvests saw a return to more customary prices. All the same, the agricultural prices continued to rise and by the beginning of the fourteenth century the cost of a quarter of wheat had risen to a steady price of 6 shillings and 1 penny.⁸¹ An interesting aspect to the price of agricultural goods in the late twelfth and thirteenth centuries is that the addition of Irish grain to the pool available in Britain did not depress prices. Rather, as the exploitation of Irish lands increased so did the cost of agricultural products in Britain. By the end of the twelfth century, these increased prices had so alarmed the officials of the royal treasury that in 1194 they attempted to stabilize livestock prices. The cost of a cow, horse or ox was set at 4 shillings, a sow or boar was 12 pence, a fine woolled sheep was placed at 10 pence and a coarse woolled sheep cost 6 pence.⁸² Unfortunately this effort at price fixing failed, as the cost of livestock then proceeded to fall, and the royal estates were undersold by their neighbours where, for example, cows were sold for only 3 shillings.

Another benefit to the Irish Sea economy was the relatively inexpensive cost of transporting goods by water in comparison with the expense of transporting bulk goods overland, which ensured a greater profit for those who produced goods close to ports.⁸³ In 1171 the officials of Henry II purchased grain in Oxfordshire and Buckinghamshire for his troops in Ireland. The 100 quarters of wheat cost 1 shilling 3 pence the quarter; when the cost of haulage from Oxford to Bristol (44 shillings and 10 pence which was almost half the price of the wheat) was added onto the cost of the grain, the total cost for a quarter had risen to 1 shilling 8 pence.⁸⁴ This was still less expensive than buying wheat in Somerset, where the price for the grain alone was 1 shilling and 10 pence. As a point of comparison, in the following year the cost of transportation by boat from Worcester to Ireland of 400 quarters of wheat, 300 quarters of oats, 100 quarters of salt, 100 quarters of beans and 200 flitches of bacon was 4 pounds, 6 shillings and 10 pence, a little more than double the cost of the carriage for only 100 quarters of wheat from Oxford to Bristol. As a side note, wheat, flour and bacon were standard issue rations for Irish troops as well as the English; the *Song of Dermot and the Earl* tells us that the attack on, and dispersal of, the Irish

---

80 *Ibid.*, p. 37.
81 Based on the tables in D. L. Farmer, 'Some grain price movements in thirteenth-century England', *Econ. Hist. Rev.*, 2nd series, 10 (1957–8), pp. 207–20.
82 A. L. Poole, 'Live-stock prices in the twelfth century', *EHR*, 55 (1940), pp. 284–95 (p. 285).
83 For a different opinion on a slightly later period see J. Masschaele, 'Transportation costs in medieval England', *Econ. Hist. Rev.*, 2nd series, 46 (1993), pp. 266–79.
84 Farmer, 'Some price fluctuations', p. 35.

army that was besieging Dublin in 1171 gained the victorious challengers enough wheat, flour and bacon to provision the city for a year.[85]

The kind of commodities being bought and sold in the Irish Sea was constantly changing and this had an influence on manufacturing. The trade in Irish clothes that had flourished since the tenth century seems to have fallen off in part due to the changes in fashion already noted, and in part due to increased wool production in Wales and England. By the twelfth century England was one of the great wool exporting regions in Western Europe. As demand for Irish clothes declined, a market for leather expanded. In the eleventh century Irish marten skins were sold at Chester and Rouen, and by the last quarter of the century Gerald of Wales notes that the Irish were sending hides, pelts and skins to Poitou.[86] In return, wine from Poitou went to Ireland, and perhaps also wine from Worcestershire, whose merits were sung by William of Malmesbury.[87] Early in the twelfth century grain was being imported into Ireland, largely for the towns such as Dublin and Wexford; Gerald remarks that the crew of a ship in Wexford harbour carrying wheat and wine from Britain attempted to flee the town as it was being attacked by Diarmait Mac Murchada and Robert fitz Stephen in 1169.[88] Wales also took substantial imports of grain, and both William of Newburgh and Gerald of Wales insist that the Welsh were dependent on foodstuffs from England.[89] By the beginning of the thirteenth century grain imports from Bristol to Waterford, Wexford and Dublin had ceased and the Irish ports were exporting grain produced on the east coast manors. This trade quickly became considerable, and from 1224 to 1225 about 8,000 bushels of wheat were purchased by the mayor of London from just the Irish estates of William Marshal.[90] In one six-month period in 1299, the town of Carlisle took delivery from Ireland of almost 25,000 bushels of wheat and more than 110,000 bushels of oats.[91] This grain trade from Ireland extended to Scotland. Sometimes it went directly to a town, such as Ayr, but an interesting aspect to this trade was the purchasing made directly by religious houses such as Cambuskenneth

---

[85] *Song of Dermot*, p. 145 (ll. 1961–4).
[86] Giraldus, *Topographia*, p. 35 (i.2); J. H. Round, *Feudal England* (London, 1895), p. 354.
[87] William of Malmesbury, *De Gestis Pontificum*, p. 292.
[88] Giraldus, *Expugnatio*, p. 34.
[89] William of Newburgh, *Historia Rerum Anglicarum*, in *Chronicles and Memorials of the Reigns of Stephen, Henry II, and Richard I*, ed. R. Howlett, 4 vols. (London, 1884–9), i, p. 107; Gerald of Wales, *The Journey Through Wales and The Description of Wales*, ed. and trans. L. Thorpe (Harmondsworth, 1978), pp. 267–70 (book II, chapter 8 of *The Description*).
[90] *NHI*, ii, p. 484.   [91] *Ibid.*, ii, p. 485.

Abbey (which had a house in Ireland) or Glenluce Abbey.[92] This trade did depend on the good relations between the Scots and English, so when it occurred it was probably considered a bonus for both buyer and seller.

By the beginning of the thirteenth century the Irish Sea was also important for its trade in timber. The deforestation which had occurred throughout much of Europe after the millennium had not affected Ireland, which was the main supplier of lumber.[93] The export of lumber was considerable from Ireland to Wales and Gascony, and the trade in timber was one of the commercial points of contact between the Gaelic Irish and the Anglo-Irish of the east coast.[94] How ancient was that trade is not certain, but Geoffrey Keating claims that William Rufus's great hall at London used oak beams imported from Ireland.[95] Further east, in 1098 the Norwegian king Magnus Barefoot was taking timber from Galloway.[96]

The changes sweeping through the Irish Sea region in the late twelfth century were not limited to production of foodstuffs, timber and woollens. There was a change in the importance of the various commercial centres. For this period saw the beginnings of Bristol's pre-eminence in the region, a superiority it would enjoy for centuries. Bristol was becoming not just a trading centre of first importance for the Irish Sea region, it was becoming a leading international trade terminus, especially with the Bay of Biscay. The marriage of Henry of Anjou with Eleanor of Aquitaine, prior to Henry's ascension to the English throne, brought Aquitaine within the economic orb of the Irish Sea. Bristol was best positioned to benefit from that happy circumstance. In addition to shipping and receiving goods, Bristol became the main processing centre for the rest of the Irish Sea. Welsh cattle provided the hides for the tanning industry at Bristol, while fish caught by fleets from the Isle of Man were brought there to be smoked or salted. From Bristol sailed the cargoes of salt and iron which were imported into Ireland. When Edward I's armies in Wales needed supplies, it was the ships from Bristol that carried the wine from Gascony and the grain from Dublin.[97] Bristol not only became the premier port for the Irish Sea region, but it was also the model for economic development in the area. The guilds

---

[92] A. A. M. Duncan, *Scotland: The Making of the Kingdom* (Edinburgh, 1975), p. 505.
[93] O'Neill, *Merchants and Mariners*, pp. 99–102.
[94] *NHI*, ii, p. 488.
[95] Geoffrey Keating, *The History of Ireland. Foras Feasa ar Éirinn*, ed. D. Comyn and P. S. Dineen, 4 vols., ITS (London, 1902–14), iii, p. 294.
[96] *Chronicle of the Kings of Man and the Isles*, ed. G. Broderick and B. Stowell (Edinburgh, 1973), p. 63.
[97] M. Powicke, *The Thirteenth Century 1216–1307* (Oxford, 1953, 2nd edn, 1962), p. 442.

established at Dublin followed the Bristol guild regulations.[98] In 1193 the liberties of Bristol were granted to Lancaster by Lord John, the beginning of its rise to economic importance.[99] The true sign of the importance of Bristol came in 1254 when Edward, the future King Edward I, set up his central exchequer at Bristol, the same year that he received the lordship of that town, Chester, Montgomery, Builth, Cardigan, Carmarthen and parts of Ceredigon and Gwent. In short, a substantial portion of the eastern shore of the Irish Sea was given to the heir to the English throne.

But if Bristol was both the main port and economic model in the Irish Sea, one man is responsible for organizing and promoting the commerce of the region into the form it would follow for centuries later: Lord and later King John of England. This is not the place to enter into the debate on his motives and/or the problem of royal finances. Suffice to say that he, not his brother Richard nor his father Henry, followed a deliberate policy of promoting economic growth in the Irish Sea province. Unlike Henry II who merely granted charters allowing continuation of economic ties between major commercial centres – for a consideration, we can be sure – John oversaw the development of commercial venues at both the local and international level. John's ties on either side of the Irish Sea placed him in a unique position for cross-sea development. Not only had John been made, unhappily, the 'king' of Ireland by his father, but he held estates across the Irish Sea in western England. He gave Bristol its charter of liberties and his patronage was crucial to the invigoration of commercial life in northwest England. He gave his permission for the first known fair to be held there, at Preston, sometime after 1189, and his role in the setting up of a fair at Lancaster in 1193 has been mentioned.[100] By the time of his death at least ten fairs or periodic trading meetings had been established in the northwest.[101] His work was not limited to the eastern shores of the Irish Sea, for the beginning of commercial fairs in Ireland was carried out under his patronage. In 1204 he ordered that fairs lasting for eight days be held at Donnybrook (now merely a neighbourhood within Dublin city, but then a village separate from the town), Drogheda, Waterford and Limerick.[102] In 1214 he had a fair established in Dublin itself.[103] The royal incentive to commercial meetings inaugurated the vast expansion of

[98] *Hist. & Mun. Doc. Ire.*, pp. 53–4.
[99] G. H. Tupling, 'The origins of markets and fairs in medieval Lancashire', *Transactions of the Lancashire and Cheshire Antiquarian Society*, 49 (1933), pp. 75–94 (p. 82).
[100] Ibid., p. 80; R. H. Britnell, 'King John's early grants of markets and fairs', *EHR*, 94 (1979), pp. 90–6.
[101] Tupling, 'Origins of markets', p. 83.
[102] *Hist. & Mun. Doc. Ire.*, p. 61. [103] Ibid., p. 62.

market franchises throughout the realm that continued throughout the thirteenth century.[104] Sometimes John's patronage was clearly not disinterested, as in 1215 when he sold the town of Dublin its freedom for 200 marks, with several reservations, such as the right to collect the wine prisage which in 1192 had been set at 2 butts of wine worth 20 shillings each from all ships carrying more than 2 tuns of wine.[105]

Economic activity in the Irish Sea province became slightly less monopolized by the great port towns or the important religious houses. At the end of the eleventh century smaller ports participated in the Irish Sea trade. In northwest England the capture and repopulation of Carlisle by William Rufus in 1092 has been mentioned. The town, helped by the discovery of silver mines, prospered so much that by the mid-twelfth century, once again in Scottish hands, it became the *de facto* capital of King David I.[106] In Ireland, Drogheda appears as a commercial centre in the twelfth century. The *Song of Dermot and the Earl* tells us that Diarmait Mac Murchada sailed to Bristol from the port of Corkeran in 1166, and when he wanted to return home to Ireland he waited without success at Bristol for an Irish ship before finally hiring a ship at St Davids.[107] Gerald of Wales informs us about harbours at Wicklow and Arklow which had some importance for trade in the Irish Sea; Arklow appears to have been a special study, for Gerald makes a comment on the ebb and flow of the tides there.[108] Some ports appear to have had patronage precisely to benefit from the Irish Sea trade. One such port is Ayr, which received its charter as a burgh in 1198, had a mint by the mid-thirteenth century, and a fair by 1260. These ports flourished and new ports were established as the physical shape of the Irish Sea region began to change. By the thirteenth century the silting in the river Dee was making it difficult for the larger merchantmen to sail into the harbour. This led to King John's establishment of a borough at Liverpool in 1207 in order to attract merchants to supply goods and boats to provision his troops in Ireland.[109] There was a similar problem in the river Liffey, and by the thirteenth century the larger merchant ships bound for Dublin were unloading their cargoes several miles south along the coast at Dalkey or north along the coast at Howth.[110] Occasionally prosperity was responsible for physical changes. Increased

---

[104] R. H. Britnell, 'The proliferation of markets in England', *Econ. Hist. Rev.*, 2nd series, 34 (1981), pp. 209–21.
[105] *Hist. & Mun. Doc. Ire.*, p. 63.
[106] I. Blanchard, 'Lothian and beyond', in *Progress and Problems in Medieval England*, ed. R. H. Britnell and J. Hatcher (Cambridge, 1996), pp. 23–45 (pp. 27–30).
[107] *Song of Dermot*, pp. 221, 369.   [108] Giraldus, *Topographia*, p. 58.
[109] Tupling, 'Origin of markets', p. 83.
[110] O'Neill, *Merchants and Mariners*, p. 52.

trade at Bristol began to overwhelm the facilities of the town, so between 1240 and 1250 the river Avon was diverted in order to allow for work on the expansion of the town.[111]

While Bristol was becoming the main commercial centre of the Irish Sea as well as one of the premier English ports, Dublin was continuing to dominate the western shores of the Irish Sea. The paucity of records from Dublin means that archaeology will have to tell us much about the development of the town, although it is clear from John's charter of 1192 that Dublin was being reorganized in conformity with the English port cities, and subsequent charters show us that the town was growing rapidly in the thirteenth century. In 1233, Dublin was given royal permission to levy tolls for three years on a wide variety of goods in order to pay for expansion of the town's fortifications, and further fortification was necessary in 1250.[112] This method of raising funds for public works was standard practice. In 1228 the burghers of Drogheda were allowed to impose tolls on grain, livestock, fish, wool, wine and other goods for the space of one year in order to pay for the construction of a bridge.[113] Dublin also was prospering from its position as the leading centre in Ireland. In 1244 it was decreed that all weights and measures in Ireland were to use those at Dublin as the standard, and in 1246 the exchequer in Ireland was fixed at Dublin.[114]

Irish Sea trade was not without its risks – the two most dangerous were piracy and shipwreck. Piracy had an ancient lineage and the Roman garrisons on the Irish Sea at Anglesey and Chester had been placed there to intercept raiders from Ireland. The semi-legendary exploits of personages such as Niall of the Nine Hostages could have been based on their careers as just such raiders, and the location of their adventures beyond Ireland could give some indication of the range of their raids. Pride of place for piracy must be yielded to the Vikings, who were considered by their victims as the most vile pirates of all, albeit more financially sophisticated than most. Of course who was a pirate in this area and at this time rather depended on the view-point of the victim, and the 'good old days' of Viking piracy lingered long in the Irish Sea. In 1218 the Manx lord, Ragnall Godredsson, was forced to bring some of his subjects to the English court in order to make amends for their excesses.[115] Late in the fourteenth century merchant ships in Ireland were ordered to remain in port because of piracy in the Irish Sea.[116] Shipwreck was another hindrance to commerce, although it

---

[111] Powicke, *Thirteenth Century*, p. 635. [112] *Hist. & Mun. Doc. Ire.*, p. 96.
[113] *Ibid.*, p. 88. [114] *Ibid.*, pp. 102, 106.
[115] *Cal. Doc. Ire.*, 1171–1251, p. 123, no. 828.
[116] *CPR*, 1321–1324, p. 126.

could be profitable to some. At the Third Lateran Council (1179) Pope Innocent II attempted to encourage shippers to supply the crusader states, and towards that end he had attacked the practice of pillaging shipwrecks; the punishment of excommunication was ordered for anyone who despoiled Christians. Gerald of Wales, in his *Instructions for Princes*, apparently had this legislation in mind when he noted that both prelates and princes in England, Ireland and Wales enriched themselves through this plunder; he notes that even if a ship remained intact when stranded on a sandbar it was considered wrecked and thus open for plunder.[117] This went against traditional attitudes towards distressed vessels, and in Irish law anything brought in from the sea was the property of its finder, although anything that washed ashore was the property of the owner of the land.[118]

The economy of the Irish Sea province was flourishing from the tenth to thirteenth centuries, but this prosperity was not shared equally. The mint that operated on the Isle of Man in the eleventh century has vanished by the twelfth. Chester was superseded as a major commercial centre in the late twelfth century by its southern rival Bristol, which became the economic powerhouse of the Irish Sea. Chester's last hurrah as a dominant port in the Irish Sea was the poem in praise of the town written by the monk Lucian. Yet even as he was describing the commercial armada anchored at Chester's docks, the silting in the river Dee was making almost impossible the passage of the larger merchantmen. Another group who did not benefit from the prosperity of the twelfth century was the Norwegians. It is a curiosity that at the time when Norse political influence in the region was being recognized by neighbouring monarchs and the papacy – as shown by the inclusion of the diocese of Sodor within the metropolitan of Trondheim – there is little specific evidence of increasing trade with Norway. Late in the twelfth century, Lucian of Chester claimed that one of the city's gates looked towards Norway, a picturesque way of signifying trade contacts. But the political turmoil in Norway during the twelfth and early thirteenth centuries meant that exploitation of its economic interests in the region were limited. Icelandic merchants set up a beacon at Sanday *c.* 1200 and Copeland Island, in Belfast Lough, was well known to Norwegian traders as 'Merchant's Island'. But traffic from Iceland declined, both because ships bound there customarily sailed round the west coast of Ireland and because Icelandic ships sailing on to Norway could not pay their harbour dues, calculated in lengths of coarse woollen cloth known

[117] Giraldus Cambrensis, *De Principis Instructione* in *Giraldus Cambrensis, Opera*, viii, pp. 119–20.
[118] Kelly, *Early Irish Law*, p. 108 (Binchy (ed.), *Corpus Iuris Hibernici*, pp. 315.4, 314.17).

as *vaðmál*, in the kingdom of Man and the Isles, although they could pay this toll in the Orkneys or Shetlands.[119] While the Manx chronicle and Norse histories record the collection of the king of Norway's taxes in the area, they have little information about trade. When the Icelanders recognized Norwegian sovereignty in the mid-thirteenth century, the monopoly of all trade with Iceland and Greenland was placed in the hands of the Norwegians. The port at Bergen had long been a rival of Trondheim, and in 1294 it was made the staple town for all trade with the Norwegian dependencies. Bergen carried out its trade with the eastern coast of England, Flanders and northern France. After 1266, the Treaty of Perth led to the ceding of the kingdom of Man and the Isles to the Scots, which effectively closed other than occasional Scandinavian commercial forays into the Irish Sea.

The importance of the Irish Sea region for international trade as well as within the economy of England, Wales and Ireland can be gauged by going slightly beyond the limits of this discussion to the establishment of the home staples for the wool trade in 1326. The Ordinance of Kenilworth set up staples in fourteen towns, of which five – Drogheda, Dublin, Cardiff, Carmarthen and Bristol – were in the Irish Sea region while another three, Cork, Exeter and Shrewsbury – had traditional economic ties to the region. The currency reform of the year 1300 set up seven mints of which two were Bristol and Dublin, later to be joined by Chester. But these privileges also show how international the Irish Sea ports had become. At Dublin the supervision of the currency exchange was overseen by the Frescobaldi of Florence and the Dublin mint itself was operated by the Riccardi of Lucca; it was the Riccardi who, before their fall in 1294, have been credited with opening up an international market for Irish wool.[120] The southern element to Irish Sea trade becomes increasingly visible throughout the thirteenth century when customs officials from Bayonne were placed at Bristol and Dublin to collect customs duties from England and Ireland.[121]

The 400-year span covered by this discussion was one of great change and development throughout Europe as a whole, and those changes can be seen in the Irish Sea province. In the tenth century the Irish Sea region was politically diverse and experienced a precocious commercial unity and vitality which is more expected in the Mediterranean than in northern Atlantic Europe. By the end of the thirteenth century, the direction of mercantile development was being dictated by the political

[119] *Hrafns saga Sveinbjarnarsonar*, ed. G. P. Helgadóttir (Oxford, 1987), p. 22 and discussion on p. 76.
[120] *NHI*, ii, p. 509.   [121] Powicke, *Thirteenth Century*, p. 650 n. 1.

affairs of the English king. This is curious in itself, for the claims of Norwegian sovereignty in the region until the mid-thirteenth century and then the Scots claims would have suggested a more diverse exploitation of the region's resources. Active Norwegian trade with the Irish Sea seems to have fallen off in the twelfth century as political chaos in Norway combined with the increasing commercial importance of Bergen to shift Norwegian trade to the eastern coast of Britain and southwards directly to Flanders. The main Scots marts – such as Perth, Dundee and Aberdeen – were on the east coast of Britain. So by the late twelfth century the economy of the Irish Sea was being directed by the English king partly through his control of lands on either side of the Irish Sea and partly through the lack of interest shown by other monarchs. The twelfth century marked a turning point in the economic affairs of the Irish Sea as manufacturing shifted from the western shores to the east and the region became less important as an international emporium and more important for the shipping of raw materials and the processing of foodstuffs and wool. The increased demand throughout Europe as well as Britain and Ireland for grain, wool and fish ensured the prosperity of the Irish Sea region.

Although the types of economic records that give information about prices and producers appear only at the end of the period under discussion, and even then infrequently and provincially, the suggestion can be offered that an economic aspect to political events around the Irish Sea needs to be considered more carefully than has been true previously. The battle of Clontarf in 1014 might have been concerned as much with control of at least part of the Irish trade as with political affairs. The expeditions into the Irish Sea of the Norwegian king Magnus Barefoot in 1098–1103 could have been prompted by the need to exploit all possible sources of revenue as the responsibilities, and cost, of government increased in the late eleventh century. The appearance of Henry II in Ireland could have owed much to the king's desire that he should exploit Irish resources and not his barons, whose loyalty was less than certain. On the western shores of the Irish Sea, King John appeased his barons with lands after his loss of Normandy; and round the Irish Sea were trained English princelings in the late twelfth and thirteenth centuries.

Finally, the place of the Irish Sea province within the context of European trade was changing. In the tenth and eleventh centuries it looked to the north, to the northern Atlantic and the Baltic, for buyers and imports. This was also the period when it was one of the regions where the northern Atlantic merchants met those from the south. By the end of the period under discussion the merchants of the Irish Sea looked south and the region had become, to a great extent, a terminus for trade. This change was less deliberate than a reflection of trade routes changing to accommodate the rise of new markets and the expansion of old ones, especially the role played by the Flemish towns in northern European trade. This very change does show, however, how important the Irish Sea province had become for the well-being and standard of living of the peoples around it.

3 Cults of Irish, Scottish and Welsh saints in twelfth-century England

Robert Bartlett

In the twelfth century the constituent parts of the British Isles came to be bound together in new ways. Sometimes this involved consciously aggressive military and political action resulting in the subordination of some areas to authorities based in other parts of the islands; sometimes it stemmed from emulation by the ruling classes of one region of the institutions, techniques and culture of elites elsewhere; and beneath all this there was a process of convergence and assimilation which can best be seen as part of the wider European scene of migration and cultural change. This increased contact can be studied in a dozen fields – coinage, kingship, vernacular literature, feudalism, urbanism and so forth, but the purpose of this paper is to look at the minor, but relatively unexplored, case of saintly cult.

In theory saints are international and hence easily transportable. In reality, of course, individual cults often had strong regional, national and other particularist associations and characters. Below the level of the great biblical saints, like Mary, Peter and John, the early medieval saints of England, Ireland, Scotland and Wales are easily distinguishable. Of the eighty-nine saints listed in the early eleventh-century inventory of saints' resting places in England, the vast majority are Anglo-Saxon kings, bishops and heads of religious communities, especially those of the conversion period.[1] The cults that predominated in Ireland, Wales and, perhaps to a significantly lesser degree, Scotland did not overlap substantially with those in England. The litany in the late twelfth-century English Psalter Gough liturgica 2 in the Bodleian contains the names of 113 saints. The majority are either biblical, early martyrs or Frankish ecclesiastical leaders, such as Amand and Radegund. Eight have a claim to be specifically English (Edmund, Alban, Oswald, Thomas of Canterbury, Cuthbert, Dunstan, Wilfrid and Hilda). One only – Brigit – is from another part of the British Isles. So,

---

[1] *Die Heiligen Englands*, ed. F. Liebermann (Hanover, 1889), pp. 9–19; for commentary D. Rollason, 'Lists of saints' resting-places in Anglo-Saxon England', *Anglo-Saxon England*, 7 (1978), pp. 61–93.

although the English coloration of this litany is not deep – only 7 per cent of the saints listed are English – the tint is English rather than British.

The twelfth century did not revolutionize this picture, but there are sufficient cases of contact and interaction to make a study worthwhile. All the permutations of influence of course deserve attention: English saints turned up in Scotland, as in the case of St Milburga, who was taken by the Stewarts from Shropshire to Paisley,[2] Ireland saw the flourishing of the Welsh saint David, who is important in later medieval Irish hagiographical collections and kalendars[3] and so on. In this chapter, however, the focus is on the saints and cults of Ireland, Wales and Scotland that had some impact in twelfth-century England.

To turn first to Irish saints, it is clear that any twelfth-century reader of Bede would know of the important part that Irish saints had played in the conversion of the Anglo-Saxons. This was the great age of copying for the *Ecclesiastical History* and also the age that, more seriously than any other, took its text as a programme for action. It is symptomatic that the Life of Aidan that circulated in Durham manuscripts at this time was composed of extracts from Bede's work.[4] Aidan's cult was not widespread, with just a single church dedication, at Bamburgh,[5] and relics at Bath, Durham, Glastonbury and Waltham in the twelfth century,[6] but his reputation was sustained by his place in the first and formative piece of English historical writing. Durham also seems to have been the centre of interest in another Irish saint of the conversion period, though one not active within England, namely Columba [Colum Cille], for Adomnán's Life was copied there in the late twelfth century[7]

---

[2] I. B. Cowan and D. E. Easson, *Medieval Religious Houses: Scotland*, 2nd edn (London, 1976), pp. 64–5.
[3] R. Sharpe, *Medieval Irish Saints' Lives* (Oxford, 1991), p. 371 and n. 4.
[4] A. J. Piper, 'The first generations of Durham monks and the cult of St Cuthbert', in *St Cuthbert, his Cult and Community to A.D. 1200*, ed. G. Bonner, D. Rollason and C. Stancliffe (Woodbridge, 1989), pp. 437–46, at p. 443.
[5] E. Cambridge, 'Archaeology and the cult of Oswald in pre-conquest Northumbria' in *Oswald: Northumbrian King to European Saint*, ed. C. Stancliffe and E. Cambridge (Stamford, 1995), pp. 128–63, at p. 136.
[6] *Two Chartularies of the Priory of St Peter at Bath*, ed. W. Hunt, Somerset Record Society 7 (London, 1893), p. lxxv; *The Relics of Saint Cuthbert*, ed. C. F. Battiscombe (Oxford, 1956), p. 113; Liebermann (ed.), *Die Heiligen Englands*, p. 17; William of Malmesbury, *De Gestis Pontificum*, p. 198; I. G. Thomas, 'The cult of saints' relics in medieval England' (Ph. D. thesis, University of London, 1975), p. 534 (from BL Harley 3776, fol. 32). Thomas seems to have been misled by a passage in the *Chronicle of Hugh Candidus*, ed. W. T. Mellowes (London, 1949), p. 52, when asserting that Peterborough also had relics in the twelfth century.
[7] BL Add. MS 35110; see the comments of Richard Sharpe in his translation of Adomnán of Iona, *Life of Columba* (Harmondsworth, 1995), p. 237.

and there was also a chapel dedicated to Columba on the Durham property of Lindisfarne.[8]

Aidan and Columba are well-attested historical figures whose lives could be studied in the twelfth century in the pages of Bede and Adomnán. There is another and more obscure group of saints with Irish connections who seem to be syncretic creations or constructs. Of course, according to some recent theorists all our supposedly self-evident and commonsense concepts and categories are constructs, not given by nature but created through a contested and deeply self-interested process of manipulation of representations. Sanctity is a category of this type and hence there is a case to be made that all saints are constructs. But some saints are more constructs than others. Several medieval saints can be shown to be built up from diverse materials, sometimes from the traditions of more than one earlier saint, a process that is especially obvious, of course, when we have the pre-existent materials from which they were constructed.

Two examples that are relevant here, as concerning saints with Irish backgrounds who had active cults in twelfth-century England, are provided by St Modwenna and St Bega. The bones of the first, Modwenna, were claimed by the Benedictine abbey of Burton-on-Trent, which was founded in the early years of the eleventh century and seems to have acquired the saint's relics during the course of that century.[9] Abbot Geoffrey of Burton, who took up office in 1114, was eager to find out as much as he could about Modwenna, evidently lacking a Life or other written traditions. He pursued his investigations far and wide; he wrote to a bishop in Ireland; and he was at last successful: 'a book (*codex*) was brought to me from Ireland', he records triumphantly. This book contained the Life of the Irish saint Monenna, also known as Moninna or Darerca, who was the foundress of the abbey of Killevy in south Armagh and whose death in 517 is recorded in the *Annals of Ulster*.[10] At some point – it is not exactly clear when, where or how – the coherent and exclusively Irish career of this early Irish abbess-saint was welded onto two other traditions, one with a Scottish, one with an English locale. The Scottish career of Monenna/Modwenna involves her in the founding of a series of churches at hill fort sites across the central belt of Scotland, and her death is actually claimed to have occurred in Scotland, at a place probably to be identified with Luncarty

---

[8] Geoffrey of Durham, *Vita Bartholomaei Farnensis* in *Symeonis Monachi Opera Omnia*, ed. T. Arnold, 2 vols., RS (London, 1882–5), i, pp. 295–325, at p. 322.
[9] What follows is based upon an edition and translation of Geoffrey of Burton's *Life and Miracles of St Modwenna* being prepared for Oxford Medieval Texts by the present writer. The principal MSS are BL Royal 15 B. iv and Add. 57533.
[10] *AU*, s.a. 517.

in Perthshire. After her death there followed a squabble over her body, a dispute which was resolved by the Scots marching off in one direction, the English in another, both convinced they were carrying the saint's remains. Like the king's two bodies, a saint's two bodies are not an unfamiliar part of the medieval scene, reflecting competition and/or conflation in the hagiological landscape. Some have even suggested that Modwenna's Scottish career can only be a distant echo of Ninian's – although the sex is different, the sites involved would fit and it is suggestive that the affectionate diminutive of his name would be Mo-ninn.[11]

Modwenna's English career, as elaborated in the extant hagiography, is designed to tie her in with her eventual resting place in the West Midlands. She supposedly cures an Anglo-Saxon prince, Alfred, son of the king of the Mercians and West Saxons, is endowed with property to found nunneries in the area of the Forest of Arden and is a mentor of St Edith of Polesworth in Warwickshire. The Burton tradition has her buried on an island in the river Trent, Andresey, whence her bones are translated into the abbey church.

The case of St Moninna/Modwenna is a clear example of the wholesale borrowing of an early Irish Life to clothe the nakedness of an English saint. In the eleventh century, Modwenna who rested at Burton was a saint with bones but no Life. The abundance of Irish hagiography could be tapped to remedy this lack. Syncretism, conflation, confusion and, probably, conscious invention resulted in the saint represented in Abbot Geoffrey's early-twelfth-century Life of Modwenna, a northern Irish royal abbess who founded churches in Ireland, Scotland and England and whose bones at Burton were still actively performing miracles in Geoffrey's own day. Given the pullulating creativity of English hagiographic writing in the late eleventh and early twelfth century, it seems entirely plausible that the bones resting at Burton could have been provided with a different origin story, but in fact they were given an Irish pedigree. We shall return to the significance of this.

A yet more remarkable instance of the syncretic construction of a saint from Irish and English materials is that of St Bega. An anonymous Life and Miracles composed in the later twelfth or early thirteenth century[12] describes how the saint was born in Ireland, the daughter of a

[11] A. Boyle, 'St Ninian and St Monenna', *Innes Review*, 18 (1967), pp. 147–51. Professor Donald Watt kindly brought this to my attention.

[12] *The Register of the Priory of St Bees*, ed. J. Wilson, Surtees Society, 126 (Durham, London, 1915), pp. 497–520. The reference to Canterbury pilgrimage (p. 518) dates the text to after 1173. One of the figures mentioned, Adam son of Ailsi (p. 514), may be identical to a man of the same name in a charter of 1211 × 1247 (Wilson (ed.), *Register of St Bees*, no. 74, p. 105; J. M. Todd, 'St Bega: cult, fact and legend',

powerful (but unnamed) king, and how from an early age she vowed to preserve her virginity. She was confirmed in this intention by a handsome figure who appeared to her in a vision and presented her with an arm-ring (*armilla*) as a token that she was a spouse of Christ. Her beauty and wealth nevertheless attracted suitors, among them the young king of Norway. The night before marriage negotiations were to be concluded, deeming that 'it is neither right nor pleasing to marry a mortal bridegroom when one is vowed to an immortal one',[13] Bega slipped away from the court, opening the doors with a touch of her magic arm-band, and boarded a ship for England. Here she lived a solitary life in Copeland in Cumbria until the region became so troubled by pirates that she moved away, leaving behind her arm-ring. Bega came to Northumbria, then ruled by King Oswald, was consecrated a nun – the first ever in Northumbria – by Aidan and ruled over a community at Hartlepool. Eventually she handed this over to St Hilda and retired to Tadcaster. While visiting the Yorkshire monastery of Hackness, Bega saw in a vision Hilda's death and reception into heaven, and it was at Hackness shortly afterwards that she herself died and was buried. The author of the Life and Miracles goes on to relate how her bones had been translated from Hackness to Whitby at some point in the twelfth century[14] and then narrates a series of miracles centred on the holy arm-ring preserved at the priory of St Bees in Cumbria. This was employed especially in the swearing of judicial oaths and worked dreadful vengeance against perjurers like the northern baron, Walter Espec, who lost his son and heir after swearing falsely on Bega's bracelet.

Some of the component elements of this legend can be identified. One starting point is a short passage in Bede, where, as part of his account of St Hilda (*Ecclesiastical History* 4. 23), he describes how a nun of Hackness called Begu saw Hilda's death in a vision. That is all Bede has to say about her, but in another passage in the same chapter he talks about a nun called Heiu, who was the first nun in Northumbria, was consecrated by Aidan, founded the monastery of Hartlepool and later retired to Tadcaster. Clearly Bega's Northumbrian career as reported in the twelfth century is a conflation of Bede's Begu and Bede's Heiu. Her Cumbrian aspect, especially the role of the holy bracelet and the

---

Transactions of the Cumberland and Westmoreland Antiquarian and Archaeological Society 80 (1980), pp. 23–35, at p. 34 n. 48). The manuscript of the Life, BL Cotton Faustina B iv, is dated by Ker to the first half of the thirteenth century (N. R. Ker, *Medieval Libraries of Great Britain*, 2nd edn (London, 1964), p. 102).

[13] Wilson (ed.), *Register of St Bees*, p. 502.

[14] There is very little evidence for a cult at Whitby, although a poem recounting the history of the abbey contains a vengeance miracle performed by Begu/Bega: A. G. Rigg, *A History of Anglo-Latin Literature 1066–1422* (Cambridge, 1992), p. 24.

admitted absence of any corporal relics at St Bees, presents an interesting possibility. The Old English word for ring or bracelet is *beag*. Oaths were sometimes taken upon holy bracelets, such as that sworn by the Viking leaders to King Alfred in 876 *on þam halgan beage*, or, as the twelfth-century Latin version of the Chronicle (F) has it, *super sacrum armillum*.[15] Bega's bracelet was clearly the central focus of the Cumbrian cult. The church at St Bees was referred to as 'the church in which the bracelet is kept',[16] while as late as 1516 offerings were being made there 'to the bracelet of St Bega' (*ad armillam sancte Bege*).[17] The suspicion naturally arises that originally St Bega *was* a bracelet and that the Cumbrian cult started from a holy arm-band that only gradually adopted a human form too, the talismanic *halig beag* undergoing a metamorphosis into the person St Bega. Whether or not this hypothesis is correct, the extant evidence of the twelfth and early thirteenth centuries shows that by then a coherent, if composite, persona had been created. By that time, in the words of John Todd, whose admirable article deals fully with these topics, 'Bega was regarded as a virgin not as a bracelet'.[18]

Two Northumbrian nuns from Bede's *Ecclesiastical History*, a Cumbrian holy bracelet and, the last ingredient in the mixture, the tale of an Irish royal origin – that is what St Bega is made of. We cannot be sure how the Irish section of her Life arose, but the complete absence of proper names or any specific localization, the general and indefinite nature of the narrative and the amount of space given to such subjects as praise of virginity or Bega's inner state make it plausible that it is pure literary invention. But it is worth noting that what was invented was an Irish virgin.

The most famous case of a newly discovered Irish childhood is that of St Cuthbert. Although he was certainly the dominant saint of the north of England and his life was reported in some of the earliest and most widely diffused English hagiography, including two Lives by Bede, Cuthbert's biography, as available to readers in early-twelfth-century England, lacked a graphic or detailed Chapter 1 – 'Family and Childhood'. The implication of the early hagiography is that he was of Northumbrian origin, but it is only an implication. A story is told about his childhood taste for games, but that is not localized. Neither relatives nor place of birth are named. This glaring omission was rectified in the

---

[15] Plummer and Earle (eds.), *Two of the Saxon Chronicles Parallel*, i, pp. 74–5 and n. 7; Todd, 'St Bega', p. 25.
[16] Wilson (ed.), *Register of St Bees*, no. 65, p. 96.
[17] Todd, 'St Bega', p. 6, citing Cumbria Record Office, D/Lons./W/St Bees 1/1.
[18] Todd, 'St Bega', p. 30.

late twelfth century by a writer, who was, in all likelihood, a monk of Durham, possibly Reginald of Durham, author of a massive collection of Cuthbert's miracles.[19] While in the case of St Bega all we know is that an Irish origin for the saint was at some point elaborated, and in the case of St Modwenna that a book was brought from Ireland, in the case of Cuthbert we have explicit evidence that an Irish informant communicated with the Durham hagiographer about the new material.

The treatise *De Ortu Sancti Cuthberti*, that expounds the story of Cuthbert's Irish origin, contains a preface in which the author explains that, while composing an account of Cuthbert's miracles, he had turned up a *quaterniuncula*, or 'small quire', 'that set forth saint Cuthbert's birth in Ireland and his royal and noble descent'. These facts were later corroborated by Eugenius, bishop of Ardmore, who met the author of the treatise and also 'revealed to us many other things which we had previously known nothing about', including the name of Cuthbert's father and mother and the city of his birth.[20] Bishop Eugenius witnessed a charter of Diarmait Mac Carthaig between 1173 and 1177[21] and is probably the same bishop of Ardmore who was paid 5 shillings a day for performing episcopal functions in the diocese of Chester (Lichfield) during a vacancy there in 1184–5.[22] As a native Irish bishop familiar with England he would be an ideal intermediary between the eager English hagiographer and the rich but linguistically inaccessible Irish traditions.

Modwenna, Bega and Cuthbert thus represent three variant ways in which saints whose primary shrines and cult centres were in England were given Irish origins. With Bega, we cannot be sure of how the Irish part of her life came to be constructed,[23] but in the case of Modwenna

---

[19] The treatise was edited under the title *Libellus de Ortu Sancti Cuthberti* by James Raine, *Miscellanea Biographica*, Surtees Society, 8 (London, Edinburgh, 1838), pp. 63–87, from York Minster MS XVI I 12; Reginald's authorship is advanced, very plausibly, by Richard Sharpe, 'Were the Irish annals known to a twelfth-century Northumbrian writer?', *Peritia*, 2 (1983), pp. 137–9; other discussions include M. H. Dodds, 'The little book of the birth of St Cuthbert', *Archaeologia Aeliana*, 4th series, 6 (1929), pp. 52–94; P. Grosjean, 'The alleged Irish origin of St Cuthbert', in Battiscombe (ed.), *The Relics of Saint Cuthbert*, pp. 144–54.

[20] Raine (ed.), *Libellus de Ortu Sancti Cuthberti*, pref., p. 63.

[21] BL Add. MS 4793, fols. 70–70v (seventeeth-century transcript by Sir James Ware); see M. T. Flanagan, 'Monastic charters from Irish kings of the twelfth and thirteenth centuries' (MA thesis, NUI Dublin, 1972), p. 284.

[22] *Pipe Roll 1184–5: The Great Roll of the Pipe for the Thirty-First Year of the Reign of King Henry II 1184–5*, ed. J. H. Round, PRS, 34 (London, 1913), p. 142.

[23] Although there was certainly a cult in the Gaelic-speaking areas of Britain by the twelfth century, as witnessed by personal names like Gillebecoc and place-names like Kilbucho, Peeblesshire: Wilson (ed.), *Register of St Bees*, no. 1, p. 28; *RRS*, ii, p. 418; J. M. MacKinlay, *Ancient Church Dedications in Scotland*, 2 vols. (Edinburgh, 1910–14), ii, pp. 261–2.

and Cuthbert we know that Irish bishops were involved as correspondents and informants and that written material – Geoffrey of Burton's *Codex de Hibernia* and the Durham author's 'little quire' – was also circulating. In the case of Modwenna we actually have the prior hagiographic material and can thus chart the process of rewriting and reinterpretation that was required to make a sixth-century Irish abbess a plausible patron of a west Midland monastery of the monastic revival period. It would be too much to say that an Irish childhood had become a topos for saints of unspecified origin, but it is clearly the case that, when English hagiographers of the twelfth century pursued the potentially endless task of elaborating the legend of their local saint, then an Irish origin and upbringing was a proposition that was acceptable, plausible and easy to substantiate.

These three saints, Modwenna, Bega and Cuthbert, each had a church and major cult focus in England, at Burton, St Bees and Durham respectively. Before turning to the subject of Welsh and Scottish saints in twelfth-century England, it is worth mentioning the compositions about Irish saints that were written in England but were not linked to primary cult centres there. In the early 1130s Laurence of Durham composed a Life of Brigit, that he dedicated to Aelred, the later abbot of Rievaulx, on the basis of a Life given to him by Aelred's father, Eilaf, who had ended his days as a monk of Durham.[24] Brigit was a relatively well-known saint in England. We have already seen that she was the unique Irish saint in the litany in Gough liturgica 2, and she appears in virtually all the English monastic kalendars of the Middle Ages. Half-a-dozen cathedrals and abbeys claimed relics in the twelfth and thirteenth centuries and there are English manuscripts of the twelfth century containing her Life in the version that Laurence used.[25]

---

[24] *Acta Sanctorum*, 1 Feb., pp. 172–85; W. W. Heist, *Vitae Sanctorum Hiberniae e Codice olim Salmanticensi nunc Bruxellensi*, Subsidia Hagiographica, 25 (Brussels, 1965), pp. 1–37; these lack the preface, which is edited by A. Hoste, 'A survey of the unedited work of Laurence of Durham with an edition of his letter to Aelred of Rievaulx', *Sacris Erudiri*, 11 (1960), pp. 249–65, at pp. 263–5.

[25] For kalendars, *English Kalendars before A. D. 1100*, ed. F. Wormald, Henry Bradshaw Society, 72 (London, 1934; repr. Woodbridge, 1988); *English Benedictine Kalendars after A.D. 1100*, ed. F. Wormald, 2 vols., Henry Bradshaw Society 77, 81, (London, 1939–46). For relics at Abingdon, Durham, Exeter, Glastonbury, Leominster, Reading, Waltham and York: *Chronicon Monasterii de Abingdon*, ed. J. Stevenson, 2 vols., RS (London, 1858), ii, p. 158; *Historiae Dunhelmensis Scriptores Tres*, ed. J. Raine, Surtees Society, 9 (Durham and London, 1839), p. ccccxxix; P. W. Conner, *Anglo-Saxon Exeter: A Tenth-Century Cultural History* (Woodbridge, 1993), pp. 186, 198, 205; William of Malmesbury, *De Gestis Pontificum*, p. 197; William of Malmesbury, *De Gestis Regum*, i, p. 27; William of Malmesbury, *De Antiquitate Glastonie Ecclesie. The Early History of Glastonbury*, ed. and trans. J. Scott (Woodbridge, 1981), pp. 60 (c. 12), 170; *The Register of Richard de Swinfield, Bishop of Hereford (1283–1317)*, ed. W. Capes, Cantilupe Society and Canterbury and York Society, 6 (London, 1909), p. 125;

It is also indicative that the Life of Modwenna and the *De Ortu Sancti Cuthberti* seek to enhance the prestige of their saints by associating them with Brigit. When we add Lawrence's Life of Brigit, composed by a Durham monk, to the evidence already cited for the copying in Durham of Lives of Aidan and Columba and the construction there of the *De Ortu Cuthberti* with the help of a specific Irish informant, a picture emerges of twelfth-century Durham as one of the English sites with the most active interest in Irish hagiography.

Patrick took second place to Brigit in English cult. There are fewer ancient dedications (seven for Patrick compared to fifteen for Brigit), fewer relics in English churches, although Glastonbury did, of course, claim the whole body, and commemoration in monastic kalendars was much less frequent.[26] Curiously, as far as the evidence of those kalendars edited by Francis Wormald is concerned, there seems to be a major decline in Patrick's standing after the Norman Conquest. Wormald edited virtually all the English kalendars prior to 1100 and, separately, a selection of post-1100 kalendars from eighteen Benedictine houses. While Patrick is commemorated in 68 per cent of pre-1100 kalendars, he occurs in only 17 per cent of the later material. At first glance, this picture does not harmonize very easily with that of hagiographic activity, because three Latin Lives of Patrick were composed in England in the twelfth century. There is the anonymous life in the Legendary in Gloucester Cathedral MS 1, which was copied around 1200,[27] a lost

D. Bethell, 'The making of a twelfth-century relic collection', in *Popular Belief and Practice*, ed. G. J. Cuming and D. Baker, *Studies in Church History*, 8 (Cambridge, 1972), pp. 61–72, at p. 68; Thomas, 'Cult of saints' relics, p. 544 (from BL Harley 3776, fol. 35); *Historians of the Church of York and its Archbishops*, ed. J. Raine, 3 vols., RS (London, 1879–94), iii, p. 107. For the cult at Glastonbury see J. A. Robinson, 'St Brigid and Glastonbury', *RSAI Jn.*, 83 (1953), pp. 97–9. Twelfth-century English manuscripts of the *vita prima* include Lincoln 149 and Lambeth 94.

[26] For dedications one still has to use F.E. Arnold-Foster, *Studies in Church Dedications*, 3 vols. (London, 1899), iii, pp. 344 (Brigid), 433–4 (Patrick), though, even after modern dedications are excluded, this can only be taken as a rough guide; relics of Patrick are recorded for the twelfth and thirteenth centuries only at Durham, Glastonbury, Leominster, Twynham (Christchurch) and Waltham: Raine (ed.), *Historiae Dunhelmensis Scriptores Tres*, p. ccccxxix; Liebermann (ed.), *Die Heiligen Englands*, p. 17; William of Malmesbury, *De Gestis Pontificum*, p. 197; William of Malmesbury, *De Gestis Regum*, i, p. 27; William of Malmesbury, *De Antiquitate Glastonie Ecclesie*, pp. 60 (c. 10), 170; Capes (ed.), *Register of Richard de Swinfield*, p. 125; Thomas, 'Cult of saints' relics', pp. 528, 534, 544 (from BL Cotton Tiberius. D VI/2, fol. 150, and Harley 3776, fols. 32 and 35). For the cult at Glastonbury, see H. P. R. Finberg, 'St Patrick at Glastonbury', in his *West Country Historical Studies* (Newton Abbot, 1969), pp. 70–88. For kalendars, Wormald (ed.), *English Kalendars*, *English Benedictine Kalendars*.

[27] 'Eine Patricksvita in Gloucester', ed. L. Bieler, in *Festschrift Bernhard Bischoff zu seinem 65. Geburtstag*, ed. J. Autenrieth and F. Brunhölzl (Stuttgart, 1971), pp. 346–63 (reprinted in his *Studies on the Life and Legend of St Patrick*, ed. R. Sharpe (London,

Life by William of Malmesbury addressed to the monks of Glastonbury[28] and, finally, that by Jocelin of Furness. Jocelin, a monk from the Cistercian monastery of Furness in Cumbria, who was active in the period *c.* 1175–1215, was something like a specialist hagiographer, composing Lives of Saints Helen, Kentigern and Waltheof of Melrose as well as the Life of Patrick.[29] This last was written at the request of Tomaltach (Thomas), archbishop of Armagh, Echmilid (Malachy), bishop of Down, and John de Courcy, the Anglo-Norman ruler of Ulster. Here we have an unusual case of Irish material being reworked in England for re-export to Ireland, for Jocelin's Life had nothing to do with Glastonbury but was designed to serve the cult at Down, where, in 1185 the remains of Patrick, along with those of Brigit and Columba, were translated under the auspices of John de Courcy.[30] Jocelin's Patrick is the first instance so far discussed in which any connection at all appears between the circulation of hagiographic material and processes of political and military subordination. John de Courcy's espousal of the native saints has long been seen as a legitimizing claim, designed to portray him as a favoured son of the great Irish trinity of Patrick, Brigit and Columba, not as an alien interloper. As the younger offspring of a baronial family with deep associations in northwest England,[31] he turned naturally to the leading hagiographer of the region when commissioning a revised Life of Patrick.

1986), XVIII, with same pagination; the MS is described in detail in N. R. Ker, *Medieval Manuscripts in British Libraries*, 3 (Lampeter, Oxford, 1983), pp. 934–9).

[28] Excerpts were copied by Leland from a manuscript at the Augustinian house of Twynham or Christchurch, Hants., which, as we have seen, possessed relics; he saw two other copies at Glastonbury: *De Rebus Brittannis Collectanea*, ed. T. Hearne, 6 vols. (London, 1774), iii, pp. 273–6; iv, p. 155; William of Malmesbury, *De Antiquitate Glastonie Ecclesie*, p. 40; C. H. Slover, 'William of Malmesbury's *Life of St Patrick*', *Modern Philology*, 24 (1926), pp. 5–20; D. Dumville, *Saint Patrick, A.D. 493–1993* (Woodbridge, 1993), pp. 265–71.

[29] *Vita Sancti Kentigerni*. *Lives of St Ninian and St Kentigern*, ed. A. P. Forbes, The Historians of Scotland, 5 (Edinburgh, 1874), pp. 159–242; J. Pinkerton, *Pinkerton's Lives of the Scottish Saints*, ed. Rev. W. M. Metcalfe, 2 vols. (Paisley, 1889), ii, pp. 1–96; *Vita Sancti Waldevi* (*Acta Sanctorum*, 1 Aug.), pp. 248–76; *Vita Sancti Patricii* (*Acta Sanctorum*, 2 Mar.), pp. 540–80 (I am grateful to Richard Sharpe for access to the text of a working edition prepared by the late Ludwig Bieler). The Life of Helen, in Gotha, Forschungs- und Landesbibliothek I 81, fols. 203v–212v, and Corpus Christi College, Cambridge MS 252, fols. 166v–183v, is unedited, apart from the translation account: *Translatio Sancte Helene*, ed. P. Grosjean, *Analecta Bollandiana*, 58, (1940), pp. 199–203.

[30] Giraldus Cambrensis [Gerald of Wales], *Topographia Hibernica* in *Giraldus Cambrensis, Opera*, v, 3.18, pp. 163–4; Giraldus, *Expugnatio*, p. 234.

[31] As well pointed out by Seán Duffy, 'The first Ulster plantation: John de Courcy and the men of Cumbria', in *Colony and Frontier in Medieval Ireland: Essays presented to J. F. Lydon*, ed. T. Barry, R. Frame and K. Simms (London, 1995), pp. 1–27.

Further examples could be cited of the Irish impact on twelfth-century saintly cults in England. At some point in the period, between the writing of the first and the second version of their *Chronicle*, the monks of Abingdon came to believe that their monastery took its name from the early Irish saint, Abbán, who had been endowed with the site in pre-Saxon times. Probably instrumental in convincing them of this was the Irish Cistercian, Ailbe Ua Máel Muaid (Albinus), bishop of Ferns (d. 1223), who was either the author or the instigator of a Latin Life of Abbán and a familiar figure in the south of England, being recorded at the Cistercian house of Waverley in Surrey in 1201 and 1214.[32] Another Cistercian nexus lay behind the transmission of material relating to St Patrick's Purgatory on Lough Derg. The *Tractatus de Purgatorio Sancti Patricii* was written in the 1180s by a Cistercian of Sawtry in Huntingdonshire at the request of the abbot of the mother house of Warden and on the basis of information supplied by Gilbert, monk of Louth in Lincolnshire and later abbot of Basingwerk in Wales, who had himself visited Ireland in an unsuccessful attempt to establish a Cistercian daughter of Louth there.[33] Finally, one of the most obscure but also among the more dramatic cases of new interest in Irish saints in twelfth-century England was the discovery in Ludlow in 1199 or 1200, while the church there was being extended, of the bodies of the father, mother and brother of St Brendan. Little more is known than the bare fact that the bodies, identified by a written label, were found in stone tombs and translated to a shrine within the church on 11 April 'until the Lord should deign to bring to pass miracles through their merit and intercession', yet it is clear that even relatives of a famous Irish saint had a high reputation among the clergy and layfolk of a Shropshire town.[34]

The story of the place of Welsh saints in twelfth-century England is rather different. Anglo-Norman penetration of Wales was early and

[32] Stevenson (ed.), *Chronicon Monasterii de Abingdon*, i, pp. 2–3; P. Ó Riain, 'St Abbán: The genesis of an Irish saint's Life', in *Proceedings of the Seventh International Congress of Celtic Studies*, ed. D. Ellis Evans *et al.* (Oxford, 1986), pp. 159–70; J. Campbell, 'The debt of the early English church to Ireland', in *Irland und die Christenheit*, ed. P. Ní Chatháin and M. Richter (Stuttgart, 1987), pp. 332–46, at pp. 338–40; Sharpe, *Medieval Irish Saints' Lives*, pp. 349–53; thanks are due to several participants at the 'Britain and Ireland' conference for pointing out the case of Abbán, to John Hudson for discussing the manuscripts of the Abingdon Chronicle and to Dáibhí O Cróinín for supplying helpful offprints.

[33] *Das Buch vom Espurgatoire S. Patrice de Marie de France und seine Quellen*, ed. K. Warnke, Bibliotheca Normannica 9 (Halle, 1938), pp. 2–168 (even pages).

[34] Leland in Hearne (ed.), *De Rebus Brittannis Collectanea*, iii, p. 407; a shorter account is found in a fourteenth-century Ludlow chronicle, BL Cotton Nero A iv, fol. 42, which was kindly brought to my attention by Chris Given-Wilson.

extensive. From the time of the establishment of the priory of Chepstow in 1070 or thereabouts, dependent upon the Norman monastery of Cormeilles and under the patronage of William fitz Osbern, earl of Hereford, religious houses had been founded in Wales that were clearly affiliates of the settler not the native society; the appointment of the Breton Hervey as bishop of Bangor in 1092 marked the beginning of a process in which clerics of French and English descent and upbringing took charge of Welsh sees, cathedral chapters came to be divided, like that of St Davids, between *Anglici* and *Walenses*, while gradually the authority of Canterbury was extended over the whole Welsh church.[35] The result, however, was not the alignment of native Welsh saints with native princes and clerics contrasted with the importation of alien saints by the incomers. For, just as in the analogous case of the Normans in England after 1066, very soon non-native clerics began to identify with the local saints associated with their churches, or to appropriate them if they had none.

The outcome of this process was a body of hagiographical material that it is hard to categorize in simply ethnic or national terms. The earliest Life of St David, written in the late eleventh century by Rhigyfarch, son of the bishop of St Davids, was, it has been argued, disseminated and possibly adapted under the auspices of Bernard, first Norman bishop of St Davids, while a revision of it was undertaken late in the twelfth century by Gerald of Wales, a good example of a cleric of mainly Norman descent who came to identify himself with a Welsh see, even if temporarily and self-servingly.[36] The earliest Lives of Dubricius, Teilo and Oudoceus are those in the Book of Llandaff, put together to bolster the claims of that see, probably under Bishop Urban (1107–34) and his successors (Teilo, incidentally, outdid Modwenna by miraculously leaving not merely two but three bodies as relics).[37] Bishop

---

[35] On Chepstow, R. Graham, 'Four alien priories in Monmouthshire', *Journal of the British Archaeological Society*, new series, 35 (1929), pp. 102–21; on Bishop Hervey, *Episcopal Acts and Cognate Documents relating to Welsh Dioceses 1066–1272*, ed. J. Conway Davies, 2 vols. (Cardiff, 1946–8), i, pp. 92–7; on *Anglici* and *Walenses*, Gerald of Wales (Giraldus Cambrensis), *De Invectionibus* 1. 2, ed. W. S. Davies, *Y Cymmrodor*, 30 (1920), p. 87. General discussion can be found in Rees Davies, *Conquest, Coexistence and Change: Wales 1063–1415* (Oxford, 1987), pp. 172–202.

[36] Rhigyfarch, *Life of St David*, ed. and trans. J. W. James, (Cardiff, 1967), pp. xxix–xxx; see also R. Bartlett, 'Rewriting saints' Lives: the case of Gerald of Wales', *Speculum*, 58 (1983), pp. 598–613, esp. p. 604.

[37] *Liber Landavensis: The Text of the Book of Llan Dâv*, ed. J. G. Evans and J. Rhys (Oxford, 1893), pp. 68–86, 97–129, 130–60. See G. H. Doble, *Lives of the Welsh Saints* (Cardiff, 1971), pp. 56–87, 162–229; C. Brooke, 'The archbishops of St Davids, Llandaff and Caerleon-on-Usk', in *Celt and Saxon: Studies in the Early British Border*, ed. N. K. Chadwick (Cambridge, 1963), pp. 258–322; reprinted in his *The Church and the Welsh Border in the Central Middle Ages* (Woodbridge, 1986), pp. 16–49.

Urban, although of a Welsh family, had previously been a priest in the diocese of Worcester. The great collection of Lives of Welsh saints in Vespasian A xiv may represent a compilation originally made at Gloucester in the 1130s.[38] It would be misleading to talk in these circumstances of the influence of Welsh saints upon England. Because England and Wales were close and contiguous, because Anglo-Norman clerical colonization was so pervasive, because English religious houses like Gloucester were endowed with lands and churches in Wales, there was a fluidity to the boundaries and a degree of overlap that we do not find in the case of Ireland.

One unusual instance of Anglo-Welsh contact in the sphere of the saints concerns St Wenefreda. This stands out as the only recorded case in this period of the physical transfer of the chief relics of a saint from one part of the British Isles to another.[39] The initiative came from the monks of Shrewsbury, a Benedictine abbey founded by Roger de Montgomery, earl of Shrewsbury, in 1083 and settled with monks from Séez in Normandy.[40] Although the house flourished, the brethren were aware that they did not have everything that a great religious house should have. In the words of their prior, Robert, 'they frequently lamented to each other that they had great need of some relics of the saints and with all their effort applied their minds to acquiring some'. They were given a goal when one of their number fell ill and the neighbouring monasteries were asked to pray for him. The sub-prior of Chester, like Shrewsbury a new Norman foundation, had a vision of St Wenefreda, telling him that if he sent two monks to celebrate mass in her church at Holywell in Flintshire, the Shrewsbury monk would be cured. So it happened and the convalescent monk himself went to pray there and drink the water of Wenefreda's well. 'Because of this the hearts of the brethren became filled with more devout remembrance of the holy virgin' and they determined to seek out the site of Wenefreda's tomb, which was at a site separate from her holy well, at Gwytherin in Denbighshire.

A first attempt was made to obtain the bones during the reign of Henry I and the consent of the bishop of Bangor and the local princes

---

On the *Book of Llandaff* in general see W. Davies, *An Early Welsh Microcosm: Studies in the Llandaff Charters* (London, 1978); W. Davies, *The Llandaff Charters* (Aberystwyth, 1979).

[38] K. Hughes, 'British Museum MS Cotton Vespasian A. XIV (*'Vitae Sanctorum Wallensium'*): its purpose and provenance', in *Studies in the Early British Church*, ed. N. K. Chadwick *et al.* (Cambridge, 1958), pp. 183–200; Wade-Evans (ed.), *Vitae Sanctorum Britanniae*, pp. viii–xiii.

[39] The following account is based on Robert of Shrewsbury, *Vita et Translatio Sanctae Wenefredae*, *Acta Sanctorum*, 1 Nov., pp. 708–31.

[40] Orderic Vitalis, *Ecclesiastical History*, iii, pp. 146–8.

was obtained, but the disturbances attendant upon King Henry's death interrupted this undertaking. 'In the second year of the reign of King Stephen', i.e. 1137, the abbot of Shrewsbury sent Prior Robert and a monk called Richard to try again. They were joined in the enterprise by the prior of Chester and a native Welsh priest. Once more the bishop of Bangor and the native ruler were well disposed, but the inhabitants of Gwytherin, where the saint lay, were less friendly, sending a messenger to say that 'they are stirred by grave indignation against you because you are trying to carry off the bodies of the saints that rest among them; know for certain that neither fear of the prince nor the threats of their lords nor desire for money will make them agree to this'. In the event, their opposition was less uncompromising. Indeed, when the Norman monks came to Gwytherin the local priest himself agreed to help them, not only because he had received supernatural instructions to do so, but also because, in his own words, 'I wish to be more closely allied with you.' Calling together the inhabitants and acting as spokesman and interpreter, the priest explained the situation to them and had almost won them over, when one man, 'a man of Belial' according to Prior Robert, said that 'it is not right that saints should be dragged away from their native soil and carried off to a land that has nothing to do with them'. His furious resistance could only be broken by bribery: 'by a gift of money', we are told, 'he was more closely allied with them', the verbal identity here with the description of the motives of the local priest perhaps having some significance.

The monks were now free to go to the holy cemetery where the saints' bodies lay, separate from the ordinary graveyard used by the community and marked by a holy oak tree and a little wooden church. Digging up Wenefreda's bones, they returned with them to Shrewsbury, miracles already occurring *en route*. Placing the remains temporarily in St Giles' church on the edge of the town, Prior Robert obtained episcopal permission for the translation and also had it publicized through the surrounding parishes. Eventually Wenefreda was carried in solemn procession to the abbey church and placed on the altar of Saints Peter and Paul. For the rest of the Middle Ages Wenefreda's cult flourished at two sites, Shrewsbury and Holywell. They are about 40 miles apart, and it was both appropriate and manageable to make a pilgrimage to both, as Henry V did, on foot, in 1416.[41] Holywell indeed continued to flourish past the Reformation. A crowd of 1,500 was supposedly there in 1629, while even in the 1990s 2,000 or so still come there on Wenefreda's day.[42]

[41] Adam Usk, *Chronicle*, ed. C. Given-Wilson (Oxford, 1997), p. 262.
[42] *Acta Sanctorum*, 1 Nov., p. 737 (and pp. 736–59 in general on the post-medieval cult);

If it is not always a straightforward task to disentangle the impact of native Welsh saints on England from the adoption of such saints by Anglo-Norman ecclesiastics within colonial Wales, it is even more difficult to draw clear lines that would enable us to talk unambiguously of the influence of Scottish saints on England. Before the thirteenth century the border between the kingdoms of Scotland and England was a shifting one. Anciently Northumbria had extended on both sides of the Tweed and the social and linguistic features of Lothian and Northumberland continued to be similar. Writing in the Berwickshire abbey of Dryburgh late in the twelfth century, Adam of Dryburgh describes his location in the telling phrase 'in the land of the English and in the kingdom of the Scots' (*in terra Anglorum et in regno Scotorum*).[43] Cuthbert's cult was important on both sides of the political frontier, and a writer like Reginald of Durham, recording Cuthbert's miracles, can tell of many in Scotland, at places like Kirkcudbright, 'Cuthbert's church', while the *De Ortu Sancti Cuthberti*, possibly written, as already mentioned, by the very same author, has long passages on Cuthbert's apocryphal activities in Scotland to balance his apocryphal childhood in Ireland.[44]

The complexity of the terms 'Scottish' and 'English' emerges clearly from a consideration of the two most important Lives of Scottish saints written, at least presumably, in twelfth-century England. These are the Life of Ninian by Aelred of Rievaulx and the Life of Kentigern by Jocelin of Furness.[45] Both authors were Cistercians from the north of England. Both Lives were addressed to Scottish bishops. Although Aelred does not give the name of the dedicatee of his Life of Ninian, the preface makes it clear that it was commissioned by a bishop of Whithorn, while Jocelin of Furness's Life of Kentigern was addressed to the writer's namesake, Jocelin, bishop of Glasgow 1174–99, who had previously been a monk and then abbot of Melrose, and who indeed died and was buried at the abbey.[46] Both Lives, Aelred's of Ninian and

J. Bord, 'St Winefride's Well, Holywell, Clwyd', *Folklore* 105 (1994), pp. 99–100; further on the cult in the sixteenth and seventeenth centuries in C. De Smedt, 'Documenta de sancta Wenefreda', *Analecta Bollandiana*, 6 (1887), pp. 305–52.

[43] *De Tripartito Tabernaculo* 2. 120, *MPL*, 198, cols. 609–792, at col. 723.

[44] *Libellus de Admirandis Beati Cuthberti Virtutibus* c. 84, ed. J. Raine, Surtees Society, 1 (London, Edinburgh, 1835), pp. 177–8; Raine (ed.), *Libellus de Ortu, cc.* 19–27, pp. 77–84.

[45] Forbes (ed.), *Vita Sancti Kentigerni. Lives of St Ninian and St Kentigern*, pp. 137–57, *Pinkerton's Lives of the Scottish Saints*, i, pp. 9–39.

[46] Aelred refers to 'the clergy and people of your church, who are moved by a wonderful affection for the holy man of God (Ninian) under whose patronage they live'. This must mean Whithorn. There are two possible candidates: Gille-Aldanus, first bishop of the revived diocese, who was active between 1128 and 1151, and his successor Christian (1154–86). For biographical details see *Series Episcoporum Ecclesiae Catholicae*

Jocelin's of Kentigern, are reworkings of earlier Lives, and some of these earlier materials are extant.

Aelred, descendant of the line of hereditary priests at Hexham, knew Scotland well, having served as steward of the royal household of David I of Scotland before he entered the monastic life around 1134. It was during his service at the Scottish court that he was presented with the Life of Brigit by its author, Lawrence of Durham. Much later Aelred was also the dedicatee of Reginald of Durham's collection of miracles of Cuthbert, and Reginald plays on the wording of Lawrence's earlier dedicatory letter, addressing Aelred, whom Lawrence had styled 'steward of the royal house', as 'royal steward of the house of the Lord'.[47] Several of the stories Reginald records had come from Aelred himself, more than one of them with a Scottish setting. There is the miracle, just mentioned, that occurred at Kirkcudbright on St Cuthbert's day 1164, when Aelred was himself present there 'in the land of the Picts' (*in terra Pictorum*), perhaps during a visitation of Rievaulx's daughter-house at nearby Dundrennan, while Aelred also transmitted stories of Cuthbert's miracles in Lothian, which he had picked up when visiting Melrose, also a daughter-house of Rievaulx besides being the place where Cuthbert himself had become a monk.[48]

The significant place of Durham as a centre of information about Irish saints has already been mentioned and the important role of Cistercian connections suggested in the cases of Abbán and St Patrick's Purgatory. We can now elaborate our picture of the network of communication and information about non-English saints by adding the northern Cistercians to our account. Aelred was a pivotal figure, deeply involved with the traditional saints of the north, including Cuthbert, the cross-border saint *par excellence*, yet also a founding father of the northern English and southern Scottish Cistercians. Cistercian affiliations cut across political boundaries. Melrose was founded from Rievaulx, Holm Cultram in Cumbria from Melrose, Grey Abbey in County Down from Holm Cultram. Aelred, dedicatee of Lawrence of Durham's Life of Brigit, had the duty of undertaking visitations of Melrose, which had been founded by his former lord, David I. At Holm Cultram, also a foundation of King David's, there were in the twelfth century copies of the Lives of Bega, the Irish virgin and bracelet, and Wenefreda, whose bones the monks of Shrewsbury had taken from Wales; while Everard, abbot of Holm Cultram from 1150 to 1192, who had previously, like

---

Occidentalis 6/1: Ecclesia Scoticana, ed. D. E. R. Watt (Stuttgart, 1991), pp. 24–7 (Gille-Aldanus and Christian), 60–3 (Jocelin).

[47] Raine (ed.), *Libellus de . . . Cuthberti Virtutibus*, c. 1, p. 1.
[48] Ibid., c. 84, pp. 177–8, c. 88, p. 188.

Bishop Jocelin of Glasgow, been a monk of Melrose, was himself credited with writing Lives of two early abbots of Iona, Cumméne Ailbe and Adomnán.[49] Christian, bishop of Whithorn, the probable dedicatee of Aelred's Life of Ninian, was a friend and patron of Holm Cultram, witnessing grants for the abbey and arranging to be buried there, as he was in 1186, during Everard's abbacy.[50] Grey Abbey, Holm Cultram's Irish daughter-house, was founded in 1193 by the wife of John de Courcy, who had commissioned Jocelin of Furness's Life of Patrick. Furness itself had a daughter-house at Inch in Co. Down.[51]

There was clearly a dense network of personal, institutional and cultural contacts binding together secular patrons, prelates and hagiographic writers in the north of England, southern Scotland and northern Ireland. Lives were being copied and rewritten, miracle accounts and stories of the saints circulated orally, active investigations undertaken by men with horizons that were not limited by kingdoms or lordships. In a curious way, the cultural geography of this world harmonized very well with that of the age of conversion, with which much of its hagiography dealt. If Cuthbert's activities ranged from Melrose to Yorkshire, so did Aelred's; if Patrick began his life in the valley of the Clyde and ended it in Ulster, as Jocelin of Furness asserted, then such vistas harmonized well with Jocelin's own. In his Cumbrian monastery, writing Lives of Patrick, of Kentigern, of his near-contemporary and fellow-Cistercian, Waltheof of Melrose, and of the first British female saint, Helen, and sending them to a bishop of Glasgow as well as an archbishop of Armagh and a bishop of Down, to the king of Scots as well as the 'ruler of Ulster' (*princeps Ulidiae*), as he terms John de Courcy, Jocelin's themes are congruent with his international network of patronage.

In conclusion, it may be worth opening up the question of what is

---

[49] BL Cotton Faustina B iv, containing the Life of Bega, and BL Cotton Claudius A v, with an anonymous Life of Wenefreda (not Robert of Shrewsbury's), are both from Holm Cultram, Ker, *Medieval Libraries*, p. 102. In a work published in 1627 Thomas Dempster maintained that Abbot Everard wrote Lives of his former abbot St Waltheof (d. 1159), Cumméne of Iona (d. 669), and Adomnán of Iona (d. 704): *Historia Ecclesiastica Gentis Scotorum*, ed. D. Irving, 2 vols., Bannatyne Club (Edinburgh, 1829), i, p. 260. Dempster's evidence for the Life of St Waltheof is probably no more than the citation of Everard's oral testimony in the Life by Jocelin of Furness. The nearest evidence that Everard wrote any antiquarian work comes from John Denton, *An Accompt of the County of Cumberland* (1610), ed. R. S. Ferguson (Kendal, 1887), p. 93, where he is cited for a place-name tradition about Thursby. This reference was kindly supplied by Richard Sharpe.

[50] The diocese of Carlisle, in which the abbey lay, was vacant during most of Christian's episcopate and he seems to have assumed responsibility for it as well as Whithorn.

[51] On Grey Abbey and Inch, see A. Gwynn and R. N. Hadcock, *Medieval Religious Houses: Ireland* (London, 1970), pp. 134–5.

implied in the English treatment of this material for the general twelfth-century English perception of the other parts of the British Isles. The twelfth century was the period when characters and narratives from Celtic literature and legend made their most profound impact on European culture prior to the age of Romanticism. By 1200 every sophisticated court in Western Europe knew of Arthur and Guinevere, of Merlin, of Tristan and Isolde. Yet it is not easy to say in what the appeal of this material lay. It is debatable whether the Matter of Britain exhibited a particular spirit or mood that captivated its audience or whether it was simply taken up by an expanding courtly literature hungry for the raw materials of narrative. The same difficulties of interpretation apply to the cultural contact that we have been examining in the sphere of cult and hagiography.

One thing that emerges at first glance is the English writers' sense of the literary inferiority of the indigenous models. Geoffrey of Burton, producing his Life of Modwenna on the basis of the book brought to him from Ireland, criticized the earlier work, lamenting that 'the style was displeasing and some parts of the book were a disorderly jumble'. His task, as he saw it, was to 'draw material with great toil from the barbarous language (*lingua barbara*) of the book and the treasure chests of the Irish, as if from hidden and obscure places, in the same way that metal is laboriously extracted from a mine with great care and effort'. Jocelin of Furness was no less displeased by the earlier Lives of Patrick and Kentigern that he was revising. 'Many people wrote saints' lives', he complains, 'who were unlettered and ignorant of the art of composition ... many find that reading saints' lives written in a clumsy style and a barbaric language (*sermo barbaricus*) provokes nausea rather than faith.' He proposes to remedy this 'confusion and obscurity of style' and 'to produce the flavour, if not of the most Latin speech, at least of Latin speech'.[52] The earlier Lives of Kentigern were 'darkened by barbaric language' (*sermo barbaricus* again) and Jocelin proposed to 'season what had been produced barbarically with Roman salt'.[53] Jocelin's phrasing had already been used earlier by Lawrence of Durham, who wrote to Aelred explaining that he was attempting to turn the 'semi-barbarous' Life of Brigit he had received from Aelred's father into 'a Latin one, even if a most Latin one is beyond my powers'. Lawrence compares himself to a sculptor attempting to refashion a badly made carving.[54]

Aelred's own preface to his Life of Ninian contains the most explicit

---

[52] *Vita Sancti Patricii*, prol., p. 540 (see note 29).
[53] Forbes (ed.), *Vita Sancti Kentigerni. Lives of St Ninian and St Kentigern*, p. 160; *Pinkerton's Lives of the Scottish Saints*, ii, p. 2.
[54] Hoste, 'A survey of the unedited work of Laurence of Durham', pp. 263–5.

statement of the theme of barbarism. Many people, he says, have been moved to record the lives of the saints for posterity. Some have done so with great style and eloquence. Others, 'who lacked the ability to compose with elegance and skill because of the barbarity of their native soil (*ob barbariem natalis soli*)' fulfilled their debt to future generations by writing in a simple style. Hence it was that the Life of Ninian was 'obscured by barbaric language (*sermo barbaricus*)'. Aelred's task was to take this earlier Life, 'which had been composed in a very barbarous style' and 'to draw it out of the shadows of its rustic language and to bring it into the light of Latin speech'.[55] Aelred's views on the barbarity of Galloway are well attested and here he makes a link between the barbarism of the region and the barbarism of its Latin.[56]

Of course hagiographers often bemoan the quality of the material they are reworking. Eadmer promised a revised Life of St Oswald, the Anglo-Saxon bishop, 'in a new and succinct style' because the earlier Lives were 'burdensome to read'.[57] In the middle years of the twelfth century, Osbert of Clare, producing a Life of Edburga, wrote, 'because the accounts of her deeds were composed in a confused style and they shone with no grace or order, I have made a diligent effort to give polish to what was neglected'.[58] William of Malmesbury began his Life of Dunstan with a condemnation of the ancient Lives, that seemed to him 'to lack literary grace' and to be full of 'rusticity (*agrestia*)'.[59] William clearly saw the conscious stylistic updating of saints' Lives as a necessary and laudable activity. He praised Goscelin, the prodigious hagiographer of the late eleventh century, for producing 'innumerable saints' Lives in a modern style (*recentium stylo*) ... renewing those that had been composed in a disordered manner'.[60]

The reworking of hagiography from the Anglo-Saxon past could thus be undertaken in the same spirit of smug cultural superiority that seems to have predominated amongst those rewriting Irish, Welsh or Scottish Lives. What seems to differentiate the two cases, however, is the terminology of barbarism employed by the latter group. It is striking that

---

[55] Forbes (ed.), *Vita Sancti Kentigerni. Lives of St Ninian and St Kentigern*, pp. 137–8; *Pinkerton's Lives of the Scottish Saints*, i, p. 9.
[56] Aelred of Rievaulx, *De Sanctis Ecclesiae Haugustaldensis*, ed. J. Raine in *The Priory of Hexham*, 2 vols., Surtees Society, 44, 46 (Durham and London, 1864–5), i, pp. 172–203, at pp. 178, 183; Aelred of Rievaulx, *Relatio de Standardo* in Howlett (ed.), *Chronicles of the Reigns of Stephen, Henry II and Richard I*, iii, pp. 179–99, at pp. 187–8, 193.
[57] Raine (ed.), *Historians of the Church of York*, ii, p. 1.
[58] S. J. Ridyard, *The Royal Saints of Anglo-Saxon England: A Study of the West Saxon and East Anglian Cults* (Cambridge, 1988), p. 259.
[59] Stubbs (ed.), *Memorials of Saint Dunstan*, p. 250.
[60] William of Malmesbury, *De Gestis Regum*, ii, p. 389.

they deride the 'barbarous language' of their predecessors, while writers like Osbert of Clare and William of Malmesbury manage to confine themselves to a vocabulary of literary abuse that has no such overtones of general social disapproval. It would, however, be misleading to see in the statements these hagiographers make a sweeping condemnation of Celtic barbarism of the kind that some twelfth-century English and Anglo-Norman writers certainly could and did utter. They are explicitly decrying earlier *writers*. Barbarity is opposed to Latinity. Their imagery of laboriously mining ore, adding salt to barbaric food, recutting misshapen carvings and bringing things from shadow to light reflects primarily literary judgements rather than views of Irish, Welsh or Scottish society. Indeed, the overall conclusion must be that there was little in the way of cultural reluctance or distancing in the encounter between English ecclesiastics and the saints of the other parts of the British Isles. In twelfth-century England it was not undesirable to give your own saint an Irish origin, and some Irish saints, such as Brigit, were widely commemorated; Anglo-Norman monks were eager to identify with, and obtain the remains of, Welsh saints; while the multiple ties across the Scottish border meant that the frontier between the kingdoms of Scotland and England was no more an Iron Curtain in hagiographical terms than it was in linguistic or tenurial ones. By the twelfth century, true, the Latin of earlier Irish, Welsh and Scottish hagiography did indeed strike some Anglo-Norman writers as, specifically, 'barbarous', but, with a few exceptions, this did not encourage them to make negative generalizations about Irish, Welsh or Scottish society. In matters of cult and hagiography the British Isles was by no means a unity but it was a unit, within which contact and communication were continual and fertile.

4 Sea-divided Gaels? Constructing relationships between Irish and Scots c. 800–1169

Máire Herbert

Study of insular history of the period between the Viking era and the twelfth century has been revitalized by focus on the inter-relationships of the peoples of the Irish Sea region. Is it possible to recover something of the contemporary perceptions of these inter-relationships? What was the perception of the relationship between the Irish and their kinsmen overseas, the descendants of those who had settled in various parts of Britain from around the late Roman period? By the tenth century, Irish settlements in Wales were a distant memory, their legacy surviving only in placenames, inscriptions and anecdote.[1] Yet an active link had been maintained over about four centuries between the homeland and the descendants of Irish settlers in the northwest of Britain, a link mediated through shared language, custom and ecclesiastical association.[2] As the period between the tenth and twelfth centuries was marked by considerable political and social change on both sides of the Irish Sea, how was the relationship between the 'sea-divided Gaels' of Ireland and of Scotland in that era configured by Irish *literati*?

In assembling the evidence I have drawn not only on sources conventionally regarded as historical documentation, such as the Irish annals, genealogical collections and synchronisms of reigns, but also on other vernacular texts, hitherto classed as 'literary', and therefore largely unexploited for their historical testimony. While it is a truism that all literary works reveal something of their contemporary context, those

---

I am grateful to my colleagues Pádraig Ó Riain and John Carey for their helpful comments.

[1] T. Charles-Edwards, 'Language and society among the insular Celts AD 400–1000' in *The Celtic World*, ed. M. J. Green (London and New York, pbk. 1996), pp. 703–36 (pp. 704–10).

[2] See, for instance, K. H. Jackson, 'Common Gaelic: the evolution of the Goedelic languages', *Proceedings of the British Academy*, 37 (1951), pp. 71–97; M. O. Anderson, *Kings and Kingship in Early Scotland* (Edinburgh, 1973, repr. 1980), pp. 119–204; Herbert, *Iona, Kells, and Derry*, pp. 9–126.

included in my survey belong to genres specifically concerned with societal and political issues. Saints' Lives and historical tales from the post-Viking era represent an early Christian past shaped by the experiences and needs of the writer's present. Conventionally, a saint stands as surrogate for his monastic successor and a dynastic ancestor is the designated literary representative of a medieval ruler. Thus, contemporary ideology is articulated in the guise of narrative about a former era, and an invented past encodes information complementary to that provided by mainstream historical documentation.[3] Further texts which project contemporary concerns onto the past are those redacted in a process of Irish self-definition, a process on-going since the early Christian era, in which native traditions of origins and identity are integrated within the larger framework provided by the Bible and Christian-Latin learning.[4] A primary value of this material is, of course, its illumination of the interaction of pagan and Christian doctrine about creation and beginnings. Yet as Irish scholars framed their subject-matter as historiography, they thereby fabricated an antiquity which reflected their political experience and outlook as well as their expertise in vernacular and Christian learning.

Up to about the late ninth century the main focus of accounts of Irish antiquity was on people rather than on territory, on the origins of the *Goídil* and of their language, and on the manner in which they succeeded, as other settlers had not, in settling and populating the country. Historical construct was closely linked to genealogical construct, as pedigrees of leading Irish kin-groups were traced back to the original immigrants, and linked through them to biblical ancestors and universal history.[5] The Irish-descended settlers of Dál Riata on the west coast of Scotland were fitted imperceptibly into this scheme as members of the Gaelic family, bonded by a common ancestry which transcended political particularism.[6] Yet by the ninth century the wide web of kinship was being supplanted by a dynastic polity, and power had accrued to the greater provincial kings, who ruled over territories rather than peoples. Around the end of the century an Irish ecclesiastical scholar prefaces a copy of the now obsolescent genealogical corpus with a reproach to

---

[3] On this topic, see also M. Herbert, 'The Death of Muirchertach mac Erca: a twelfth-century tale', in *Celts and Vikings: Proceedings of the Fourth Symposium of Societas Celtologica Nordica*, ed. F. Josephson (Goteborg, 1997), pp. 27–39 (pp. 27–8).

[4] J. Carey, *The Irish National Origin-Legend: Synthetic Pseudohistory*, Quiggin Pamphlets on the Sources of Mediaeval Gaelic History, 1 (Cambridge, 1994).

[5] J. V. Kelleher, 'The pre-Norman Irish genealogies', *IHS*, 16 (1968–9), pp. 138–53; Carey, *Irish National Origin-Legend*, p. 10.

[6] *CGH*, 140 b 2; 143 a 6.

imprudens Scottorum gens, rerum suarum obliuiscens, 'the foolish Irish people, forgetful of its history'.[7] Indeed, as the Annals of Ulster award the title of 'king of all Ireland' to the Uí Néill over-king in the year 862, and refer to the successor of Patrick, the abbot of Armagh, as *caput religionis totius Hiberniae* in the year 874, does this imply accelerated change?[8] Has the further stage of national authority been attained? Was the collective community of the Irish itself becoming defined in terms of place rather than of people?

In fact, neither outcome could be accounted as *fait accompli* even a century later. While over-kings of the Uí Néill held the most powerful position in Ireland, other provincial kings had not conceded subordinacy. Moreover, Armagh clerics, the likely authors of both ecclesiastical and secular titles of overlordship of 'all of Ireland', were themselves ambivalent about how that realm of authority was to be constituted.[9] In the Tripartite Life of Patrick, probably completed by the end of the tenth century, depiction of the saint's progress around Ireland includes a meeting in the north with Fergus Mór, son of Erc, elsewhere identified as a founding father of Scottish Dál Riata. Patrick's prophecy, that Fergus would beget a line of kings 'in this country and over Fortriu', is said to have been fulfilled by Áedán mac Gabráin's taking of Alba.[10] The statement initially betokens Patrician influence over the whole kindred of the Gael, in Ireland and across the sea. However, the central focus of the Armagh hagiographer is on kingship rather than on kinship. Moreover, he has tailored his material to take account of contemporary politics. The prophecy cited above states that the Dál Riata line of kings are to have power in Fortriu, the formerly Pictish kingdom, associated with Dál Riata at least by the ninth century.[11] Furthermore, the ultimate fulfillment of the prophecy, the taking of Alba by Áedán mac Gabráin, represents, in terms of the Patrician past, the achievement of Cináed

---

[7] Byrne, *Irish Kings and High-Kings*, pp. 254–66; Byrne, Review of *CGH* in *ZCP*, 29 (1962–4), pp. 381–5.

[8] *AU*, pp. 318–19, 330–1. It should be noted, of course, that even in the seventh century the Uí Néill claim to 'monarchy over the kingdom of all Ireland' was being asserted in the *Vita Columbae*, while seventh-century Patrician hagiography was promoting the primatial claims of Armagh.

[9] On Armagh as a site of annal-keeping see G. Mac Niocaill, *The Medieval Irish Annals* (Dublin, 1975), pp. 21–4.

[10] *Bethu Phátraic: The Tripartite Life of Patrick*, ed. K. Mulchrone (Dublin, 1939), p. 97, lines 1884–91.

[11] For divergent views on the subject see, for instance, M. O. Anderson, 'Dalriada and the creation of the kingdom of the Scots', in *Ireland in Early Medieval Europe*, ed. D. Whitelock, R. McKitterick and D. Dumville (Cambridge, 1982), pp. 106–32; D. Dumville, *The Churches of North Britain in the first Viking-Age*, Fifth Whithorn Lecture (Whithorn, 1997), pp. 34–6.

mac Ailpín and his line, whom the genealogists represent as descendants of Áedán.[12]

The writer of the Tripartite Life thus seeks to incorporate the new kingdom of Alba[13] within the political sphere of Gaeldom (and the ecclesiastical hegemony of Armagh) by including it along with kingdoms in Ireland whose dynastic rulers were favoured by Patrick. That Irish *literati* by the end of the tenth century regard the greater territorially based kingships as being at the core of political life is further indicated by the author of the versified biblical history, *Saltair na Rann*. The latter reveals his year of writing (988) by listing contemporaneous kings, both native and foreign. The king of Alba is included in the former category, a further indication that the new kingship, which united Pict and Gael, was now being given place in the conceptual scheme of Irish politics.[14] What was this to mean in practical terms? As the Uí Néill were once more claiming to be kings of Ireland, and seeking authority over other rulers, was this desired overlordship to extend to Alba as well? By the early eleventh century, the Uí Néill had, in fact, been supplanted from premier position in Ireland by Brian Bóruma, a ruler from a hitherto unregarded Munster dynasty.[15] When Brian visited Armagh in the year 1005 the occasion was noted in the *Book of Armagh in conspectu Briain imperatoris Scottorum* [in the presence of Brian, emperor of the Irish]. Is the formulation 'emperor of the Irish' chosen here to affirm that all the far-flung kindred of the Gael are included in Brians's realm? Or did monastic links with Irish foundations in Germany provide a context in which the title *imperator Romanorum* used by Otto III found an Irish imitator?[16] Even if this be so, use of the title need not imply concomitant familiarity with the politics of imperial claims abroad. The full text of the entry suggests that the secular overlordship of Brian was the correlative of the ecclesiastical primacy of Armagh.[17] That Alba was

---

[12] *CGH*, 162 c 50.
[13] For the extent of the kingdom of Alba 'south of the Moray, east of the central Highlands, and north of the Forth' see D. Broun, 'The birth of Scottish history', *SHR*, 76 (1997), pp. 4–22. See also Dumville, *The Churches of North Britain*, p. 3, n. 7; D. N. Dumville, 'Ireland and Britain in *Táin Bó Fraich*', *Études Celtiques*, 32 (1996), pp. 175–87.
[14] *Saltair na Rann*, ed. W. Stokes (Oxford, 1883), p. 34, lines 2349–76. This conclusion is not hindered by textual difficulties, for which see G. S. Mac Eoin, 'The date and authorship of Saltair na Rann', *ZCP*, 28 (1960–1), pp. 51–67. I take the view that the exigencies of the metrical form of the list militate against the proposition that the placement of the king of Alba in the list means that its compiler had links with that kingdom (Mac Eoin, pp. 59–60).
[15] For a narrative of Brian's career, see Ó Corráin, *Ireland before the Normans*, pp. 120–8.
[16] A. Gwynn, 'Brian in Armagh, 1005', *Seanchas Ardmhacha*, 9 (1978–9), pp. 35–50.
[17] *Sanctus patricius iens ad caelum mandauit totum fructum laboris sui tam baptismi tam causarum quam elemoisinarum deferendum esse apostolicae urbi quae scotice nominatur*

part of the *imperium* being claimed both for Armagh and for Brian is indicated by the evidence so far, as well as by the evidence of the Uí Néill riposte.

In the year 1007 the reconvening of the Fair of Tailtiu, and the installation there of a new successor of Colum Cille, invoked in ritual the traditional primacy of the Uí Néill dynasty, and of its ecclesiastical *confrères*, the Columban *familia*. In the same year the preface to the poem *Amra Coluim Cille* projected a similar message in another medium.[18] Its fictive account of the sixth-century Convention of Druim Cet was mimetic of the historical event, not only in so far as Uí Néill king and Iona abbot were at the forefront of Irish affairs, but also in that relations between the Uí Néill and the Gaels of Scotland were a Convention issue.[19] In the fictive account, however, eleventh-century interest in overlordship replaces sixth-century interest in alliance. The text states that 'expedition and hosting' from the Scottish kingdom should be accorded to the men of Ireland, while 'tax and tribute' were to be retained by the men of Alba.[20] That this formulation reflected current political ambition is further suggested by the fact that the *Amra* preface material was subsequently adapted to suit the interest of Munster (and, implicitly, of Brian and his family). While the original text called upon sixth-century historical precedent to support Uí Néill overseas designs, the revised version, in an adroit reinterpretation of genealogical doctrine, reached back to pre-migration times to contrive an association between 'the men of Munster' and 'the men of Alba'.[21]

To what extent was the claim on Alba, sanctioned by pseudo-history, considered realizable? Annal evidence that the Uí Néill ruler, Máel Sechnaill, had a son who bore the epithet *In tAlbanach*, and that the allies of Brian Bóruma at the battle of Clontarf included *mormhaer Marr*

---

ardd macha. Sic reperi in bibliotics scotorum, ego scripsi id est caluus perennis in conspectu briain imperatoris scotorum et quod scripsi finiuit pro omnibus regibus maceriae. (Text published in Gwynn, 'Brian in Armagh', p. 42.)

[18] M. Herbert, 'The preface to *Amra Coluim Cille*', in *Sages, Saints and Storytellers: Celtic Studies in Honour of Professor James Carney*, ed. D. Ó Corráin, L. Breathnach and K. McCone (Maynooth, 1989), pp. 67–75.

[19] *Ibid.*, pp. 69–71.

[20] W. Stokes, 'The Bodleian Amra Choluimb Chille', *Revue Celtique*, 20 (1899), pp. 30–55, 132–83, 248–87, 400–37 (pp. 132–3) (Preface from the twelfth-century manuscript, Rawlinson B 502, fols. 54a–59b. Other copies are in *Lebor na hUidre: Book of the Dun Cow*, ed. R. I. Best and O. Bergin (Dublin, 1929: repr. 1970), fols. 5a–15a33, and Trinity College Dublin, *Liber Hymnorum*, fols. 26a–28b).

[21] Text from *The Yellow Book of Lecan*, cols. 683–4, published by Stokes, 'The Bodleian Amra', pp. 423–6. For genealogical doctrine linking Dál Riata with particular peoples in Munster see, for instance, 'De shíl Chonaire Mór', ed. L. Gwynn, *Ériu*, 6 (1912), pp. 130–43, 'De maccaib Conaire', *ibid.*, pp. 144–53. By generalizing from the particular, a relationship with the kingdom of Munster (and implicitly, with its rulers) is forged.

i nAlbain, suggests that both contenders for the high-kingship in the early eleventh century had sought to involve themselves in the affairs of the overseas kingdom.[22] Clearly, achievement was considerably less than aspiration. Yet the inclusion of Alba within the Irish political community was evidently a tenet of contemporary learned circles. For example, synchronisms of rulers from Patrick's time to the eleventh century categorize holders of Tara kingship from the fifth century as 'kings over Ireland' and match their reigns with those of provincial kings, implicitly their subordinates. The latter constituency includes kings of Alba, a title retrospectively extended to all who ruled in the overseas kingdom from the period of the settlement of Dál Riata.[23] The synchronisms had presented an Uí Néill-dominated kingship of Ireland with final acknowledgement of the reign of the Munster ruler, Brian. In fact, Brian's accession had changed Irish political life by showing that rule over Ireland might be achieved through main force by any of the provincial kings. In the inter-dynastic competition of the following decades, was Alba still theoretically subsumed within the coveted over-kingship? Certainly, concern with establishing genealogical relationships between particular Irish royal dynasties and those of the Scots is discernible in the literature. What does scrutiny of this material reveal?

The literary legend of Muirchertach mac Erca, dynastic ancestor of Cenél nEógain, reinterpreted his given name as a metronymic, thereby identifying the king as son of Erc, daughter of Loarn.[24] In the eleventh century we find that the identity of this Erc has been further specified as *inghean ríg Alban*, 'daughter of the king of Alba'.[25] Thus, learned doctrine was now asserting family relationship between the royal line of Cenél nEógain, of the Irish Northern Uí Néill, and the royal line of Loarn, whose contemporary representatives, the rulers of Moray, were claiming kingship over Alba.[26] The main historical documentation of

---

[22] *AI*, s.a. 1013; *AU*, s.a. 1014.
[23] R. Thurneysen, 'Synchronismen der irischen könige', *ZCP*, 19 (1931), pp. 81–99; A. Boyle, 'The Edinburgh synchronisms of Irish kings', *Celtica*, 9 (1971), pp. 169–79. Though the longer version (Thurneysen, 1931) continues to the death of Muirchertach Ua Briain in 1119, I incline to the view that the final section (1014–1119) represents a later addition, which departs from hitherto formulaic statements about the kingship of Ireland. The shorter version (Boyle, 1971) breaks off incomplete, but I suggest that its unfinished final section may represent the final section of the original compilation.
[24] M. E. Dobbs, 'References to Erc daughter of Loarn in Irish MSS', *Scottish Gaelic Studies*, 6 (1947), pp. 50–7; Byrne, *Irish Kings and High-Kings*, p. 102.
[25] *Lebor Bretnach: The Irish Version of the Historia Britonum ascribed to Nennius*, ed. A. G. van Hamel (Dublin, 1932), pp. 40–1.
[26] For an Irish genealogical record of the descent of eleventh-century Moray rulers from Loairn, see *CGH*, 162 e 1; 162 e 21. On the kingdom and its rulers, see also B. T. Hudson, *Kings of Celtic Scotland* (Westport, CT, 1994), pp. 127–47; *Moray: Province and People*, ed. W. D. H. Sellar (Edinburgh, 1993).

the contest between the incumbent dynasty and that of Moray through the eleventh century and into the twelfth is found in another northern Irish source, the Annals of Ulster. Indeed, the Annals award the title of king of Alba to Moray rulers in the years 1020 and 1058.[27] The indications are that influential opinion in the north of Ireland viewed with favour a power-shift in favour of the Moray dynasty. But the claim of kinship with the dynasty by Cenél nEógain does not involve a claim to extraneous sovereignty over the Scots. Rather, it may be supposed that Cenél nEógain propagandists confront political reality. Alliance with an emergent royal dynasty overseas, negotiated on particular grounds of relationship, might assist the recovery of sovereignty in Ireland.[28] With Uí Néill power in decline, the grand designs of the past appear to be giving way to present pragmatism.

Another instance of claimed relationship by an Irish royal dynasty involves Leinster. By the mid-eleventh century, Diarmait mac Máel na mBó of the Uí Chennselaig dynasty of Leinster had become a leading contender for Irish over-kingship, having gained power over the Dublin Norse, extended his family's sway into the Isle of Man, and involved himself in the affairs of exiled dynasts from Wales and Wessex.[29] Contemporary story, moreover, linked Diarmait's dynasty with the main ruling dynasty of Alba. The tale, set in the sixth century, portrays Diarmait's ancestor, Brandub mac Echach, and Áedán mac Gabráin, ancestor of Alba's main ruling line, as brothers. Their mother, wife of the king of Leinster, had exchanged one son for one of twin daughters born at the same time to the wife of the king of Alba, so that both fathers should have an heir. The sons duly succeeded to the kingships of Leinster and of Alba, but Áedán, king of Alba, thereafter came on an expedition to contest the kingship of Ireland, 'for he had a right by virtue of descent from Gabrán'. His threat to Leinster was averted only by the intervention of Brandub's mother, who revealed the king of Alba as her son.[30] The author of this tale seems to take the view that, if Alba

---

[27] *AU, s.a.* 1020, 1058. The *Annals of Tigernach* also accord the title to a Moray dynast in 1029. See *AT, s.a.* 1029.

[28] The further tradition (*Lebor Bretnach*, p. 53) that Muirchertach murdered his grandfather, Loarn, may reflect a souring of relations between the kingdoms.

[29] S. Duffy, 'Irishmen and Islesmen in the kingdoms of Dublin and Man, 1052–1171', *Ériu*, 43 (1992), pp. 93–133.

[30] 'Gein Branduib maic Echach ocus Aedáin maic Gabráin inso sís', ed. K. Meyer, *ZCP*, 2 (1899), pp. 134–5. For another version, and discussion of the text tradition, see 'The Birth of Brandub and of Aedan son of Gabran', ed. R. I. Best, in *Medieval Studies in Memory of Gertrude Schoepperle Loomis*, ed. P. Rajna *et al.* (Paris, New York, 1927), pp. 381–90. A verse rendering of the tale is edited by M. A. O'Brien, 'A Middle-Irish poem on the birth of Áedán mac Gabráin and Brandub mac Echach', *Ériu*, 16 (1952), pp. 157–70.

were regarded as an Irish province, then rulers of Alba, like powerful provincial kings in Ireland, could have both the genealogical right, and the potential might, to challenge for Irish over-kingship. The claim that Leinster's royal dynasty shared kinship with the royal line of Alba takes on a defensive aspect in the tale. It may be that eleventh-century Leinster adventures in the politics of the Irish Sea regions led to the realization that Alba was no longer a quiescent constituent of Irish political life. The goodwill of the kingdom might be gained by demonstration of shared kinship. It could not simply be taken for granted.

As the eleventh century progressed, the theory that Alba, at some level, was implicated in Irish sovereignty was being confronted by the reality that both Alba and Ireland were embarked on their separate paths of development towards national kingship. Professional learned men sought to harmonize ideal and reality as they continued the scholarly tradition of interpreting the origins and history of the Irish. After the mid-eleventh century, Irish political horizons were being redefined. The versified history, *Ériu ard, inis na ríg*, 'Noble Ireland, island of the kings', focuses on the island territory, on the manner in which successive settlers sought its possession, on the institution of kingship over 'the land of Ireland', and on the attainment of this kingship by over a hundred rulers before the coming of Christianity.[31] Thus, the political cosmos is made to coincide with the geographical entity, and sovereignty of the island of Ireland is represented as a political goal sanctioned by antiquity. The most enduring version of the Irish national origin-legend, the text which came to be known as *Lebor Gabála*, was also shaped around this time.[32] The surviving twelfth-century recension reinforces the political message of the poem above. Moreover, it represents post-invasion Irish history as a history of kings who gained *regnum Hiberniae*.[33] National territory and national institution had become twin pillars of political ideology.

As the Irish body politic was being delineated by the learned order, the manner in which an individual Irishman defined his identity is illustrated in the contemporary chronicle of Marianus Scottus.[34] In the

---

[31] *Bk. Leinster*, iii, pp. 471–90; *The Codex Palatino-Vaticanus, No. 830*, ed. and trans. B. McCarthy (Dublin, 1892), pp. 142–213. On the poet, Gilla Coémáin, and his floruit, *c.* 1072, see *ibid.*, p. 98.

[32] *Lebor Gabála Éirenn*, ed. and trans. R. A. S. Macalister, 5 vols., ITS (London, 1938–56); Carey, *Irish National Origin-Legend*.

[33] *Bk. Leinster*, i, pp. 1–99.

[34] 'Mariani Scotti Chronicon', ed. G. Waitz, *MGH Scriptorum*, vol. V, ed. G. Pertz (Hanover, 1844) pp. 481–562; *Codex Palatino-Vaticanus*, pp. 3–36, 93–8; B. Ó Cuív, 'The Irish marginalia in *Codex Palatino-Vaticanus*, no. 830', *Éigse*, 24 (1990), pp. 45–67.

year 1072, Marianus, in monastic exile in Mainz, was joined by a fellow-countryman who had come via Alba 'on his pilgrimage'. In a marginal note on the codex, the newcomer tells Marianus that he writes 'pro caritate tibi et Scotis omnibus, id est Hibernensibus, quia sum ipse Hibernensis'.[35] Why does the writer perceive a need to redefine the broad term *Scoti* in order to specify Irishness? From whence comes his awareness of the particularity of his identity as *Hibernensis*? It seems reasonable to conjecture that his precision may have been honed by his acquaintance with the political life of Alba, for he notes in the chronicle of Marianus the reigns of some of its eleventh-century rulers, styled as *rex Scotiae*.[36] Yet if personal experience of the separate status of the kingdom of Alba/Scotia was a factor in the writer's individual assertion of identity, nevertheless, his self-definition also reflects the view currently being espoused by *literati* in Ireland, that the national realm was constituted in territorial rather than in tribal terms. The redescription of the realm of Irish kingship meant that the place of Alba within the theoretical scheme of Irish politics had to be revised. In the early twelfth century we see an attempt to do so within the conservative framework of the Irish genealogical corpus, which maintained the early, all-inclusive record of kinship alongside the contemporary narrowed pedigrees of leading kingships. The latter record includes genealogies of rulers of Alba up to the second half of the eleventh century, including both dynasties in contention for kingship in that century. Yet these pedigrees, headed *ríg Alban*, are placed at the end of the collection, followed only by those of the Fomoire, figures from Ireland's mythic prehistory.[37] Thus, in its attempt to align past and present, the genealogical corpus situates Alba in a position both attached to, and detached from, the Irish political world.

Historical tales constitute another site in which Alba's political relationship with Ireland is refigured. The seventh-century battle of Mag Rath, involving Scottish Dál Riata in conflict with the Northern Uí Néill, became the subject of literary recreation both in the tenth and in the twelfth centuries.[38] The tenth-century version, rewriting the scenario from the perspective of that era, depicts the men of Alba not as initiating hostility in Ireland, but rather as participants on the side of the

---

[35] Full text and translation, *ibid.*, pp. 50–1.
[36] Waitz (ed.), 'Mariani Scotti Chronicon', pp. 556–8.
[37] Bodleian Library Oxford, MS Rawlinson B 502, fol. 87v. Facsimile ed. Kuno Meyer, (Oxford, 1909), 162 c 44–g. For edited text, see *CGH*, pp. 328–33. On the Fomoire, see, for instance, P. Mac Cana, *Celtic Mythology* (London, 1970), pp. 57–64.
[38] M. Herbert, '*Fled Dúin na nGéd*: A reappraisal', *Cambridge Medieval Celtic Studies*, 18 (1989), pp. 75–87 (pp. 76–7).

king of Ulster against the Uí Néill king.[39] It is taken as self-evident from a tenth-century viewpoint that Alba should be the place of first recourse for allies to assist neighbouring kin in Ulster. The twelfth-century retelling of the tale, however, indicates that alliance between an Irish kingdom and Alba could no longer be assumed, but rather had to be demonstrated on particular grounds. The Ulster king is advised to go to seek the king of Alba, 'for a daughter of his is your mother'.[40] Though the men of Alba agree to assist the Ulster king, their druid remains hostile to the venture 'as Ireland is not your own land'.[41] Alliance across the Irish Sea, therefore, is no longer a given, determined by common ancestry, but rather is contingent on specific family ties. In the enactment of twelfth-century political relationships, synchronic connection took precedence over diachronic descent.

Yet connection at this level between Ireland and Alba was facilitated by continuing links of language and culture. These are epitomized in the twelfth-century Irish narrative, *Acallam na Senórach*, which vividly depicts the transinsular adventures of the Fianna, legendary hunters and fighting-men.[42] The Fianna of the *Acallam* are shown to be based in Ireland, but active throughout Gaeldom.[43] Indeed, their leader is married for seven years to a daughter of the king of Alba.[44] The text, with its tales of daring deeds untrammelled by national boundaries, clearly reflects a linguistic community uncircumscribed by political definition. The author of the *Acallam* is aware, moreover, that the linguistic community in the Irish Sea regions in the twelfth century is not neatly definable in terms of the extended genealogical kindred of the Gaels. The Viking wife of the king of Alba is represented as having been seduced by tales of the Fianna recounted by visiting Irish poets.[45] The enumeration of a warrior-band of the Fianna includes nobles not only from Irish kingdoms and from the kingdom of Alba, but also from Islay, the Hebrides and Galloway.[46] Thus, the cultural realm mirrored in the *Acallam* extends beyond ethnic Gaeldom to all who became affiliated

---

[39] 'A new version of the Battle of Mag Rath', ed. and trans. C. Marstrander, *Ériu*, 5 (1911), pp. 226–47.
[40] *Fled Dúin na nGéd*, ed. Ruth Lehmann (Dublin, 1964), lines 432–4. On contemporary aristocratic marriage, see M. T. Flanagan, *Irish Society, Anglo-Norman Settlers, Angevin Kingship. Interactions in Ireland in the Late Twelfth Cenury* (Oxford, 1989), pp. 91–5.
[41] Lehmann (ed.), *Fled Dúin na nGéd*, lines 641–2. See *Dictionary of the Irish Language*, Royal Irish Academy (Dublin, 1983) *s.v. flesc*, 164.45–6.
[42] *Silva Gadelica: A Collection of Tales in Irish*, ed. S. H. O'Grady, 2 vols., ITS (London, 1892), i, pp. 94–233, ii, pp. 101–265; 'Acallamh na Senórach', ed. W. Stokes, in *Irische Texte*, 4.1, ed. W. Stokes and E. Windisch (Leipzig, 1900).
[43] 'Acallamh na Senórach', lines 329–60; *Silva Gadelica*, ii, pp. 108–9.
[44] 'Acallamh na Senórach', lines 3055–103; *Silva Gadelica*, ii, pp. 180–1.
[45] 'Acallamh na Senórach', lines 4658–752; *Silva Gadelica*, ii, pp. 214–16.
[46] 'Acallamh na Senórach', lines 4544–62; *Silva Gadelica*, ii, pp. 211–12.

with the Gaels through adoption of their language. It makes a point of including those whom the annalists termed *Gallgoídil*, the Hebridean descendants of inter-marriage between Gael and Viking.

It would seem, therefore, that Irish men of learning in the mid-twelfth-century outline two coexisting spheres in which the relationship between the inhabitants of Ireland and those of Irish ancestry in Northern Britain might be articulated. The Irish political community was now defined by the island territory. Insular interconnections were no longer the assured outcome of common descent, but might be mediated through marriage alliances between royal families. Irish political relationships with overseas Gaels had become a matter of decision and negotiation. Cultural relationships, on the other hand, continued to affirm the centuries-old transinsular bonds. The linguistic and literary community transcended political territoriality and linked Gaeldom on both sides of the Irish Sea. Moreover, the Irish cultural world was a world of permeable boundaries, of free movement of poets and their lore, of open access through the medium of shared language. It was a sphere of inclusiveness rather than of delimitation, encompassing peoples of different political affiliation and descent.

The idea that political and cultural identities were not necessarily coterminous seems to have had useful implications for Irish *literati* of the mid-twelfth century.[47] An Annals of Ulster death notice in the year 1165 describes Malcolm, king of Alba, as *in Cristaidhe as ferr do bai do Gaidhelaibh re muir anair* [the best Christian among the overseas Gaels to the east].[48] On the other hand, an Irish verse composition, setting out foreign parallels for the peoples of the leading Irish provincial kingdoms, counts *Albanuigh*, the people of Alba, among the foreigners.[49] Yet as men of learning defined varieties of Irishness in an Irish Sea world much changed over two centuries, they did not realize that even greater change was imminent. After 1169, Norman intrusion into Ireland would force further revision of the way in which membership of the Irish nation could be conceptualized, both politically and imaginatively.

---

[47] The present focus on attitudes of Irish *literati* points up a need for further study of works of debated provenance, such as *Duan Albanach* and the so-called 'Prophecy of Berchán', with a view to establishing their perspectives on transinsular relationships.
[48] *AU, s.a.* 1165. I have revised the published translation.
[49] 'Two Middle-Irish poems', ed. and trans. K. Meyer, *ZCP*, 1 (1897), p. 112.

5 The 1169 invasion as a turning-point in Irish–Welsh relations

Seán Duffy

It goes virtually without saying that the arrival in Ireland in the late 1160s of the first smallish contingents of Anglo-Norman adventurers and mercenaries marks a turning-point of some sort in the history of Ireland's relationship with Wales. Frequently the invaders had cut their teeth in Wales, many had won estates in Wales or in the Welsh marches and some had found wives there.[1] They brought with them to Ireland, and employed in their wars against the Irish, valuable experience gained in comparable warfare against the Welsh.[2] They countered Irish arms with bands of Welsh archers and colonized their newly acquired swordland with ship-loads of tenants from their Welsh and Marcher lordships, some of whom were undoubtedly of native Welsh extraction.

The invasion established, therefore, a new nexus of involvement between Ireland and Wales, which interrupted, though it certainly did not obliterate, earlier patterns of contact between the two countries. This operated at different levels – ecclesiastical and scholarly, political and military, commercial – and also, and equally significantly, with different degrees of intensity. For instance, if one were to draw a line on a map of Ireland running from Galway to Dundalk, the evidence would indicate that the area north of that line, as geography if nothing else dictated, had long-established lines of communication with northern Britain and was by comparison relatively isolated from contact with Wales. It is, with few exceptions, south of this line that one must look for traces of Welsh links. Furthermore, even within Wales, contact with Ireland was not uniform: the people of Deheubarth or south Wales were

---

[1] The best discussion of this subject is Flanagan, *Irish Society, Anglo-Norman Settlers, Angevin Kingship*, ch. 5; see also, G. H. Orpen, *Ireland under the Normans, 1169–1333*, 4 vols. (Oxford, 1911–20, repr. 1968), i, chs. 5 and 7; and the excellent genealogical table by Kenneth Nicholls of the 'Descendants of Nesta' in *NHI*, ix, p. 166.

[2] See L. H. Nelson, *The Normans in South Wales 1070–1171* (Austin, 1966); I. W. Rowlands, 'The making of the March. Aspects of the Norman settlement of Dyfed', in *Proceedings of the Battle Conference*, vol. iii, ed. R. A. Brown (Woodbridge, 1981), pp. 142–57; W. E. Wightman, *The Lacy Family in England and Normandy* (Oxford, 1966).

most frequently found in connection with Munster and south Leinster, and the men of Gwynedd or north Wales with north Leinster and Dublin. This distinction between south Welsh and north Welsh involvement with Ireland is important in assessing the reaction in Wales to the Anglo-Norman invasion of Ireland.

Their geographical proximity meant that the inhabitants of the southeast coast of Ireland and of the west coast of Wales had always rubbed shoulders.[3] Early church connections, especially the transmigrations of saints and missionaries,[4] Irish colonies in Wales,[5] the rise to power in Ireland of what may have been returned emigrant dynasties,[6] Irish kings, heroes and apical figures said to have been the sons of British mothers[7] – these are all the familiar stock-in-trade of immediate prehistoric and early medieval Hiberno-Welsh relations. When the Welsh chronicle tradition begins to blossom in the eleventh century we find Irishmen active in Welsh politics, toppling Welsh kings and seeking to grab power there themselves.[8] From these and other sources we find Welsh princes seeking refuge at the courts of Irish kings, being supplied with armies and fleets to try to secure their restoration,[9] and, in at least one case, a title being given to an Irish province-king which suggests that he claimed suzerainty over Wales or part of Wales.[10]

Since they had the best fleets and monopolized much of the trade, contact between Ireland and Wales in this period was channelled largely

---

[3] The two full-scale, and now rather dated, studies of this subject are C. O'Rahilly, *Ireland and Wales. Their Historical and Literary Relations* (London, 1924) and B. G. Charles, *Old Norse Relations with Wales* (Cardiff, 1934).

[4] There is a considerable body of literature on this subject, but perhaps the most stimulating study is E. G. Bowen, *Saints, Seaways and Settlements in the Celtic Lands* (Cardiff, 1977), which also has an extensive bibliography.

[5] M. Richards, 'Irish settlements in south-west Wales: a topographical approach', *RSAI Jn.*, 90 (1960), pp. 133–62; C. Thomas, 'Irish settlements in post-Roman western Britain', *Journal of the Royal Institution of Cornwall*, 6 (1972), pp. 251–74; M. Dillon, 'The Irish settlements in Wales', *Celtica*, 12 (1977), pp. 1–11; B. Coplestone-Crow, 'The dual nature of the Irish colonization of Dyfed in the Dark Ages', *Studia Celtica*, 16–17 (1981–2), pp. 107–19; T. Ó Cathasaigh, 'The Déisi and Dyfed', *Éigse*, 20 (1984), pp. 1–33; W. Davies, *Wales in the Early Middle Ages* (Leicester, 1982), pp. 87–9. See W. Davies, *Patterns of Power in Early Wales* (Oxford, 1990), where she concludes: 'In short, contacts between west Wales and Ireland must have been frequent, if not the norm, and the early evidence seems to prefigure the establishment of a long-term pattern' (p. 40).

[6] Byrne, *Irish Kings and High-kings*, pp. 72, 184.

[7] T. F. O'Rahilly, *Early Irish History and Mythology* (Dublin, 1946), pp. 49 (n. 3), pp. 216–17.

[8] S. Duffy, 'Ostmen, Irish and Welsh in the eleventh century', *Peritia*, 9 (1996), pp. 378–96.

[9] K. L. Maund, *Ireland, Wales, and England in the Eleventh Century* (Woodbridge, 1991), ch. 4.

[10] *AT*, s.a. 1072.

through the towns established by the Vikings or Ostmen, principally, Dublin, Waterford and Wexford.[11] There was a Waterford contingent at the crucial Welsh battle of Mynydd Carn in 1081, supplied by the Ua Briain royal house of Munster.[12] This battle paved the way to power in Gwynedd of Gruffudd ap Cynan and in Deheubarth of Rhys ap Tewdwr. When Rhys was expelled from Deheubarth in 1088 he fled to Ireland, gathered a fleet there, returned and defeated his opponents.[13] When he was killed by intruding Normans in 1093, along with what appears to have been an Ostman from Ireland, his death was reported in the Munster Annals of Inisfallen.[14] The Normans quickly overran Dyfed, which William Rufus conferred on Arnulf de Montgomery. Rhys's son Gruffudd then fled to Ireland where he appears to have spent the next twenty-two years, only returning to Wales in 1115, and his exile did him no harm, since he thereupon recovered part of his ancestral kingdom, and at least one other period of enforced exile began in 1127.[15]

As for the Normans who were occupying the Pembrokeshire part of south Wales at this point, the de Montgomery family, it is well known that when they got into hot water with Henry I in 1102 they sent the steward of Pembroke, Gerald of Windsor, ancestor-figure of the Irish Geraldines, to Muirchertach Ua Briain of Munster, formed a marriage-alliance with him (Arnulf de Montgomery married Muirchertach Ua Briain's daughter) and won military aid to assist them in their rebellion.[16] It is interesting to note that the Welsh *Brut* chronicles state of these developments that the Normans 'thought to make peace with the Irish', implying that relations had earlier been strained, and 'exalted themselves with pride because of those events', a measure, it seems, of Muirchertach Ua Briain's status in contemporary eyes.[17] Now, we do not know what Muirchertach's aims were in forming this alliance, but Pembroke was a focal point on the trade route from Waterford to south Wales and the Bristol Channel. Strongbow's capture of Waterford in 1170 is, therefore, in one sense at least, paralleled by the Ua Briain and

---

[11] D. Moore, 'Gruffudd ap Cynan and the medieval Welsh polity', in *Gruffudd ap Cynan. A Collaborative Biography*, ed. K. L. Maund (Woodbridge, 1996), pp. 23–31.
[12] *A Mediaeval Prince of Wales. The Life of Gruffudd ap Cynan*, ed. D. S. Evans (Felinfach, 1990), pp. 35, 66; *AI*, s.a. 1080.
[13] *Brut*, p. 18. [14] *AI*, s.a. 1093.
[15] *Brut*, p. 39; *Annales Cambriae*, ed. J. Williams ab Ithel, RS (London, 1860), s.a. 1127.
[16] For the Montgomery family, see J. F. A. Mason, 'Roger de Montgomery and his sons (1067–1102)', *TRHS*, 5th series, 13 (1963), pp. 1–28; for Arnulf, see E. Curtis, 'Murchertach O'Brien, high-king of Ireland, and his Norman son-in-law, Arnulf de Montgomery, circa 1100', *RSAI Jn.*, 51 (1921), pp. 116–34; Flanagan, *Irish Society, Anglo-Norman Settlers, Angevin Kingship*, pp. 67–8.
[17] *Brut (RHB)*, p. 43.

de Montgomery alliance of 1102, and the aim may have been in part the same: the controller of one end of this vital navigational path was trying to make secure the other end. With the collapse of the rebellion, Arnulf de Montgomery sought to evade Henry I's wrath by, according to the chronicler Orderic Vitalis, fleeing to Ua Briain in Ireland.[18] There is some evidence to support this, since Muirchertach later wrote to Archbishop Anselm of Canterbury thanking him for interceding with King Henry on Arnulf's behalf.[19] Orderic also claims that Arnulf brought his retainers with him and that they saw action in Ireland. There is not the least mention of this in the Irish annals, but it is worth pointing out that when the exiled Leinster king, Diarmait Mac Murchada, returned from banishment in August 1167, he brought a band of strange and ferocious Flemings from Pembrokeshire in tow, yet neither the Annals of Inisfallen nor the Annals of Ulster bother to mention them: chroniclers were obviously used to witnessing small contingents of alien mercenaries walking on and off the Irish stage. Orderic's statement, therefore, is not altogether beyond belief, and the implication – the possibility that Ireland played host to Pembrokeshire Normans two-thirds of a century before their full-scale invasion – provides, at least, food for thought. The same can be said for Orderic's claim that Arnulf de Montgomery, in fleeing to Ireland, hoped to secure his father-in-law's kingdom in his wife's right. One is tempted to dismiss this out of hand, but, then, a more famous successor as lord of Pembroke was to do just that two generations on.

These events owe their origin, in large part, to the disruption caused by the death of Rhys ap Tewdwr, and the quickening advance of Norman settlement throughout Wales that followed it, something which had previously been spasmodic and half-hearted.[20] With this new Norman influx we get a good deal more detail on Welsh contacts with Ireland. Whether this is merely the product of the thickening out of the chronicles at this point, or whether Welsh leaders, now squeezed by the Normans' westward expansion, found themselves with little choice but to make recourse to Ireland, one cannot with certainty say. In either case, it is possible to build up for this period quite a comprehensive picture of the subsequent transmigrations to Ireland of discomfitted Welshmen, and of the activities in Wales of men from Ireland. These events have been well rehearsed elsewhere,[21] but one might perhaps

[18] Orderic Vitalis, *Ecclesiastical History*, vi, pp. 48–51.
[19] Ussher, *Whole Works*, iv, p. 526.
[20] The best recent analysis is Davies, *Conquest, Coexistence and Change*, pp. 27–45.
[21] Flanagan, *Irish Society, Anglo-Norman Settlers, Angevin Kingship*, pp. 63–7; Maund, *Ireland, Wales, and England*, pp. 169–70; Moore, 'Gruffudd ap Cynan and the medieval Welsh polity', pp. 23–7.

make a couple of observations on the matter. When the Normans invaded Anglesey in 1098, its ruler Gruffudd ap Cynan, and his son-in-law Cadwgan ap Bleddyn, fled to Ireland. They returned in the following year and the *Brut* tells us that 'after making peace with the French, they received a portion of the land and the kingdom'.[22] A decade or so later Cadwgan's son Owain spent several brief periods of exile in Ireland, and we are told that 'King Muirchertach, the chief of the Irish, received him honourably for it was him that he had been with before when the war in Anglesey had been waged.'[23] Owain used the backing he received in Ireland to launch several damaging campaigns in Wales and we are told that the outcome was that in 1111 Henry I 'promised peace to Owain, and he bade messengers be sent after him to Ireland', while at the same time he restored Owain's father's forfeited lands.[24]

In both these instances, men who detached themselves from their transmarine alliances were rewarded. This suggests that Henry I was aware of the dangers of having recalcitrant Welshmen receive a sympathetic hearing across the Irish Sea, where Muirchertach Ua Briain seems to have gone out of his way to set himself up as protector of displaced Welsh dynasts. Muirchertach fell from power in 1114, and it may just be worth mentioning that it was in that same year that King Henry chose to make his massive expedition to Wales in an effort to subdue it. It is just possible that he did so confident in the knowledge that the Welsh were without their long-standing prop across the Irish Sea. Sure enough, none of the Welsh made what had formerly been an almost instinctive response on their part to such pressure, the voyage to Ireland. Instead, they stayed put and came to terms.[25] In each of these cases, therefore, from Rhys ap Tewdwr, to Arnulf de Montgomery, Gruffudd ap Cynan, Cadwgan ap Bleddyn and his son Owain, and on the part of Henry I himself, there was an awareness that Ireland had a role to play *vis-à-vis* Wales, a place where one could find refuge among friends, a place where one's enemies could take cover beyond one's reach, a land, perhaps, of opportunity. And in the considerations of the Irish (at least, those of the south and east), whose connections with Wales now extended beyond the native Welsh to the new Norman settlers, and, directly or indirectly, to the king of England, Wales must have loomed large. Though these events may precede the Anglo-Norman invasion of Ireland by a couple

---

[22] *Brut*, p. 21. [23] *Ibid.*, p. 30. [24] *Ibid.*, p. 35.
[25] R. R. Davies, 'Henry I and Wales', in *Studies in Medieval History presented to R.H.C. Davies*, ed. H. Mayr-Harting and R. I. Moore (London, 1985), pp. 132–47; C. P. Lewis, 'Gruffudd ap Cynan and the Normans', in Maund (ed.), *Gruffudd ap Cynan*, pp. 61–77.

of generations, they have remarkably strong parallels with it, and are a reminder of the need not to view the invasion in too sharp a focus.

Native Welshmen undoubtedly participated in the invasion, in response to the famous offer broadcast in Wales on Diarmait Mac Murchada's behalf that 'Whoever shall wish for soil or sod, richly shall I enfeoff them.'[26] Large numbers of Welshmen settled in the newly conquered lands. Charters of Irish lands are addressed in a significant minority of cases to 'Francis et Anglis, Wallensibus et Hybernensibus', or a variant thereof. The surviving Irish monastic registers and cartularies, and other voluminous records such as the proceedings of the justiciar's court, throw forth a whole host of native Welsh names, and of individuals with a cognomen such as 'Walensis' or 'Bretnach'. Indeed, one charter dated 1282 describes the invasion as 'the arrival of the English and Welsh in Ireland'.[27] This is reminiscent of a poem composed in honour of Cathal Crobderg Ua Conchobair of Connacht, which its editor tentatively dates to 1191, and which refers to the invaders in the following terms: 'The ugly coarse shoal who are assailing the bright salmon [i.e., the Irish] are the Welsh with abundance of weapons and the English and French from over the fair sea.'[28] The reigning king of Deheubarth was Rhys ap Tewdwr's grandson, the Lord Rhys ap Gruffudd, and he seems to have supported the venture. Gerald of Wales tells us that when Diarmait Mac Murchada was in Wales in 1167 Rhys 'took pity on the exile's misfortune'. Rhys facilitated Robert fitz Stephen's contribution to the ensuing invasion by releasing him from imprisonment, on the express condition that he take part.[29] According to an entry in the *Annals of the Four Masters*, in the first encounter which Mac Murchada faced when he returned to Ireland with his new foreign allies, those killed on his side included 'the son of the king of Wales, who was the battle-prop of the island of Britain, who had come across the sea in the army of Mac Murchada'.[30] This seems to have been one of Rhys's own sons. Those of mixed Norman-Welsh blood were, of course, to the forefront, principal among them being the brood of Rhys's aunt Nest. In Ireland these men exhibit an extraordinary degree of reverence for St David. The *Song of Dermot and the Earl* has them invoking David's aid whenever danger threatened, thus seeking the sanction of the Welsh patron for their conquests.[31] Gerald of Wales

[26] *Song of Dermot*, lines 431–6.
[27] 'Calendar to Christ Church deeds', ed. M. J. McEnery, in *Report of the Deputy Keeper of the Public Records of Ireland*, 20 (1888), no. 130.
[28] B. Ó Cuív, 'A poem composed for Cathal Croibhdhearg Ó Conchobhair', *Ériu*, 34 (1983), pp. 157–74, quatrain 50.
[29] Giraldus, *Expugnatio*, pp. 28–31.   [30] *AFM*, s.a. 1167.
[31] See, for instance, *Song of Dermot*, lines 987, 1938, 3442–55.

uses the prophesies of Merlin Silvester to justify Norman-Welsh participation in the subjugation of Ireland. He quotes: 'A knight [i.e., Robert fitz Stephen], sprung of two different races, will be the first to break through the defences of Ireland by force of arms.'[32] There is a strong inference being made here, and that is that the Welsh should have little sympathy for the Irish since it is their own prophecy that is coming true. For these and other reasons, therefore, the men of south Wales and the Norman-Welsh collaborated in a venture that had something to offer both.

It seems likely, however, that the men of north Wales responded differently to the invasion. Our knowledge of Irish–Welsh relations in the pre-Norman period, and about the relationship in particular between the ruling house of Gwynedd and the Ostmen of Dublin, derives to a large extent from the text known as *Historia Gruffud vab Kenan*, about which it is fashionable to be sceptical, though I have attempted elsewhere to prove that one can place some degree of reliance on what this tract says about Ireland.[33] To summarize the matter, the *Historia* claims that its hero, Gruffudd ap Cynan, founder of a dynasty who ruled as princes of Gwynedd until the conquest of Wales in the late thirteenth century, was born in Dublin in the middle years of the eleventh century, and was reared in Swords in north County Dublin. His father was a man called Cynan ab Iago, who was a contender for the kingship of north Wales but who was forced to flee Gwynedd and to seek refuge in Dublin with the family of the famous king Sitriuc Silkenbeard. Cynan married Sitriuc's granddaughter, Ragnhild, and Gruffudd was a product of this marriage. The *Historia* describes how, when he came to manhood, Gruffudd enlisted support in Dublin, invaded Anglesey and conquered north Wales from his enemies. From time to time he got into difficulty in Wales, at the hands of Welsh enemies and of the Normans, and on each occasion took refuge in Ireland, gathered fleets from Dublin and elsewhere, and managed to recover his grip on Gwynedd. Now, in the aftermath of the Anglo-Norman invasion, the descendants of Gruffudd ap Cynan, the family of his son Owain Gwynedd, are found holding land in the city of Dublin and in its northern hinterland, Fingal. It is not easy to establish, of course, whether they acquired these lands as a result of the invasion or were already landholders in the Dublin area before the Anglo-Normans arrived. However, we know from Welsh genealogies that Owain Gwynedd had an Irish wife, who was the mother of the poet Hywel.[34] Furthermore, Welsh genealogical collections, based on compilations

[32] Giraldus, *Expugnatio*, p. 31.   [33] Duffy, 'Ostmen, Irish and Welsh', pp. 378–96.
[34] *Early Welsh Genealogical Tracts*, ed. C. C. Bartram (Cardiff, 1966), p. 97.

that date from the first half of the thirteenth century, also refer to 'Rhirid ab Owain [Gwynedd], who owned Cloghran, the town which was given to the old Gruffudd ap Cynan, which is between the city of Dublin and Swords'.[35] Now, if the latter is independent of *Historia Gruffud vab Kenan*, it is corroborating evidence for Gruffudd's association with north Co. Dublin, and for the family's continued possession of that land in the post-invasion period.

The Rhirid in question, described as Richerid Macchanan (presumably Mac or ap Cynan) can be proven to have held lands in the modern barony of Balrothery West in north Co. Dublin in the early thirteenth century, as Dr Marie Therese Flanagan has shown, building on earlier foundations laid by Edmund Curtis.[36] Indeed, Dr Flanagan has suggested, following Eric St John Brooks, that Balrothery itself may take its name from a member of the family.[37] She suggests Rhirid, that is, 'Baile Rhirid', 'the town of Rhirid'. However, Rhirid had a brother Rhodri whom we know to have had a connection with Ireland: he was expelled from Anglesey about 1190 and when he returned to reclaim his position three years later, the campaign that followed was dubbed by a Welsh chronicler, 'the summer of the Irish (*haf y gwydyl*)'.[38] It is likely that 'Baile Rhodri' would give us Balrothery more easily than 'Baile Rhirid'. Be that as it may, the addition of Rhodri to the list of others of his family to be mentioned shortly only serves to increase the evidence for the connection between the rulers of Gwynedd and Dublin. And the occurrence of the place-name Balrothery, if we accept its association with Rhodri ab Owain Gwynedd, is significant in another respect. Its earliest occurrence is in the Dublin *Guild Merchant Roll*, at about the year 1200, where it is rendered 'Baliretheri'.[39] The fact that this place-name in north Co. Dublin, at the heart of the new Anglo-Norman colony, is rendered in Irish form, rather than 'villa Retheri' or 'Retheristown', suggests that it is a survival from the days when Irish was the language of that area, from the pre-invasion period. A brother of Rhirid and Rhodri, Maelgwn ab Owain, held lands in the city of Dublin, and these too seem to date to the period before the establishment of the English lordship of Ireland, because an inquisition was held in 1218 to

---

[35] *Ibid.*, p. 97.
[36] M. T. Flanagan, '*Historia Gruffud vab Kenan* and the origins of Balrothery, Co. Dublin', *Cambrian Medieval Celtic Studies*, 28 (1994), pp. 71–94.
[37] *The Irish Cartularies of Llanthony Prima and Secunda*, ed. E. St John Brooks, Irish Manuscripts Commission (Dublin, 1953), p. xix.
[38] *The Text of the Bruts from the Red Book of Hergest*, ed. J. Rhys and J. G. Evans (Oxford, 1890), p. 405.
[39] *The Dublin Guild Merchant Roll, c. 1190–1265*, ed. P. Connolly and G. Martin (Dublin, 1992), pp. 45, 78, 92.

determine if seisin should be granted to Maelgwn's famous nephew and heir, Llywelyn ab Iorwerth, or to Adam le Savonier, probably a new Anglo-Norman citizen who had disseised him.[40] We know that Maelgwn was in Ireland as early as 1173, when he was expelled from Gwynedd by his brother Dafydd.[41] Where in Ireland was Maelgwn in 1173? I would suggest that he was holed up in his house in Dublin or in his estate in Fingal, whence he returned to Wales in the following year, presumably having recruited a force of armed men, to challenge his brother for the kingship, albeit unsuccessfully. Incidentally, a later member of the family, a certain Rericius Makanan (perhaps the Richerid Macchanan already mentioned), held lands at some point before 1281 in the villa Ostmannorum, the transpontine suburb of Dublin.[42] Oxmantown, as its name suggests, is where the Ostmen are said to have been banished after the Anglo-Norman seizure of the town, and that one of Gruffudd ap Cynan's descendants held land there may be significant.

The cumulative evidence for Venedotian links with Dublin city and the north Dublin area of Fingal is extensive, and it seems unreasonable to resist the plausible conclusion that those links antedate the Anglo-Norman seizure of Dublin. If that is the case, then the house of Gwynedd had much to lose from the assertion of Anglo-Norman lordship over Ireland. Their links were with the Ostmen of Dublin and with the inhabitants of the Dublin hinterland, and those links were under threat after 1169. The imminent collapse of the Ostman kingdom spelt danger for a dynasty which had intimate links with it stretching back perhaps as much as a century. It would, however, be wrong to see the invasion as marking a thorough break in the traditional pattern of contact between Wales and Ireland. Because the eastern seaboard of Ireland was the area most densely colonized, it formed a wedge securely driven between native Wales and Ireland. But some level of contact was maintained. We have seen above that when Maelgwn ab Owain Gwynedd was banished from Anglesey in 1173 by his brother Dafydd, he found refuge in Ireland, though he was back in Wales within a year. As Maelgwn's Irish holding was in Dublin, we may assume that the recent changeover in power there had not yet altered its long-standing receptiveness to Welsh refugees. This fits in with the impression gained from other sources that the Ostmen of Dublin maintained some level of independence during the 1170s at least. There are a few obvious instances of this. After the Anglo-Norman invasion of Ireland the term

---

[40] *Cal. Doc. Ire.*, 1171–1251, no. 830.   [41] *Brut*, p. 70.
[42] *Chartularies of St Mary's Abbey, Dublin*, ed. J. T. Gilbert, 2 vols., RS (London, 1884–6), ii, p. 486.

Gall, 'foreigner', came, in the course of time, to describe the new invaders, rather than the Ostmen as had formerly been the case. Thus, one might have imagined that a reference after 1170 to the activities of *Gaill Átha Cliath* ('the foreigners of Dublin') had the new settlers there in mind, but not so, or at least not exclusively so: when the petty ruler of Cairbre was killed by *Gaill Átha Cliath* in 1174, the latter were led by a 'Mac Turnin', almost certainly an Ostman.[43] In the same year Strongbow was defeated at Thurles by Domnall Mór Ua Briain. The *Four Masters* tell us that before the battle Strongbow and his men 'solicited to their assistance the *Gaill Átha Cliath*', and again these appear to be Ostmen, because the Cottonian annals refer to this as a clash *cum Anglicis et Dublinniensibus*.[44]

It seems, therefore, that some Ostman families managed to salvage part of their former autonomy even after the annexation of their city-state. It must have been men like these whom Maelgwn ab Owain brought back to Anglesey with him in 1173, and, as already noted, his brother Rhodri, who may have been lord of Balrothery in Co. Dublin, brought another army to Anglesey from Ireland in the early 1190s. Therefore, it had been a feature of Irish–Welsh relations in the pre-invasion period that men from Ireland participated in warfare in Wales. One assumes that this was seriously disrupted as a result of the invasion, but, as this evidence indicates, the flow of men from Ireland to military service in Wales had not entirely abated. And it was not confined to the reigning dynasty in Gwynedd alone. One of the successors of the Lord Rhys of Deheubarth, his son Maelgwn, employed the services of 'a certain Irishman', and his battle-axe, to have some of his enemies assassinated in 1205.[45] That, unfortunately, is as much as we are told: just a casual mention by a Welsh chronicler, but it may be a clue both to the continuing military contribution of Ireland to Welsh warfare, and to a more widespread Irish presence in Welsh society than is usually allowed.

In the immediate aftermath of the invasion, the stock of the Lord Rhys and of his principality, Deheubarth, was rising. Within Wales, the native kingdoms of Gwynedd and Powys were in disarray through succession disputes. In Ireland the high-king, Ruaidrí Ua Conchobair, had by any standards been worsted in his dealings with the newcomers. It was in these circumstances that the Lord Rhys held his two famous contests for poets and musicians at Cardigan Castle at Christmas 1176

---

[43] *AFM, s.a.* 1174.
[44] A. M. Freeman, 'Annals in Cotton MS Titus A. XXV', *Revue Celtique*, 41–44 (1924–7); at 42 (1925), p. 290.
[45] *Brut*, p. 82.

and had them announced a year in advance throughout Britain and Ireland, a clear attempt to parade the pre-eminence of his court,[46] and not, we may presume, merely over the rest of Wales, but over Ireland, under whose cultural shadow Wales had sometimes remained hidden. The question arises, therefore, as to whether, in the aftermath of the invasion, the Welsh and Irish can be assumed to have shared any measure of affinity or empathy, and, if so, whether it influenced their actions. No Irish chronicler bothers to record Rhys's death, though the *Song of Dermot and the Earl*, in its account of earlier events, calls him 'a very brave and courteous king'.[47] Neither do the Irish sources bother much about events in Wales. Welsh chronicles for their part report in journalistic fashion the early stages of the invasion of Ireland, expressing neither approval nor censure. Whether, therefore, these tumultuous events strengthened or weakened the bonds between the Welsh and Irish is a moot point. There seems little reason to call into question the commonly held view that, in providing a new target for the aggression of Anglo-Norman marcher barons, the invasion of Ireland relieved the pressure felt by the native Welsh.[48] Add to that the co-operation of the Lord Rhys in the early stages of the enterprise, and the settlement in Ireland as a result of large numbers of Welshmen, and one would be foolish indeed to speculate on Welsh sympathy for the Irish in their plight.

Yet, clearly no Welshman, however short-sighted, could be blind to the similarities in their situation. It was a truism of the age. The Anglo-Norman chronicler, Ralph of Coggeshall, concludes his obit of Henry II by saying that he 'conquered the Welsh, always rebels of the kings of England, and at last subjugated the unwilling, but not without great loss of his leading men and expenditure of his army. Moreover, a large part of Ireland was subdued both by him and his barons.'[49] Gerald of Wales's views are, of course, often contradictory and always jaundiced. But he makes no bones about warning those who might find themselves getting involved in Welsh or Irish affairs that 'there is a great difference between warfare in France on the one hand, and in Ireland and Wales on the other'.[50] He is referring, of course, to such simple matters as difficulties in the terrain, and similarities in Irish and Welsh politics and forms of warfare. But it ran much deeper. Gerald was convinced that vital errors had been made in the handling of both the Irish and the Welsh problem

---

[46] *Ibid.*, p. 71; Davies, *Conquest, Coexistence and Change*, p. 221.
[47] *Song of Dermot*, p. 31.
[48] See, for example, Davies, *Conquest, Coexistence and Change*, p. 271.
[49] *Chronicon Anglicanum*, ed. J. Stevenson, RS (London, 1875), pp. 25–6.
[50] Giraldus, *Expugnatio*, pp. 245–7.

by Anglo-Norman kings and policy-makers. Central to it was a basic failure of understanding, an inability to comprehend the motivation of the native peoples in resisting attempted domination: 'The English', he says, 'are striving for power, the Welsh for freedom; the English are fighting for material gain, the Welsh to avoid a disaster; the English soldiers are hired mercenaries; the Welsh are defending their homeland.'[51] Welsh belief in a glory-filled past was what motivated them, he believed:

> they boast and confidently predict that they will soon reoccupy the whole island of Britain. It is remarkable how everyone in Wales entertains this illusion ...
>
> The memory which they will never lose of their former greatness may well kindle a spark of hatred in the Welsh and encourage them to rebel from time to time; for they cannot forget their Trojan blood and the majesty of their kings who once ruled over Britain ...[52]

As for the Irish, even in Gerald's eyes they had been shabbily treated. His account of the infamous beard-pulling incident, when those Irish nobles who met the Lord John at Waterford in 1185 were treated with mockery and personal abuse, is well known. This, if we take Gerald's word for it, produced a reaction, among even those Irish who had initially cooperated with the invaders, which was of long-term consequences:

> they deduced that these small injustices would be followed by greater ones, and debated among themselves how the English must intend to act against the overweening and rebellious, when men of goodwill, who had kept the peace, received this treatment. So with one accord they plotted to resist, and to guard the privileges of their ancient freedom even at the risk of their own lives ... they made pacts with each other throughout the country, and those who had previously been enemies now became friends for the first time.[53]

According to Gerald's rather paranoiac state of mind the tide was turning. In Wales, because of the preoccupation of the Anglo-Normans with continental affairs, he says, 'the Welsh have been able to raise their heads a little higher, recover their lands, and cease to bear the yoke which once weighed so heavily upon them'.[54] In Ireland, as a result, as he sees it, of broken promises, of betrayed loyalties, and of bestowing upon new arrivals land held by Irish who had all along proved cooperative, what few friends the Anglo-Normans had 'immediately went over to our enemies, and, changing their role, spied on us and guided the enemy to us'.[55]

---

[51] Gerald of Wales (Giraldus Cambrensis), *The Journey through Wales and the Description of Wales*, p. 274.
[52] *Ibid.*, pp. 265, 274.   [53] Giraldus, *Expugnatio*, pp. 237–9.
[54] Gerald of Wales (Giraldus Cambrensis), *The Journey through Wales and the Description of Wales*, p. 267.
[55] Giraldus, *Expugnatio*, p. 239.

If Gerald was aware of these similar and simultaneous responses to Anglo-Norman domination in Ireland and Wales, it would be surprising if the indigenous inhabitants themselves were not. People who share the same enemies can, of course, be allies almost without knowing it. They can find themselves taking advantage of a common enemy's moment of weakness without any measure of coordination in their actions. And this appears to be what sometimes happened in Ireland and Wales after 1169. The Irish and Welsh rarely if ever colluded in their efforts to counter the thrust of Anglo-Norman royal and baronial policy in their areas. They responded, however, to the same set of stimuli. Rebels rise up when the defences of their would-be master are down. For the Irish and Welsh that sometimes meant timing their insurgency to coincide with a moment when the Anglo-Normans were distracted elsewhere, or taking advantage of the disturbed conditions of a troubled reign, or the incapacity of a weak or unpopular king, or taking the outbreak of hostilities on the other side of the Irish Sea as the cue to rise.

An example of this sort of phenomenon occurs in the immediate aftermath of the invasion. According to Gerald of Wales, when the full extent of the invasion facing the Irish became known to Ruaidrí Ua Conchobair, he sent emissaries to assemble together the country's leading men, in order to coordinate a response. As usual, we have only Gerald's word for this, but we do know from other sources that Ruaidrí did assemble something like a national army on more than one occasion in the early stages of the campaign.[56] Gerald has Strongbow's uncle, Hervey de Montmorency, declare: 'the whole population of Ireland has joined in plotting our destruction',[57] and that plot found its opportunity in the summer of 1173. When Henry II's oldest son, the young king Henry, rebelled in league with Louis of France, large numbers of the new settlers in Ireland, including their leaders, Strongbow and Hugh de Lacy, withdrew to Normandy to their lord's aid. This was the signal for an Irish revolt: 'The Irish', Gerald says, 'had got to hear of the serious disturbances which had lately broken out in the lands across the sea, and as they are a race consistent only in their fickleness ... [the earl (Strongbow), on his return] found almost all the princes of that land in open revolt against the king and himself.'[58] What is interesting is that this revolt in Ireland was matched by disturbances by both the Scots and Welsh. King William of Scotland had been in Louis' camp in 1168 when his envoys were at the French court seeking to keep Anglo-French hostilities alive. In 1173 William invaded

[56] *Song of Dermot*, lines 1570–4, 1734–49, 3184–319; see also, A. J. Otway-Ruthven, *A History of Medieval Ireland* (London, 1968), pp. 44–7, 54–5.
[57] Giraldus, *Expugnatio*, p. 63.   [58] *Ibid.*, p. 135.

England, as William of Newburgh says, 'having learned how greatly the king of the English laboured in Normandy'. His invasion was a well-timed onslaught taking full advantage of Henry's difficulty, though it ultimately proved disastrous for him and he was humiliatingly captured in July 1174.[59] In Wales, meanwhile, following the death of Owain Gwynedd in 1170, the Lord Rhys had emerged as the leading figure in the Welsh polity, and maintained loyalty to Henry II throughout the crisis, even sending his son to join Henry's forces. But another, lesser Welsh princeling, Iorwerth ab Owain of Gwynllwg (in the southeast marches, between Morgannwg and Gwent), along with his son Hywel, launched a revolt, in pursuance of the family claim to Caerleon.[60] Gerald of Wales links the Gwynllwg rising with King William's abortive assault on England and Henry's continental troubles:

Hywel, the son of Iorwerth of Caerleon, attacked the neighbourhood and destroyed the whole area. A little later Henry II, king of the English, captured the king of Scotland and so restored peace to his own realm. As a result Hywel had good reason to fear that Henry would be free to take vengeance on him for the war which he had waged ... [But Meilyr the soothsayer assured him:] 'You need not fear the king's anger ... One of the cities, the noblest which he possesses across the Channel, is being besieged by the king of the French. He will be forced to put aside all other preoccupations and to cross the sea without losing a moment.[61]

If the revolt of Iorwerth and Hywel was thus indirectly linked with the Scottish invasion, it had a much closer bearing on the Irish situation. The insurgents in both cases were motivated by the same impulse. The object of the Irish offensive led by King Ruaidrí Ua Conchobair in the early 1170s was to overcome some of the recent successes of the Anglo-Norman adventurers there, successes which Strongbow personified. Therefore, we find Domnall Mór Ua Briain attacking Strongbow's garrison in Waterford in 1173, and in the same year a disinherited grandson of Diarmait Mac Murchada revolting against his new uncle, Strongbow, by doing battle with the Anglo-Norman settlers in Leinster.[62] But Strongbow was also the target of the Welsh rising. Its high-point was reached in mid-August 1173, when the insurgents swept as far as the very walls of Chepstow, the principal castle of the lordship of Strigoil. When the tide turned against Iorwerth and Hywel it was Strongbow's men who seized the castle of Usk from

---

[59] Duncan, *Scotland. The Making of the Kingdom*, pp. 228–9.
[60] For the revolt, see J. E. Lloyd, *A History of Wales from Earliest Times to the Edwardian Conquest*, 2 vols. (London, 1911), ii, pp. 545–6.
[61] Gerald of Wales (Giraldus Cambrensis), *The Journey through Wales and the Description of Wales*, pp. 119–20.
[62] *AT*, s.a. 1173.

them,[63] and when Henry II decided to reach a moderate settlement, Strongbow was ordered to restore to them the main bone of contention, Caerleon.[64]

There is no evidence of any collaboration between the organizers of the Irish and Welsh revolts, and no reason to suspect such, though it would be surprising if one was initiated entirely in ignorance of the other. The essential point is that the convenient absence from both arenas of Strongbow, and of much of the colonists' defensive strength, happened to combine with an all but identical sense of grievance, and a common target, to produce enough tinder to spark off simultaneous revolts on both sides of the Irish Sea. It is of significance only because it represents the first instance of such synchronous insurgency in the period after the Anglo-Norman expansion into Ireland, but it was to become a perennial concern.

In the period before the Anglo-Norman invasion of Ireland, therefore, there was a very considerable input by Irishmen into Welsh affairs. The Irish had ambitions in Wales and there was high-level political contact, so that the Welsh princely dynasties were closely aligned with the Irish provincial kings, particularly of Munster and Leinster, and the latter intervened decisively to secure the succession of Welsh allies to the various principalities. It is possible that these connections were on the wane even before 1169: it is quite difficult to assess since there is a thirty-year period immediately prior to it in which some of the main Irish annal compilations are defective. But from what we can tell there was indeed a decline in contact. After the fall of Muirchertach Ua Briain power shifted northwards to Connacht and Ulster, which, as noted earlier, tended to lack communication with southern Britain. William of Malmesbury, for instance, in discussing the affairs of Ireland in this period mentions Muirchertach, and then adds, 'and his successors whose names have not come to our notice'.[65] The year 1169 did represent a turning-point. After it, the element of the equation which mattered most and which helped shape the course of Hiberno-Welsh relations in succeeding generations was the fact that many of the new adventurers in Ireland, particularly in Munster and Leinster, were the sons of men who had conquered lands in Wales, and now they and their sons would attempt the same in Ireland. In so doing, certain cross-channel links were disrupted, if not ended, but others were greatly reinforced. Many marcher lords ended up with landed interests on both

---

[63] Lloyd, *History of Wales*, ii, p. 546, n. 50.
[64] For these events, see Davies, *Conquest, Coexistence and Change*, p. 275; Flanagan, *Irish Society, Anglo-Norman Settlers, Angevin Kingship*, p. 157, n. 88.
[65] William of Malmesbury, *De Gestis Regum*, ii, pp. 484–5.

sides of the Irish Sea. They used the profits of their estates on one side to finance campaigns of conquest and colonization on the other. When they found themselves in difficulties in their marcher lordships in Wales, they fled for refuge to Ireland, and vice versa. They brought Welsh armies to Ireland and Irish armies to Wales.

When Welshmen were on good terms with the marcher barons one suspects that they cared little about their aggressive expansion in Ireland. But in those periods when the Welsh themselves felt the brunt of baronial and royal aggression, the similarities in the Welsh fate and the experience of the native Irish became obvious to all. And it spurred men into action. In 1282–3, during the course of Edward I's conquest of Wales, Thomas fitz Maurice, the head of the Munster Geraldines, reported that 'because of the war in Wales, the Irish are more exalted than usual; some have been incited to make war, others are preparing to do so'.[66] The year 1169 may have brought big changes to Ireland and Wales, and the Welsh and Irish may have been growing apart, but some things still united them, and one was a common experience of colonial domination and attempted conquest.

[66] *Cal. Doc. Ire.*, 1285–1292 no. 360.

6 Killing and mutilating political enemies in the British Isles from the late twelfth to the early fourteenth century: a comparative study

John Gillingham

The convention of sparing the life and limb of defeated high-status enemies visible in Germany and France (the Frankish heartland of Europe) from the end of the tenth century onwards entered English political *mores* in part at least as a consequence of 1066 and the influx of a new French ruling class. The diffusion of this chivalrous code is just one aspect of that much wider process of cultural homogenization which Robert Bartlett has called 'the Europeanization of Europe'.[1] Very likely the chivalrous 'Europeanization of England' would have happened without the 1066 factor – there are signs that it was beginning to happen in late Anglo-Saxon England south of the Humber – but, in the event, it was in the wake of the Norman Conquest that politics in England became chivalrous. Thus change was perceived not as Europeanization but as Frenchification.[2] But although chivalrous compassion became fashionable in twelfth-century England, bloodier political *mores* continued to prevail in the rest of the British Isles.[3] Elsewhere I have suggested that the rise of chivalrous compassion may be connected with the rising stone walls of European – and English – economic growth, that the proliferation of the towns and castles of the new landscape meant a proliferation of strong-points from which men of high status could control territory, and hence a proliferation of assets which they could, in the event of defeat, use as bargaining counters in exchange for

---

[1] R. Bartlett, *The Making of Europe* (Harmondsworth, 1993), ch. 11.
[2] See, for example, Orderic Vitalis, *Ecclesiastical History*, ii, p. 256. Both William of Malmesbury and Gerald de Barri would almost certainly have accepted Guibert de Nogent's belief that tranquillity of temperament (*serenitas*) was most becoming to a gentleman (*quae prima ingenuitatem decet*) and would have understood why he contrasted the 'moderation of the French kings' with the savageness of other rulers. J. F. Benton, *Self and Society in Medieval France* (New York, 1970), pp. 59, 195; Guibert, *De Vita Sua*, ed. G. Bourgin (Paris, 1907), pp. 62, 390.
[3] J. Gillingham, '1066 and the introduction of chivalry into England', in *Law and Government in Medieval England and Normandy*, ed. G. Garnett and J. Hudson (Cambridge, 1994), pp. 31–55.

a promise to spare their lives and/or limbs. In societies where there were few such strongpoints – as still in the less wealthy peripheries of the British Isles in the twelfth century – there was less to be gained from showing mercy; there was correspondingly more to be gained from directly targeting the persons of enemies, killing, mutilating or imprisoning them, or taking hostages from among them.[4] In this chapter I wish to look a little more closely at the further diffusion of this aspect of the Europeanization of the British Isles in the later twelfth and thirteenth centuries than I have done hitherto.[5]

By the mid-thirteenth century political struggles in Wales and Scotland were conducted 'English fashion', but in Gaelic Ireland traditional ways continued. Why was this? As Rees Davies put it: 'Developments which are taken for granted in one country might appear much more surprising – and therefore demanding of an explanation – if we are forced to contrast them with what happened (or did not happen) elsewhere in the British Isles.'[6] Given that this was a period of English expansion, it is only natural that the further diffusion of this relatively humane political style should have been interpreted as an 'anglicization' of the Celtic world, and that the Irish who, unlike the Welsh and the Scots, stoutly stood out against the fashion for compassion, should have borne the brunt of a condescending and condemnatory attitude characteristic of English historians.[7] In the words of J. H. Round: 'We went to Ireland because her people were engaged in cutting one another's throats; we are there now because, if we left, they would all be breaking one another's heads ... The leaders of the Irish people have not so greatly changed since the days when "King" MacDonnchadh blinded "King" Dermot's son, and when Dermot, in turn, relieved his feelings by gnawing off the nose of his butchered foe.' Round associated this bloodiness with what he termed Ireland's 'tribal polity' and doubted 'whether Ireland, left to itself, would even yet have emerged from the tribal stage of society'.[8] In an attempt to fight off my natural tendency to

---

[4] J. Gillingham, 'Conquering the barbarians: war and chivalry in twelfth-century Britain', *Haskins Society Journal*, 4 (1993), pp. 67–84.
[5] As an exercise it is very like that carried out by Alexander Grant in his comparison of levels of, and attitudes towards, political violence in late medieval Scotland and England, 'Crown and nobility in late medieval Britain', in *Scotland and England 1286–1815*, ed. R. A. Mason (Edinburgh, 1987), pp. 34–59.
[6] R. R. Davies, 'In praise of British history', in *The British Isles 1100–1500: Comparisons, Contrasts and Connections*, ed. R. R. Davies (Edinburgh, 1988), pp. 9–26 (quote at p. 19).
[7] Chivalrous compassion, however, because it is class-specific, is clearly distinct from humanity as such.
[8] J. H. Round, 'The conquest of Ireland' in Round, *The Commune of London and other Studies* (London, 1899), pp. 137–70 (quotes at pp. 164, 169–70). For the reaction of recent Irish scholars to Round's influence see F. J. Byrne and F. X. Martin in *NHI*, ii,

a feeling of English superiority, I shall conclude with the strange death of chivalrous England – the reversion to a more brutal political style in the reigns of Edward I and Edward II.

I begin with some well-known observations made by Gerald de Barri, an author who attached great importance to compassion, as can be seen from the way he chose to conclude his first major work, *The Topography of Ireland*, with a paean of praise to Henry II for the 'mercy and laudable clemency you as victor showed to the kings and chiefs (*principes*) whom you had subdued'.[9] In works written in 1189 and in the early 1190s Gerald contrasted war and chivalry in France (*Gallica militia*) with warfare in Ireland and Wales. Part of the contrast lay in the conventions which governed the treatment of knightly prisoners. 'There in France knights are held in captivity; here they are decapitated. There they are ransomed; here killed.'[10] In *The Topography* Gerald emphasized the bloodshed generated in Ireland by rivalries within the family and by the code of honour which then demanded vengeance. 'Woe to kinsmen. When they are alive they are relentlessly driven to death. When they are dead and gone, vengeance is demanded for them.'[11] In his work on Wales, Gerald explicitly placed the shedding of the blood of kin within the context of succession disputes. 'After the death of a father ... the most terrible disturbances occur, people are murdered, brothers kill each other or put each other's eyes out and, as everyone knows, it is very difficult to settle disputes of this sort.'[12] His views on Scotland are less explicit since he never carried out his intention of writing a *Topographia Britannica*. He did, however, assert that the Scots living in the north of Britain still exhibited an affinity with their Irish kinsmen in matters of arms and customs as well as language and dress.[13] Moreover, in the Life of Geoffrey of York, which he wrote in 1193–4, he referred to the

pp. 5, 46–7; also D. Ó Cróinín, *Early Medieval Ireland 400–1200* (London, 1995), pp. 272–3, 290.

[9] *Topographia Hibernica* in *Giraldus Cambrensis, Opera*, v, pp. 190–1; the passage is on p. 177 in the text of the first recension: 'Giraldus Cambrensis in Topographia Hibernie', ed. J. J. O'Meara, *RIA Proc.*, 52 (1948–52) C, pp. 113–78; Giraldus, *Topographia*, pp. 124–5. According to this, Henry always had a copy of Seneca's *De Clementia* to hand. By the time Gerald wrote *The Conquest of Ireland* he had ventured to become slightly more critical of Henry II.

[10] Giraldus, *Expugnatio*, p. 246, and repeated in his *Descriptio Kambrie* in *Giraldus Cambrensis, Opera*, vi, p. 220; Gerald of Wales, *The Journey Through Wales and The Description of Wales*, p. 269.

[11] *Topographia Hibernica* in *Giraldus Cambrensis, Opera*, v, pp. 167–8; Giraldus, *Topographia*, p. 108.

[12] *Descriptio Kambrie* in *Giraldus Cambrensis, Opera*, vi, pp. 211–12; Gerald of Wales, *The Journey through Wales and the Description of Wales*, p. 261.

[13] *tam lingue quam cultus, tam armorum etiam quam morum, usque in hodiernum probat affinitas*, *Topographia Hibernica* in *Giraldus Cambrensis, Opera*, v, p. 161; Giraldus, *Topographia*, p. 99. See R. Bartlett, *Gerald of Wales* (Oxford, 1982), pp. 182 n. 17, 188.

1173–4 Scottish invasion of the north of England as the work of barbarians.[14] Evidently he thought that Scottish political *mores* were very like those of Ireland and Wales.

At the time he was writing there were good grounds for Gerald's comments. In Scotland, Wales and Ireland political enmities had recently ended in the kind of bloodshed which, though it earned the disapproval of churchmen, was evidently acceptable to secular society. In Scotland, Gilbert of Galloway had blinded and murdered his half-brother Uhtred in 1174, but was able to rule Galloway until his own death, of natural causes, ten years later. The revival of the mac William claim to the Scottish throne in the 1180s led to an act of bloodshed in November 1186 when 'the peace of the holy church was outraged at Coupar by the violence of Malcolm, earl of Atholl'. Although the exact meaning of this entry in the *Holyrood Chronicle*, probably at this time being compiled at Coupar, is obscure, it is none the less clear that someone of high status, probably Aedh (or Heth) son of Donald son of Malcolm mac Heth, was beheaded before the altar of the church; and that the rest of his band, fifty-eight in number, were burned and killed in the abbot's dwelling.[15] It may be that in the middle decades of the century David I had presided over a relatively 'civilized' period of Scottish politics; if so, it had ended by the time Gerald was writing.

In Wales, the murder of Owain ap Caradog, nephew of lord Rhys, by his brother Cadwallon, occurred, in Gerald's words, 'in our own times'.[16] According to the *Brut y Tywysogyon*, in 1187 Owain ap Madog (i.e. Owain Fychan) of Powys 'was slain by [his cousins] the two sons of Owain Cyfeiliog, namely Gwenwynwyn and Cadwallon, and that through betrayal and treachery at night. And then Llywelyn ap Cadwallon was unjustly seized by his brothers and his eyes were gouged out of his head.' In 1191 the *Brut* reported that 'Einion of Porth [ruler of Elfael and probably son-in-law of Rhys] was slain by his brother.'[17] In 1193 'Anarawd in his greed for worldly power seized his two brothers, Madog and Hywel, and had their eyes gouged out of their heads.'[18] When he came to produce a second edition of his *Itinerarium Kambrie* in

---

[14] *Vita Galfridi* in *Giraldus Cambrensis, Opera*, iv, pp. 358, 365, 367.
[15] Discussion by Barrow in *RRS*, ii, pp. 11–12 esp. note 47. Duncan, *Scotland. The Making of the Kingdom*, pp. 193–4.
[16] *Itinerarium Cambriae* in *Giraldus Cambrensis, Opera*, vi, bk. 1, ch. 7, p. 69; Gerald of Wales, *The Journey Through Wales and The Description of Wales*, p. 128. The incident is dated to 'some time before 1183' in J. E. Lloyd, *A History of Wales from Earliest Times to the Edwardian Conquest*, 3rd edn (London, 1939), p. 572.
[17] *Brut (RHB)*, s.a. 1191; Lloyd, *History of Wales*, pp. 545, 567, 585.
[18] 'Cronica de Wallia and other documents from Exeter library MS. 3514', ed. T. Jones, *BBCS*, 12 (1946–8), p. 30, which shows that it was Anarawd ap Einion ap Anarawd and that he took his brothers 'by a trick'.

the late 1190s, Gerald added a new passage lamenting terrible events, blindings, which occurred in the region between the Wye and the Severn 'in our days'.[19]

In Ireland the 'bloody realities' – Donnchadh Ó Corráin's phrase[20] – of twelfth-century political life included the killing and blinding of close kin, often brothers.[21] The Annals of Loch Cé report that in 1185 Diarmait, son of Toirrdelbach Ua Briain, was blinded by his brother Domnall – a very successful ruler; in 1186 Conchobar Ua Flaithbertaig was killed by his brother; in 1187 a son of Cathal Ua Ruairc was blinded as an act of revenge; in 1188 Ruaidrí Ua Canannain was slain by treachery by Flaithbertach Ua Máel Doraid and one of the perpetrators was then killed in revenge; in 1189 Conchobar Máenmaige Ua Conchobair was killed at the instigation of his brother, another Conchobar, who was then killed in revenge by Cathal Carrach son of Conchobar Máenmaige.[22] So far as I am concerned this kind of conduct cannot be assumed to be evidence of anarchy, let alone of 'tribal anarchy'.[23] Rightly or wrongly, my assumption is that conflict in Ireland was as much bound by informal rules of acceptability as conflict elsewhere. It seems clear that in the twelfth century lay society took it for granted that rivalry among kinsmen for kingship was so intense that the killing and blinding of rivals remained well within the rules of acceptable conduct, even more so than the tone of contemporary authors, mostly annalists, would indicate.[24] Katharine Simms has detected a very different tone in later authors such as Seaán Mac Craith, the mid-fourteenth-century author of *The Triumphs of Turlough* who described the late thirteenth-century 'Carnage of Clare' with its killing of women, children and servants as well as of warriors with 'not a trace of outrage' and who seems to have revelled in 'battle scenes which include dying warriors, with both arms lopped off, attempting to chew off their opponents' noses, and the routine stacking and counting of decapitated heads after each conflict'. Simms contrasts this with the tone of earlier authors and

---

[19] *Itinerarium Cambriae* in *Giraldus Cambrensis, Opera*, vi, p. 19, bk. 1, ch. 1; Gerald of Wales, *The Journey Through Wales and The Description of Wales*, p. 80.
[20] D. Ó Corráin, 'Prehistoric and early Christian Ireland', in *The Oxford Illustrated History of Ireland*, ed. R. F. Foster (Oxford, 1989), p. 51.
[21] Contrast the absence of fratricide in Icelandic saga noted by W. I. Miller, *Bloodtaking and Peacemaking. Feud, Law and Society in Saga Iceland* (Chicago, 1990), p. 160.
[22] *ALC*, s.a. 1185, 1186, 1187, 1188, 1189.
[23] A. L. Poole, *Domesday Book to Magna Carta 1087–1216*, 2nd edn (Oxford, 1955), p. 302, 'bewildering anarchy' a 'sordid chapter of Irish history in which battles and raids, murder and mutilation were of daily occurrence'.
[24] An adequate assessment of tone requires, of course, a knowledge of the relevant languages. Hence the comments that follow, relying upon translations, are by definition inadequate. Even so they would have been much worse but for the help and advice of Marie Therese Flanagan and Katharine Simms.

suggests that this may be because 'Irish literature passed out of the hands of churchmen to the laity, to bardic poets and historians whose values reflected those of their patrons.'[25] Before the survival of new and more secular literary genres, the attitudes of lay rulers to bloodshed still have to be inferred from patterns of successful political conduct.[26] Thus Ruaidrí Ua Conchobair's expedient of securing his own position by blinding his brother and chief rival in a succession struggle fits so snugly into an established pattern of behaviour that it has been described as 'time-honoured'. Presumably then the apparently widespread feeling that Muirchertach Mac Lochlainn offended against the rules in 1166 was not because he blinded Eochaid Mac Duinn Sléibe, but because in so doing he violated guarantees given by Donnchad Ua Cerbaill and many other notable persons.[27]

By contrast, when men of high status were defeated in the conflicts within the English and French parts of the Angevin Empire they were in little danger of suffering bodily harm – not even when they were dealt with as traitors. None of the traitors who rebelled against Henry II in 1173–4 and 1183 were punished in life or limb – hence Gerald's praise for Henry's clemency. Nor were those nobles who rebelled against Richard in 1193. Whereas Richard had 'mere' sergeants hanged for fighting against him, their leaders, such as Gerard de Camville and Jollanus de la Pumerai, escaped with their bodies intact. So too did John, Richard's brother and rival for the throne, despite the fact that he had made a treacherous alliance with the king of France.[28] This restraint effectively continued the practices of Stephen's reign. Christ and his saints may have slept during those nineteen years of civil war and 'anarchy', but it should be noted that even in their sleep they could look after the high-born. Nor would the struggle for kingship in England in 1215–17 undermine this chivalrous pattern. John's murder of his nephew Arthur in 1202 was exceptional and John quickly paid a heavy price. All in all, when Gerald wrote there was good reason for the

---

[25] K. Simms, 'Gaelic warfare in the Middle Ages', in *A Military History of Ireland*, ed. T. Bartlett and K. Jeffery (Cambridge, 1996), pp. 104–6. Mac Craith clearly disapproved of killings outside battle; this might, of course, simply be a function of the cases which he chose to describe, *Caithréim Thoirdhealbhaigh*, ed. S. H. O'Grady, 2 vols., ITS (London, 1925), ii, pp. 50, 52.

[26] I emphasize 'successful' because this contrasts the frequent kin-slaying aimed at obtaining power with the frequent kin-slaying occurring within the modern nuclear family.

[27] Ó Corráin, *Ireland before the Normans*, p. 165; Ó Cróinín, *Early Medieval Ireland*, p. 285.

[28] Roger of Howden, *Chronica*, ed. W. Stubbs, 4 vols., RS (London, 1868–71), iii, pp. 239, 241–2, 249. Though for a possible exception see the fate of Robert Brito, starved to death in prison according to a marginal addition in Ralph of Coggeshall, *Chronicon Anglicanum*, ed. J. Stevenson, RS (London, 1875), p. 63.

contrast he drew between *Gallica militia* and practices in Wales and Ireland.

Of course what Gerald 'the Englishman' did not draw attention to, although it is implicit in his commentary on the 1170 massacre of Baginbun, is that in Wales and Ireland the English were already inclined to treat the native aristocracy with much less than chivalrous respect.[29] In Ireland this story began in 1171 with the treatment which Strongbow meted out to Murchad Ua Brain. In the words of *The Song of Dermot*, 'Because the felon had betrayed Dermot his rightful lord, the earl had him beheaded and his body then thrown to the hounds. The dogs wholly devoured him and ate up his flesh.'[30] Shortly afterwards, the captured Askulv of Dublin was beheaded for his *desmesure* and *fous dis*.[31] In Wales a number of incidents involving the invaders and members of Welsh princely families had clearly angered native opinion: Henry II's treatment of hostages in 1165; the killing of Owain ab Iorwerth of Caerleon in 1172; the massacre at Abergavenny in 1175; the killing of Cadwallon ap Madog of Maelienydd in 1179.[32]

What happened 'after Gerald'? I shall, as before, restrict myself to the shedding of blood of people of high status when they were at their enemies' mercy and when it seems that the act was committed in the pursuit of territorial or political power. This means, for example, that I shall exclude the hanging of William de Braose by Llwelyn ap Iorwerth in 1230, because the fact that that was followed by so little in the way of political repercussion suggests that it was indeed carried out, as alleged, as a punishment for William's adultery with Llywelyn's wife Joan. Nor am I concerned with battle casualties.[33] Inevitably there are a few cases which are hard to classify. One such is the killing of Áed Ua Conchobair in 1228. According to the Annals of Connacht, he 'was killed with one

---

[29] Gillingham, 'Conquering the barbarians', pp. 67–8, 83–4.

[30] And one of Murchad's sons was put to death as well, *Song of Dermot*, lines 2168–80, pp. 159–61. This incident was omitted by Gerald. It is noteworthy that the *Song*, composed in the secular vernacular, though in general less condescending in tone than Gerald, is also more casual in its account of killing, as for example in its account of the massacre of Baginbun.

[31] *Song of Dermot*, lines 2466–71, p. 181; on account of his 'insolence' according to Gerald, Giraldus, *Expugnatio*, pp. 76–9.

[32] *Brut (RHB)*, s.a. 1165, 1172, 1175; Ralph of Diceto, *Opera Historica*, ed. W. Stubbs, 2 vols., RS (London, 1876), i, pp. 437–8; Giraldus, *Expugnatio*, pp. 122–4, 128, 220. For discussion of Gerald's attitude to 1175 see J. Gillingham, 'Henry II, Richard I and the Lord Rhys', *Peritia*, 10 (1996), pp. 227–9.

[33] Except when the number of high-status casualties on one side only was so high as to suggest that the victors may have adopted a policy of taking no prisoners. For comment on Evesham see below pp. 131–2. The battles of Ardee in 1159 and Callann in 1261 might be other examples.

blow of a carpenter's axe in the court of Geoffrey de Marisco while the carpenter's wife was giving him a bath'. If it was motivated by sexual jealousy then this murder should be excluded. On the other hand, both the Annals of Connacht and Loch Cé imply a political motive in saying that it was a treacherous act instigated by the English.[34] Another awkward case is the killing of Adam, bishop of Caithness, in 1222 – pelted with stones, fatally wounded by a blow from an axe and then finished off by being roasted in his own kitchen in the episcopal manor house at Hallkirk. The author of the *Melrose Chronicle* portrayed Adam as a martyr for the faith, who had angered the people of Caithness only because he saw it as his duty to save their souls by insisting that they pay tithes. But if, as narrated in papal letters, an agreement about the payment of tithes had recently been reached in the presence of the king of Scotland, then there may well have been a political dimension, and one which concerned a competition for power in Caithness between Alexander II and Earl John of Orkney and Caithness. Although Alexander punished the malefactors he could not touch the earl.[35] It is clear, at any rate, that when Earl John was 'killed in his own house, and burnt' in 1231, the Melrose chronicler thought that it served him right.[36] But the difficulties in classifying a few incidents such as these do not, I think, affect the overall pattern. A more serious problem is the patchiness, both regionally and chronologically, of the narrative sources on which this study principally relies. Even so, some broad trends emerge very plainly. In Wales and Scotland the pattern of political bloodshed becomes an English – or European – one; in Ireland the tradition endures.[37]

In Wales political bloodshed remained fairly common until the early 1190s, though it is worth noting that the most successful political leader of the later twelfth century, the Lord Rhys, seems not to have mutilated or killed his high-status enemies – in this respect unlike Owain Gwynedd, who certainly did. It may be that in addition to being a great patron of native culture Rhys was also, as Henry II's justiciar for South Wales, a principal conduit whereby English political – if not sexual –

---

[34] *AC, ALC* both *s.a.* 1228.
[35] Anderson, *Early Sources*, ii, p. 451. See discussion by Barbara Crawford, 'The earldom of Caithness and the kingdom of Scotland, 1150–1266', in *Essays on the Nobility of Medieval Scotland*, ed. K. J. Stringer (Edinburgh, 1985), pp. 25–43.
[36] *Chronica de Mailros*, ed. J. Stevenson (Edinburgh, 1835), pp. 139, 142. However saga evidence suggests John was killed in an inheritance dispute, Anderson, *Early Sources*, ii, pp. 480–1.
[37] On the basis of the material in the Chronicle of the Kings of Man and the Isles, the last 'action highlight' there was the killing of Reginald Olafsson in 1249. Magnus Olafsson was knighted in England in 1256.

values entered Wales.[38] From the mid-1190s on, political bloodshed was rare, though in Deheubarth Maelgwyn ap Rhys seems to have been exceptionally wedded to the old ways. In 1204 Hywel Sais ap Rhys was fatally wounded by followers of his brother Maelgwyn, and in 1205, according to the *Brut*, 'Maelgwyn ap Rhys put to death Cedifor ap Griffri, a worthy man of rank, and along with him his four eminent sons, who were sprung from a high-born lineage.'[39] It was then to be more than thirty years before the *Brut* next reported a kinslaying or maiming. The most successful Welsh political leader of this next generation, Llywelyn ap Iorwerth, imprisoned his uncle, Dafydd ap Owain in 1197 but, so far as I can see, he put no one of high status to death – except, of course, William de Braose in 1230. Indeed Gerald de Barri remarked on Llywelyn's mercifulness – and linked it with that other mark of the 'modernizing' Welshman: avoidance of incest.[40] Then in 1238 Maredudd ap Madog of Powys killed his brother Gruffudd. The consequence was that, in the words of the *Brut*, 'forthwith Lywelyn ap Iorwerth dispossessed him because of that'. As Rees Davies puts it, Maredudd had 'stepped out of line'.[41] I know of no more incidents of this sort after 1238.[42] In 1274 Dafydd ap Gruffudd was accused of plotting to murder his brother Llywelyn. According to a letter composed by the chapter of Bangor, the plan had been that Dafydd would get into Llywelyn's chamber and kill him, but he had been defeated by storms and rain. Obviously this may have been no more than a false accusation contrived to blacken Dafydd's reputation, for it portrayed him both as a murderer at heart and as a wimp who failed to carry out his intentions because of a spot of bad weather.[43] The absence of political bloodshed in thirteenth-century Wales is all the more striking because feuds and disputes between kin continued to occur. One Welsh author was clearly struck by the way in which, in the Marches in 1245, the division of the Marshal inheritance was peacefully carried through.[44] Not so in native Wales. In Gwynedd, for example, both Dafydd ap Llywelyn and Llywelyn ap Gruffudd seized brothers and nephews, rivals for power, and kept them

---

[38] Davies, *Conquest, Coexistence and Change*, p. 54 and see pp. 77–80 for observations on less exultingly brutal forms of political conduct and a new model of Welsh kingship.

[39] In its account of the killings of 1205 the *Brut (RHB)* noted that they were carried out 'by a certain Irishman with an axe'.

[40] *Itinerarium Cambriae* in *Giraldus Cambrensis, Opera*, vi, bk. 2, ch. 8, pp. 133–4; Gerald of Wales, *The Journey Through Wales and The Description of Wales*, pp. 192–4.

[41] Davies, *Conquest, Coexistence and Change*, p. 244.

[42] Although Matthew Paris calls Dafydd ap Llywelyn a fratricide, that seems to be only because he managed to blame him for Gruffudd's death while escaping from the Tower of London; Matthew Paris, *Chronica Majora*, ed. H. R. Luard, 7 vols., RS (London, 1872–83), iv, pp. 323, 518.

[43] *Foedera*, i, p. 532.   [44] *Brut, s.a.* 1245.

in prison. In Deheubarth too, the practice of partible inheritance led to what have been described as 'bitter quarrels' after 1245.[45] Bitter they may well have been, even so, they did not lead to bloodshed as they might well have done in the previous century.

Turning to Scotland, in 1242 at Haddington, Patrick of Atholl, in the words of the *Melrose Chronicle*, 'was foully slain in his lodgings while he slept, and so were two of his companions, and the house in which they lay was burned down so as to make it seem that the crime had been an accident'.[46] John and Walter Bisset were then accused of murder. Whether or not they really were guilty of the crime – a matter on which modern historians disagree – the accusation was sufficiently plausible for John Bisset to flee and his uncle Walter to be exiled by Alexander II. That in 1242 it was plausible is not surprising. It was this episode which led A. A. M. Duncan to brood on 'the sombre side' of thirteenth-century Scotland, reflecting, for example, on 'the brutal death of an infant member of the mac William family, her brains dashed out against the stone pillar of the market cross of Forfar in 1230'.[47] In 1215 another of the mac William dynasty, Donald, had been killed together with his allies, Kenneth mac Aht and the son of an Irish king, and their decapitated heads had been sent, in the words of the *Melrose Chronicle*, 'as new gifts to the new king'. This is a doubtful case since the chronicler's account does not make it clear whether they were killed in battle or afterwards.[48] But in the case of Godfrey mac William, put to death in 1212, there is no doubt. He was 'captured and chained and presented to the lord Alexander, the king's son ... and was hanged by the feet after his head had been cut off'.[49] Tensions caused by William I's advance north into Caithness in 1197 – which may also have been linked with the mac William claim since Earl Harald of Orkney and Caithness was married to a daughter of Malcolm mac Heth – led to the blinding and castration of Earl Harald's son Thorfinn (held as hostage by William I) as well as to John bishop of Caithness being blinded and having his tongue cut out.[50] There was also the killing of the earl of Caithness at Thurso in 1231 and the probable case of the burning of the bishop of Caithness in 1222. One way or another all of these were incidents in struggles for power, whether for the Scottish throne or

---

[45] Lloyd, *History of Wales*, pp. 710–11, 742; Davies, *Conquest, Coexistence and Change*, pp. 226–7.
[46] Stevenson (ed.), *Chronica de Mailros*, pp. 154–5. A similar story was told in the Chronicle of Lanercost, Anderson, *Early Sources*, ii, pp. 530–1; *Chronicon de Lanercost*, ed. J. Stevenson (Edinburgh, 1839), pp. 49–50.
[47] Duncan, *Scotland. The Making of the Kingdom*, p. 546.
[48] Stevenson (ed.), *Chronica de Mailros*, p. 117.
[49] Anderson, *Early Sources*, ii, p. 389.   [50] *Ibid.*, pp. 348–50.

between earl, church and king for power in Caithness. Against the background of the previous fifty years it would seem that there was nothing very surprising about the death of Patrick of Atholl in 1242 – indeed, given that Patrick was the son of Thomas of Galloway, it may be that murder even at so courtly an occasion as a tournament at Haddington can be tied in with the traditionally bloody politics of Galloway.[51] It is noticeable that those high-status enemies whom William I and Alexander II killed or mutilated were all of Gaelic or Scandinavian affiliation. In treating enemies from outside their own Anglo-French Scotland in this manner, the Scottish kings could be said to have modelled their behaviour on the English pattern.

Yet what strikes me most about the 1242 incident is that if Patrick was indeed the victim of a political murder, then it was to be the last such act in Scotland for half a century. Perhaps then by 1242 such acts were already less acceptable than earlier – which could have made it all the more urgent to try to pass a killing off as an accident. When Alexander II suppressed the Galloway rising of 1235 and chose to spare the lives of its leaders, Thomas of Galloway, Gilrodh and the 'son of a certain king from Ireland', he was, according to the Melrose chronicler, exercising his '*solita pietas*' – the kind of mercy which had not been shown in 1212 and 1230.[52] That new rules of political conflict were accepted by the mid-thirteenth century is suggested by the character of the fierce factional struggles which dominated Scottish politics in the 1250s during the minority of Alexander III. Even though the young king and queen were kidnapped twice, and even though, to judge from the account in the *Melrose Chronicle*, the word 'traitor' was much bandied about from 1251 onwards, none of the participants in these struggles for power ever paid for defeat in life or limb; the worst they suffered was being ousted from the council and from sources of patronage.[53] Political rivalries were similarly restrained in the years following the death of Alexander III in 1286. In 1288 Earl Duncan of Fife was ambushed and killed by his kinsman Hugh Abernethy, but apparently this act did not trigger further bloodshed either within the family or amongst the wider Scottish political elite.[54] Thirteenth-century Scottish politics was be-

---

[51] As suggested in Duncan, *Scotland. The Making of the Kingdom*, pp. 544–5.
[52] Stevenson (ed.), *Chronica de Mailros*, pp. 135–6.
[53] *Ibid.*, pp. 179, 183–4.
[54] Hugh fled abroad and one of his accomplices was executed. Earl Duncan was allegedly 'cruel and greedy beyond all that we have commonly seen, abstaining from no injustice whereby he could minister to his avarice. And when curses without number had accumulated upon him, and enmities provoked by his deeds had been deservedly roused against him, he was slaughtered on horseback by his own men and kinsfolk.' *The Chronicle of Lanercost 1272–1346*, trans. H. Maxwell (Glasgow, 1913), p. 59.

coming 'anglicized' and this was helping the Guardians to maintain aristocratic solidarity in face of increasing pressure from a king of England. That there were fierce rivalries to be contained is clear from an English spy's vivid report of a quarrel between Sir David Graham and Sir Malcom Wallace in the Scottish camp in 1299:

> the two knights gave the lie to each other and drew their daggers. And since Sir David Graham was of Sir John Comyn's following and Sir Malcolm Wallace of the earl of Carrick's following, it was reported to the earl of Buchan and John Comyn that a fight had broken out without their knowing it; and John Comyn leaped at the earl of Carrick and seized him by the throat, and the earl of Buchan turned on the bishop of St Andrews declaring that treason and lese-majeste were being plotted. Eventually the Stewart and others came between them and quietened them.[55]

However difficult it was, the fact remains that those who tried to restrain the rivalries succeeded in doing so until 12 February 1306 – hence Robert Bruce's murder of the Red Comyn and his followers' killing of Sir Robert Comyn shocked partly because they came after so long a period free from this kind of violence. If Bruce survived the civil war which he brought upon himself by this act, it was thanks to Edward I's over-ferocious reaction, the reign of terror he unleashed in the summer of 1306.

If Wales and Scotland joined the European club, however, Ireland, did not. Traditional patterns of violence continued unabated throughout the thirteenth century and beyond. Irish blood continued to be spilt both by the English and by the Irish themselves. By contrast, although the English in Ireland often quarrelled between themselves, leading F. J. Byrne to write 'a cynic would be tempted to say merely that feudal anarchy had replaced tribal',[56] it was very rare that their disputes were taken to the point of killing one of the main protagonists, hence the furore when Richard Marshal was killed in 1234. So far as conflict between and within the Irish kingdoms is concerned, Katharine Simms has suggested that between the eleventh and fifteenth centuries there may have been a trend away from killing and towards mutilating.[57] If so, it was a trend which had hardly got under way by the early fourteenth century. Consider, for example, J. F. Lydon's summary of events in Connacht: 'Between 1274 and 1315 there were no less than thirteen kings of Connacht of whom nine were killed by their own brothers or cousins.'[58] Although it seems that in Irish politics it was business as

---

[55] Cited in G. W. S. Barrow, *Robert Bruce*, 2nd edn (Edinburgh, 1976), p. 152.
[56] *NHI*, ii, p. 5.
[57] K. Simms, *From Kings to Warlords. The Changing Political Structure of Gaelic Ireland in the Later Middle Ages* (Woodbridge, 1987), pp. 50–1.
[58] *NHI*, ii, p. 249.

usual, it may be worth taking a closer look at the first half of the thirteenth century, partly because, in the context of the question asked here, this has been shown to have been the crucial period in Scotland and Wales, and partly because in Irish history this was when English pressure on the native Irish was at its most intense, when the process of conquering was being driven forward most vigorously and when a number of Irish rulers, facing the choice between accommodation and resistance, appear to have chosen accommodation – at any rate to a greater extent than during the Gaelic resurgence of the mid-thirteenth century and later. Of course, given the fragmentary character of the evidence, any attempt to plot changes in attitudes is bound to be, as Robin Frame has observed, 'a treacherous business'.[59] None the less it is at least conceivable that at this time some Irish leaders were attracted by the values of chivalrous politics, so, even at the risk of pressing the evidence too hard, it seems a question worth considering.[60]

The annals for this period have little to say about the north. Hence the fact that Áed Ua Néill, the dominant figure in the north for the first three decades of the thirteenth century, is not recorded as having shed the blood of any of his rivals – except in battle – may be nothing more than a reflection of the relative lack of interest of any surviving annalist in the internal politics of the north.[61] Certainly, in the better documented Desmond of the Annals of Inisfallen and Mac Carthy's Book, there is little sign of a new restraint; the rivalry between the brothers, Diarmait, Cormac and Domnall Got Cairprech Mac Carthaig led to all three being recorded as spilling blood. In Connacht, similarly, the famous panegyric on Cathal Crobderg Ua Conchobair in the Annals of Connacht for 1224 appears to show that it was by 'time-honoured' means that he had dominated Connacht politics since the 1190s. According to this he was 'the king whom of all kings in Ireland God made most perfect in every good quality ... the king who was the fiercest and harshest towards his enemies that ever lived; the king who most blinded, killed and mutilated rebellious and disaffected subjects'. However, given that churchmen tended to approve of the blood of criminals being shed in the interests of what they saw as law and order, it

---

[59] R. Frame, 'England and Ireland, 1171–1399', in *England and her Neighbours 1066–1453*, ed. M. Jones and M. Vale (London, 1989), p. 146; reprinted in R. Frame, *Ireland and Britain 1170–1450* (London and Rio Grande, 1998), pp. 15–30.

[60] The English might have liked to believe so. Ralph of Diceto, *Opera Historica*, i, p. 350 had believed that one of the reasons the Irish submitted to Henry II was that they regretted their mutual slaughters. Any such regret may, of course, have been principally an ecclesiastical view.

[61] On Áed's 'considerable statesmanship and military skill' see K. Simms, 'The O Hanlons, O Neills and Anglo-Normans in 13th Century Armagh', *Seanchas Ardmhacha*, 9 (1978), pp. 74–7.

may be that by 'rebellious and disaffected subjects' the author of the Connacht annals intended not so much segmentary rivals, as rather the sort of people whom shorter versions of the panegyric in the Annals of Loch Cé (as also in the Annals of Ulster) seem to have in mind when they praise him as 'the corrector of culprits and transgressors; the destroyer of robbers and evil-doers'.[62] It is arguable that despite all the troubles of his reign Cathal Crobderg preferred to imprison and exile his high-status enemies, for example, Toirrdelbach in 1203 and Cathal Mac Diarmata in 1208. However it is also undeniable that there were two occasions, in 1204 and 1220, when the Connacht annalist held him responsible for killings.[63]

If there was an Irish king willing to be influenced by new 'English' values then the most plausible candidate is probably Donnchad Cairprech Ua Briain, who in the first half of the thirteenth century dominated Thomond until his death in 1242. So far as can be seen from all the Annals, including the Annals of Inisfallen and Mac Carthy's Book, neither in taking nor in holding the kingship did he shed the blood of a single rival.[64] The annals also indicate that politically he chose to be closely associated with the English. He fought with English allies in Desmond and Connacht as well as in internal Thomond conflicts in 1201, 1206, 1208, 1210, 1212, 1214, 1225 and 1230. He stepped out of line in 1234–5 when he attacked Limerick (presumably tempted by the turbulence in the English establishment after the death of Richard Marshal) but soon paid a fine to the English crown to be restored to favour. He allowed an Englishman to be elected bishop of Killaloe in 1217.[65] His claim to be an early patron of the Franciscans may be another indication of his openess to new fashions coming from England.[66] According to Mac Carthy's Book, in 1210 King John 'came with a great fleet to Waterford. Donnchad Cairbreach Ó Briain came to him and he knighted him (*e-sin do deanum ridiri de*).'[67] What, if anything, should we read into this knighting? Rees Davies has argued that historians, a 'puritanical and severely academic' lot, have been slow to

---

[62] *AC* and *ALC*, both *s.a.* 1224. Both sets of annals go on to describe the succession of Cathal's son Áed in terms of the stern maintenance of law and order – the mutilation of robber and rapist.

[63] Though on both occasions the language of the annalist suggests a concern (both the author's and Cathal's?) to spread responsibility for these acts more widely.

[64] But he had earlier been involved in the killing of Donnchad Ua Donnocáin, *A.I, s.a.* 1196.

[65] Orpen, *Ireland under the Normans*, iv, pp. 55–7.

[66] *Medieval Religious Houses, Ireland*, pp. 249–50; J. A. Watt, *The Church and the Two Nations in Medieval Ireland* (Cambridge, 1970), pp. 177–8.

[67] *Misc. Ir. Annals, s.a.* 1210. John also gave him the lordship of Carrigogunnel (Co. Limerick) in return for a rent of 60 marks and the liberation of his brother.

realize that the 'world of chivalry and courtoisie ... must have been attractive and intoxicating for many of the native Welsh, Irish and Scottish dynasties and magnates' and that the order of knighthood 'opened the door into an exhilarating international world of aristocratic fellowship and customs'. As he points out, the kings of Scotland were early 'admitted into the charmed circle' but very few of the native rulers of Wales and Ireland were. Indeed in the twelfth and thirteenth centuries there was only one Irish king who was knighted: Donnchad Cairprech Ua Briain of Thomond.[68] Did admission to this charmed circle indicate a readiness to abide by chivalrous values, including the sparing of the life and limb of men like oneself? Were 'time-honoured' political *mores* going out of fashion at the court of early thirteenth-century Thomond? It would be ironic if John, the least chivalrous of English kings, was the one who did most, however little that was, to introduce chivalry into Ireland.

If there was a moment in Irish history when chivalrous compassion was attracting a few adherents (and it is, of course, a big 'if'), the moment was momentary. Although the succession to Donnchad Cairprech seems to have been remarkably peaceful – perhaps more by biological accident than anything else – the period of relative internal peace in Thomond came to an abrupt end in 1268 when Muirchertach's son Diarmait committed the deed, the killing of Conchobar and his son Ioan, which unleashed a bloody civil war. Overall, and irrespective of whether or not there was a chivalrous interval in Thomond, it can be seen that from the perspective of political violence, Scotland and Wales 'entered Europe' in the thirteenth century, but Ireland did not. Historians commonly bracket Ireland and Wales together – in part perhaps the enduring influence of Gerald – and almost as commonly bracket Scotland with England. In this context the pair that go down the same road is Scotland and Wales.

Why did thirteenth-century politics become more chivalrous in Scotland and Wales, but not in Ireland? Doubtless the establishment of greater political unity in both Scotland and Wales helped. Former kingships became estates within a greater whole. Increasingly disputes were settled by 'higher' authorities, and relatively peacefully.[69] As Sir John Lloyd put it, 'Time was transforming these turbulent raiders into feudal barons.'[70] Lloyd's phrase has a wistful ring to it – yet there was no

---

[68] Davies, *Domination and Conquest*, pp. 49–51. I think the next Irish ruler to enter the charmed circle was Ó Conchobhair Donn of Connacht, knighted by Richard II in 1395, Otway-Ruthven, *A History of Medieval Ireland*, p. 333.
[69] Davies, *Conquest, Coexistence and Change*, pp. 230–6.
[70] Lloyd, *A History of Wales*, ii, p. 713. Cf. the Mac Gilla Mo Cholmóc, in R. Bartlett,

reason for most of the inhabitants of Wales to lament the transformation. But in thirteenth-century Ireland there was no such transformation – only the continuing appeal of 'sovranty' and hence of the transformation of the hag at the well from the bestial and loathsome to the beautiful and goodly.[71] However, the emergence of political unity in north and west Britain cannot explain why the struggle for the biggest prizes, for rule over the kingdom of Scotland and over the principality of Wales, became more chivalrous. Did ecclesiastical disapproval contribute to the way political bloodshed went out of fashion? Or was it the influence of English cultural values? What, for example, was the effect when Welsh princes such as Dafydd ap Owain and Llywelyn ap Iorwerth possessed manors in England and took wives from the English royal dynasty? Not surprisingly an Englishman like Matthew Paris believed that Alexander III was keen to see the manners and customs of the English accepted in his realm.[72] But what was it that put the rulers of Scotland and Wales into a receptive frame of mind so that they were now ready to listen to old teaching, whether it came from the church or from their powerful neighbours? (It could, of course, be argued that by 1200 both international church and English national kingdom were more powerful than before.) If chivalry was indeed a code appropriate to the new Europe of towns and stone castles, one attractive line might be that it was only *c*. 1200 that Scotland and Wales reached the critical stage of socio-economic development. In Rees Davies's judgement it was from the 1180s onwards that castles proliferated in native Wales.[73] By 1200 the language of the *Brut y Tywysogyon* – phrases such as the characterization of Llandovery and Dinefwr as 'the keys to all his (Maelgwyn's) territory' and of Cardigan as 'the key to all Wales' – reveals the author's recognition of the strategic importance of strong-points for control of territory.[74] Whereas in lowland Scotland, Anglo-French Scotland, this stage had probably been reached by the mid-twelfth century, it came later in those parts of Scotland involved in most of the thirteenth-century incidents of political bloodshed and where Scandinavian and Irish influence remained strong.

How does Ireland fit into this scheme? Marie Therese Flanagan has made a strong case for the importance of fortifications in twelfth-century Ireland before the coming of the English. She shows that both temporary campaign fortifications (*longphoirt*) and more permanent

'Colonial aristocracies of the high Middle Ages', in *Medieval Frontier Societies*, ed. R. Bartlett and A. Mackay (Oxford, 1989), pp. 27–8.
[71] For the tale of Niall's encounter with the hag, Simms, *From Kings to Warlords*, 43.
[72] Matthew Paris, *Chronica Majora*, v, pp. 573–4.
[73] Davies, *Conquest, Coexistence and Change*, p. 255.
[74] According to the *Brut (RHB)*, castles were exchanged for hostages in 1194 and 1198.

fortresses (*dun*, *caistel* or *cais*) had a role to play in the management of major campaigns by Irish kings. Victorious kings, as she points out, took the trouble to dismantle their enemies' fortresses. What does not seem to have happened is that the victors retained fortresses and garrisoned them as part of a long-term strategy of occupation of conquered territory. There were major sieges: Limerick, Dublin, Cork, Waterford and Armagh were each under Irish siege on occasion in the twelfth century.[75] A siege carried to a successful conclusion meant that the inhabitants of these towns agreed to give their allegiance to the victor; but he did not build castles in towns in order to secure that allegiance in the way that William the Conqueror, for example, did in the years after 1066.[76] There were strongpoints but perhaps not as yet in sufficient number to be usable as means of controlling territory. A comment made by Flanagan on the subject of arms and armour may be relevant here. She points out 'that a certain amount of prestige equipment was available in or imported into Ireland for use among the highest ranks of the aristocracy; more critical, however, is whether the economic or technological resources for the mass production of weapons and armour were available in twelfth-century Ireland'.[77] That same critical question has also to be asked of castles and fortified towns in those parts of Ireland which the English had not occupied. Not until the fifteenth and sixteenth centuries was native Ireland the most castellated society in Europe.[78]

The story of what happened in early fourteenth-century England demonstrates, however, that whatever the stage of socioeconomic development, chivalrous conventions could not be taken for granted. John at Rochester in 1215 allegedly wanted to put nobles to death and had to be talked out of it by Savari de Mauleon.[79] In 1322 no one was able to talk Edward II out of his determination to execute two dozen English nobles headed by his own cousin, Thomas of Lancaster, after the battle of Boroughbridge. According to the English *Brut*, Edward II 'brought all

---

[75] M. T. Flanagan, 'Irish and Anglo-Norman warfare in twelfth-century Ireland', in *A Military History of Ireland*, ed. T. Bartlett and K. Jeffrey (Cambridge, 1996), pp. 54, 60–2, 66.
[76] Though for the increasingly significant attempts to rule Dublin by other means see Duffy, 'Irishmen and Islesmen in the kingdoms of Dublin and Man', pp. 93–133.
[77] Flanagan, 'Irish and Anglo-Norman warfare', p. 72.
[78] T. Barry, 'Rural settlement in Ireland in the Middle Ages: an overview', in *Ruralia I, Pamatky archeologicke – Supplementum 5* (Prague, 1996), p. 140; Simms, 'Gaelic warfare in the Middle Ages', pp. 112–14; R. Frame, 'War and peace in the medieval lordship of Ireland', in *The English in Medieval Ireland*, ed. J. F. Lydon (Dublin, 1984), pp. 122–5; reprinted in Frame, *Ireland and Britain 1170–1450*, pp. 221–40.
[79] Matthew Paris, *Chronica Majora*, ii, p. 626.

the chivalry of England unto death'.[80] Contemporaries were in no doubt that in 1322 Edward II exacted revenge for the killing of his friend, Piers Gaveston, beheaded in 1312 as a 'public enemy' after his return from the exile imposed upon him in the previous year. But the killings of 1312 and 1322 were far from remaining isolated incidents. Rather they ushered in a period of several centuries dominated by a new code of political violence which Maitland called the 'ages of blood'.[81] Hence most historians have preferred to think that the executions of Edward II's reign were due to more profound causes than the passions aroused for and against Gaveston – even if they have rarely agreed with the *Brut* author's belief that 'too much intermarriage with other nations had spoiled the kind blood of the English'.[82]

What brought about so profound a change is not easy to understand. Arguably the story begins with the death of Simon de Montfort and his sons at the battle of Evesham – killings which precipitated a vendetta and the murder of Henry of Almain at Viterbo in 1271.[83] Langtoft believed that before Evesham Edward and Gilbert de Clare had sworn a mutual oath that 'They would take Earl Simon and his sons and without accepting ransom they would put them to death.'[84] The battle-field became a killing ground – perhaps the victors of Evesham had calculated that their enemies had to be killed in a battle precisely because it was still morally impossible to execute them after the battle. Hence it was, in Robert of Gloucester's words (*c.* 1270), 'the murder of Evesham, for battle it was none'.[85] There is here, as David Carpenter has pointed out, a tremendous contrast with what had happened at the battle of Lincoln in 1217 when there had been only one noble fatality, the count of Perche, and no one could quite believe it for no one had wanted him dead. Surely he had fainted.[86] But at Evesham, according to the report

---

[80] *The Brut, or Chronicles of England*, ed. F. W. D. Brie, 2 vols. (London, 1906–8), i, pp. 224–5, where the author also observed that Edward confiscated so many estates that he was now the richest king since William I. See N. Fryde, *The Tyranny and Fall of Edward II* (Cambridge, 1979), pp. 58–63.

[81] F. Pollock and F. W. Maitland, *The History of English Law before the Time of Edward I*, 2 vols. (Cambridge, 1898), ii, p. 506.

[82] Brie (ed.), *The Brut, or Chronicles of England*, i, p. 220.

[83] As he stabbed Henry, Gui de Montfort was believed to have cried out, 'You had no mercy on my father and brothers', *Flores Historiarum*, ed. H. R. Luard, 3 vols., RS (London, 1890), iii, p. 22.

[84] *The Chronicle of Pierre de Langtoft*, ed. T. Wright, 2 vols., RS (London, 1866–8), ii, pp. 144–5.

[85] *The Metrical Chronicle of Robert of Gloucester*, ed. W. A. Wright, 2 vols., RS (London, 1887), ii, p. 736, line 11.

[86] D. A. Carpenter, 'From King John to the first English duke: 1215–1337', in *The House of Lords, a Thousand Years of British Tradition*, ed. R. Smith and J. S. Moore (London, 1994), p. 29. In writing this chapter I gained much from discussions with David Carpenter.

of the Osney annalist, the royalists advanced shouting 'Old traitor, old traitor, no way can you live longer', and they then had Simon put to 'a shameful and unheard of death'.[87]

The same annalist made a similar comment when the victor of Evesham presided over the execution of David of Wales in 1283. David, drawn, hanged and disembowelled, his entrails burned and his body quartered, was, wrote the Osney annalist, 'judicially sentenced to a death unheard of in times past'.[88] Yet kings of England had long shown themselves capable of treating the Welsh more ferociously than they treated enemies from within their own Anglo-French political and cultural community. To the anger of Gerald de Barri, Henry II had castrated and mutilated hostages, including daughters as well as sons of Welsh princes in 1165.[89] In 1212 John and his commanders hanged hostages including a six-year-old Rhys ap Maelgwyn.[90] Not surprisingly, such ferocity came more to the forefront in Edward I's reign as a consequence of his policies towards Wales and Scotland. In 1292 Rhys ap Maredudd went the way of David and so did Cynan ap Maredudd and two associates in 1295. Finally, Edward I began to treat the Scots in similar fashion – not a moment too soon for Langtoft whose view of the king's 1303 policy towards the Scots was that it was far too kind, and who believed that in the past the downfall of the Britons had been caused by their compassion towards their enemies.[91] In 1306 Edward had John, earl of Atholl, and other high-status prisoners, including three of Robert Bruce's brothers and three of his brothers-in-law, put to death. John of Atholl was both Edward's (distant) kinsman, and the first earl to be put to death since the execution of Waltheof in 1076. Up to a point the brutality of Edward I's new policy towards Scottish noblemen (as opposed to his slightly earlier treatment of William Wallace) can probably be explained in terms of a reaction to Bruce's murder of the Red Comyn in Greyfriars Kirk – an event as shocking as the killing of Gaveston. It may also be that Bruce's association with the Gaelic Irish world made it easier to treat Bruce's adherents as though they were Irish.[92] Bruce himself was to take an active part in developing the new

---

[87] *Annales Monastici*, ed. H. R. Luard, 5 vols., RS (London, 1864–9), iv, p. 170. Whereas Wykes lamented the losses to the chivalry of England, *ibid.*, iv, p. 174.
[88] *Ibid.*, iv, p. 294.
[89] Giraldus, *Expugnatio*, p. 220. For details of the fate of the hostages, Roger of Howden, *Chronica*, i, p. 240. See also F. Suppe, 'The cultural significance of decapitation in high medieval Wales and the Marches', *BBCS*, 36 (1989), pp. 147–60.
[90] *Brut (RHB), s.a.* 1212.
[91] Wright (ed.), *The Chronicle of Pierre de Langtoft*, ii, p. 326.
[92] On the cultivation of that association see S. Duffy, 'The Bruce brothers and the Irish Sea world, 1306–29', *Cambridge Medieval Celtic Studies*, 21 (1991), pp. 55–86. By 1307 Edward I was being warned of a Scotto-Welsh alliance prophesied by Merlin.

political style. At the Black Parliament of 1320 he condemned three knights to being drawn, hanged and beheaded.

Focusing on a British Isles context it might be tempting to link the new style of English politics with England's increasingly close and violent relationship with the 'Celtic' world, were it not for the fact that a similar trend away from chivalry is also perceptible in early fourteenth-century France. The reaction of an anonymous Parisian chronicler to the execution of Jourdain de Lisle in 1323 is reminiscent of reaction in England to the bloodbath after Boroughbridge in the previous year. 'One cannot remember nor find written in the *gestes* of France that a man as high-born as my lord Jourdain has ever suffered such a death since the time of Ganelon.'[93] Since Maitland's day this new readiness to shed the blood of high-status opponents in both England and France has conventionally been perceived as part of a much more fundamental development, the origins of the 'modern state'. According to this interpretation Edward I had introduced a new concept of treason. Until his reign, it is said, rebels who took up arms against their sovereign were not regarded as traitors. This alleged change in the law of treason occurred at about the same time in France and in both countries has been associated with other alleged developments. 'As kingship moved towards sovereignty and as Roman law theories of public authority exercised in the common good entered the mainstream of European political thought, fighting against the king increasingly appeared as an offence against the symbol and guarantor of public peace.' Until that time, so the argument runs, 'the chivalric classes' had posed a serious threat to public order. Thus the long tradition which allowed private warfare buttressed by the ethos of chivalry had to be ended before a state claiming effective control of legitimate force could emerge.[94] In these executions then we are said to be witnessing the baptism of that sturdy infant, the modern state, baptized in the blood of noblemen. To a remarkable degree this political bloodshed has been seen as a 'good

[93] Cited in S. H. Cuttler, *The Law of Treason and Treason Trials in Later Medieval France* (Cambridge, 1981), pp. 116, 144–5. A new ferocity had already been apparent in Philip IV's way with those who offended him. According to Barbour's *Bruce*, in 1320 Sir Ingram Umfraville had protested against the condemnation of a knight as chivalrous and worthy as Sir David Brechin to so disgraceful a death; he therefore asked for, and obtained, Bruce's permission to return to Edward II's England, before being last heard of in France. If he witnessed the executions after Boroughbridge and then got to Paris by 1323 he must have felt the world of chivalry was collapsing around him. John Barbour, *The Bruce*, ed. and trans. A. A. M. Duncan (Edinburgh, 1997), pp. 702–5.

[94] R. W. Kaeuper, *War, Justice and Public Order: England and France in the Late Middle Ages* (Oxford, 1988), p. 229. The chronology accepted by the European Science Foundation project on the Origins of the Modern State reflects the view that key developments occurred *c.* 1300.

thing'. In trying to explain the change Maitland wrote, 'in part perhaps we may account for this by saying that men became more cruel as time went on; but also we ought to see that there has been a real progress, treason from being the betrayal of the ruler has become a crime against the state, the development of a new political idea ... and this is well'.[95]

There are problems, however, with this mode of interpretation. Rulers had always regarded rebellion as unlawful and had punished rebels as traitors.[96] The question is not so much about new concepts of what constituted treasonable conduct as about new and bloodier punishments for treason. But the history of shedding blood has not been much studied. In part this may well reflect the discomfiture of historians in general – not just 'revisionist Irish historians' – when faced by the violence of history; hence they often resort to tacit evasion or to sociological euphemisms such as 'segmentary competition'.[97] Moreover, when studying political structures, historians of Scotland, Wales and Ireland, like historians of England, have preferred to concentrate on the growth of the state and have looked for 'modernizing' trends which involved the emergence – or the prospect of the emergence – of united kingdoms ruled over by dynasties of kings, high-kings or princes. But whether or not, as historians have liked to believe, the emergence of the 'state' helped in the maintenance of 'law and order', is one thing; quite another, as the history of England and France *c.* 1300 shows, is the extent to which the state sets – or does not set – limits to the shedding of blood for political ends. It is also clear that the 'anglicization' of political values in the fourteenth and subsequent centuries when, as Alexander Grant pointed out, there were more lurid acts of violence in English politics than in Scottish, would carry entirely different implications for the health of the leading players than did the process of 'anglicization' in the twelfth and thirteenth centuries.[98]

[95] Pollock and Maitland, *History of English Law*, ii, p. 506.
[96] Gillingham, '1066 and the introduction of chivalry', pp. 44–51; Carpenter, 'From King John to the first English duke', pp. 31–2; M. Strickland, *War and Chivalry: The Conduct and Perception of War in England and Normandy, 1066–1217* (Cambridge, 1996), pp. 247–57.
[97] B. Bradshaw, 'Nationalism and historical scholarship in modern Ireland', *IHS*, 26 (1988–9), pp. 329–51.
[98] Grant, 'Crown and nobility in late medieval Britain', pp. 34–6.

7 Anglo-French acculturation and the Irish element in Scottish identity

Dauvit Broun

It is well known that in the central Middle Ages the native populations of Ireland and most of Scotland shared the same language, 'high culture' and major saints' cults. Indeed, it would be no exaggeration to say that they formed a single people – identified in their own language as *Gáedil* – who stretched from Munster in the south to Moray in the north, and whose élite interacted with each other culturally and politically irrespective of any division into Ireland and Scotland.[1] We should not be surprised, for instance, that the first record of a *mormaer* of Mar (a region straddling the rivers Dee and Don in Aberdeenshire) is as a casualty fighting for Brian Bóruma at the battle of Clontarf (1014).[2] Another example of this pan-Gaelic vision is King Ruaidrí Ua Conchobair's famous endowment, in 1169, of funds to assist the *fer léginn* (lector) of Armagh in the instruction of students from Ireland and Scotland.[3] And when Robert Bruce faced his destiny in 1306–7, he asked Irish kings to support him because 'we come from the seed of one nation'.[4]

By the time Robert Bruce dispatched his words of pan-Gaelic fraternity to Ireland, however, what being *Scoti* was understood to mean – at least as articulated by the kingdom's *literati* – had taken a new form. The wars of independence witnessed the first extant attempts to portray the

---

I am very grateful to Professor Robert Bartlett, Dr Sonja Cameron and Dr Keith Stringer for suggesting improvements to earlier drafts of this chapter, and to the perceptive comments and criticisms received from delegates at the 'Britain and Ireland' conference. I am also very grateful to Dr Nerys Ann Jones for her continual encouragement and support.

[1] See esp. Duffy, 'The Bruce brothers and the Irish Sea world', pp. 55–86.
[2] *AU*, s.a. 1014; Anderson, *Early Sources*, i, p. 536.
[3] *AU*, s.a. 1169; Anderson, *Early Sources*, ii, p. 267. Those who came to study there would not have been disappointed, for the *fer léginn* at the time was highly qualified, having spent twenty-one years training in France and England. *ALC* and *AFM*, s.a. 1174; Anderson, *Early Sources*, ii, p. 267 n. 6.
[4] '*ab uno processimus germine nacionis*': R. Nicholson, 'A sequel to Edward Bruce's invasion of Ireland', *SHR*, 42 (1963), pp. 30–40, at 38; see also Barrow, *Robert Bruce* (3rd edn), p. 379 n. 9. For the dating of Robert I's letter, see now Duffy, 'The Bruce brothers and the Irish Sea world', pp. 64–5.

Scots as a nation in their own right quite separate from the Irish. The idea of being one people with the Irish did not necessarily die out,[5] but by 1306 some Scots, at least, would seem to have recognized only a distant association. When the Declaration of Arbroath was drafted in 1320 its account of the Scots' mythical wanderings from Greater Scythia to Scotland made no mention whatever of any link with Ireland.[6] How distant the connection with Ireland could subsequently become is suggested by the bigoted remarks of Abbot Walter Bower (1385–1449), for whom the Irish were noted for their 'propensity for theft, plundering and murder'.[7]

These changes in how being Scottish was articulated suggest a reorientation of Scotland's place within Britain and Ireland as perceived by the kingdom's *literati* (and, we may presume, the élite in general). The novel idea of Scots as a nation in their own right may have had the war with Edward I as its immediate cause. On the face of it, however, it could conceivably have signified an active wish to dilute, if not reject, the age-old identification with the Irish. Could this have had its roots in an earlier redefinition of Scottishness in which the élite turned its gaze from the west and looked eagerly to the south for its most meaningful cultural and social contacts? This, indeed, is what might be expected from some aspects of the kingdom's recent history. The twelfth and thirteenth centuries witnessed an influx of clerics, knights and merchants from England and the continent and a fundamental restructuring of life in court and castle, cloister and cathedral, and town and country, not only in the south but in the kingdom's heartland in the Gaelic east.

---

[5] See, for example, *CGS*, p. 149 (Bk. 4, ch. 6); 'Hyberniensis vicina nobis, ac ejusdem nostri generis natio...' It has been argued, however, that much of *Chronica Gentis Scottorum* was already in existence by 1301; Broun, 'Birth of Scottish history', pp. 4–22. Note also the comment in *The Scottis Originale* (mid-fifteenth century) that Ireland was 'callit efter Scota Scocia maior vnto the tyme that part of ws come out of it in our Scotland that now is inhabit and was callit Scocia minor' ; *The Asloan Manuscript: a Miscellany of Prose and Verse written by John Asloan*, ed. W. A. Craigie, 2 vols., STS (Edinburgh and London, 1923), i, p. 187.

[6] Sir James Fergusson, *The Declaration of Arbroath* (Edinburgh, 1970), p. 9. Robert I's chancellor, Bernard de Linton, was credited as the Declaration's author by T. M. Cooper (Lord Cooper of Culross), *Supra Crepidam* (London, 1951), pp. 62–71, but the grounds for this have been challenged by Professor Duncan (*RRS*, v, pp. 164–6): Barrow, *Robert Bruce* (3rd edn), p. 308, has suggested Master Alexander Kinninmonth, one of King Robert's ambassadors to the Curia, as the author. The Declaration's chief source for its brief account of Scottish origins was (ironically) Henry of Huntingdon's *Historia Anglorum*: see D. Broun, 'The Scottish origin-legend before Fordun' (Ph.D. thesis, University of Edinburgh, 1988), pp. 144–5.

[7] *Scotichronicon*, i, pp. 46–7 (Bk. 1, ch. 19). In the same passage Bower even managed to find a discreditable explanation of Ireland's purity – famed since Bede remarked that 'almost everything that comes from that island is an antidote to poison' – by declaring that it was 'so that the people might have a polished mirror for the contemplation of their own appearance and the reformation of their uncouth and uncivilised behaviour'.

In the same period Gaelic language and culture began its retreat in the lowlands. It is not surprising, therefore, that aspects of this process have been characterized as 'anti-Celtic',[8] and summed up by Professor Duncan with the pithy sentence: 'Scotland, which had been created as a Celtic kingdom, had become an English kingdom.'[9]

At the same time, however, it is generally recognized that all things Gaelic were not rejected willy-nilly, and that, although Gaelic culture suffered a mortal decline in status in the east where it had once been predominant, the social fabric of the kingdom's heartlands at the end of this period was woven from Gaelic as well as Anglo-French strands.[10] In particular, it has been observed that in Scotland 'there was no conflict between old "Celtic" law on the one hand and new "feudal" law on the other, and no institutionalized form of apartheid similar to the exceptions of Irishry and Welshry to ensure that Anglo-Norman and older native laws followed separate paths of development'.[11] Leading members of the native aristocracy – the earls/*mormair* – not only survived, but their position was in some respects consolidated and two in particular (Fife and Strathearn) benefited from royal favour.[12] The development of Fife and Strathearn is particularly illustrative of how acculturization did not displace the Gaelic heritage. In both cases cadet branches were successfully excluded as a result of adopting primogeniture as the rule of succession. In Fife this may have occurred as early as the reign of Donnchad I (d. 1154), in whose time the relationship with the kingship was redefined so that the earldom was held of the king;[13] certainly none of the descendants of Donnchad's predecessor, Gille

[8] E.g. Barrow, *Robert Bruce* (3rd edn), p. 6: 'If Scotland [in Alexander III's reign (1249–86)] was thus a Celtic country, it was also a country of non-Celtic developments and anti-Celtic tendencies.' Also, G. W. S. Barrow, *Kingship and Unity: Scotland 1000–1306* (London, 1981), p. 105, describes these changes as a reorientation of mind and *mores*: 'The feudal kingdom of David I and his descendants turned away from the western modes of thought and action which linked the country to Ireland and also, by the sea-route of the Minch and the Northern Isles, to Norway.'
[9] A. A. M. Duncan, *The Nation of Scots and the Declaration of Arbroath*, Historical Association Pamphlet no. 75 (London, 1970), p. 9.
[10] In general, see Duncan, *Scotland: the Making of the Kingdom*, chs. 7–17; Barrow, *Kingship and Unity*.
[11] H. MacQueen, 'Scots law under Alexander III', in *Scotland in the Reign of Alexander III, 1249–1286*, ed. N. H. Reid (Edinburgh, 1990), pp. 74–102, at 95.
[12] G. W. S. Barrow, *David I of Scotland: the Balance of Old and New*, Stenton Lecture 1984 (Reading, 1985), pp. 15–16; reprinted in Barrow, *Scotland and its Neighbours in the Middle Ages* (London, 1992), pp. 45–66, comments that the 'earldoms formed a necessary, systematic and completely integrated element of political geography'. The first earl from an incoming family was William Comyn in or soon after 1211, who obtained Buchan through marriage. See also the brief survey in Duncan, *Scotland: the Making of the Kingdom*, pp. 164–8. For examples of royal grants to earls of Fife and Strathearn, see *RRS*, ii, pp. 258, 435.
[13] Duncan, *Scotland, the Making of the Kingdom*, p. 138.

Mícheil, became earl.[14] In Strathearn the crucial generation would appear to have been the sons of Earl Gilbert (Gille Brigte) (1171–1223) who were eight in number; after Gilbert's death, however, the senior line prevailed in possession of the earldom.[15] In both earldoms the successful application of primogeniture coincided with a marked tendency to call the eldest son of each generation by the same choice of one or two names.[16] It is notable, however, that it was Gaelic names which were thus associated with this redefinition of the family according to Anglo-French practice. As a result, in Fife Donnchad (*anglice* Duncan) (d. 1154) was succeeded by Donnchad (1154–1204), then Máel Coluim (*anglice* Malcolm) (1204–28), then Máel Coluim (son of the previous Máel Coluim's brother, Donnchad) (1228–66), then Colbán (1266–70), then Donnchad (1270–88), and last of the line was Donnchad (1288–1353); in Strathearn the first earl to succeed by primogeniture was Robert, fourth son of the long-reigning Gilbert (Gille Brigte), who was succeeded by Máel Ísu (*anglice* Malise) (1244–71), then Máel Ísu (1271–*c*. 1313), Máel Ísu (*c*. 1313–*c*. 1333), and the last of the line was Máel Ísu (d. *c*. 1353). Both these families were open to Anglo-French influence, became knights and founded houses of the new monastic orders;[17] in neither case, however, did they think it incongruent to make Gaelic names so prominent a part of their new identity as a lineage.[18]

[14] For Fife see *The Scots Peerage*, ed. Sir James Balfour Paul, 9 vols. (Edinburgh, 1904–14), iv, pp. 5–12, and J. Bannerman, 'MacDuff of Fife', in *Medieval Scotland: Crown, Lordship and Community*, ed. A. Grant and K. J. Stringer (Edinburgh, 1993), pp. 20–38.

[15] For earls of Strathearn, see *Charters, Bulls, and other Documents Relating to the Abbey of Inchaffray*, ed. W. A. Lindsay et al., Scottish History Society (Edinburgh, 1908), pp. lx–lxx.

[16] A similar pattern can be discerned in the Lennox and Ross, where in the aftermath of acculturation a particular name was favoured for the eldest son: in the Lennox 'Máel Coluim' was used in this way for three generations from the early thirteenth century until the father of the last of the direct male line; in Ross 'William' was used in this way in four out of five generations from the mid-thirteenth century until the direct male line died out in 1372 (see *Scots Peerage*, v, pp. 331–7; vii, pp. 232–9). This naming pattern is not apparent in earldoms where the (legitimate) male line(s) of descent died out before acculturation had taken root (e.g. Angus and Atholl; *Scots Peerage*, i, pp. 160–6, 415–19) or where the succession was disputed as late as the mid-thirteenth century (e.g. Mar; *Scots Peerage*, v, pp. 573–6).

[17] Gilbert earl of Strathearn (re)founded Inchaffray as an Augustinian priory in 1200, Máel Coluim earl of Fife (re)founded Culross as a Cistercian house in 1218 (I. B. Cowan and D. E. Easson, *Medieval Religious Houses: Scotland*, 2nd edn (London, 1976), pp. 74, 91; and n. 22, below).

[18] Bartlett, *Making of Europe*, pp. 274–7, points to the naming patterns of the descendants of Donnchad ua Maíle Choluim (Duncan I) (1034–40) as an example of 'transformation and convergence' in which 'the early generations exhibit indisputably regional names' (in a European context), but 'a major transformation occurs' resulting in 'a very syncretistic pattern, in which Gaelic names are unusual'. This important observation

Some Gaelic institutions in the kingdom's historic heartland did, at least in the long term, suffer a permanent reverse. Even so, this does not seem to have been as a result of any deliberate attempt to eradicate them. For example, the native judicial official (*brithem*, or *judex* in Latin) – including *judex regis*, the king's *brithem* – continued into the thirteenth century to play an important part in the settlement of disputes and the passing of legislation.[19] Another member of the learned orders, the king's poet (*ollam ríg*), has also been identified as late as 1249 performing his customary role as the chief official at a royal inauguration.[20] As for the church, there were no doubt some instances in which members of old ecclesiastical establishments were uprooted for the sake of a new foundation, or forcibly made to adopt a regular lifestyle.[21] There were, however, a number of cases where change did not occur until the mid-thirteenth century and was probably voluntary.[22] A number of important Gaelic churches, therefore, continued to function in the east midlands into the thirteenth century.[23] Putting all this

may be taken a stage further (at least for Scotland) by noting that the 'syncretistic pattern' includes three generations in which the eldest son was named Alexander (d. 1249, d. 1286 and d. 1284 respectively). This subsequent development may be compared with naming patterns among earls observed above (especially given that when Alexander (d. 1249) was recognized as William I's heir in 1201 this was the first occasion when an immature eldest son was preferred despite the existence of an adult male in the royal family, in this case William I's brother David, earl of Huntingdon, d. 1219; this may therefore be regarded as the first certain instance of primogeniture; see W. D. H. Sellar, 'Celtic law and Scots law: survival and integration', *Scottish Studies* 29 (1989), pp. 1–27, at p. 13.

[19] G. W. S. Barrow, *The Kingdom of the Scots: Government, Church and Society from the Eleventh to the Fourteenth Century* (London, 1973), pp. 69–82, esp. 70–2.

[20] J. Bannerman, 'The king's poet and the inauguration of Alexander III', *SHR*, 68 (1989), pp. 120–49; see also pp. 138–49 for further discussion of Gaelic learned orders in eastern Scotland in this period.

[21] Possible examples are Scone (Augustinian, daughter-house of Nostell, *c.* 1120), Culross (Cistercian, daughter-house of Kinloss, 1218) and Deer (Cistercian, daughter-house of Kinloss, 1219), but it is not known whether communities or colleges still functioned immediately prior to these refoundations. See Cowan and Easson, *Medieval Religious Houses: Scotland*, pp. 97, 74, 47. For Culross as earlier foundation see A. Macquarrie, '*Vita Sancti Servani*: the Life of St Serf', *Innes Review*, 44 (1993), pp. 122–52, esp. 127. A more gradual displacement was enforced at Loch Leven, which was made dependent on the Augustinian priory of St Andrews about 1150, and its Céli Dé compelled to become canons regular. An attempt to foist a similiar arrangement on Céli Dé at St Andrews failed. See Barrow, *The Kingdom of the Scots*, pp. 212–32, and Cowan and Easson, *Medieval Religious Houses: Scotland*, pp. 93, 96.

[22] For instance Monymusk (by 1245) and Abernethy (possibly 1272/3) became Augustinian priories; the Céli Dé of Brechin became a cathedral chapter (1218 × 42); and Céli Dé at St Andrews were reconstituted as a secular college (probably 1248/9). Ibid., pp. 93, 89, 203, 225. For St Andrews' complicated history, see Barrow, *Kingdom of the Scots*, pp. 212–32.

[23] Including Abernethy, Brechin, Dunblane, Dunkeld, Methven, Monymusk, Muthill: Cowan and Easson, *Medieval Religious Houses: Scotland*, pp. 46–7, 50–1; see also

together, it appears that Gaelic *literati* remained socially significant into the reign of Alexander II (1214–49). It is notable, moreover, that the names of these *literati* are overwhelmingly Gaelic up to the mid-thirteenth century,[24] which suggests that Gaelic culture retained its vitality for them up to that point. A case can be made, therefore, for seeing Gaelic's loss of status in the east as, in an immediate sense, a phenomenon of the mid-thirteenth century, and not simply the result of acculturation initiated a century earlier.

This suggests that Anglo-French acculturation in Scotland need not have been predominantly 'anti-Celtic' in intention. Those Gaels – not least the kings of Scots themselves – who espoused the *mores* and manners of a new international élite may have regarded these as complementing rather than eradicating their native culture. Not only would Gaelic language and law have continued for some time to remain important to them in a local context, but they would also have given them an identity within the cosmopolitan world they sought to join. Until the mid-thirteenth century, therefore, there may have been a kind of *modus vivendi* between Anglo-French and Gaelic culture among the upper echelons of society, at least in the kingdom's historic heartland in the east, north of the Forth and south of Moray. Such a balancing-act might seem improbable, however, from what may be gauged about Anglo-French attitudes to native Scots and Irish. John Gillingham has highlighted what he has described as 'one of the most fundamental ideological shifts in the history of the British Isles' which saw, by the mid-twelfth century, the emergence of a strongly expressed view among English commentators that their Celtic neighbours were uncivilized barbarians.[25] It must be wondered, therefore, whether this view was

K. Veitch, 'The Scottish material in *De domibus religiosis*: date and provenance', *Innes Review*, 47 (1996), pp. 14–23.

[24] Bannerman, 'King's poet', pp. 138–49: note also, for instance, Gaelic-named priors of Céli Dé found 1235×9 at Abernethy and 1204×14 at Brechin; and Gaelic-named 'kings' of schools (the phrase is *rex scholarum*, probably for *fer léginn*) at Dunblane and Muthill 1214×23 (Cowan and Easson, *Medieval Religious Houses, Scotland*, pp. 46–7, 51). For *judices* see list in Barrow, *Kingdom of the Scots*, pp. 74–80: before 1250 the only *judices* listed in the east midlands who did not have Gaelic names were Henry, *judex* in Fife and Fothriff *c.* 1170×80 and Adam, *judex* in Angus recorded in 1219 and 1228 (though he was in fact a Gael, so his name may have been Áed: his brother was Cairell, *judex* of Angus recorded in 1228 and 1244, and his father was Máel Coluim, also a *judex* in Angus, recorded *c.* 1220). For a more wide-ranging discussion of Gaelic survivals in eastern Scotland in this period, see G. W. S. Barrow, 'The lost Gàidhealtachd', in *Gaelic and Scotland: Alba agus a' Ghàidhlig*, ed. W. Gilles (Edinburgh, 1989), pp. 67–88; reprinted in Barrow, *Scotland and its Neighbours in the Middle Ages* (London, 1992), pp. 105–26. For evidence of Gaelic literacy in this area into the thirteenth century, see D. Broun, 'Gaelic literacy in eastern Scotland, 1124–1249', in *Literacy in Medieval Celtic Societies*, ed. H. Pryce (Cambridge, 1998), pp. 183–201.

[25] J. Gillingham, 'The beginnings of English imperialism', *Journal of Historical Sociology*, 5

taken to heart by Scotland's acculturizing kings, and travelled north with the Anglo-French immigrants they invited to their realm. The charge of Celtic barbarity, after all, was not simply the idle invective of an insufferable neighbour, but carried with it the threat of damnation in the eyes of a resurgent church and exclusion from the charmed circles of an international aristocracy.[26] Certainly, to a contemporary English observer it seemed that, by the early thirteenth century, 'the most recent kings of Scots profess themselves to be rather Frenchmen in race (*genere*), manners, language and culture; and, having reduced the Scots to utter servitude, admit only Frenchmen to their service and following'.[27]

A tendency to regard native Scots as barbarians can, moreover, be detected in the *Chronicle of Melrose* – the most extensive source which survives from the Scottish kingdom in this period.[28] Melrose was a torch-bearer for the new dispensation and, although it was situated in an area which had never been Gaelicized (and did not regard itself as 'Scottish' until the mid or late thirteenth century[29]), it was the mother-house of new foundations in the kingdom's Gaelic heartland and beyond.[30] The *Chronicle*'s record of events in Galloway in 1235 included recycled details about sacrilegious savagery committed by some Scots, presumably soldiers from Menteith, whose earl had been left by Alexander II to police the lordship after the first risings that year.[31] We need not doubt that acts of brutality were in fact committed – the prior and sacrist of the recently founded abbey of Tongland were

---

(1992), pp. 392–409; Gillingham, 'The English invasion of Ireland', in *Representing Ireland: Literature and the Origins of Conflict, 1534–1660*, ed. B. Bradshaw *et al.* (Cambridge, 1993), pp. 24–42 (quotation at 24).

[26] On the latter, see Davies, *Domination and Conquest*, esp. pp. 50–1. In general, see Bartlett, *Making of Europe*, pp. 243–91.

[27] *Memoriale Fratris Walteri de Coventria: the Historical Collection of Walter of Coventry*, ed. W. Stubbs, 2 vols., RS (London, 1872–3), ii, p. 206 (translation based on Davies, *Domination and Conquest*, p. 20). Walter of Coventry here reproduces the words of the Barnwell Chronicle, the contemporary source used for the period 1201–25 by the compilation abridged by Walter 1293 × 1307. See Stubbs (ed.), *Memoriale Fratris Walteri de Coventria*, i, pp. xix–xxii, xxxi–xxxii, xxxvii–xxxviii; see also pp. xlv–xlvii.

[28] The chronicle is the principal contemporary Scottish source from 1171 to 1263. See *The Chronicle of Melrose*, ed. A.O. Anderson *et al.* (London, 1936), p. xi.

[29] D. Broun, 'Defining Scotland and the Scots before the wars of independence' in *Image and Identity: the Making and Remaking of Scotland through the Ages*, ed. D. Broun, R. Finlay and M. Lynch (Edinburgh, 1998), pp. 4–17, at p. 9.

[30] Kinloss (Moray), 1150; Coupar Angus, ×1164; Balmerino, *c.* 1227. Kinloss was, in turn, mother-house of Culross (1218) and Deer (1219) (Cowan and Easson, *Medieval Religious Houses: Scotland*, pp. 72–9).

[31] Anderson (ed.), *Chronicle of Melrose* [84]; Anderson, *Early Sources*, ii, p. 497. The 'common army' was raised by earls from their earldom: see Duncan, *Scotland: the Making of the Kingdom*, pp. 378–82; *RRS*, ii, pp. 56–7.

killed – but the chronicler has garnished his account with a passage repeated from the *Chronicle*'s report of an earlier outrage in 1216.[32] This suggests that a prejudice against indigenous Scots as uncivilized barbarians moved the chronicler responsible for writing up 1235 to record details which did not actually occur.[33] If Melrose chroniclers viewed native Scots as barbarians as late as 1235, then this was presumably a significant current of opinion within the kingdom. Even in southern and eastern Scotland, however, where royal authority was strongest and Anglo-French immigration and influence was most in evidence, the élite were not so homogeneous that it can be assumed that Melrose chroniclers spoke for them all. In particular, the *Chronicle of Melrose* may only represent a viewpoint from the English south-east of the kingdom, and is not direct evidence therefore for the idea of Celtic barbarity among the Gaelic élite who embraced Anglo-French culture and came into regular contact with immigrant knights, merchants, monks and clerics. It might be suspected, indeed, that a different perspective prevailed in the east midlands where Gaelic had been long-established and deeply entrenched and (unlike so much of the Celtic world) Anglo-French acculturation was experienced without military confrontation between native and immigrant élites. The question of how far the stereotype of Gaelic barbarity was adopted by the acculturized élite will not be tackled in this chapter, however.[34] Instead, the focus will be on how acculturization may have affected the age-old link with the Irish, specifically with regard to the Irish element in the kingdom's identity. I will argue that, before the wars of independence, Scottish

[32] The similarity of the two passages was pointed out by Anderson, *Early Sources*, ii, p. 497, nn. 2, 3. G. W. S. Barrow, 'The army of Alexander III's Scotland', in *Scotland in the Reign of Alexander III 1249–1286*, ed. N. H. Reid (Edinburgh, 1990), pp. 132–47, at p. 136 suggested that the *Scoti* who committed atrocities in 1216 were 'probably Gallovidians to whom raiding in Cumbria was not unfamiliar' (the attack was on Holm Cultram). Elsewhere in these parts of the *Chronicle* (Anderson (ed.), *Chronicle of Melrose*, [63], [84]), however, *Scoti* seems to refer specifically to the inhabitants of *Scotia*, i.e. north of the Forth, e.g., when later in 1216, following the atrocities committed by *Scoti*, Alexander II set off for Carlisle and ultimately Dover with his whole army with the exception of *Scoti* from whom he took an aid: these *Scoti* included men inhabiting Arbroath Abbey's tofts in royal burghs, whose contribution Alexander II confirmed would not create a precedent against the abbey's immunity from aids (which they claimed had been granted in a charter of William I, no doubt *RRS*, ii, no. 448): see *Liber S. Thome de Aberbrothoc Registrum Abbacie de Aberbrothoc*, ed. P. Chalmers and C. Innes, 2 vols., Bannatyne Club (Edinburgh, 1848), i (1848), p. 80 (no. 111): see also p. 79 (no. 110).

[33] As far as the chronicle's regard for Ireland, the Isles and the Highlands is concerned, this is typified by a tendency to be dismissive. Note, for instance, the way that Diarmait Mac Murchada is described (*s.a.* 1169) merely as 'a certain kinglet [*regulus*] of that land', without even being named; Anderson, *Chronicle of Melrose* [38].

[34] I will discuss this in a forthcoming article on prejudices against Scots found in Scottish literature before John of Fordun.

men of letters identified the Scottish kingdom and its people with Ireland, and that this identification was not adversely affected by Anglo-French influence. The continuing vitality of this Irish element in Scottish identity may, therefore, be regarded as another instance where acculturation in the kingdom's historic heartland did not involve the rejection of obvious manifestations of Gaelic culture and society.

The Irish element in Scottish identity under discussion can be found particularly in accounts of Scottish origins written by the kingdom's acculturized men of letters. As a genre, such accounts of necessity sought to identify the Scots in relation to other peoples, and did so in a way which could have reflected any pressing social and cultural concerns held by the acculturized élite to which their authors and redactors belonged.[35] Such accounts have the potential, therefore, to reveal key aspects of what Scottish men of letters thought it was to be Scottish. If these accounts are to be useful as a source, however, it is important to analyse more than one or two of them. Only by comparing a number over a significant period is it possible to identify innovations, distinguish those elements which were entrenched from those which failed to catch on, discern how radical or conservative a scholar has been with his materials, and to hazard a view about an account's popularity and significance. It is regrettable, therefore, that there is such a paucity of Scottish origin-legend material of Scottish provenance before the fourteenth century. No extended account of Scottish origins written using Scottish sources survives until Thomas Grey's *Scalacronica* of the 1360s, or John of Fordun's *Chronica Gentis Scottorum*, which may be dated to the mid-1370s.[36] The only chance of making good this dearth of

[35] See in general S. Reynolds, 'Medieval *origines gentium* and the community of the realm', *History*, 68 (1983), pp. 375–90.

[36] *Chronica Gentis Scottorum* (which is represented in Skene's edition as running from Scottish origins to David I's death in 1153) is coupled in most MSS with a sequence of annals (known as *Gesta Annalia*) which run from St Margaret's royal ancestors to 1363 (with a perfunctory continuation in some MSS to 1385): see Donald Watt's discussion in *Scotichronicon*, iii, pp. xvi–xvii. There is considerable uncertainty about whether *Gesta Annalia* may safely be regarded as Fordun's work. It seems that 1371–7 is the likeliest date for the *Chronica* itself (I intend to explore this issue on a future occasion).

Scalacronica survives in a single manuscript (Cambridge, Corpus Christi College MS 133: the account of Scottish origins runs from fol. 190vb22 to 191va22): for edition, see *Scalacronica: a Chronicle of England and Scotland from A.D. MLXVI to A.D. MCCCLXII*, ed. J. Stevenson, Maitland Club (Edinburgh, 1836) (pp. 112–14 for account of Scottish origins). A translation of the latter part has been published: *Scalacronica: the Reigns of Edward I and Edward II and Edward III by Sir Thomas Gray of Heton*, trans. Sir H. Maxwell, bart. (Glasgow, 1907): at p. viii he explains that Grey began work on *Scalacronica* during his captivity in Edinburgh Castle, 1355–7, but it continues to the early 1360s. The majority of the text is a version of the *Brut* running from the Creation to the death of Henry III which Grey has continued from his own

material is by examining Grey's *Scalacronica* and Fordun's *Chronica Gentis Scottorum* to see if anything can be said about their sources in the hope that some, at least, may be identified as Scottish accounts written before the fourteenth century.

This is a demanding and complex operation which requires much more analysis than I can offer on this occasion: what follows is necessarily a rather simplified discussion.[37] There are obvious difficulties to beware of, not least the problem of identifying interference by Grey or Fordun themselves, or other medieval scholars who may have encountered this material in the interim. The task, however, is rather less awesome than might be supposed. It appears that Grey has translated a Latin text datable to the reign of King John (1292–1304)[38] which, by joining origin-legend to king-list, covered the whole sweep of Scottish history (if in a rather skeletal form).[39] *Chronica Gentis Scottorum* presents more problems, but also more scope for uncovering lost accounts. A particular stroke of luck is that it has not been composed as a single,

knowledge and from what he found while in Edinburgh Castle (including the account of Scottish origins, no doubt). His text of the *Brut* has been described as 'certainement le moins traditionnel de nos cinque manuscrits' in the Parker Library, Corpus Christi College, Cambridge: D. B. Tyson, 'Les manuscrits du Brut en prose française', in *Les Manuscrits Français de la bibliothèque Parker, Actes du Colloque 24–27 mars 1993*, ed. Nigel Wilkins (Cambridge, 1993), pp. 101–20, at p. 111. (I am grateful to Professor David Dumville for drawing this article to my attention.) The account of Scottish origins (and following king-list) have been published and translated separately in *Chronicles of the Picts, Chronicles of the Scots, and other early Memorials of Scottish History*, ed. W. F. Skene (Edinburgh, 1867), pp. 194–208.

[37] A full treatment will appear in my forthcoming book, *The Irish Identity of the Kingdom of the Scots in the 12th and 13th Centuries* (Woodbridge, forthcoming). This material is also discussed in detail in Broun, 'Scottish origin-legend', pp. 28–183, although this is unsatisfactory in a number of respects, especially its rather uncritical use of Skene's edition of CGS. R. James Goldstein, *The Matter of Scotland: Historical Narrative in Medieval Scotland* (Lincoln, NE, 1993), pp. 104–32, takes a different view which sees Fordun as the innovator and Grey's account as closer to the original. This, however, cannot be sustained (see my review in *Nottingham Medieval Studies*, 39 (1995), pp. 205–7). For a different analysis of the nameless sources in *Chronica Gentis Scottorum* see *Scotichronicon*, i, pp. xxiii–xxx (see further nn. 42 and 45, below).

[38] John surrendered to Edward I in an abjectly humiliating ceremony in 1296 (see G. G. Simpson, 'Why was John Balliol called "Toom Tabard"?', *SHR*, 47 (1968), pp. 196–9) and after a spell as a prisoner in England was eventually allowed to retire to his ancestral estates in Picardy, never to return to Scotland. Despite this, significant areas of Scotland continued to be governed in his name in opposition to Edward I until the final Comyn surrender of 1304. F. Watson, 'The enigmatic lion: Scotland, kingship, and national identity in the wars of independence', in *Image and Identity: the Making and Remaking of Scotland through the Ages*, ed. D. Broun, R. Finlay and M. Lynch (Edinburgh, 1998), pp. 18–37. John may not have ruled after 1296, therefore, but as far as most Scots were concerned he certainly reigned beyond that. For this period see Barrow, *Robert Bruce* (3rd edn), pp. 80–131.

[39] Edited in Skene, *Chronicles of the Picts, Chronicles of the Scots*, pp. 197–208. The king-list section, known as king-list K, has been edited more recently (filleted of interpolated passages) in Anderson, *Kings and Kingship in Early Scotland*, pp. 286–9.

homogeneous narrative, but consists of a collection of passages, episode-by-episode up to the arrival of *Scoti* in Ireland, which have evidently been culled from different sources. It has been argued, in fact, that this compilation from disparate sources was not composed by Fordun himself, but by an earlier scholar[40] who may have been responsible for another part of *Chronica Gentis Scottorum* which seems to have been known to the Scottish procurators at the Curia in 1301, long before Fordun's time.[41]

Most of the passages which make up the treatment of Scottish origins in *Chronica Gentis Scottorum* are simply attributed to 'a chronicle' or 'another chronicle'. The contradictions which are frequently thrown up between passages, however, may serve as reassurance that this was not simply a device designed to create a spurious air of authenticity. For instance, the first episode, Gaedel Glas's emigration from Greece to Egypt and marriage to Scota, is given four times: only in one does Gaedel receive a good press, claiming that he was sent to Egypt with an army to help Pharaoh against the Ethiopians; in two he is described as an arrogant youth who exasperated his father, a Greek king, and his subjects so much that he was expelled and ended up in Egypt; in the fourth account it is even said that Gaedel tried to usurp the kingship but was successfully resisted by Egyptians who refused to bow to his tyranny. Discrepancies of this sort make it possible to analyse all the passages attributed to nameless sources and identify particular idiosyncrasies shared by two or more extracts across different episodes.[42] In this way key elements in two accounts can be reconstructed as far as the arrival of the *Scoti* in Ireland (though only in as much detail as has been derived from them). One account had Gaedel's son Éber leading the Scoti to Ireland; the other gave this role to Partholón. I will therefore refer to these respectively as the 'Éber' and 'Partholón' accounts.

[40] Brown, 'Scottish origin-legend', pp. 64–71. John and Winifred MacQueen (*Scotichronicon*, i, pp. xxvii–xxx) agree with this, and suggest that Fordun may have depended on this source for more than his account of Scottish origins (and king-list).
[41] Broun, 'Birth of Scottish history', where it is argued that the innovatory chronological framework in the *Chronica* (at least from the first Scottish settler in Scotland to an early-ninth-century Pictish king) can be detected in a draft by the Scottish procurators in Rome in 1301. This would suggest that the origin-legend material containing Fergus mac Ferchair is likely to have also been part of the *Chronica* by this time, especially in view of the evidence for its construction which has been taken to show that the origin-legend material was put together by a scholar earlier than Fordun (see note above).
[42] John and Winifred MacQueen (*Scotichronicon*, i, p. xxiii) employ a different method, based on what they describe as 'possibly over-bold assumptions ... that when he [Fordun] quoted from more than one chronicle-source he usually kept the order A, B, C', and that A was regarded as the 'primary authority' which was 'usually quoted first or solely'. This does not take account of the contradictions in detail which allow idiosyncrasies to be identified between passages.

As well as these nameless sources (and at least one other),[43] material on Scottish origins in *Chronica Gentis Scottorum* is also attributed to a 'legend of St Brendan' and a 'legend of St Congal'.[44] The former is very similar in outline to what I have dubbed the 'Éber' account, and traces the *Scoti* from Gaedel through to Éber's colonization of Ireland. It is clearly related to Irish accounts of Irish origins, though it is significantly different in detail and casting. The 'St Congal' account, however, is rare and unusual: it concerns Símón Brecc, a son of a Spanish king,[45] who is given a stone inaugural throne which he takes with him when he conquers Ireland, in due course placing it at Tara, the chief royal site in Ireland; later his descendant, Fergus mac Ferchair, brings this stone throne to Scotland, where he becomes king of the *Scoti* who migrated there; the stone is eventually placed at Scone. It can be shown with some confidence that the *Scalacronica*'s account has been derived ultimately from the same source as the material in *Chronica Gentis Scottorum* attributed to legends of St Brendan and St Congal. It is possible, therefore, to add to the tally of recoverable accounts of Scottish origins a composite text drawn from hagiographical works on St Brendan and St Congal. I do not know of any extant Life or Legend of a St Brendan or a St Congal which contained this origin-legend material, so at this point the trail goes cold.[46]

The tally of lost, but recoverable, accounts of Scottish origins can still be increased, however. The account shared (ultimately) by Fordun

---

[43] Which described Éremón and Éber, sons of Míl Espáine, leading the exodus from Spain to Ireland. This corresponds with Irish accounts of the legend.

[44] The name may alternatively have been originally 'Cougal' for *Comgall*.

[45] The manuscript of *Scotichronicon* which Professor Watt identified as written and revised under Bower's supervision (Cambridge, Corpus Christi College MS 171) has glossed the text's notice of Símón Brecc's father with *Milo nomine* (*Scotichronicon*, i, p. 64). As a result, Símón's father was identified as Míl in all subsequent manuscripts of *Scotichronicon*. *Scotichronicon* is here simply a copy of *Chronica Gentis Scottorum* which does not identify Símón's father (though Míl appears as a gloss in British Museum, MS Cotton Vitellius E. XI: this manuscript has, however, been partially collated with a copy of *Scotichronicon*). There is no warrant, therefore, for the MacQueens' conclusion (*Scotichronicon*, i, p. 144) that Míl was an original feature of the St Congal hagiographical source to which the passage is attributed. It appears, rather, that 'Milo' has been introduced by Bower from the Scottish poem in *Liber Extravagans* (the 'supplementary book' attached to *Scotichronicon*) in a section datable to 1296 × 1306 (ed. D. Brown with A. B. Scott in *Scotichronicon* ix, ed. D. E. R. Watt).

[46] To my knowledge it is rare to find accounts of Scottish or Irish origins in Irish or Scottish hagiography, though a striking parallel is provided by the Life of the tenth-century recluse St Cathroe, who hailed from Scotland but emigrated to Metz where he was buried and where his Life was written (see A. Boyle, 'St Cadroe in Scotland', *Innes Review*, 31 (1980), pp. 3–6: for text see Skene (ed.), *Chronicles of the Picts, Chronicles of the Scots*, pp. 106–16, at 108–9, taken from *Acta Sanctorum Veteris et Majoris Scotiæ seu Hiberniæ*, ed. J. Colgan (Louvain, 1645), pp. 494–507). See comments by John and Winifred MacQueen, *Scotichronicon*, i, pp. xix–xx.

and Grey also appears in Andrew of Wyntoun's *Original Chronicle*, written and twice rewritten during the first quarter of the fifteenth century.[47] There are, therefore, three independent witnesses of a lost account, which makes it possible, by analysing more closely their relationship to each other, to examine how this account may have been developed. It emerges that Grey's represents a version which has endeavoured to improve on the original account. It may be recalled that Grey's exemplar combined the origin-legend with a king-list, enabling it to be dated to King John's reign (1292–1304). It can be shown that Wyntoun also used an earlier version of this combined origin-legend and king-list text, and that Fordun (or, rather, his source) probably did likewise. This means that the text which brought together the accounts of Scottish origins from hagiographical works on a St Brendan and a St Congal probably also included a copy of the Scottish king-list. This list belonged to Marjorie Anderson's X group, whose archetype she dated to the reign of Alexander II (1214–49).[48] Returning to what I dubbed the 'Éber' and 'Partholón' accounts, the former can be identified as yet another rewriting of the source shared by Fordun, Grey and Wyntoun. The 'Partholón' account, however, stands outside this tradition. Its chief sources can be identified as *Historia Brittonum* (not necessarily directly) and Geoffrey of Monmouth's *Historia Regum Britannie*. Its author has not followed these slavishly, however, and has (for instance) removed material from Geoffrey of Monmouth which was designed to show that Ireland came under the authority of the king of Britain. It may be only the beginning of a much more extensive work, identified in other parts of *Chronica Gentis Scottorum* by John and Winifred MacQueen, in which Geoffrey's material has been modified to give a pro-Scottish slant.[49]

In Figure 7.1, then, we have three accounts of Scottish origins (denoted in bold) which can be shown to have refashioned their sources in some way. All can be traced to some time either during or after the

[47] See Brown, 'Scottish origin-legend', pp. 139–83. The first and third editions have been edited in *The Original Chronicle of Andrew of Wyntoun*, ed. F. J. Amours, 6 vols., STS (Edinburgh, 1903–14); the second edition in *Androw of Wyntoun's The Orygynale Cronykil of Scotland*, ed. D Laing, Historians of Scotland, 3 vols. (Edinburgh, 1872–9). In Amours' edition the account of Scottish origins under discussion is in vol. ii, bk. II, ll.631–768 and bk. III, ll.1039–88.
[48] Anderson, *Kings and Kingship*, pp. 53–67, esp. pp. 63–4, and pp. 212–15.
[49] *Scotichronicon*, i, xxviii–xxix. The MacQueens suggest (at p. 378) that *tribuni* (at p. 250) could suggest a date later than 1347 for this source because the title was uniquely applied to Cola di Rienzo, tribune of the Roman people, 1347–54. The term can be found earlier, however, used for instance by Orderic Vitalis: he says of Edward, the victorious commander of David I's forces at the battle of Stracathro (1130), 'sub Eduardo rege tribunus Merciorum fuit', Orderic Vitalis, *The Ecclesiastical History*, iv, pp. 276–7.

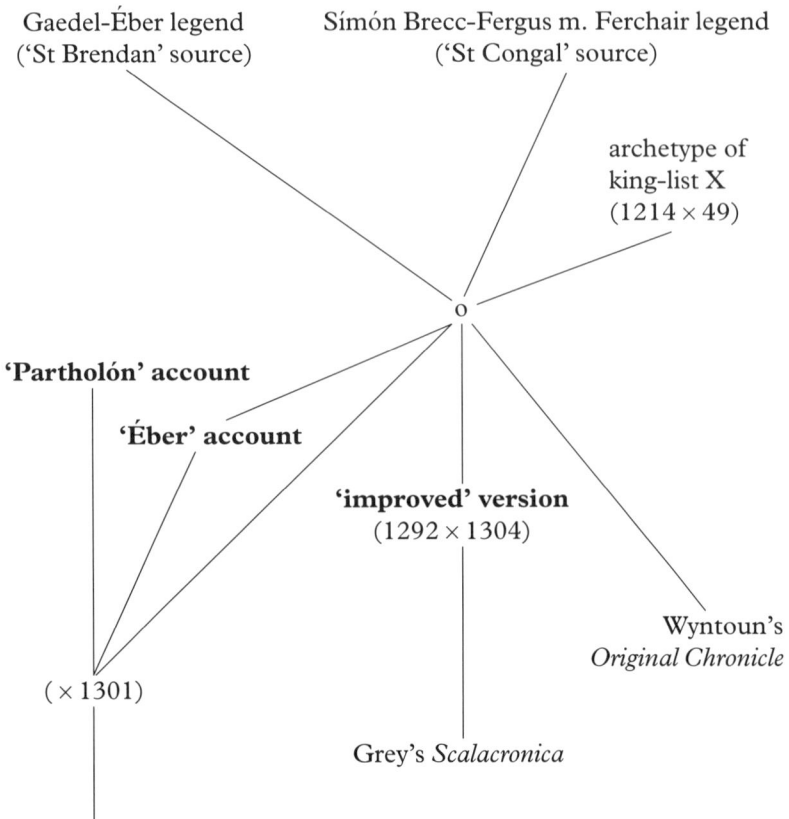

Fig. 7.1 Lost accounts of Scottish origins traceable in Fordun's *Chronica Gentis Scottorum*, Grey's *Scalacronica* and Wyntoun's *Original Chronicle*

period of Anglo-French acculturation. There is the improved version which Grey translated, which may be dated to some time between 1292 and 1304; the 'Éber' account, which is likely to be earlier than 1301 and significantly later than 1214; and the 'Partholón' account which is certainly no earlier than 1136 and likely to be no later than 1301. None of these is likely to have been composed by a Gaelic man of letters.[50] A

[50] In Brown, 'Scottish origin-legend', pp. 76–7, I argued that the *ollam ríg* may have brought the accounts together in *Chronica Gentis Scottorum*. I now think this is unlikely. The prologue to the Book of Coupar version of Bower's *Scotichronicon* (no earlier than 1440s) described Fordun as touring Ireland and England in his hunt for material (*CGS*, pp. xlix–l). There is nothing to suggest that he ever made contact with a Gaelic *literatus*.

striking feature of all these accounts is that, although they share some, if not many elements with Irish accounts of Irish origins, they are entirely ignorant of *Lebor Gabála Érenn*, the 'Book of the Taking of Ireland', which dominated this aspect of Irish historiography from the second half of the eleventh century.[51] It might legitimately be expected, given the close cultural ties among men of letters throughout the Gaelic world, that any Scottish *judex* or cleric, poet or *fer léginn* who still read Gaelic would have betrayed some familiarity with contemporary Irish origin-legend material.[52] The source-base for all but the 'Partholón' account appears to have been limited solely to material drawn initially from two hagiographical works. If these were not written in Latin, the text which first brought the two accounts together certainly was. The 'Partholón' account itself, of course, used no material of recent Gaelic vintage.

What makes these Scottish accounts of the thirteenth century (or earlier) particularly significant is what they all have to say about Ireland.[53] Not only is the link maintained between Ireland and the Scots, but in two of them it has been given renewed emphasis. This is most obvious in the case of the 'Éber' account. Because its source can be reconstructed from three independent witnesses, it is possible to identify where its author has been most innovative. The most important innovation is the notion that every nation had a divinely designated virgin territory as its homeland. The account's narrative was organized around this idea, so this can not plausibly be regarded as a later interpolation. According to the 'Éber' account, the divinely ordained homeland of *Scoti* was not Scotland, but Ireland. Another example of a fresh emphasis on Ireland as the homeland of *Scoti* is provided by the Partholón account. Its central theme was the wretched plight of *Scoti* in their search for somewhere where they could settle and be free. Its climax comes when Partholón leads the *Scoti* to 'perpetual settlements in freedom':[54] these 'perpetual settlements' were not in Scotland, but Ireland. Again, this seems to be too important a part of the plot to be a later addition. As for the 'improved version' of 1292 × 1304 translated by Grey, it may have included a declaration that Fergus mac Ferchair

---

[51] Brown, 'Scottish origin-legend', 73–5. The St Brendan and St Congal hagiographic sources were probably written by literate Gaels, but it is impossible to say when. There is a formal possibility that they were actually written in Gaelic, which would mean that whoever compiled the source shared by *Chronica Gentis Scottorum*, Grey and Wyntoun would have been literate in Gaelic. This remains open to doubt for the same reason as the other texts are unlikely to be the work of literate Gaels: there is no sign of any knowledge of *Lebor Gabála* itself.
[52] See now Carey, *The Irish National Origin-Legend*, pp. 17–24.
[53] Brown, 'Scottish origin-legend', 397–9.   [54] 'perpetuas cum libertate mansiones'.

(first king in its succession of Scottish kings) 'was entirely of the nation of Ireland';[55] the status of this passage as an original feature of Grey's source is not beyond doubt, however.

Susan Reynolds has perceptively observed that accounts of a people's origins such as these were 'myths not only in the popular sense that they were not based on real evidence ... but in a more profound sense that they were developed to explain the present and promote its values'.[56] What aspect of the 'present' in thirteenth-century Scotland and its values could such accounts of Scottish origins have been deemed to explain? A proper answer would require a fuller consideration of this material than can be attempted on this occasion.[57] One feature, however, seems clear: the conclusion of the primeval exodus of *Scoti* was deemed to be their arrival in Ireland. Ireland, not Scotland, was apparently the place identified at that time as the homeland of *Scoti*.[58] Scotland in this scheme was regarded unambiguously as an Irish colony, its current inhabitants as simply an offshoot of *Scoti* from their Irish homeland. This may appear particularly perplexing to the modern reader who is used to thinking of the Scots and Irish as separate peoples. It is not a case, however, of one people identifying with the homeland of another which they had conquered (as, for instance, the English identified with Britain).[59] It was evidently a sense of being one people with the Irish, the same sense that allowed Robert I to refer to *nostra nacio*, 'our nation', when he made his famous address to Irish kings in 1306/7.[60] It may be premature to draw hard-and-fast conclusions about this without a proper consideration of the function(s) of this sense of Irishness in the context of the thirteenth-century Scottish kingdom. It does, however, have the potential to be recognized as a (perhaps fading) reflection of the Gaelic world which stretched from Munster to Moray.[61] These accounts composed by non-Gaelic *literati* could therefore be a potent example of continuity with their Gaelic predecessors, pointing to the

---

[55] 'tout estoit il du nacioun de Ireland'.
[56] Reynolds, 'Medieval *origines gentium*', p. 380.
[57] It will be tackled more fully in Broun, *The Irish Identity of the Kingdom of the Scots*, where I will argue that Irish identity served to endow the Scottish kingship with the lustre of antiquity: in a nutshell, being Irish conferred legitimacy.
[58] Some accounts, indeed, went on to say that Ireland was named *Scotia*, further emphasizing its role as homeland of *Scoti*.
[59] Neither is it a case of two kingdoms/peoples sharing a supposed common descent; that occurred later once Scottish *literati* refashioned the legend to portray Scotland as the homeland of *Scoti*.
[60] See n. 4 for reference.
[61] A new development by the end of the thirteenth century was the construction of an ancient history for the Scottish kingdom, which may have had the effect of reducing the emphasis on an appeal to Irish origins for the kingdom's lustre of antiquity. This will be discussed further in Broun, *The Irish Identity of the Kingdom of the Scots*.

continuing validity of the Irish element in how Scottish men of letters defined Scottishness.

It is important to emphasize that these accounts were not created simply by repeating old doctrine unthinkingly. Each has involved refashioning the legend in some way. Had there been a desire to alter the same legend in order to present a different view, and portray Scotland itself as the homeland of the Scots, then presumably the legend would have been remodelled in these accounts in order to express this: there are accounts in the early fourteenth century in which such a recasting indeed occurred.[62] Moreover, the non-Gaelic-literate authors who quite deliberately portrayed Ireland as the Scottish homeland did not do so as an idle antiquarian fancy. These accounts, after all, were concerned to justify Scottish claims to freedom and/or provide an anchor for the ancient succession of Scottish kings.[63] One way in which this identification with Ireland could have endured despite the loss of Gaelic itself was that the royal genealogy, from which the kingship gained its lustre of antiquity, was studded with legendary Irish figures who each stood at key points in the matrix of power and prestige portrayed in Gaelic high culture.[64] It is impossible to be sure, however, about how generally their vision of Ireland as the homeland of the Scots was shared even in the east midlands. A possible indication of some controversy can be traced in a potpourri of extracts from Isidore written sometime between 1202 and 1214 in what was probably a second rank ecclesiastical establishment in the east midlands.[65] Its author, who added only a few of his own

[62] The Declaration of Arbroath has already been mentioned as omitting Ireland altogether (see p. 136 above). Another example is the material drafted by the Scottish procurators at the Curia in 1301 (discussed in Brown, 'Scottish origin-legend', pp. 231–7). The final text of their Pleading recounted how Scota, eponym of *Scotia*, journeyed from Egypt to Scotland with a large force, recruiting some reinforcements in Ireland on the way. Bringing Scota herself to Scotland clearly signals that Scotland was regarded as the homeland, while Ireland is presented as not much more than a staging-post. Making Scotland Scota's destination was a new idea: Scota and Gaedel are described taking the stone of Scone to Scotland in an Anglo-French song not earlier than 1296 (D. Legge, 'La piere d'Escoce', *SHR*, 38 (1959), pp. 109–13: see also Brown, 'Scottish origin-legend', pp. 225–37).

[63] There was no shortage of occasions, even before the disastrous decade of the 1290s, which might have provoked justifications of the king of Scots' sovereignty (for instance, attempts to acquire the right to coronation and anointment made in 1221, 1233, 1251 and 1259, which floundered against objections by the king of England or the archbishop of York who claimed that this would infringe their rights over Scotland: see Duncan, *Scotland: the Making of the Kingdom*, pp. 554, 559, 576).

[64] See Broun, 'Birth of Scottish history'.

[65] Edited in Anderson, *Kings and Kingship*, pp. 243–5; discussed in M. Miller, 'Matriliny by treaty: the Pictish foundation-legend', in *Ireland in Medieval Europe*, ed. D. Whitelock, R. McKitterick and D. Dumville (Cambridge, 1982), pp. 133–61, at pp. 138–42. She suggests Scone as a possible provenance. See also D. Broun, 'The seven kingdoms in *De situ Albanie*: a record of Pictish political geography or imaginary

words to Isidore, grumbled that '*Scoti* are now wrongly called *Hibernienses*'; unfortunately it is difficult to determine in this case whether *Scoti* as Gaels or *Scoti* as inhabitants of *Scotia* was at issue.[66] There were also, of course, other ways of presenting the kingdom's past which addressed different aspects of its identity: it was possible, for instance, to focus on the reigning dynasty by tracing their history from the family's beginnings with St Margaret (d. 1093) and Máel Coluim Cenn Mór (1058–93) and even to take St Margaret's English royal ancestors as a line of descent with which kings of Scots could (and should) identify.[67]

What these accounts of Scottish origins illustrate, however, is what appears in the thirteenth century to have been the current detailed explanation of who *Scoti* were – presumably intended as an exposition of the kingdom's identity as *regnum Scottorum*. It is possible, however, that the view of Scottish identity in these accounts was the only one articulated as an origin-legend, and that any divergent opinion remained comparatively incoherent. Indeed, the attempts during the wars of independence to find an origin-legend of the Scots as a nation in their own right show every sign of refashioning origin-legend (and king-list) material afresh, rather than simply copying, summarizing or polishing up texts which had already achieved this objective.[68] These accounts, therefore, point to the existence of a sustained and articulate current of acculturized opinion in which the Irish element in how the kingdom and its people were perceived was apparently unaffected by the devastating stereotype of the Irish (and Gaels in general) as uncivilized barbarians. This has implications for the more general question of whether the Gaelic identity of acculturized aristocratic *Scoti* – and indeed the Gaelic import of the kingdom's identity as *regnum Scottorum* – was ever seriously threatened. Rather than supposing that the acculturization of the native Gaelic élite (including presumably the king himself) – particularly in the east midlands – involved the determined rejection of 'old' for 'new', this adds weight to other indications that there was a *modus vivendi*, a cultural and social accommodation, between Anglo-French and Gaelic.[69]

map of ancient Alba?', in *Alba: Celtic Scotland*, ed. E. J. Cowan and R. A. McDonald (East Linton, forthcoming).

[66] The situation is made worse by the scholar's own lack of consistency: *Scotia*, for instance, is found referring to Scotland north of the Forth, Scotland north of the Forth but east of Argyll, and as an alternative name for Ireland.

[67] Particularly influential was Aelred's *Genealogia Regum Anglorum* in *MPL*, 195 (Paris, 1855), cols. 711–38, which was used, for instance, by Adam of Dryburgh in his *De Tripartito Tabernaculo* (*MPL*, 198, cols. 609–792, at 722–3). See Broun, 'Birth of Scottish history'.

[68] See Broun, 'Birth of Scottish history'.

[69] This formulation is indebted to Davies, *Domination and Conquest*, p. 62. See also Broun, 'Gaelic literacy in eastern Scotland'.

There may, of course, have been a distinction drawn by the acculturized élite between themselves as 'civilized Gaels' as opposed to those who were unacculturized. The acquisition of Anglo-French culture and *mores* may have been seen by those who sought membership of élite international society as a necessary addition to Gaelic culture without this implying any active desire to displace their Gaelic heritage. This would be different from regarding native Scots as inherently barbarous, in which case Anglo-French acculturation would be seen as the defeat and rejection of native culture. As noted already, English *literati* were accustomed to regard their Celtic neighbours as savages: to be 'civilized' meant becoming English or French and turning away from the Celtic. It should not be surprising, therefore, that an English commentator saw the distinction between acculturized and unacculturized Gaels in Scotland in terms of those (like the king) who he imagined regarded themselves as racially French, and those who remained 'Scottish' (whom he viewed as reduced to servitude, no doubt because he could not conceive of them as members of the kingdom's élite).[70] This racial frame of reference was particularly stark in Ireland where those who belonged to Anglo-French society were treated as 'English' and those who were 'Irish' were excluded.[71] As already observed, however, in Scotland there was no attempt to draw a legal distinction between the acculturized and unacculturized.[72] Gaelic culture, instead of being spurned, could retain a presence among the élite (which it seems to have done until the mid thirteenth century).[73] Gaelic's eventual decline in the east may therefore have had other, more immediate, causes than acculturation itself.

The relationship between acculturation and Gaelic identity which evolved in eastern Scotland may therefore serve as yet another example of the 'balance of old and new' which scholars have drawn attention to in many other areas of Scottish society in this period.[74] What is especially striking, however, is the continuing identification with Ireland by Scottish men of letters as late as the thirteenth century despite the decline of Gaelic – testimony to the presence of the Gaelic world as a feature of the history of Britain and Ireland in the period 900–1300. When a new sense of the Scots as a nation in their own right was articulated during the struggle for independence against Edward I this marked a crucial change in the perception of interrelationships within Britain and Ireland, a change which signified the beginning of the modern configuration of four national identities.

---

[70] See p. 141 above.   [71] Bartlett, *Making of Europe*, pp. 214–17.
[72] See p.137 above.   [73] See pp. 138–40 above.
[74] The phrase is Geoffrey Barrow's, in the title of his Stenton lecture *David I: the Balance of Old and New*.

8 John de Courcy, the first Ulster plantation and Irish church men

Marie Therese Flanagan

In an important article Seán Duffy highlighted that John de Courcy, although traditionally described as having hailed from Somerset, in fact had important connections with the north of England, more particularly Cumbria, via his maternal relatives, and that he drew many of the tenants for his lordship of Ulster from that region rather than from Somerest. The filiations of the religious houses which he founded in Ulster similarly reflected a Cumbrian connection.[1] John de Courcy shared with Richard fitz Gilbert, earl/lord of Pembroke/Strigoil, alias Strongbow, and with Hugh de Lacy the distinction of having succeeded to a virtually intact pre-Norman Irish lordship: just as Strongbow succeeded to the lordship of Leinster, and Hugh de Lacy to that of Mide, so John de Courcy acquired the Dál Fiatach kingship of Ulaid.[2] What distinguished de Courcy from either Strongbow or Hugh de Lacy, however, was his status prior to his intervention in Ireland, for, unlike either of these men, John de Courcy, whom Giraldus described as 'pauperum et mendicum',[3] was not a tenant-in-chief of the English crown. That distinction had a bearing on the creation, the settlement, and ultimately, also, his loss of the lordship of Ulster.

Just how limited de Courcy's resources were before his intervention in Ireland is reflected in the fact that historians have failed to identify landholdings of de Courcy in England beyond a modest manorial estate in Middleton Cheney in Northamptonshire, which came to him via his maternal relatives. In his dower charter in favour of his wife, Affrica, daughter of Godred II (Olafsson), king of Man, drawn up on the

---

I wish to thank Dr Nollaig Ó Muraile, Department of Celtic, the Queen's University of Belfast, for his very helpful comments on this chapter.

[1] Duffy, 'The first Ulster plantation', pp. 1–28.
[2] In contrast with the pattern of grants to Anglo-Normans in the pre-Norman kingdoms of Desmond (Cork), Thomond (Limerick), Airgialla, or Connacht, which were not granted as unitary lordships. On the signification of Ulaid see D. Flanagan, 'Transferred population or sept-names: Ulaid (*a quo* Ulster)', *Bulletin of the Ulster Place Name Society*, series 2, 1 (1978), pp. 40–3.
[3] Giraldus, *Expugnatio*, pp. 176–7.

occasion of their marriage, John de Courcy granted her 'totam terram meam quam habeo in Middiltun cum omnibus pertinentiis suis'.[4] This indicates that Middleton Cheney was a demesne estate of John de Courcy, since only land held in demesne could be granted as dower. In fact, this solitary English grant to Affrica suggests that it was the only demesne estate which de Courcy held in England, and, while there is no precise indication of its size, such evidence as there is suggests that it was not of great extent. From his Middleton Cheney estate de Courcy made a grant of 1 virgate of land to the Augustinian house of Canons Ashby in Northamptonshire.[5] It was this grant which determined the fortuitous transcription of Affrica's dower charter into the Canons Ashby cartulary, as pertinent to de Courcy's Canons Ashby grant. Another charter relating to de Courcy's Middleton Cheney estate, transcribed into Sir Christopher Hatton's book of seals, recorded a grant to one Robert Bruton and his heirs of 2 virgates of land in the fields of Middleton Cheney to be held for an annual rent of 12 d. payable to John de Courcy and his heirs at Easter.[6] Notable, again, is the small amount both of the land grant and of the income deriving from it. When relations between de Courcy and the crown deteriorated in 1201, and his Middleton Cheney estate was sequestrated, it was yielding an annual income of £8.[7] John de Courcy was not a man of substantial property and, while Duffy has effectively demonstrated that he drew the greater number of his Ulster tenants from his Cumbrian connections, it remains the case also that none of them were major magnates and that the majority did not hold extensive landed estates in England or elsewhere in Henry II's dominions. De Courcy, then, was

---

[4] A. J. Otway-Ruthven, 'Dower charter of John de Courcy's wife', *Ulster Journal of Archaeology*, 3rd series, 12 (1949), pp. 77–81; E. Curtis, 'Two unpublished charters of John de Courcy, *princeps Ulidiae*', *Belfast Natural History and Philosophical Society Proceedings* (1928), pp. 2–10.

[5] At the dissolution the priory possessed a rent of 13s 4d from land in Myddleton Chaynay: W. Dugdale, *Monasticon Anglicanum*, ed. J. Caley, H. Ellis, and B. Bandinel, 6 vols. in 8 (London, 1817–30; repr., 6 vols., 1846), vi, I, p. 444.

[6] *Sir Christopher Hatton's Book of Seals*, eds. L. C. Loyd and D. M. Stenton, Northamptonshire Record Society, 15 (1950), no. 364, p. 250. A virgate was equivalent to a $\frac{1}{4}$ carucate, i.e. between 20 and 30 acres: R. E. Latham, *Revised Medieval Latin Word-list from British and Irish Sources* (London, 1965), p. 514. The name Bruton does not occur either as tenant of de Courcy in Ulaid or as a witness to his charters.

[7] *Pipe Roll 1201: The Great Roll of the Pipe for the Third Year of the Reign of King John*, ed. D. M. Stenton, PRS, new series, 14 (London, 1936), p. 187; *Pipe Roll 1202: The Great Roll of the Pipe for the Fourth Year of the Reign of King John*, ed. D. M. Stenton, PRS, new series 15 (London, 1937), p. 152; *Pipe Roll 1203: The Great Roll of the Pipe for the Fifth Year of the Reign of King John*, ed. D. M. Stenton, PRS, new series, 16 (London, 1938), p. 186. On 22 May 1205 the sheriff of Northampton was directed to put Warin fitz Gerold in seisin of the manor of Middleton which Warin had by the king's precept delivered to John de Courcy 'ad se sustenandum': *RLC*, i, p. 33b.

not in a position to draw on significant resources, or indeed tenants who were themselves substantial landholders in England, for the creation of his Anglo-Norman lordship of Ulaid, such as were available to Strongbow and Hugh de Lacy in setting up their respective lordships in Leinster and Mide.

De Courcy offset this deficiency by adopting a policy of active cooperation with a number of Irish churchmen and by using monastic foundations as a colonizing agency: he introduced six new monastic communities with English filiations into Ulaid.[8] It is noteworthy that although, in general, Giraldus criticized the Anglo-Norman colonists in Ireland for their lack of generosity to the church, this was not a failing which he attributed to de Courcy, whom he described as giving 'the church of Christ that honour which was its due'.[9] De Courcy enjoyed a notably cooperative relationship with Echmilid, bishop of Down (c. 1176–1202), who adopted the latinized name Malachias, hereafter referred to as Malachy III. Malachy III had succeeded to the bishopric of Down about 1176, that is shortly before de Courcy's incursion into Ulaid. He was taken captive by de Courcy at the storming of Downpatrick in early 1177,[10] but was released almost immediately. This violent introduction does not seem to have had any permanently adverse effects on the subsequent close collaboration between the two men. There is a concentration of de Courcy's ecclesiastical benefactions in the vicinity of the cathedral city of Downpatrick and these, in particular, must have required the consent and cooperation of Bishop Malachy III. An original letter issued by him is still extant, granting an indulgence to persons willing to make benefactions to de Courcy's Cistercian foundation ('ad abbatiam construendam') at Inch.[11]

Why Bishop Malachy III proved so willing to cooperate with John de Courcy may be more readily understood by taking account of the history of his episcopal see in the immediate pre-Norman period. Down-

---

[8] Duffy, 'The first Ulster plantation', pp. 5–10. A seventh foundation, that of the Hospital of St John the Baptist, Downpatrick, probably originated from the Hospital of St John the Baptist, Dublin: *ibid.* For the suggestion that there was an unusually high proportion of church lands relative to secular settlement in this area in the pre-Norman period see F. McCormick, 'Farming and food in medieval Lecale', *Down: History and Society*, ed. L. Proudfoot (Dublin, 1997), pp. 33–46.

[9] Giraldus, *Expugnatio*, pp. 180–1.

[10] Roger of Howden, *Gesta Regis Henrici Secundi Benedicti Abbatis*, ed. W. Stubbs, 2 vols., RS (London, 1867), i, p. 138; Roger of Howden, *Chronica*, ii, p. 120. Giraldus made no mention of his capture. *Misc. Ir Annals*, s.a. 1178 recorded the capture of the archbishop of Armagh, but not the bishop of Down.

[11] PRO, DL1 25/L219 edited in H. G. Richardson, 'Some Norman monastic foundations in Ireland', in *Medieval Studies presented to Aubrey Gwynn, S.J.*, ed. J. A. Watt, J. B. Morrall and F. X. Martin (Dublin, 1961), pp. 29–43 with plate. The letter passed from Furness at the Dissolution to the Duchy of Lancaster.

patrick was the secular *caput* of the Mac Duinn Sléibe kings of Ulaid in the twelfth century.[12] But it was also an ecclesiastical site in continuous use from at least the eighth century onwards.[13] The Synod of Ráith Bressail, 1111, which sought to establish a nationwide territorially delimited diocesan structure for the Irish church, had designated two episcopal sees within the kingdom of Ulaid, Downpatrick and Connor,[14] reflecting the political sub-division within Ulaid between the Dál Fiatach and Dál nAraide spheres of influence. The history of the churches of Connor and Downpatrick in the immediate post-Ráith Bressail period is obscure. Flann ua Sculu, styled bishop of Connere, and Máel Muire, styled bishop of Dún dá Lethglas, are each recorded to have died in 1117.[15] Whether these men had been elevated to episcopal orders following the deliberations of the Synod of Ráith Bressail, or were already bishops by 1111, is not certain,[16] but following their chronologically coincident deaths in 1117 the territorial designation 'bishop of Ulaid' replaces description by episcopal see or cathedral church. Despite the fact that the Synod of Ráith Bressail had envisaged two episcopal sees within the kingdom of Ulaid, there appears to have been only one reformed episcopal pastorate after 1117. The first recorded

[12] So described in Roger of Howden's *Gesta*, i, pp. 137, 138 and *Chronica*, ii, p. 120, and supported by annalistic entries. In 1170 Magnus Mac Duinn Sléibe, king of Ulaid, was slain by his brother in Downpatrick: *AU*, *ALC*, *AFM* Cf. earlier killings of kings of Ulaid at Downpatrick in 1007 and 1081: *CS*, *s.a.*1005 = 1007, *AFM*, *s.a.*1005 = 1117, *AU*, *s.a.* 1007, *AU*, *s.a.*1081, *AI*, *s.a.*1081, *ALC*, *s.a.* 1081. The [peaceful] death of Cú Ulad Mac Duinn Sléibe, king of Ulaid, at Downpatrick is recorded in 1157: *AT*, *AFM*. The formation of two distinct name-compositions, Dún Lethglaise and Dún dá Lethglas, has been interpreted as signifying the development of both an ecclesiastical and a secular settlement at the same location with precedence gained by the primarily civic name during the course of the eleventh century: D. Flanagan, 'The names of Downpatrick', *Dinnseanchas* 4 (1971), pp. 89–112. The distinction between the ecclesiastical enclosure and the secular settlement is suggested also by the annalistic entry which records – that lightning burnt Dún dá Lethglas in 1111 'both *ráith* and *trían*': *AU*, *s.a.* 1111; *ALC*, *AFM*. For the identification of the so-called English Mount at Downpatrick as the secular centre of the Dál Fiatach kings of Ulaid see J. P. Mallory and T. E. McNeill, *The Archaeology of Ulster from Colonization to Plantation* (1991), pp. 240–1.
[13] Cf. *AU*, *s.a.* 780 which records the death of an abbot of Downpatrick. An ecclesiastical site in the seventh century may be presumed from Muirchú's Life of Patrick which locates Patrick's burial at Downpatrick: *The Patrician Texts in the Book of Armagh*, ed. L. Bieler (Dublin, 1979), pp. 120–1. The death of Fergus, bishop of Druim Lethglaisse, is recorded in *AU*, *s.a.* 584, *CS*, *AT*, *AFM* all *s.a.* 583 = 584.
[14] Geoffrey Keating, *The History of Ireland*, iii, p. 303. I have followed the emendation proposed by J. Mac Erlean, 'Synod of Ráith Bresail: boundaries of the dioceses of Ireland', *Archivium Hibernicum*, 3 (1914), pp. 1–33 at p. 21. Cf. A. Gwynn, *The Irish Church in the Eleventh and Twelfth Centuries* (Dublin, 1992), pp. 187, 203–4.
[15] *AU*, *s.a.* 1117.
[16] Bishops of Downpatrick and of Connor are recorded in the annals before 1111: For Downpatrick cf. *AU*, *s.a.* 956; *AFM*, *s.a.* 954 = 956; *CS*, *s.a.* 1041; *AFM*, *s.a.* 1043; for Connor cf. *AU*, *s.a.* 659, 726.

'bishop of Ulaid' in the post Ráith Bressail period was Óengus Ua Gormáin, abbot of Bangor, who died on pilgrimage in Lismore in 1123. It is not known whether his episcopal see was located at Connor or Downpatrick; he may, in fact, have remained resident at the monastery of Bangor of which he was abbot.[17] His death at Lismore suggests contacts with the church reform movement, for Lismore can be identified as a reform centre by the early twelfth century.

The next recorded bishop in Ulaid was to be the prominent reformer, Máel Máedóc Ua Morgair, who adopted the Latin name Malachias, hereafter referred to as Malachy I. Bernard of Clairvaux in his Life of Malachy I depicted him inaugurating his public career as an ecclesiastical reformer at the monastery of Bangor by acquiring the actual site of the conventual buildings from his uncle, a 'rich and powerful man who owned Bangor and its holdings'. Malachy I proceeded to build a new wooden church on the site, but the extensive land holdings of the monastery remained under the control of another who continued to bear the title of abbot 'preserving in name, but not in fact, that which had once been'.[18] Bernard's rather cryptic account indicates just how difficult it may have been for reform minded clerics intent on restoring conventual life to recover appropriated church lands. The initial arrangement proved unsatisfactory 'for he to whom Malachy had yielded the possessions of the monastery of Bangor, was not grateful for that benefice, and, from that time on, behaved most arrogantly towards him and his disciples, being troublesome to them in all things, plotting everywhere and disparaging his deeds'.

Eventually, the possessions of Bangor 'reverted peaceably to the place where they belonged', but not before the son of the possessor had died as a result of opposing Malachy I in the construction of a new church and the man himself had complained of Malachy 'coram duce et maioribus Ulidiae', in divine punishment for which he was possessed of a demon from whom, however, Malachy magnanimously chose to rid him.[19]

Having set about reestablishing conventual life at Bangor, Malachy I

[17] *AU*, s.a.1123 and *AFM* record 'the death of Óengus ua Gormáin, successor of Comgall, on pilgrimage at Lismore'; *AI*, s.a. 1123 simply records the death of 'the Ulidian bishop' at Lismore. *NHI*, ix, p. 280, lists him as bishop of Down. See *AU*, s.a. 1175 for the death notice of Malachias II styled 'bishop of Ulaid' and compare his attestation as 'bishop of Ulaid' in Muirchertach Mac Lochlainn's charter of 1157 to Newry Abbey: Dugdale, *Monasticon Anglicanum*, vi, II, p. 1133; *AU*, *ALC*, *AFM*, all s.a. 1174 for use of the term 'bishop of Connor and Dál nAraide'.
[18] *Sancti Bernardi Opera*, ed. J. Leclercq, C. H. Talbot and H. M. Rochais (Rome, 1957–), iii (1963), pp. 321–4; Bernard of Clairvaux, *The Life and Death of St Malachy the Irishman*, ed. R. Meyer (Kalamazoo, 1978), pp. 30–1.
[19] Leclercq, *et al.* (eds.), *Sancti Bernardi Opera*, iii, pp. 365–6; Bernard of Clairvaux, *Life and Death of Malachy*, pp. 77–9.

was then elevated to episcopal status. According to Bernard he was consecrated bishop for the *civitas* of Connor 'which was then vacant and had been so for a long time'. Bernard implied that Malachy I took up residence at Connor, although he did not explicitly say so; then, after a few years, an unnamed king of the northern part of Ireland destroyed the *civitas* and Malachy was forced into exile in the Munster kingdom of Cormac Mac Carthaig.[20] On 1 April 1129 Cellach, archbishop of Armagh, died having 'made a sort of last testament with the provision that Malachy should succeed him'.[21] However, the intention that Malachy I should succeed Cellach at Armagh met with strong opposition from the secularized and hereditarily entrenched clerical family of Uí Sínaich: Malachy was not consecrated until 1132 and it was not until 1134 that he succeeded in taking control of the insignia of office and the temporalities of the see.[22] In 1136 he resigned the see of Armagh and consecrated in his stead Gilla Meic Liac (latinized Gelasius), abbot of the important Columban church of Derry for the previous sixteen years. This was clearly a compromise strategy designed to secure support from the northern Uí Néill king, Muirchertach Mac Lochlainn, newly succeeded to the kingship of Cenél nEógain in 1136: the Mac Lochlainn power base was at Derry and Gilla Meic Liac might be expected to enjoy the support of Muirchertach. According to Bernard, Malachy

> then went back to his own diocese, but not to Connor. Listen to his reason, which is worth mentioning here: that diocese is said to have had two episcopal sees from very early times and therefore to contain two bishoprics. This seemed better to Malachy. He re-divided those two sees which ambition had welded into one, by giving the one to another bishop and keeping the other for himself. This was why he did not come to Connor, because he had already ordained a bishop there. But he took himself to Down, settling the diocesan bounds as in the old days. Oh pure heart! Oh dove-like eyes! He handed over to a new bishop the place which seemed to be better provided and more prestigious, the place in which he himself had been enthroned.[23]

Bernard does not name Malachy's see again. It is therefore uncertain whether Malachy I actually succeeded in installing himself at Downpatrick, or whether, as is possible, he may have chosen, or been obliged, to return to Bangor. Noteworthy, however, is Bernard's remark that the see of Down was not well endowed.

[20] Under his protection, Malachy built the monastery of 'Ibracense'; its precise location remains unknown: Gwynn and Hadcock, *Medieval Religious Houses: Ireland*, p. 365.
[21] Leclercq *et al.* (eds.), *Sancti Bernardi Opera*, pp. 325–29; Bernard of Clairvaux, *Life and Death*, pp. 33–7.
[22] *AT, Misc. Ir. Annals, AFM,* all *s.a.* 1134.
[23] Leclercq *et al.* (eds.), *Sancti Bernardi Opera*, iii, pp. 338–9; Bernard of Clairvaux, *Life and Death of Malachy*, p. 47. The identity of this bishop of Connor is unknown: *NHI*, ix, p. 277.

Sometime after Malachy's death on 2 November 1148, and certainly before the synod of Kells, 1152, he was succeeded by Máel Ísu mac in Cléirig Chuirr, who likewise adopted the Latin name Malachias, hereafter referred to as Malachy II.[24] It is not known where Malachy II chose to reside as bishop since in the Irish annals he is invariably described territorially as 'bishop of Ulaid'. It is possible that he may not have been able to take possession of the church at Downpatrick because it was still in the hands of secularized and unreformed clergy. This may be inferred from the charter of Muirchertach Mac Lochlainn, king of Cenél nEógain, and claimant to the high-kingship, issued to the Cistercian abbey of Newry in 1157: Malachy II witnessed as 'bishop of Ulaid' while the witness list also included Gilla Aodar Ua Cathasaig, *airchinnech* of Dún dá Lethglas, that is Downpatrick.[25] Not only his title, which may be translated as 'administrator' or 'land steward', but, even more significantly, his location in the witness list indicates that he was classed as a layman rather than a cleric.[26] The Uí Cathasaig appear to have been hereditarily entrenched at Downpatrick, for a Domnall Ua Cathasaig is recorded as *airchinnech* of Dún in 1068.[27] The surname may derive from Cathasach son of Fergusán who died as *comarba* or head of the church of Dún in 972.[28] In 974 the death of Máel Brígte son of Cathasach, bishop and abbot of Dromore is recorded.[29] Cathasach may have established an ecclesiastical dynasty which sought to control not only the church of Downpatrick, but also that of Dromore. The Uí Cathasaig, however, had rivals at Downpatrick, for the Uí Cairill are found in the office of *airchinnech* there in 988, 1083 and 1102.[30] The Uí Cairill were descended from Cairell, king of Ulaid (810–19), during whose reign existed a strong link between secular and ecclesiastical institutions: Cairell's brother, Loingsech, died as abbot of Dún Lethglaise in 800.[31] It is not unlikely,

---

[24] The earliest secure date for Malachy II is afforded by his presence at the Synod of Kells in March 1152. The presence at Kells is also recorded of Máel Pátraic Ua Bánáin, whose death as 'bishop of Connor and Dál nAraide' is recorded at Iona in 1174: *ALC, AU, AFM*. Máel Pátraic apparently had resigned by 1171–2 when Nehemias, bishop of Connor, is recorded by Roger of Howden as having sworn an oath of loyalty to Henry II: Roger of Howden, *Gesta*, i, p. 26; *Chronica*, ii, p. 30.

[25] Dugdale, *Monasticon Anglicanum*, vi, II, p. 1133.

[26] The laicization of the office of *airchinnech* is also evidenced in the eleventh- and twelfth-century charter material in the *Book of Kells*, where *airchinnig* of the monasteries of Dulane, Donaghpatrick, and Ráth Lugdach are listed among the laity: M. Herbert, 'Charter material from Kells', in *The Book of Kells: Proceedings of a Conference at Trinity College, Dublin, 6–9 September 1992*, ed. F. O'Mahony (Aldershot, 1994), pp. 60–77 at 73.

[27] *AU, AFM, s.a.*1068.   [28] *AU, s.a.* 972.   [29] *AFM, s.a.* 972 = 974.

[30] *AFM, AU, s.a.* 1083, 1102.

[31] *AU, s.a.* 800; Byrne, *Irish Kings and High-Kings*, pp. 119–24; M. E. Dobbs, 'The history of the descendants of Ir', *ZCP*, 14 (1923), pp. 45–144 at 83.

therefore, that both Bishop Malachy I and Bishop Malachy II would have faced opposition from secularized clerical lineages, such as the Uí Cathasaig and the Uí Cairill, in attempting to locate their cathedral church in Downpatrick.

Malachy II died in 1175 and was succeeded as 'bishop of Ulaid' by Gilla Domangairt Mac Cormaic, abbot of Bangor, who died in the same year.[32] Since the annals referred to him by the territorial designation, 'bishop of Ulaid', the location of his cathedral church, once again, remains unknown. Gilla Domangairt, however, was not the only bishop of Ulaid who died in 1175. According to the Annals of Ulster 'The son of the successor (*comarba*) of Finnian, namely Amlaím, abbot of Saul, died in the episcopacy of Ulaid (*i n-escopoiti Uladh*).' The phrase '*i n-escopoiti Uladh*' is noteworthy and contrasts with the description of Gilla Domangairt as 'bishop of Ulaid'; it suggests a disputed episcopal election in 1175 and that the annalist did not recognize the validity of Amlaím. The description of Amlaím as 'son of the successor of Finnian' denotes that his father was, or had been, head of the church of Movilla. Amlaím had also been the subject of an unusually detailed entry in the Annals of Ulster in 1170:

A great unbecoming deed was done by the monk, namely by Amlaím, son of the successor [*comarba*] of Finnian of Movilla, and by Magnus Mac Duinn Sléibe, king of Ulaid, along with the *toísig* of Ulaid and with the men of Ulaid as well, excepting the bishop, Máel Ísu [Malachy II], and Gilla Domangairt Mac Cormaic, successor of Comgall [of Bangor], and Máel Martain, successor of Finnian [of Movilla], with their communities; that is, the congregation [*comtinól*] of canons regular, with their abbot, whom Máel Máedóc Ua Morgair [Malachy I], legate of the successor of Peter, instituted in Saul, were expelled out of the monastery which they themselves had built and were despoiled completely, both of books and furniture, cows and persons, horses and sheep and all things they had collected therein from the time of the aforesaid legate until then, excepting only the tunics and capes which they were wearing at that time. It was through jealousy and lustful love and greed of honour for himself [that he did this]. For the monks of Droichat Átha [Mellifont] deposed him from the abbacy for lawful causes. Alas! alas! alas! Woe to him who did this deed and to the territory in which it was done. But it did not go unavenged by the Lord; for the *toísig* who did it were killed at one and the same time by a few enemies, and the king was unhappily wounded and unhappily died a little while after in the place where that unrighteous counsel (*comairle*) was decided upon, namely in Dún [Downpatrick]. Now it was on a Tuesday that the congregation (*comtinól*) was expelled; on a Tuesday at the end of a year that the nobles (*maithi*) of Ulaid were killed and their king was wounded, and on a Tuesday a little later that he himself was killed by his brother in Dún.[33]

---

[32] *AT, AU, AFM*. His episcopacy was of such short duration that the Latinized version of his name remains unknown.

[33] *AU, ALC* and cf. censored version in *AFM*. Magnus was a son of Cú Ulad Mac Duinn

In 1170 Amlaím, with the support of Magnus Mac Duinn Sléibe, king of Ulaid, obviously had been intruded into the abbacy of Saul and an attempt made to expel the Augustinian canons whom Malachy I had introduced there.[34] Amlaím's opponents, whom it may be presumed presented themselves as supporters of reform, had been Bishop Malachy II, Gilla Domangairt, abbot of Bangor, and Máel Martain, abbot of Movilla. Máel Martain indeed may have been placed in the abbacy of Movilla as a reform candidate at the expense of Amlaím who may have expected to succeed his father in that office. Amlaím can be assumed to be a member of a hereditary ecclesiastical family who sought to seize first the abbacy of Saul in 1170 at the expense of the reform community which had been installed there, and then in 1175 the bishopric of Ulaid. Since, on the evidence of the Annals of Ulster, Amlaím had enjoyed the support of Magnus Mac Duinn Sléibe in his bid to seize the abbacy of Saul in 1170, Amlaím's attempt to take the bishopric of Ulaid in 1175 most likely centred on the church of Downpatrick, which was contiguous to the secular royal residence of the Meic Duinn Sléibe (where Magnus had been assassinated by his brother, Donn Sléibe, in 1171), and also just a few miles from Saul. Downpatrick and Saul were also linked by strong Patrician associations.

The short-lived Bishop Gilla Domangairt was succeeded as bishop of Ulaid around 1176 by Malachy III, who was to become such a close associate of John de Courcy. Since Malachy III was in the city of Downpatrick when it was attacked and captured by de Courcy early in 1177,[35] it may be assumed that the chosen location for his cathedral church was at Downpatrick. Just how much progress his immediate

Sléibe, king of Ulaid (*d.* 1157) of whom it is said in a praise poem on the kings of Ulaid that 'he partook before death of the Lord's Body, he committed no crime, he did not billet troops on churches': F. J. Byrne, 'Clann Ollaman Uaisle Emna', *Studia Hibernica*, 4 (1964), pp. 54–94 at pp 73, 92. Such a laudatory death notice, emphasizing Cú Ulad as a patron of the church, does not accord with his apparent lack of support for Malachy I: below p. 170. In the bitter contest for the kingship which ensued between the five sons of Cú Ulad after his death pro- and anti-reform parties may have been implicated in supporting rival candidates. On Movilla see A. Hamlin, 'The early church in County Down to the twelfth century', in *Down: History and Society*, ed. L. Proudfoot (Dublin, 1997), pp. 47–70 at 49–50.

[34] The annalistic entry may be read in a number of ways. Fr Colmcille, OCSO, *The Story of Mellifont* (Dublin, 1958), pp. 35–6, interpreted Amlaím as having been abbot of the Cistercian house of Mellifont (Co. Louth), which had been founded as a reform house in 1142 under the auspices of Malachy I, and as having been deposed by the monks of Mellifont from the office of abbot at Mellifont rather than Saul, presumably because of a difficulty in explaining why the monks of Mellifont should have been involved in a deposition at Saul. But cf. below p. 165. In his later 'Abbatial succession of Mellifont, 1142–1539', *Co. Louth Archaeological Journal*, 15 (1961–4), pp. 23–8, Fr Colmcille did not list Amlaím as abbot of Mellifont.

[35] Above, note 10.

episcopal predecessors had made in procuring an adequate landed endowment, and how secure Malachy III's control of the temporalities may have been, is another matter; nor is anything known of the circumstances of his election, but this also may have been the subject of a rival challenge. From his death notice, which refers to him as 'Echmilid, son of the *comarba* of Finnian, bishop of Ulaid',[36] it may be inferred that Malachy III was the son of a head of the church of Movilla, conceivably even of Máel Martain who, together with Bishop Malachy II, had sought to prevent the expulsion of the Augustinian canons from Saul in 1170. If this identification is correct, it is only too likely that Malachy III's candidacy may have been opposed by a non-reform grouping.

Malachy III may have had to contend with opposition not only from unreconstructed clergy like the infamous Amlaím, but also within reform circles. In 1244 Pope Innocent IV gave judgement in a case brought by the Augustinian community of Bangor (established by Malachy I), claiming a right against the Benedictine chapter of Downpatrick to elect the bishop of Down.[37] The pope ruled in favour of the Benedictines at Downpatrick, but the origins of Bangor's claim to a right of election may go back as far as the time of Malachy I, and may derive from the circumstance that he had been obliged to reside at Bangor rather than Downpatrick; it may perhaps even have dated back to the episcopate of Malachy's predecessor, Bishop Óengus (d. 1123), who also had been abbot of Bangor.[38] The Bangor community may be presumed to have played a role in securing the election as bishop of Ulaid in 1175 of their abbot, Gilla Domangairt Mac Cormaic, Malachy III's immediate predecessor, although Gilla Domangairt may never have succeeded in taking up residence at Downpatrick, because the infamous Amlaím may have been *in situ* there.[39] It is also conceivable that the Augustinian canons of Bangor may have sought to claim not only a role in episcopal elections, but also that the episcopal see of Ulaid should be located at Bangor.

A desire of Bishop Malachy III to locate his cathedral church at Downpatrick, in accordance with the original intention of the Synod of Ráith Bressail, 1111, and the opposition which he may have faced both from reformed and unreformed clerical circles, as well as inadequacies

---

[36] *ALC, s.a.* 1204.
[37] *Pontificia Hibernica: Medieval Papal Chancery Documents concerning Ireland, 640–1261*, ed. M. P. Sheehy, 2 vols. (Dublin, 1962–5), i, no. 259.
[38] See above p. 158.
[39] In 1212 one Óengus Mac Cormaic succeeded as abbot of Bangor: *AU*. His name lends support to the view that the Bangor community was involved in the election in 1175 of Gilla Domangairt Mac Cormaic.

in the landed endowment and income of his see, provide a context for his endorsement of de Courcy's monastic endowments. John de Courcy may have been instrumental in helping Malachy III to secure the church of Downpatrick as the episcopal church of the bishopric of Down. Certainly, both men collaborated in a policy of enhancing the prestige of the church at Downpatrick by emphasizing its Patrician connections. This may have been motivated, in part, by the recent attempt by the abbot of the Patrician church of Saul to seize the church of Downpatrick, as well as by a possible challenge from the monastery of Bangor to have the episcopal see located there. Giraldus recounted that about 1185–6 the bodies of Patrick, Brigit and Colum Cille were discovered at Downpatrick, and a translation ceremony staged under the auspices of John de Courcy.[40] The liturgical office of the feast of the Translation, which came to be celebrated on 9 June,[41] attributed the discovery of the bodies of the three saints to Bishop Malachy III who undertook a series of night vigils in the cathedral church until the precise spot at which digging should take place was revealed to him. One measure of Malachy III's and de Courcy's success in promoting the Patrician associations of the church of Down is the eventual English name-form, Downpatrick. Although not attested before 1617,[42] its origin stems from a change in the dedication of the cathedral church at Downpatrick from Holy Trinity to Saint Patrick which was effected during the episcopate of Malachy III. John de Courcy's earliest charter relating to the cathedral church of Downpatrick records a confirmation 'episcopo et ecclesia sanctae Trinitatis de Dun'.[43] Subsequent to that charter, however, Bishop Malachy III was associated with a cathedral church dedicated to St Patrick, to which a community of Benedictine monks was attached.[44] Whether this was the church of the Holy Trinity, of which the dedication had been changed, or whether another church dedicated to St Patrick had been constructed, is uncertain.[45]

---

[40] Giraldus, *Expugnatio*, pp. 234–5; O'Meara (ed.), 'Giraldus Cambrensis in *Topographia Hibernie*', p. 165; *Giraldus Cambrensis, Opera*, v, pp. 163–4.

[41] The office, which takes the form of six historical lessons, was first printed by T. Messingham, *Officia SS. Patricii, Columbae, Brigidae* (Paris, 1620), pp. 54–67, reprinted in his *Florilegium Insulae Sanctorum seu Vitae et Acta Sanctorum Hiberniae* (Paris, 1624), pp. 206–7 (recte 208–9); also in *Trias Thaumaturgæ seu Divorum Patricii, Columbæ et Brigidæ ... Acta*, ed. J. Colgan (Louvain, 1647), [pp. xix–xx], Ussher, *Whole Works*, vi, pp. 452–4; Colgan (ed.), *Acta Sanctorum*, iii, p. 10, under 1 February.

[42] That is the year in which the manor of Downpatrick was created: Flanagan, 'Names of Downpatrick', p. 89.

[43] G. Mac Niocaill, 'Cartae Dunenses XII–XIII Céad', *Seanchas Ardmhacha*, 5 (1969–70), pp. 418–28 at p. 419, no. 1.

[44] *Ibid.*, no. 3.

[45] The fifteenth-century Laud annals recounted that John de Courcy had expelled secular canons from the cathedral of Downpatrick, and replaced an image of the Holy Trinity

About 1183 a Benedictine community, headed by a prior, was introduced from St Werburghs, Chester, to Downpatrick. Malachy III and his episcopal successors were to be 'abbas et custos sicut fit in ecclesiaie Wyntoniensi vel Coventrensi' and a substantial landed endowment (forty-six named places and six churches) was attached. Malachy III's charter confirming this arrangement and reserving for the use of the bishop the offerings of the feasts of Christmas, the Purification, St Patrick, Easter and Pentecost, was witnessed by Lorcán (latinized Laurentius) Ua Tuathail, archbishop of Dublin, in his capacity as native papal legate, and by Tomaltach (latinized Thomas and used hereafter) Ua Conchobair, archbishop of Armagh.[46] The introduction of a Benedictine chapter at the cathedral church of Downpatrick therefore was supported both by the archbishop of Armagh, to whose province the diocese of Down was attached, and by the native papal legate. The reference to the custom of Winchester or Coventry indicates the establishment of a cathedral priory, the monks of which were intended to form the electoral chapter. Malachy III may have been pursuing a reform strategy of Malachy I (and his choice of the Latin Malachias suggests that he self-consciously aimed to do so) in seeking to deploy monastic chapters as a means of ensuring canonical episcopal elections that would be less amenable to external pressures. Canon 28 of the Lateran Council of 1139 had accorded a role in episcopal elections to *viri religiosi*.[47] Malachy I, who visited the continent in that year, would have been aware of this ruling. This may serve to explain why the abbot of the Cistercian community of Mellifont turned up for the election of an archbishop of Armagh in 1201, armed with a privilege which he avowed gave him 'first voice' in the election.[48] Although an unusual claim, it is possible that it did indeed date back to the time of Malachy I, who, in light of the decree of the second Lateran Council, may have envisaged Cistercian and Augustinian communities having an impact as *viri religiosi* not only on the transformation of monasticism in Ireland, but also on episcopal elections. It is possible too that the claim advanced by the Augustinian community of Bangor in 1244 to elect the bishop of Ulaid originated from the time of Malachy I. Malachy III, in cooperating

which had enjoyed place of honour in that church, with one of St Patrick; Gilbert (ed.), *Chartularies of St Mary's Abbey, Dublin*, ii, p. 309. De Courcy's charter in favour of Holy Trinity affords no indication of the existence of a chapter of canons.

[46] Mac Niocaill, 'Cartae Dunenses', pp. 419–20; A. Gwynn, 'Tomaltach Ua Conchobair, coarb of Patrick (1181–1201)', *Seanchas Ardmhacha*, 8 (1975–7), pp. 231–74 at pp. 244–6.

[47] Lateran III can. 28 in *Decrees of the Ecumenical Councils*, ed. N. P. Tanner (London, 1990), p. 202; *Sacrorum Conciliorum Nova et Amplissima Collectio*, ed. G. D. Mansi, 31 vols. (Florence, 1759–98), pp. xxi, 534.

[48] Sheehy (ed.), *Pontificia Hibernica*, i, no. 52.

with John de Courcy in the introduction of a Benedictine chapter at Downpatrick, may have been seeking to preclude an electoral role for the Augustinian community of Bangor; he may have been pitting one body of reform-minded *viri religiosi* against another so as to confine the electoral body to clergy at Downpatrick. The participation of clergy from different churches might create tensions and divisions. The involvement of the Bangor community, in particular, raised the likelihood that one of their number might be elected (as happened in 1175),[49] and that the electee might opt to remain resident at Bangor, for which a precedent could reasonably have been argued dating back to the episcopates of Óengus Ua Gormáin and Malachy II.

Another means by which John de Courcy advanced the cause of church reform in the diocese of Ulaid, and specifically the endowment of its episcopal see at Downpatrick, was in respect of tithes. Bernard of Clairvaux had stated that one of the difficulties which Malachy I had faced was that the Irish did not pay tithes, a complaint which is corroborated by other contemporary Irish sources.[50] De Courcy made generous grants of the tithes of his lordship of Ulaid to Bishop Malachy III and to his church at Downpatrick, grants so comprehensive that they included a tithe of all cattle preys, and all acquisitions and purchases of animals.[51] It is possible that this may have been a reflex of a royal or seigneurial prerogative of the Mac Duinn Sléibe kings of Ulaid, for Irish over-kings might claim a proportion of cattle preys of subordinate kings who acknowledged their overlordship; if so, by voluntarily conceding such a tithe to Malachy III, de Courcy would have presented himself as a more acceptable lord of Ulaid from a reform perspective than the Mac Duinn Sléibe kings. On the other hand, it may reflect the legislation of the provincial synod of Dublin held by Archbishop John Cumin in 1186, or another similar but now unknown synod, which prescribed that tithes should be paid, not only on agricultural produce, but also on the profits of military exploits and trade.[52] De Courcy granted to the Benedictine community installed in the church of St Patrick, Downpatrick, free crossings of the waterways in his lordship, again conceivably

---

[49] Above p. 161

[50] Leclercq et al. (eds.), *Sancti Bernardi Opera*, iii, p. 325; Bernard of Clairvaux, *Life and Death of Malachy*, p. 33; cf. the death notice of Malachy's patron, Donnchad Ua Cerbaill, king of Airgialla (d. 1168), copied into the so-called Antiphonary of Armagh which claimed that in his time 'tithes were received': *St Bernard of Clairvaux's Life of St Malachy of Armagh*, ed. H. J. Lawlor (London, 1920), p. 170.

[51] 'decimam vaccam et quodlibet decimum animale de omnibus predis meis et de omnibus adquisitis et purchaciis meis de animalibus', Mac Niocaill, 'Cartae Dunenses', p. 420.

[52] 'Etiam de militia, de negotiatione, de artificio et venatione', Sheehy (ed.), *Pontificia Hibernica*, i, no. 16.

a pre-Norman royal or seigneurial prerogative, as well as the profits of justice relating to all its lands and men 'in toto dominio et in omni potestate mea' [in my whole lordship and over all people in all my power], in effect, instituting an ecclesiastical immunity.[53] To the Augustinian hospital priory of St John 'extra civitatem de Dun' [beyond the city of Down] de Courcy confirmed a measure of ale from each brewing in the city, and although his charter stated that it was to be rendered 'sicut fit in civitate Duveline', there is some evidence to suggest that in the immediate pre-Norman period a brewing render may have operated at sites where an ecclesiastical settlement and a secular royal residence were co-located.[54]

John de Courcy's introduction of a Cistercian community at Inch, within sight of Downpatrick, also advanced the cause of church reform. Inch was a pre-Norman church site. In 1971 an extensive earthen enclosure, typical of early Irish ecclesiastical sites, was identified by aerial photography at Inch; the Cistercian abbey buildings were to occupy only a small portion of the earlier enclosure.[55] That Inch was a pre-Norman ecclesiastical site which had been secularized is indicated by the occurrence of an *airchinnech* of Inis Cúscraid as a witness to Muirchertach Mac Lochlainn's charter to Newry Abbey in 1157; significantly his position in the witness list among the laity alongside the *airchinnech* of Dún dá Lethglas (Downpatrick), indicates that he was not accorded clerical status; but the fact that he occurs as a witness at all suggests that he was a substantial landholder.[56] Little is known of the pre-Norman history of Inis Cúscraid. MoBíu of Inis Cúscraid is listed in the main text of the early ninth-century Martyrology of Óengus at 22 July, to which a later gloss adds that Inis Cúscraid was beside Downpatrick.[57] The martyrology of Tallaght lists Dobí of Inis Causcraid at 22

---

[53] Mac Niocaill, 'Cartae Dunenses', p. 421.
[54] *Ibid.*, p. 419. Cf. the charter of Diarmait Mac Murchada, king of Leinster, issued about 1162–5 to the Augustinian community at the ecclesiastical and royal settlement of Ferns, which included a brewing render, Dugdale, *Monasticon Anglicanum*, vi, II, pp. 1141–2. In 1107 when the dual function ecclesiastical and royal settlement of Kincora was struck by lightning sixty vats both of mead and bragget were destroyed, *AU, s.a.* 1107.
[55] A. Hamlin, 'A recently discovered enclosure at Inch Abbey, Co. Down', *Ulster Journal of Archaeology*, 40 (1977), pp. 85–8. The fact that De Courcy's other Cistercian foundation at Grey Abbey was by comparison with Inch less elaborate, seems to have taken much longer to build, and had its plans changed in the course of building has been attributed to the fact that Inch already had an organized estate, Mallory and McNeill, *The Archaeology of Ulster*, p. 277.
[56] Dugdale, *Monasticon Anglicanum*, vi, II, pp. 1133–4 and cf. note 26 above; it has not proved possible to reconstruct his name which is rendered 'Edri Maglanha' (? Artrí Mac Fhlannchada) in the early seventeenth-century transcript of the charter-text.
[57] *Félire Óengusso*, ed. W. Stokes, Henry Bradshaw Society, 29 (London, 1905), p. 170.

July and Botí of Inis Caumscraid at 29 July.[58] The earliest annalistic reference to Inis Cúscraid occurs in 1001 when it was plundered by a fleet of Sitriuc mac Amlaím, king of Dublin.[59] The death of Ócán ua Cormacáin, *airchinnech* of Inis Cúscraid, is recorded in 1061.[60] In 1149 Inis Cúscraid was among a number of locations plundered by Muirchertach Mac Lochlainn, leading an army drawn from Cenél nEógain, Cenél Conaill and Airgialla, against the king of Ulaid.[61] This suggests its economic importance as a landed estate in the twelfth century. So also does the occurrence of the place-name in the twelfth-century Book of Leinster recension of the *Táin*, where Inis Cúscraid is depicted as the royal residence of the Ulaid dynast, Cuscraid Mend Macha, son of Conchobar, king of Ulster, who resided at Emain Macha.[62] There is no warrant for this association other than a similarity of name forms, but, along with the annalistic entries, it does suggest the prominence of the site in the twelfth century, by which time, however, it appears to have been a secularized landed estate. John de Courcy's decision to install a Cistercian community at Inch, fortified by the indulgence of Bishop Malachy III, ensured that secularized church lands were reclaimed for the church.[63] It is possible indeed that the Synod of Ráith Bressail had envisaged that some, if not all, of the lands of the adjacent Irish ecclesiastical site of Inch were to be used to endow the reformed episcopal see at Downpatrick.

Nendrum was another early Irish ecclesiastical site to which John de Courcy introduced a new monastic community drawn from the Benedictine house of St Bees in Cumberland, a daughter house of St Mary's, York. The annalistic evidence relating to Nendrum suggests that, like Inch, it had become a secularized ecclesiastical estate: there is no evidence for conventual monastic activity at Nendrum beyond the tenth century.[64] De Courcy granted two-thirds of the lands and churches of

---

[58] *The Martyrology of Tallaght*, ed. R. I. Best and H. J. Lawlor, Henry Bradshaw Society, 68 (London, 1931), pp. 57, 58.
[59] *AFM*.   [60] *AU, AT, AFM*, all s.a.1061.
[61] Inis Cúscraid, Movilla, Bangor and all the other churches of Ulaid were plundered excepting Downpatrick and Saul, *AFM*; cf. *AT*
[62] *Táin Bó Cúalgne from the Book of Leinster*, ed. C. O'Rahilly (Dublin, 1970), lines 211, 702; K. Muhr, 'The location of the Ulster cycle: part 1: tóchustal Ulad', in *Ulidia*, ed. J. Mallory and G. Stockman (Belfast, 1994) pp. 149–58 at 155, no. 30.
[63] Above note 11. The lands of Inch abbey were calculated by the late Fr Colmcille OCSO, Mellifont Abbey, at the Dissolution at an acreage of 5,794 acres, 3 roods, 28 perches (personal communication). While this may not reflect the twelfth-century acreage, there is little evidence for substantial endowments subsequent to the twelfth century.
[64] The latest reference to Nendrum in the annals records the burning to death of the *airchinnech* in his house in 976: *AU, s.a.* 976. Hamlin, 'Early church in Co. Down', pp. 54, 58, 64.

pre-Norman Nendrum to St Bees, reserving the remaining third for the use of Malachy III as bishop of Down.[65] The early tenth-century Tripartite life of Patrick claimed a relationship of dependency between St Patrick and St Mochoí, the reputed founder of Nendrum, who owed an annual tribute of a pig to Patrick, since he had been a swineherd before his consecration as bishop by Patrick.[66] Jocelin of Furness in his life of Patrick, *c.* 1200 elaborated on this anecdote that the pig was paid to the church of Downpatrick from the territory (*territorium*) of Nendrum.[67] A tradition linking Patrick and St Mochoí may have prompted those charged with implementing the decision of the Synod of Ráith Bressail to locate an episcopal see at Downpatrick to allocate at least some of the lands of Nendrum for the endowment of the see. Malachy III confirmed de Courcy's benefactions of two-thirds of the Nendrum lands and churches to the Benedictine community of St Bees as he stated 'non compulsus ab aliquo sed bene devotus in domino spontanea voluntate' [not compelled by anyone but in ture devotion to the Lord of my own free will] in a ceremony which took place in the church of Holy Trinity, Downpatrick

in praesentia domini Johannis de Curci coram Reginaldo episcopo Dalnard [Dál nAraide alias Connor], et coram Uroneca [Ua Ruanada] episcopo de Uvehe [Uí Echach alias Dromore] et coram Patricio abbate de Saballo [Saul] et coram priore S. Johanne de Duno et Willielmo priore de Sancto Patricio et Johanne capellano episcopi ...[68]

[In the presence of Lord John de Courcy before Reginald, bishop of Dalnard, Dál nAraide, Ua Ruanada, bishop of Uí Echach, Patrick, abbot of Saul and William, the prior of St Patrick and John, the bishop's chaplain.]

John de Courcy's re-foundation of Nendrum both restored the lands of Nendrum to church use and augmented the endowment of Bishop Malachy III's episcopal see. Certainly, from the standpoint of the

---

[65] *Ecclesiastical Antiquities of Down, Connor, and Dromore: Consisting of a Taxation of those Dioceses compiled in the Year MCCCVI*, ed. W. Reeves (Dublin, 1887), pp. 190–1; Wilson (ed.), *Register of the Priory of St Bees*, pp. 520–1.

[66] *The Tripartite Life of St Patrick*, ed. W. Stokes, 2 vols., RS (London, 1887), i, pp. 40–1; ii, pp. 452–3.

[67] Messingham (ed.), *Florilegium*, 18; Colgan (ed.), *Acta Sanctorum*, Mart. II, p. 544.

[68] Reeves (ed.), *Ecclesiastical Antiquities of Down, Connor and Dromore*, p. 192; Wilson (ed.), *Register of St Bees*, pp. 522–3. A formal ecclesiastical court may be inferred. The division between the monks of St Bees and Bishop Malachy III was confirmed by Thomas, archbishop of Armagh, and by his successor Eugenius, as well as by the papal legate, Cardinal John of Salerno, during his visit to Down on 9 June 1202: Reeves (ed.), *Ecclesiastical Antiquities*, pp. 192–3; Wilson (ed.), *Register of St Bees*, p. 523. This series of confirmations, as well as a reference in the charter of Archbishop Eugenius to a *convencio et composicio* between the monks of St Bees and Malachy III, suggests that there may have been some dispute over the division, though it need not necessarily have originated between Malachy III and the monks of St Bees; the division may have been contested by other clerical parties.

church reform party, which sought to delimit clear boundaries between the sacred and the secular, de Courcy's ecclesiastical endowments brought notable benefits for Malachy III: the status of Downpatrick was emphasized by highlighting its Patrician links; the location at Downpatrick of the cathedral church of the episcopal see of Ulaid, as envisaged by the Synod of Ráith Bressail, was endorsed, which in itself headed off possible claims from Bangor; and Downpatrick was endowed materially with lands and tithes. Additionally, the pre-Norman church sites of Inch and Nendrum were restored to ecclesiastical use. Also advantageous may have been that de Courcy did not retain the city of Downpatrick as the *caput* of his new lordship and build a major castle there, although it certainly had been the *caput* of the pre-Norman kingship of Dál Fiatach. De Courcy erected his principal strongholds at Dundrum and at Carrickfergus, leaving Downpatrick as a predominantly ecclesiastical settlement under the jurisdiction of the bishop. While allowing that de Courcy had strategic maritime reasons for placing strongholds at coastal locations, it may none the less have been advantageous to Bishop Malachy III in diverting unwelcome military attention away from Downpatrick.[69] De Courcy proved to have a better record on church reform than the pre-Norman Mac Duinn Sléibe kings, who had been notably unsympathetic to Malachy I's endeavours. Malachy I's royal patrons ought to have been the Mac Duinn Sléibe kings, but it was their political rival, Donnchad Ua Cerbaill, king of Airgialla, who proved his most supportive royal patron, and it was in the kingdom of Airgialla, and not Ulaid, that Malachy I was to introduce both the first Cistercian and Augustinian communities of the Arrouaisian observance.[70] The disapproval in certain clerical circles of Magnus Mac Duinn Sléibe, who was slain in Downpatrick by his brother Donn Sléibe in 1171, may be inferred from the annals which offered by way of explanation of his murder that

great evils had been done by him, namely, after leaving his own wedded wife, and after taking the wife of his foster-father, that is from Cú Maige Ua Flainn, and she had previously been the wife of his own brother, Áed, and after inflicting violence upon the wife of his other brother also, that is of Eochaid, and after profanation of bells, and croziers, clerics and churches.[71]

[69] The son of the king of Ulaid was killed 'in Brigit's church in the middle of Dún dá Lethglas in 1007'; *AU*, s.a. 1007; *CS*, s.a. 1005 = 1007; *AFM*, s.a. 1105 = 1007; in 1010 the *princeps* of Dún Lethglais was outraged, abducted and blinded: *AU*, s.a. 1010; *AFM*, s.a. 1009 = 1010; in 1016 Dún Lethglaise was 'totally burnt': *AU*, s.a. 1040; *ALC*, *AFM*, s.a. 1015 = 1016; in 1040 it was again burnt 'and many other churches': *AU*, s.a. 1040; *ALC*, *AFM* Cf. also above note 12.

[70] M. T. Flanagan, 'St Mary's abbey, Louth, and the introduction of the Arrouasian observance into Ireland', *Clogher Record*, 10 (1980), pp. 223–34.

[71] *AU*; *ALC*; *AFM*.

By contrast, John de Courcy's marital fidelity appears to have been exemplary, although ultimately inadequate since his marriage to his wife Affrica, to whom he assigned dower 'on the day when he took her as lawful wife at the door of the church', as his charter so charmingly puts it,[72] did not result in any legitimate offspring who survived him.

John de Courcy was associated not only with Malachy III but also with his archiepiscopal superior, Thomas, archbishop of Armagh (1180–1201). The association is attested in the preface of Jocelin's Life of St Patrick. Jocelin attributed the impetus for the life to Malachy, bishop of Down, Thomas, archbishop of Armagh, styled primate of all Ireland, and John de Courcy, 'who is well known as having a most especial love and veneration for St Patrick'.[73] Archbishop Thomas's association with de Courcy is also attested by the charter which he issued confirming de Courcy's foundation at Nendrum.[74] Thomas (Tomaltach Ua Conchobair) was a nephew of Ruaidrí Ua Conchobair, king of Connacht, and claimant to the high-kingship, who was translated from the see of Elphin to Armagh in 1180.[75] As a Connacht man he was an outsider, with no previous connections with Armagh, who owed his appointment to Ruaidrí Ua Conchobair's determination to demonstrate his high-kingship by securing his nominee in the primatial see. Thomas, however, had difficulty in establishing himself at Armagh. He had to contend with opposition from a more local candidate, Máel Ísu Ua Cerbaill, bishop of Clogher, who, supported by his kinsman, Murchad Ua Cerbaill, king of Airgialla, as well as by Hugh de Lacy I (d. 1186), managed to intrude himself into the see of Armagh in 1184.[76] The situation was complicated by a dispute over diocesan boundaries between the sees of Armagh and Airgialla (Clogher/Louth),[77] and such recognition and support for his archiepiscopate as Thomas could derive from John de Courcy as lord of Ulaid would have been most welcome.

Thomas may have had to contend with more than local opposition, however, for the see of Armagh may have faced a challenge to its primacy from the archiepiscopal see of Dublin. An innovation in

---

[72] Above, note 4.
[73] Messingham (ed.), *Florilegium*, p. 2; Colgan (ed.), *Acta Sanctorum*, Mart. II, p. 536. For de Courcy's issue of halfpennies with the name of Patrick see W. A. Seaby, 'A St Patrick halfpenny of John de Courci', *British Numismatic Journal*, 29 (1958–9), pp. 87–90 and cf. Duffy, 'First Ulster plantation', pp. 8–10.
[74] Reeves (ed.), *Ecclesiastical Antiquities of Down, Connor and Dromore*, p. 193; Wilson (ed.), *Register of St Bees*, pp. 523–4.
[75] Gwynn, 'Tomaltach Ua Conchobair, coarb of Patrick', pp. 231–74.
[76] *ALC*, s.a. 1181, 1183, 1184, 1185, 1201; *AU*, s.a. 1185, 1187; *Misc. Ir. Annals*, s.a. 1184; Giraldus, *Expugnatio*, pp. 198–9.
[77] A. Gwynn, 'Armagh and Louth in the 12th and 13th centuries', *Seanchas Ardmhacha*, 1 (1954–55), no. 1 (1954), pp. 1–11; 2 (1955), pp. 17–37.

Jocelin's Life of St Patrick was a highly coloured and wholly anachronistic account of how Patrick had converted the king and the citizens of Dublin, and how Dubliners, in return for the gift of Christianity 'bound themselves and their successors by oath to the service of Patrick and the primacy of the archbishop of Armagh', and promised payment of tribute, including a measure of ale from every tavern.[78] A challenge to the primacy of the archbishop of Armagh by the see of Dublin predated Anglo-Norman intervention, and is attested, for example, in 1121.[79] Tensions may have been exacerbated, however, by the Treaty of Windsor, 1175, which delimited two distinct spheres of lordship between Henry II and Ruaidrí Ua Conchobair. Since Thomas had been installed in 1180 as primate at Armagh in consequence of the high-kingship of Ruaidrí Ua Conchobair, and since Ruaidrí, by the Treaty of Windsor, had acknowledged the over-kingship of Henry II, it could conceivably have been argued that the archbishopric of Dublin, and more particularly Henry II's appointee, John Cumin, who succeeded Lorcán (latinized Laurentius) Ua Tuathail (alias Laurence O'Toole), in 1180, ought not to be subject to the primacy of Armagh.[80] Lorcán, furthermore, had been native papal legate in Ireland, 1179–80, a role which, in an English context, was associated with the office of primate.[81]

Bishop Malachy and Archbishop Thomas, in their various difficulties,

---

[78] Messingham (ed.), *Florilegium*, p. 33; Colgan (ed.), *Trias Thaumaturga*, fols. 80–01 (misprinted fols. 90–01). J. Szoverffy, 'The Anglo-Norman conquest of Ireland and Saint Patrick', *Reportorium Novum*, 2 (1958), pp. 6–16, rightly draws attention to the importance of Jocelin's Dublin material, but his interpretation strains the evidence. Cf. the poem in *Lebor na Cert* which details tribute due to Patrick from the city of Dublin, *Lebor na Cert: the Book of Rights*, ed. M. Dillon, ITS (London 1962), pp. 115–19. A longer unpublished version of this poem is to be found in the Book of Uí Maine 125d 53.

[79] See the letter of the people of Dublin to Ralph, archbishop of Dublin, in that year: Ussher, *Whole Works*, iv, pp. 532–3; *AU, s.a.*1121; Flanagan, *Irish Society, Anglo-Norman Settlers, Angevin Kingship*, p. 30.

[80] Cf. the papal privilege secured by John Cumin in April 1182, which included that no other archbishop or bishop should hold meetings, conduct causes or ecclesiastical business in his diocese unless by the command of the pope or of his legate: Sheehy (ed.), *Pontificia Hibernica*, i, no. 11; cf. also nos. 13, 14. The temporary abdication in 1183 of Ruaidrí Ua Conchobair, king of Connacht, may have precipitated the challenge to Thomas's archiepiscopate in 1184.

[81] The office of native papal legate subsequently was to be held by Henry of London, archbishop of Dublin, who was the first archbishop of Dublin to use the title 'primate of Ireland' on his seal: Sheehy (ed.), *Pontificia Hibernica*, i, no. 148 and note 1. On tensions between Armagh and Dublin over primacy see M. P. Sheehy, *When the Normans Came to Ireland* (Cork, 1975), pp. 91–8. In 1190 William, bishop of Ely, was appointed papal legate in England and Wales and *et in illis partibus Hiberniae in quibus nobilis vir Johannes comes Moritoniensis ... iurisdictionem habet et dominium*': Sheehy (ed.), *Pontificia Hibernica*, i, no. 22.

stood to benefit from John de Courcy's support, but John de Courcy also gained from his cooperation with them. His monastic foundations served a practical colonizing function for a man of limited resources: taking grip of a new area was materially assisted by drawing religious houses into the venture. A more remarkable though ultimately fruitless instance of ecclesiastical support was papal intervention in 1205 in support of John de Courcy, an intervention which his clerical associates may be presumed to have been instrumental in procuring.[82] On 1 July 1205 Pope Innocent III directed a letter to the archbishop of Armagh, the bishop of Down and the abbot of Inch ordering them to examine the dispute which had arisen between John de Courcy and Hugh de Lacy II, younger brother of Walter de Lacy, lord of Meath.[83] The train of events which led to this papal intervention dated back to at least 1201, when there is clear evidence that de Courcy had incurred King John's displeasure; by that date de Courcy's English estate of Middleton Cheney had already been taken into the king's hand.[84] On 29 May 1205 King John created Hugh de Lacy II earl of Ulster, to hold Ulster as it had been held by John de Courcy on the day of his capture.[85] Knowledge of this confiscation and regrant, however, almost certainly had not reached Innocent III by 1 July when he issued his letter appointing the three churchmen as papal judges delegate to investigate the dispute between Hugh de Lacy and de Courcy.

What was the justification for papal intervention in what was on the face of it a purely secular dispute? Innocent's letter rehearsed the events which led to the papal commission: Hugh de Lacy had waged war on de Courcy, and had captured him. Through the mediation of unnamed ecclesiastics de Courcy had sworn to leave Ireland permanently, and had renounced any right to avenge himself. He had resigned to Hugh de Lacy fortifications and *homagia authentica* previously conferred on him by the Apostolic See as well as by others, and had vowed to go on crusade. De Lacy had refused to let him go because the archbishop of Armagh and a number of his suffragans had excommunicated those who

---

[82] On 26 May 1204 the prior and monks of de Courcy's foundation of St Andrew in Ards had secured a protection and confirmation of their possessions from Pope Innocent III. On 11 June 1204 Pope Innocent III issued letters of protection and confirmation of their possessions to the prior and monks of St Andrew in Ards and the prior and monks of St Andrew of Stoke Courcy: *Ibid.*, i, nos. 59, 60. Members of one or other of these communities could have made representations in Rome on de Courcy's behalf.

[83] *Ibid.*, i, no. 64.

[84] Above, note 7. The course of this dispute cannot be pursued here. See further Orpen, *Ireland under the Normans*, ii, pp. 136–44.

[85] *Cal. Doc. Ire.*, 1171–1251 no. 263; *Rotuli Chartarum in Turri Londonensi Asservati, 1199–1216*, ed. T. D. Hardy (London, 1837), i, p. 151a; *Calendar of the Gormanstown Register*, ed. J. Mills and M. J. McEnery (Dublin, 1916), pp. 189–90.

had been harassing de Courcy. Hugh then swore that as soon as de Courcy had delivered to him the castles and his charters, he would allow de Courcy, and his two nephews whom he had captured, to go free and that he would not disinherit those who had held in fee of de Courcy, but would allow them to move freely with their arms and chattels. De Courcy swore again that he would leave both his own lands and the land of Ireland, but swore also that if Hugh failed to abide by their agreement, he would feel free to do all in his power to ruin him. Since Hugh had acted in disregard of his oath, John de Courcy now sought papal permission to be absolved from his. Papal intervention appears then to have been justified on the breaching of oaths, probably sworn before clerical mediators, although Innocent also briefly adverted to the notion of a just war. He directed the judges delegate to investigate whether Hugh had waged an unjust war on de Courcy, and if they found that this was so, de Courcy should be absolved from the oath which he had sworn. There was to be no right of appeal.

Innocent's letter dealing with the feud between de Courcy and Hugh de Lacy stands out as exceptional among his sixty-eight extant papal letters relating to Ireland; thirty-nine dealt with ecclesiastical affairs, eighteen were grants of privileges, protections and confirmations, and a mere ten can be classified as bearing on secular politics, chiefly on King John's difficulties with his baronage. Innocent's letter in support of de Courcy is not known to have had any material impact, but it is testimony to the degree of support from churchmen which he enjoyed. Intriguing is the statement in Innocent's letter that de Courcy held certain privileges from the pope. Summaries of lost letters from the register of Pope Innocent III provide evidence for earlier papal contacts with de Courcy. The fourteenth-century rubrics, or table of contents, for the third year of Innocent's pontificate, that is February 1200 to February 1201, contain the heading of a letter to John de Courcy *super donatione denarii sancti Petri*, and a similar letter to the king of the Isle of Man.[86] The collection of Peter's Pence had been one of the conditions laid down by Pope Adrian IV in the privilege *Laudabiliter*; and it may be that John de Courcy had sought to make himself a vassal of the papacy, and had offered to collect Peter's Pence on its behalf.[87]

---

[86] Sheehy (ed.), *Pontificia Hibernica*, i, no. 46. A third, with the heading 'to the prior and monks of the church of St Patrick', may refer to the church of Downpatrick.

[87] *Ibid.*, i, no. 4. It is noteworthy that the church of St Patrick in Downpatrick was one of only three Irish churches listed as subject to papal census in 1192: *Le Liber Censuum de l'église Romaine*, ed. P. Fabre and L. Duchesne (Paris, 1910), i, p. 233. In what circumstances this came about is unknown; it could conceivably date back to the papal legation of Cardinal Vivian who was in the city of Downpatrick when it was captured by John de Courcy. Recourse to the papacy by clerical associates on de Courcy's behalf

Other evidence of papal contact with de Courcy is afforded by the legation of Cardinal John of Salerno, *titulus* of the Coelian Mount, who was sent to Ireland in 1202. On 9 June 1202 at Downpatrick, John of Salerno issued a confirmation to the Benedictine community at Nendrum of the grants of the *nobilis vir*, John de Courcy.[88] The date and place of this confirmation is noteworthy, for 9 June was also the feast day of St Colum Cille. It was also the day on which the feast of the Translation of the bodies of Patrick, Brigit and Colum Cille subsequently was to be celebrated in Ireland. The liturgical office for the feast of the Translation states that the solemn translation took place during the legation of Cardinal John in the presence of fifteen bishops, as well as abbots, priests, deacons, archdeacons, priors and other religious men.[89] This apparently contradicts Giraldus's account that the bodies of Patrick, Brigid, and Colum Cille were translated about 1185–6.[90] Giraldus, however, may actually have been referring to the *inventio*, or discovery in 1185–6, rather than the *translatio*, although he used both terms. In a late twelfth-century calendar of St Werburghs, Chester, whence John de Courcy introduced Benedictine monks to Downpatrick, the feast of the *inventio corporum sanctorum Patricii Columb(a)e et Brigid(a)e* was listed on 24 March, that is, within the octave of the feast of St Patrick on 17 March.[91] In Ireland, however, the feast of the *inventio* appears to be unknown, probably because it was superseded after 1202 by the feast of the *translatio*, celebrated on 9 June.[92] Lections in liturgical offices are not renowned for their historicity. Yet John of Salerno's precisely dated confirmation in favour of Nendrum indicates that he was in Downpatrick on 9 June 1202.[93] It was the feast of St Columba, and it

may have been inspired by the notion that the pope had jurisdiction over islands, as claimed in *Laudabiliter*.

[88] Reeves (ed.), *Ecclesiastical Antiquities of Down, Connor and Dromore*, pp. 193–94; Wilson (ed.), *Register of St Bees*, pp. 524–55.

[89] Above, note 41.   [90] Above, note 40.

[91] Wormald (ed.), *English Benedictine Kalendars after A.D. 1100*, i, p. 97. The same calendar referred to 'Sancti Patricii archiepiscopi Hiberniensium apostoli' rather than the more usual 'sanctus Patricius episcopus (et confessor)': J. Hennig, 'The place of Irish saints in medieval English calendars', *Irish Ecclesiastical Record*, 5th series, 82 (1954), pp. 93–106 at 101.

[92] In the diocese of Dublin it was subsequently moved to 10 June so as not to coincide with the feast of St Colum Cille on 9 June: *The Book of Obits and Martyrology of the Cathedral Church of Holy Trinity*, ed. J. H. Todd (Dublin, 1844), p. xlv; the sixteenth-century Antiphonary of Armagh has an addition at the foot of the page for the month of June which states that the feast of the translation of the bodies of Patrick, Brigid and Colum Cille was celebrated on the Sunday following 9 June, clearly so as to avoid the feast of Colum Cille: A. Gwynn, 'The antiphonary of Armagh', *Journal of the Co. Louth Archaeological Society*, 9 (1945), pp. 1–12 at p. 9 (though I have interpreted the evidence differently).

[93] Above, note 88.

fell, furthermore, on a Sunday in 1202. It would have been a particularly appropriate feast and day for the legate to preside at a solemn ceremony of translation. There is a striking detail in the office of translation which suggests the historical authenticity of its account. The presence of fifteen bishops is mentioned, but there is no reference to an archbishop, and yet the archbishop of Armagh might have been expected to have been in attendance.[94] On 9 June 1202, however, there was no accepted archbishop of Armagh because the incumbent had been suspended by the legate: a disputed episcopal election at Armagh was one of the issues that John of Salerno's legation was intended to resolve.

Following the vacancy created by the death of Archbishop Thomas in 1201, Echdonn (Eugenius), Mac Gilla Uidir, abbot of Bangor, had been elected and consecrated as archbishop. There were, however, canonical irregularities pertaining to the electoral procedure and to the elect himself, and, additionally, King John sought strenuously to have his own nominee, Humphrey of Tickhill, installed, though eventually the king was to acquiesce and, no later than August 1206, had accepted Echdonn as archbishop of Armagh.[95] Archbishop Echdonn issued an undated confirmation in favour of Nendrum which was witnessed by de Courcy,[96] so their association is attested. Echdonn must also have been the archbishop of Armagh mentioned in Innocent III's letter of 1 July 1205 as involved in negotiations between de Courcy and Hugh de Lacy II. It is just possible that support for Echdonn's candidacy by John de Courcy in 1202 may have been a contributory factor in the tensions between him and King John. Innocent III, in his letter rehearsing the circumstances of Echdonn's election and consecration, stated that he had been supported by the suffragans as well as by 'ipsius terre principum'.[97] John de Courcy may have been among the latter: *princeps* was the title accorded him by Jocelin of Furness.[98]

---

[94] The office states that Bishop Malachy III communicated his discovery of the bodies to John de Courcy and that together they had petitioned Pope Urban III for permission to hold a translation ceremony and asked him to send a delegate, Messingham (ed.), *Florilegium*, pp. 206–7; Colgan (ed.), *Trias Thaumaturga*, pp. xix–xx. Urban was elected pope on 25 November 1185 and died 20 October 1187. The chronological coincidence of his short pontificate with Giraldus's dating of the discovery of the bodies is impressive and argues also in favour of an accurate basis for the account in the office of translation.
[95] See Watt, *Church and the Two Nations in Medieval Ireland*, pp. 226–30.
[96] Reeves (ed.), *Ecclesiastical Antiquities of Down, Connor and Dromore*, p. 192; Wilson (ed.), *Register of St Bees*, p. 523. The charter must be dated either 1202–3 before Echdonn left for Rome, or 1204 after his return and before the final defeat and exile of John de Courcy.
[97] Sheehy (ed.), *Pontificia Hibernica*, i, no. 52.
[98] Messingham (ed.), *Florilegium*, p. 2; Colgan (ed.), *Acta Sanctorum*, Martii II, p. 536; 'Johanne de Curci regnante in Ulvestrre', Roger of Howden, *Chronica*, iv, p. 162.

Innocent III's intervention proved of little avail to de Courcy who was deprived permanently of his lordship of Ulaid by King John in 1205. Hugh de Lacy II, in turn, was to be deprived by King John in 1210, but had managed to recover a substantial portion of the lordship of Ulster by 1227. Both Strongbow and Hugh de Lacy I ran into difficulties in their relations with the English crown, but there is a notable difference between the crown's treatment of Strongbow, Hugh de Lacy I and Hugh de Lacy II, compared with John de Courcy. Henry II chose to honour the lengthy minority of Strongbow's heirs in Leinster between 1176 and 1189 when he could have used the royal *vis et voluntas* to install another in the lordship of Leinster.[99] Although Hugh de Lacy I died in 1186 under royal disapproval, and succession to the lordship of Mide at first was withheld by John, son of Henry II, as lord of Ireland from Hugh's heir, Walter, who had come of age by 1189, Walter had recovered Mide by 1194 following the intervention of King Richard I.[100] By contrast, John de Courcy lost all in Ulaid. Of course, he was facing King John and not Henry II; nor did he have any legitimate issue to succeed him. It was also the case, however, that royal control of John de Courcy's actions in Ireland by distraint of his possessions in England was not feasible, since de Courcy held no lands of consequence; hence it was necessary for King John to wage war on him vicariously in Ireland via Hugh de Lacy II. Conversely, confiscation and regrant of John de Courcy's lordship of Ulaid in 1205 did not have serious destabilizing repercussions in England, since neither de Courcy, nor his followers, were men of sufficient status or wealth.

John de Courcy's relations with individual Irish churchmen have a wider interest beyond his own career: they bear on the role of the Irish clergy in advancing English colonization in Ireland. Churchmen in twelfth-century Ireland were at a critical stage in the evolution of a new corporate identity, both within an Irish context, and within the wider context of the supranational medieval church. There were tensions between reformed and unreformed clergy. Economic pressures were generated by competition for landed resources not only between reformed and unreformed churches, but also between reformed churches. The diocesan hierarchy was of relatively recent origin, having received papal endorsement from Cardinal John Paparo as recently as 1152 at the Synod of Kells, less than twenty years before Anglo-Norman intervention in Ireland. Issues of primacy, precedence and status, and episcopal electoral procedures were still being negotiated and defined.

---

[99] Flanagan, *Irish Society, Anglo-Norman Settlers, Angevin Kingship*, pp. 123–36. J. E. A. Jolliffe, *Angevin Kingship*, 2nd edn (London, 1963), pp. 50–86.
[100] Flanagan, *Irish Society, Anglo-Norman Settlers, Angevin Kingship*, pp. 282–3.

Anglo-Norman intervention subjected the neophyte structures of the twelfth-century Irish church to additional divisive pressures. There was no clear fractioning along reformed versus unreformed, nor, notwithstanding the subsequent emergence of the terms *ecclesia inter hibernicos* and *ecclesia inter Anglicos*, along racial, or two-dimensional lines; rather it generated different forms and varying degrees of cooperation and confrontation between Irish churchmen and Anglo-Norman incursors at local level. Giraldus and Roger of Howden depicted the Irish episcopate unanimously endorsing Henry II's intervention at the Synod of Cashel in 1171–2, thereby creating a misleading impression of the Irish clergy committed as a collectivity to the cause of reform and to endorsement of Anglo-Norman intervention to that end. It appears to have been Gilla Críst Ua Connairche, bishop of Lismore, and native papal legate, acting in the latter capacity as head of the Irish church, who sought to present a collective response on the part of the Irish episcopate to both Henry II and to Pope Alexander III in 1171–2, which, however, obscured the fragility of corporate solidarity in the twelfth-century Irish church.[101]

Irish churchmen did play a part in advancing English interests in Ireland, but it was less the unanimity of their response which facilitated the Anglo-Norman advance than the tenuousness of their corporate action which determined that individual Irish clergy at local level were to respond in differing ways and in varying degrees to Anglo-Norman intervention in Ireland. What the career of John de Courcy also illustrates is that some Anglo-Normans needed the suppport of Irish clergy more than others. Giraldus praised John de Courcy for his generosity to the church, which is confirmed by the evidence of his monastic foundations as recorded in his unusually full series of charters. The Annals of Ulster, however, attributed his downfall in Ulaid to his destruction of churches. In 1205 it recorded 'John de Courcy, destroyer of the churches and territories of Ireland, was expelled by Hugh de Lacy into Tír Eógain to the protection of the Cenél nEógain.'[102] Perhaps nothing could illustrate better the differing clerical standpoints in twelfth-century Ireland. A further perspective is offered by the fifteenth-century Anglo-Irish annals kept in Dublin which attributed de Courcy's downfall to the fact that he had presumed to replace the Almighty with St Patrick at Downpatrick![103]

[101] Flanagan, 'Henry II, the Council of Cashel and the Irish bishops', *Peritia*, 10 (1996), pp. 184–211.
[102] *AU*; *AFM*.   [103] See above, note 45.

9 Coming in from the margins: the descendants of Somerled and cultural accommodation in the Hebrides, 1164–1317

R. Andrew McDonald

One result of the current trend towards 'British' history has been an increasing interest in the geographically peripheral or outer zones of medieval Britain, including Border societies, the Isle of Man, the Irish Sea world and the Scottish highlands and islands.[1] In both a British and a more narrowly Scottish context, the integration of the margins of the Scottish kingdom – Argyll and the Isles, Galloway and Moray – forms a major theme for the twelfth and thirteenth centuries.[2] Not surprisingly, many of the milestones in this process are violent ones: the 'slaughter of the Men of Moray' at Stracathro in 1130; the uprisings in Galloway following the decision of the Scottish king to dismember that province on the death of its lord, Alan, in 1234; or the fighting at Largs in 1263, which paved the way for the political settlement at Perth in 1266. It has been noted, perhaps facetiously but with a certain amount of truth, that terminology such as the 'Winning of the West', 'connotes images of palefaces and natives, not to mention a shootout at Largs'.[3] Yet as enduring as the theme of conquest has proven – and not just in Scottish history, of course – historians are increasingly devoting their attention to

---

I would like to thank Jacqueline Buchanan, who read the manuscript and offered some very helpful advice on stylistic matters.

[1] R. Frame, *The Political Development of the British Isles 1100–1400* (Oxford, 1990), ch. 9; A. Grant, 'Scotland's "Celtic Fringe" in the late Middle Ages: the Macdonald lords of the Isles and the kingdom of Scotland', in *The British Isles 1100–1500: Comparisons, Contrasts and Connections*, ed. R. R. Davies (Edinburgh, 1988), pp. 118–141; K. Stringer, 'Periphery and core in thirteenth-century Scotland: Alan son of Roland, lord of Galloway and constable of Scotland', in *Medieval Scotland: Crown, Lordship and Community*, ed. A. Grant and K. Stringer (Edinburgh, 1993), pp. 82–113; Duffy, 'The Bruce Brothers and the Irish Sea World', pp. 56–86.

[2] Duncan, *Scotland: The Making of the Kingdom* (Edinburgh, 1975); Barrow, *Kingship and Unity: Scotland 1000–1306*.

[3] E. J. Cowan, 'Norwegian sunset – Scottish dawn: Hakon IV and Alexander III', in *Scotland in the Reign of Alexander III 1249–1286*, ed. N. Reid (Edinburgh, 1990), p. 105. In the same vein, we might also note that, 'There was even a Marshal Vigleikr on hand who took time out during the expedition to mosey a little in the cave on the west side of Arran's Holy Isle where he scratched out his name in runes.' *Ibid.*

other, more subtle processes which also shaped interactions between societies and the domination of one society by another. In a European context, not only conquest but also colonization, accommodation and acculturation have been emphasized by Robert Bartlett as important elements in what he has called the 'Europeanization of Europe'.[4] In a British setting, the work of Professor Davies has demonstrated how military invasion and conquest may follow a lengthy period of social and economic domination, or how more subtle means of domination such as overlordship and intermarriage may succeed where other methods fail.[5] Although Davies's work is concerned with relations between England and its Celtic neighbours, there are many parallels to the processes he describes and those whereby the margins of the Scottish kingdom were drawn into the centre, in what might be termed 'internal colonialism'.[6] Recent research on Galloway, for instance, has pointed to the roles of colonization and accommodation in bringing that region into conformity with the centre of the kingdom even before the events of the 1230s.[7] But examinations of Argyll and the Isles, in contrast, continue to stress the military aspects of the process, especially the various expeditions, both Scottish and Norwegian, to subdue the region, which resulted in the fighting at Largs in 1263.[8] My aim in this chapter, therefore, is to move away from military and political milestones and to determine whether processes of cultural accommodation were at work in the Hebrides, and to establish how these processes contributed to the integration of the descendants of Somerled into the Scottish kingdom between the deaths of Somerled in 1164 and his descendant, John of Argyll, in 1317, midway through the reign of King Robert I (1306–29).

By the late thirteenth century the descendants of Somerled, collectively known as the Mac Sorleys, were represented by three major kindreds. The Mac Dougall lords of Argyll claimed descent from Dugald, the son of Somerled, an obscure figure whose activities are almost wholly unknown. Dugald's son, Duncan, who appears on the record in the 1230s, is also a shadowy individual, but his son, Ewen, was a dominant figure in the monumental events of the two decades spanning 1248 to 1268. By 1275 Ewen's son, Alexander, appears on the

---

[4] Bartlett, *Making of Europe*.   [5] Davies, *Domination and Conquest*, passim.
[6] M. Hechter, *Internal Colonialism: The Celtic Fringe in British National Development 1536–1966* (London, 1975), discusses internal colonialism in a post-industrial context, but many of the concepts he considers are thought-provoking when applied to the pre-industrial era.
[7] R. Oram, 'A family business? Colonisation and settlement in twelfth- and thirteenth-century Galloway', *SHR*, 72 (1993), pp. 111–45.
[8] Cowan, 'Hakon IV and Alexander III'; G. Donaldson, *A Northern Commonwealth: Scotland and Norway* (Edinburgh, 1990).

scene, and he and his son, John, were prominent in the west for some forty years, until their respective deaths in 1311 and 1317. As lords of Argyll, the Mac Dougalls possessed, before their downfall at the hands of Robert I in 1308–09, vast insular and mainland territories, including Lorn, Benderloch, Lismore, north Jura, Mull, the Treshnish Isles, and Coll and Tiree. The Mac Donald lords of Islay claimed descent from Donald, the son of Ranald, the son of Somerled. Donald was probably dead by 1263, when his son, Angus Mór, was active in Hebridean politics. A shadowy figure at best, Angus Mór disappears from the record by 1293–6; his sons were Alexander Óg and Angus Óg, the latter of whom is well known as a prominent Bruce supporter and who seems to have died shortly after the Scottish victory at Bannockburn. The Mac Donald holdings comprised Kintyre, Islay, south Jura and probably also Colonsay and Oronsay. The third Mac Sorley kindred, and the most obscure, was that of the Mac Ruairi, lords of Garmoran. Descended from Ruairi, also the son of Ranald, Somerled's son, they were represented in the 1260s by Dugald Mac Ruairi, who was noteworthy for his freebooting activities in the Irish Sea and his steadfast Norwegian allegiance in the 1260s; after his demise in 1268 little is heard of this branch for a decade, but in 1275 Dugald's brother, Alan, played a prominent role in a Scottish expedition to the Isle of Man. Alan had two illegitimate sons, Ruairi and Lachlan, who were active in the late thirteenth and early fourteenth centuries, and a legitimate daughter, Christiana, who was a consistent Bruce supporter. The far-flung Mac Ruairi Lordship of Garmoran comprised Moidart, Arisaig, Morar, Knoydart, Rhum and Eigg, and possibly Barra, the Uists and Harris.[9]

The events which resulted in the extension of Scottish royal authority into Argyll and the Hebrides fall outside the scope of this chapter. The Treaty of Perth, which ceded the Western Isles and Man to Scotland in 1266, represented the culmination of some forty years of intermittent Scottish efforts to subdue the region, and the political integration was virtually complete by the time John Balliol's first parliament carved three new sheriffdoms out of the former kingdom of the Isles in 1293.[10] One of the noteworthy features of the new sheriffdoms was that

[9] On the MacSorley territories see A. A. M. Duncan and A. L. Brown, 'Argyll and the Isles in the earlier Middle Ages', *Proceedings of the Society of Antiquaries of Scotland*, 90 (1956–57), pp. 204–5; D. Gregory, *History of the Western Highlands and Islands of Scotland from AD 1493 to AD 1625*, 2nd edn (London and Glasgow, 1881), pp. 18–19, 22. The descendants of Somerled are discussed at greater length in R. A. McDonald, *The Kingdom of the Isles: Scotland's Western Seaboard, c. 1100–c. 1336* (East Linton, 1996).

[10] Creation of sheriffdoms in 1293: *Acts of the Parliaments of Scotland*, ed. T. Thomson and C. Innes, 12 vols. (Edinburgh, 1814–75), i, p. 447. For the extension of Scottish royal authority into the west, see: Duncan and Brown, 'Argyll and the Isles', passim; Cowan,

Alexander of Argyll, the son of Ewen, as a prominent landholder in the region, was appointed sheriff of Lorn; we thus see a west-coast chieftain 'coming in from the cold' (to borrow a phrase from John LeCarré) to play a role in the administration of the kingdom and to act as an agent in the process of the extension of royal authority.[11] The case of Alexander and his role as sheriff leads nicely into the important but neglected issue of the place of the descendants of Somerled within the community of the realm of Scotland.

During the thirteenth century, the abstract concept of a community of the realm gradually took hold, first in England and then, later in the century, in Scotland. It is generally agreed that this concept acquired meaning in the reign of Alexander III (1249–86), although it did not receive its first written expression until 1286. While the nature of the makeup of the community of the realm remains contentious, it is usually thought to have received its best expression when the king sought the counsel of his barons. It is through this medium that we can trace the integration of the Mac Sorleys into the community of the realm, both in their involvement in councils and parliaments and in the internal affairs of the kingdom. One of the more striking points to emerge from an examination of the history of the western seaboard between 1100 and 1266 is that, before the events of the 1260s, the Mac Sorleys seldom figured in Scottish domestic affairs. Their activities, though wide-ranging, were maritime-oriented and encompassed not only the Hebrides but also the Irish Sea world, Ireland and Scandinavia; when they did appear on the Scottish mainland scene, it was usually as the opponents of the Scottish kings, as in Somerled's 1164 invasion, or the involvement of his grandson Ruairi in the mac Heth and mac William uprisings of the early thirteenth century. It is a rare thing indeed to find one of Somerled's descendants involved in the internal politics of the Scottish kingdom, as (possibly) in 1175 when Dugald, the son of Somerled, was present at Durham; or in 1237 when Duncan of Argyll was named in a Scottish letter to the pope; or, perhaps, in 1255, when Ewen of Argyll profited from the troubled minority of Alexander III to regain his territories in the west. But following the treaty of Perth in 1266 the Mac Sorleys were integrated into the community of the realm and came to play a role in Scottish politics alongside other well-established noble families.

'Hakon IV and Alexander III', passim; and McDonald, *Kingdom of the Isles*, chs. 3, 4, and 5.

[11] The other sheriffs were those of Skye and Kintyre: William, the grandson of Farquhar Maccintsaccairt, the earl of Ross, and James the Steward, respectively. See McDonald, *Kingdom of the Isles*, p. 131.

Although the evidence is sparse for the Mac Sorleys in the decades after 1266, two episodes highlight the extent to which their integration had pressed forward. In 1275, the Scottish king raised an army and a fleet from Galloway and the Western Isles in order to contend with an uprising in the Isle of Man. Two of the leaders of this fleet and army were Mac Sorleys: 'Alexander Fitz John, of Argyle', that is, Alexander, the son of Ewen (whose name was often Anglicized as John), and 'Alan fitz Rother,' or Alan, the son of Ruairi, the Lord of Garmoran.[12] It seems likely that these men would have been responsible for summoning and leading the host from Argyll and the Isles, but even more importantly, the fleet of galleys that transported the army was, in all likelihood, provided by these western chieftains. Moreover, they may well have provided galloglasses, fighting men from the Hebrides, and it is difficult to believe that the extensive knowledge they could provide of the western seaboard did not also play a role in their selection as leaders of the expedition.[13] If conflict between the descendants of Somerled and the Manx kings was nothing new in the Isles, the situation in 1275 nevertheless represents a novel state of affairs. In the first instance, it stands in marked constrast to the events of 1263, when, in the face of King Hakon's might, most of the Mac Sorleys had gone over, however reluctantly, to a Norwegian allegiance and had, along with the Manx king, taken part in the plundering of the Scottish mainland. How ironic that only twelve years later, two descendants of Somerled figured prominently among the leaders of an army sent to reassert Scottish royal authority in the Isle of Man. Moreover, we see the Mac Sorleys acting in concert with other Scottish nobles like John de Vescy, John Comyn and Alan the son of Thomas of Galloway, who were also named as leaders of the expedition. As Professor Duncan has so aptly summarized the situation, we see represented in this collection of names 'a small group of fully armed knights, the "common army," footmen or serjeants of Galloway, and the ships of the Islesmen, all bent to the purposes of the king'.[14] Instead of opposing royal authority in the west, Somerled's kin had become agents of its enforcement, and it would be difficult to find a better example of their integration into the mainstream of Scottish politics.

The second illustration of the manner in which the Mac Sorleys were

---

[12] See the Annals of Furness, in *Scottish Annals from English Chroniclers, 500 to 1286*, ed. A. O. Anderson (London, 1908), pp. 382–3.

[13] On the galloglass, and the MacSorleys as suppliers, see G. A. Hayes-McCoy, *Scots Mercenary Forces in Ireland (1565–1603)* (Dublin and London, 1937), pp. 4–35; A. McKerral, 'West Highland mercenaries in Ireland', *SHR*, 30 (1951), pp. 1–14; and McDonald, *Kingdom of the Isles*, pp. 154–6.

[14] Duncan, *Scotland. The Making of the Kingdom*, p. 582.

drawn in from the margins dates from 1284. In January of that year, the Lord Alexander, the eldest son of King Alexander III, died after a long illness. The king had already lost his second son and his daughter, Margaret, the queen of Norway, and this crisis prompted a council to be held at Scone. This council acknowledged Margaret, the king's infant granddaughter, the 'maid of Norway', as 'our lady and right heir of our said lord king of Scotland'.[15] Among the nobles of the realm who were present and gave their grudging assent were three Mac Sorleys: 'Alex. de Ergadia', 'Anegus filius Douenaldi' and 'Alanus filius Rotherici', that is, Alexander of Argyll, Angus the son of Donald and Alan the son of Ruairi. This council, or, more accurately, the inclusion of the Mac Sorleys within it, is of great significance for any assessment of the position of the descendants of Somerled within the late thirteenth-century community of the realm. In the first instance, it is noteworthy that all three branches of the Mac Sorleys – the Mac Dougalls, Mac Donalds and Mac Ruairis – were present at the council as equal and integral members of the community of the realm, where they rubbed shoulders with other prominent members of the nobility like Alexander Comyn, earl of Buchan, Patrick, earl of Dunbar, Malise earl of Strathearn, Malcolm, earl of Lennox, Robert Bruce, earl of Carrick, Walter, earl of Menteith, John Balliol, John Comyn and James Stewart. Although it is true that the three Argyll magnates are named last in the list of thirty-eight nobles who were present, they are the only magnates from the western seaboard so represented and, in any event, their appearance at the end of the list nicely exemplifies their newly found position within the Scottish kingdom and the community of the realm. Also important is the inclusion of the Mac Sorleys as 'barons of the realm of Scotland' by the document. Considering that only thirty years earlier the descendants of Somerled had been styled kings of the Isles, the change in terminology is significant and reflects the extent to which their position and status had changed as they were drawn into the nexus of Scottish politics dominated by the core of the kingdom.

These, then, were some of the ways in which the Mac Sorleys were bound to the centre of the Scottish kingdom. The contrast between the position of Ewen of Argyll, for example, as king of the Isles in the late 1240s, and that of his son, Alexander, as sheriff of Lorn in 1293, half a century later, could not be more striking, and nicely encapsulates the transition from sea-kings to barons. Consciously or not, the Hebridean chieftains of the line of Somerled had trimmed their sails to the winds of change, and had taken a significant step in from the margins. Just how

---

[15] Thomson and Innes (eds.), *Acts of the Parliament of Scotland*, i, p. 424; trans. from *Scottish Historical Documents*, ed. G. Donaldson (Edinburgh, 1970), pp. 37–8.

Coming in from the margins 185

big that shift had been would become evident when the succession crisis of the late 1280s exploded into Scottish civil war and Anglo-Scottish conflict in the 1290s, from which not even the Mac Sorleys could remain aloof. The roles of the descendants of Somerled in the wars of independence provide a further illustration of the newfound place of the western seaboard in the community of the realm; indeed, the Scottish civil conflicts and Anglo-Scottish wars of the late thirteenth and early fourteenth centuries were the crucible in which the integration of the west was tested.[16]

So much, then, for the integration of the descendants of Somerled into the Scottish kingdom in a more or less political sense. It remains to explore in more detail the cultural world within which these Hebridean chieftains moved in the thirteenth century in an endeavour to understand whether, in social and cultural terms, they were moving in from the margins before the political settlement imposed by the treaty of Perth. There are several areas that can be profitably explored to illuminate this problem, including the patterns of naming and matrimony among the west coast chieftains; the problematic but important issue of west highland feudalism; knighthood and its adoption by the western nobles; and the use of charters and seals by these same men. When these issues are explored it becomes apparent that, by the time the Western Isles were ceded to Scotland, a hybrid society which fused Gaelic and Anglo-French (or European) impulses was either already in existence or well on its way towards formation.

Names and patterns of naming are among the best indicators of cultural change. They were not chosen arbitrarily, and provide important clues to lineage and ancestry. Indeed, in the early Middle Ages, many regions of Europe had localized repertoires of names which make it easy to identify the region or ethnic group under consideration.[17] But in the eleventh and twelfth centuries this began to change, sometimes as a result of conquest, sometimes as a result of cultural accommodation, and so there began the circulation of a common body of names throughout much of Western Europe.[18] The process is well known for the Scottish kings descended from Duncan I, for example, where the early generations reveal names like Duncan, Donald and Malcolm, that are virtually unique to Scotland. But by the fifth generation after Duncan only two of the twelve names in the genealogy are Gaelic.[19] Is it

[16] For which see McDonald, *Kingdom of the Isles*, ch. 6.
[17] See G. Duby, 'Lineage, nobility and knighthood', in Duby, *The Chivalrous Society*, trans. C. Postan (London, 1977), pp. 60–3; also Bartlett, *Making of Europe*, 270–8.
[18] *Ibid.*, p. 271.
[19] *Ibid.*, pp. 274–7; I. F. Grant and H. Cheape, *Periods in Highland History* (London, 1987), p. 36.

possible to detect similar patterns of naming in the western seaboard? Somerled's own name was, of course, Norse, and at least two of his sons, Olaf and Ranald (Raghnall, a borrowing from Old Norse Ragnvald), bore Scandinavian appellations. The names of others of his offspring – Dugald, Angus and Gillebrigde – were Gaelic, however.[20] Considering the mixed Gaelic and Norse milieux of the twelfth-century Hebrides this is hardly surprising, and it is also no surprise that in the thirteenth century many more of his descendants bore Gaelic names: Donald, the son of Ranald; Angus Mór, the son of Donald; Duncan, the son of Dugald; and Ewen, the son of Duncan.

Up until the middle of the thirteenth century, then, Gaelic names were predominant among the kindred of Somerled. But beginning in the middle decades of that century a new generation of Mac Sorleys appeared on the scene bearing names indicative of a change in cultural orientation. Donald, the son of Ranald, named his second son Alexander,[21] and both Angus Mór and Ewen named their first-born sons Alexander, probably after King Alexander III, since it is unlikely that either was born before the death of Alexander II in 1249. In any event, which Scottish monarch these men were named for is of much less import than the fact that a name associated with the Scottish royal dynasty had been adopted by the ruling families of the western seaboard for their first-born sons. Thereafter, there is evidence of both Gaelic-Norse and Scottish or European influences in the names chosen by these dynasties. Having named their first-born sons for the Scottish king, both Angus Mór and Ewen reverted to Gaelic appellations for subsequent children; Angus Mor's second son was Angus Óg, and Ewen's second son was Duncan. It cannot be mere coincidence that the name Alexander appears among first-born sons of the dynasties of the west at exactly the same moment when Scottish royal authority was intensifying in the region, and it is therefore reasonable to suppose that the new names emerging into the kindred of Somerled reflect the spread of Scottish influence to the west, and also a new orientation on the part of the nobles of the region. Just as the Scots of the twelfth century began to name their children William and Henry, after the Norman kings of England, so too did the rulers of the western seaboard partake in what has been called the 'cultural emulation of a powerful neighbour'[22] by naming their eldest sons Alexander. By way of contrast, we may note that the kinsmen, neighbours and rivals of the Mac Sorleys, the seafaring

---

[20] I am grateful to Dr Seán Duffy for advice on the form of some names.
[21] *Registrum Monasterii de Passelet*, ed. C. Innes (Edinburgh, 1832), p. 127, where Alexander appears as a witness to one of his brother's charters.
[22] Bartlett, *Making of Europe*, p. 277.

Manx kings, who were also open to similar cultural influences, displayed a marked preference for Scandinavian personal names such as Godred, Olaf, Ragnvald and Harald throughout the twelfth and thirteenth centuries. Perhaps this pattern of nomenclature represents an attempt to assert a self-consciously Scandinavian identity despite efforts to appear up-to-date in other respects, or perhaps the Mac Sorleys were remarkably adaptable, but whatever the case may be, the Manx kings present a stark contrast to the descendents of Somerled in their choice of personal names in our period.[23]

Patterns of matrimony also provide striking illustrations of the world in which the ruling order of medieval society moved. The marriage alliances forged by Somerled in the middle of the twelfth century, for example, point to an Irish Sea orientation – Somerled himself had married a daughter of King Olaf of Man, and his sister married Malcolm mac Heth, another Gaelic figure associated with uprisings against the Mac Malcolm kings of Scots. Indeed, the nexus of matrimonial politics in the Irish Sea in the twelfth century was fixed firmly on the Isle of Man: a daughter of Fergus of Galloway married King Olaf of Man, and even Anglo-Normans like the adventurer John de Courcy were keen to bind themselves to the Manx sovereigns, no doubt, at least in part, because of the formidable fleets of galleys which lay at their disposal.[24] It is therefore unfortunate that the matrimonial politics of the west in the late twelfth and early thirteenth centuries are largely obscured by the fragmentary nature of the evidence. But when the mists clear and the sources permit some light to be shed on these questions in the middle decades of the thirteenth century, the contrast to the patterns that prevailed in the time of Somerled could not be more striking. Thus we find that in about 1268 Ewen of Argyll married his daughter to the earl of Strathearn. This is a particularly significant episode because her first husband had been Magnus, the king of Man who died in 1265, and her second marriage reflects the greatly altered political situation after the settlement of 1266.[25] Equally significant is the marriage of Ewen's son, Alexander, to a daughter of John Comyn (the Red), lord of Badenoch, a kinsman of John Balliol and a prominent member of the Scottish nobility; it was this alliance that made the Mac Dougalls supporters of John Balliol and the

---

[23] See *Cronica Regum Mannie & Insularum*, ed. G. Broderick, Manx Museum and National Trust (Douglas, 1991), passim.

[24] For more detail see R. A. McDonald, 'Matrimonial politics and core–periphery interactions in twelfth- and early thirteenth-century Scotland', *Journal of Medieval History*, 21 (1995) pp. 227–47.

[25] *Scotichronicon*, v, p. 345; Paul (ed.), *Scots Peerage*, viii, p. 246. Ewen appeared as a witness to one of the earl's charters at Crieff in *c.* 1268: Lindsay *et al.* (eds.), *Charters, Bulls, and Other Documents Relating to the Abbey of Inchaffray*, no. 68.

implacable enemies of Robert Bruce in the Wars of Independence.[26] Donald, the son of Ranald, is said to have married a daughter of Walter, the high steward of Scotland,[27] a not unnatural alliance given the proximity of the great Stewart lordship to the Mac Donald territories, and, according to seventeenth-century tradition, Angus Mór, the son of Donald, married a daughter of Sir Colin Campbell.[28] Finally, Alan of Garmoran's heiress, Christiana, married Duncan, a younger son of Donald, the earl of Mar, another prominent eastern Scottish noble; this marriage is particularly noteworthy because it made Christiana a kinswoman of Robert Bruce, since Duncan's sister, Isabella, was Bruce's first wife.[29] By the third quarter of the thirteenth century, then, all three branches of the Mac Sorleys were actively forming marriage alliances with prominent members of the Scottish nobility, which underlines their inclusion as 'barons of the realm of Scotland' in 1284 and their newfound position within the community of the realm. Indeed, the contrast with the patterns of a century earlier could hardly be more pronounced; the nexus of the matrimonial politics of the west had shifted decisively from the Isle of Man and the Irish Sea towards the Scottish kingdom itself. Even the occasional exception seems to prove the rule. Dugald Mac Ruairi, who remained steadfast in his Norwegian allegiance throughout the 1260s, married his daughter to Áed Ua Conchobair, king of Connacht, in 1259, in an alliance which, by then, cut across the grain of matrimonial politics prevalent among the Mac Sorleys.[30]

A major theme in the history of the medieval Scottish kingdom is the process whereby it was feudalized in the twelfth and thirteenth centuries.[31] While it may be true that by the end of the twelfth century feudalism itself remained largely unknown in the west highlands, the influences which had prevailed in the southern and eastern regions of

---

[26] Laing (ed.), *Androw Wyntoun's, Orygynale Cronykle of Scotland*, bk. VIII, ch. VI, l. 1187–1189.
[27] Paul (ed.), *Scots Peerage*, v, p. 33.
[28] *Highland Papers*, ed. J. R. N. MacPhail, 4 vols. (Edinburgh, 1914–34), i, p. 17.
[29] Duncan, *Making of the Kingdom*, p. 583.
[30] McDonald, *Kingdom of the Isles*, p. 118.
[31] A precise definition of feudalism is difficult because, as R. Allen Brown has observed, 'having been invented by writers of a later age to describe a state of affairs already past, it tends to mean different things to different people' (*The Normans and the Norman Conquest* (London, 1969), p. 85). Some would expunge it from our vocabulary altogether on the basis that it is an artificial construct (E. A. R. Brown, 'The tyranny of a construct: feudalism and the historians of medieval Europe', *American Historical Review*, 79 (1974), pp. 1063–88; S. Reynolds, *Fiefs and Vassals: The Medieval Evidence Reinterpreted* (Oxford, 1994)). In treating of feudalism I accept the commonly used definition: 'An institution based on the holding of a fief, unually a unit of land, in return for stipulated honourable service, usually military, with a relationship of homage and fealty existing between the grantee and the grantor' (C. W. Hollister, *The Military Organization of Norman Britain* (Oxford, 1965), p. 11 n. 3).

the Scottish kingdom, and which had been adopted so readily by native earls in the east, were beginning to spread in concentric rings from these regions and to be felt in the more remote peripheral or outer zones. Unfortunately, plotting the spread of feudalism into the west highlands is particularly problematic. This is due in large measure to the scarcity of documents pertaining to the west before the time of King Robert I (1306–29), and the old problem, aptly summarized by Professor Barrow, 'of whether they are scarce because feudalism made little headway or because historical accident has deprived us of documentary evidence for that region'.[32] What little evidence there is suggests that feudalism was eagerly and easily adapted and utilized by the magnates of the west by the early fourteenth century, and in many cases we see those same nobles adopting the conventions of feudal society, including knighthood, the building of castles, and the utilization of charters to record transfers of land.

The earliest infeftment for knight service in the west dates from 1240, when King Alexander II granted Gillascop Mac Gilchrist extensive territories around Lochawe and Loch Fyne. The lands were held for half a knight's service in the host and a full knight's service in aid, and also for 'Scottish service as the barons and knights on the north side of the Sea of Scotland do it for their lands'.[33] The reference to Scottish service has been regarded as representing the introduction of the customs of Scotia proper into Argyll, for Scottish service was otherwise known as *forinsec* service, service outside or additional to what was due the lord, often identified as common army service for the defence of Scotia.[34] Although it is true that this grant was made as part of an attempt by King Alexander II to impose royal authority on the western seaboard, we see, for the first time, a native magnate of the west entering into a feudal relationship. It is, of course, unlikely that this document was unique, or that no further feudalization occurred in the west in the next twenty or so years.[35] Unfortunately, apart from one document which has been discussed in detail by Professor Barrow,[36] it was not until the time of King Robert I that the evidence for the feudalization of the west rises above the level of patchiness and allows a more coherent picture to

---

[32] G. W. S. Barrow, *The Anglo-Norman Era in Scottish History* (Oxford, 1980), p. 137.
[33] MacPhail (ed.), *Highland Papers*, ii, pp. 121–4. 'Et faciendo servicium scoticanum sicut Barones et milites nostri ex aquilonali parte maris scocie pro terris suis faciunt.'
[34] Duncan, *Making of the Kingdom*, pp. 378–82.
[35] Barrow, *Anglo-Norman Era*, p. 138.
[36] In 1262, Dugald Mac Sween granted to Walter Stewart, the earl of Menteith, Skipness and other extensive lands in Knapdale, Kintyre, and Cowal, to be held for the service of two-thirds of a knight in the king's army: see Barrow, *Anglo-Norman Era*, p. 138 for discussion and references.

be drawn. By then a feudal relationship between the crown and the nobles of the west appears to have been taken for granted, but at the same time it is possible to view the adaptation of feudalism to the unique conditions of the western seaboard. Enough charters survive from Robert I's reign to illustrate that the typical unit of military service in the west, at least among the greatest nobles, was not the knight, but rather the highland galley of a set number of oars; that of twenty-six oars was the most common type of service stipulated. A charter granted to Ruairi the son of Alan sometime in the reign of Robert I gave extensive lands for the service of one twenty-six-oared ship; Colin the son of Neil Cambell held Lochawe and Ardskeodnish in barony for a ship of forty oars; and Thomas Randolph was granted the Isle of Man for the service of six twenty-six-oared vessels. Many of these grants also stipulate that men and supplies are to accompany the vessel.[37] The heavy service due from the Isle of Man no doubt reflects the formidable fleets that the kings of Man had been able to command in the thirteenth century. When King Ragnall assisted his brother-in-law, John de Courcy, in his attempt to win back Ulster in 1205, he is said to have brought with him a fleet of 100 warships, and when the king of Man submitted to Alexander III and performed homage in 1264, he was bound to provide five 24-oared and five 12-oared galleys.[38] Professor Duncan, who has edited the acts of King Robert I, has sounded a cautionary note by suggesting that on the western seaboard charters were only sought by the greatest landowners; this perhaps gives the illusion that galley-service was more typical than it actually was, and it is worthwhile bearing in mind that this was the most substantial type of service.[39] But whatever the case might have been, it seems certain that none of the chieftains of the western seaboard held their lands as a fief in return for fixed military service before the time of Alexander III, although they were obligated to provide a set number of ships for royal expeditions, as, perhaps, in 1275. It was the achievement of Robert I to bring many of these men into a feudal relationship with the crown by granting, regranting or confirming estates as fiefs in return for a fixed number of galleys of so many oars, thereby grafting an older obligation onto the feudal one and creating a blend of old and new in west highland feudalism.[40]

Regardless of how it was adapted to the maritime culture of the west

---

[37] *Registrum Magni Sigilli Regum Scotorum*, ed. J. M. Thomson *et al.*, 11 vols. (Edinburgh, 1882–1914), i, Appendix I, nos. 9, 32, 105, 107; *RRS*, v, nos. 46, 239, 366.
[38] *Scotichronicon*, v, pp. 347–9.
[39] *RRS*, v, p. 54; see also Barrow, *Robert Bruce* (3rd edn), p. 289.
[40] Barrow, *Anglo-Norman Era*, p. 139.

of Scotland, feudalism was, in origin and in essence, all about knights. In the words of R. Allen Brown, it originated for 'the provision, maintenance and training of this particularly expensive and therefore exclusive, type of warrior, with his costly warhorses and equipment, who required from early youth up a lifetime of dedication to horsemanship and the military arts'.[41] In medieval society the knight came to represent a military élite, and soon thereafter a social élite as well. And, while not all knights were great men, it is certainly true to say that, in England and on the continent, all great men were knights, a trend which seems to have been followed in Scotland as well. By the late twelfth century the cult of knighthood had reached its zenith and had been introduced into Scotland by its francophile monarchs, the descendants of Malcolm Canmore and Queen Margaret. The Scottish kings David I (1124–53), Malcolm IV (1153–65), William the Lion (1165–1214) and the two Alexanders (1214–49, 1249–86), were all knighted, and Malcolm and William, as is well known, were particularly ardent devotees of the cult of knighthood. Indeed, by the early part of the thirteenth century, it was possible for one contemporary English chronicler to remark that 'more recent kings of Scots profess themselves to be rather Frenchmen, both in race and in manners, language and culture'.[42] Interest in knighthood and chivalry and in the Anglo-French culture of which these things were part and parcel was not, however, the exclusive preserve of the Scottish kings and their Anglo-French retainers. It was also expressed, from an early date, by many members of the native Scottish nobility, especially the earls of Fife, Dunbar and Strathearn, all of whom aspired to the manners and status of knighthood and portrayed themselves as equestrians with knightly accoutrements on their seals as well.[43] Indeed, as Professor Davies has shown, knighthood permitted Gaelic nobles entry into 'an exhilarating international world of aristocratic fellowship and

---

[41] R. Allen Brown, *Castles*, Shire Archaeology (Aylesbury, 1985), p. 7. There is a vast literature on medieval knighthood. A good, recent study of English knighthood is P. Coss, *The Knight in Medieval England 1000–1400* (Stroud, 1993); David Crouch addresses knighthood in his book *The Image of Aristocracy in Britain 1000–1300* (London, 1992). Another important work is that of Duby, *The Chivalrous Society*. Although feudalism has been much discussed in a Scottish context, knighthood in Scotland lacks a comprehensive examination.
[42] Chronicle attributed to Walter of Coventry in Anderson (ed.), *Scottish Annals from English Chroniclers*, p. 330 n 6.
[43] For some seals of these nobles see H. Laing, *Descriptive Catalogue of Impressions From Ancient Scottish Seals*, 2 vols. (Edinburgh, 1850), no. 333 (Malcolm, earl of Fife); J. H. Stevenson and M. Wood, *Scottish Heraldic Seals* (Glasgow, 1910), ii, p. 354 (Duncan and Malcolm, earls of Fife); W. Greenwell and C. H. Hunter-Blair, *Catalogue of Seals in the Treasury of the Dean and Chapter of Durham* (Newcastle upon Tyne, 1911–21), ii, p. 358 for Dunbar seals.

customs', and became an important agent in acculturation and assimilation between peoples in medieval Britain.[44]

This then raises the issue of whether the ideals, manners and status of knighthood spread to the western seaboard, and were practised by any of the noble families of the region. We certainly need not search far for members of the native Scottish nobility who were influenced by these ideals. Lachlann, the son of Uhtred, the son of Fergus of Galloway, for instance, is better known by the French name of Roland – and he also held the title constable of Scotland.[45] A more significant episode occurred in 1215, when one of the Gaelic leaders in the north, Farquhar Maccintsacairt, was rewarded with knighthood and later made earl of Ross for his role in quashing an uprising against King Alexander II.[46] Given these well-known examples of Gaelic nobles from the western highlands (broadly conceived) adopting the outward trappings, at least, of feudal society, it would hardly be surprising to find the Mac Sorleys doing the same, although once again the sparse nature of the evidence means that any such examination is bound to be patchy and, to a certain extent, speculative. I have argued elsewhere that the seal of Ranald Mac Sorley provides strong evidence that, as early as c. 1200, ideals of knighthood and chivalry were penetrating the western seaboard, far earlier than has been previously thought.[47] Ranald's seal was double-sided and depicted its owner on one side as a mounted knight with a drawn sword, while the other side displayed a highland galley. The portrayal of Ranald as a knight does not necessarily indicate that he was in fact knighted, and thereby inaugurated into the 'sophisticated, international world of chivalry'; indeed, some Gaelic princes and magnates are known to have portrayed themselves as equestrians without having been dubbed knights.[48] But the use of the equestrian device indicates that Ranald, in common with other Scottish, Welsh and Manx rulers of the day, was expressing a desire to be a thoroughly modern and up-to-date magnate in a time when the 'Brave New World' of French civilization was driving all before it.[49] Indeed, given the evident lapping of the

---

[44] Davies, *Domination and Conquest*, p. 51.
[45] Anderson, *Early Sources*, ii, p. 347 n. 2.
[46] *Ibid.*, ii, p. 404; see also W. C. Dickinson, *Scotland from the Earliest Times to 1603*, revised and edited by A. A. M. Duncan (Oxford, 1977), p. 74.
[47] R. A. McDonald, 'Images of Hebridean lordship in the twelfth and early thirteenth centuries: the seal of Raonall Mac Sorley', *SHR*, 74 (1995), pp. 129–43.
[48] Davies, *Domination and Conquest*, pp. 50–1, quotation on p. 51.
[49] Ranald can hardly have been unaware that his cousin and namesake, Ragnall, the king of Man, was in the habit of utilizing a double-sided seal, and it seems quite likely that it was from this quarter that the influence came. However, what is worth bearing in mind here is that, 'the form of the Manx and Hebridean seals was certainly based on the fashions prevailing in contemporary Anglo-French court circles, where the equestrian

waves of feudal influence on the shores of the western seaboard in the thirteenth century, it might have been more unusual if the Mac Sorleys had remained completely uninfluenced by them, and by the middle of the thirteenth century knighthood seems to have become something of a norm among the ruling class in the west.[50] Unfortunately, the evidence for knighthood being adopted by the Mac Sorleys is less abundant for Ranald's descendants than it is for the Mac Dougalls, and it is difficult to say how the trend set by Ranald might have been perpetuated by his descendants. However, in 1293, when Alexander of Argyll was instructed to ensure that Angus the son of Donald performed homage to King John, the document described Angus as *miles*,[51] so it would seem that, whether or not Ranald was actually knighted, his grandson, Angus Mór, certainly had been.

The evidence for the adoption of knighthood by the Mac Dougalls of Argyll is both more abundant and more convincing, and from the time of Ewen until that of his grandson, John, these prominent west-coast nobles were consistently described as knights. Ewen of Argyll is described in both narrative and charter material in a manner that leaves little doubt he had been knighted. Matthew Paris, who narrated Ewen's relations with the Scottish king in 1249, described him as a 'vigorous and very handsome knight', (*militem strenuum et elegantissimum*).[52] While this might be attributed to literary convention, there are several reasons for thinking that this is not the case. First, although he had spent most of his life at St Albans, Paris had excellent means of obtaining information, including many informants who were important public figures. This means that he was familiar with the conventions of knighthood, and it is not likely that he would have attributed them to Ewen unless he had, in fact, been knighted. Moreover, there is a very good chance that Matthew Paris had actually met Ewen, since both had been in Norway in 1248, and so he should be considered well informed on this issue. Indeed, the journey to Norway opens up the possibility that the English chronicler had first-hand information on the matter of Ewen's status,

---

type ... was the norm during the twelfth century'. See B. R. S. Megaw, 'The ship seals of the kings of Man', *Journal of the Manx Museum*, 6, no. 76 (1959–60), passim, quotation at p. 80; and my comments in 'The seal of Raonall MacSorley', passim.

[50] It is worth noting that several generations of Manx kings had been knighted at the hands of the Angevin monarchs: King Olaf the Black had been knighted by Henry III, as had his sons Harald in 1247 and Magnus in 1256. See Broderick (ed.), *Cronica Regum Mannie & Insularum*, fol. 46r. and fol. 49v; the chronicle's statement that Magnus had been knighted is corroborated by a document in *Foedera*, i, pt. ii, p. 12.

[51] Thomson and Innes (eds.), *Acts of the Parliament of Scotland*, i, p. 448.

[52] Matthew Paris, *Chronica Majora*, v, pp. 88–9; translated in Anderson (ed.), *Scottish Annals from English Chroniclers*, p. 360.

and his narrative should not, therefore, be dismissed out of hand.[53] It is certainly corroborated by other evidence. In 1240, Ewen granted lands in Lismore to the bishopric of Argyll, and in his charter he referred to himself as *Eugenius miles*.[54] This is significant in several respects. In the first instance, the term *miles* in the twelfth century was coming to designate not just a soldier but a knight trained to fight on horseback. Sparing use was made of it in documents of the eleventh and twelfth centuries, but by the thirteenth century it was beginning to be recognized as a mark of status.[55] Moreover, because its use appears in one of his own charters, it provides us with an insight into how Ewen viewed himself and how he wished to be portrayed. Finally, in a document from 1255 which details the terms of his restoration to his lordship, Ewen is described as *dominus*, a term of status which usually, by this time, implied that its holder had been knighted.[56] Taken altogether, then, the evidence in favour of Ewen having been knighted is overwhelming; he therefore appears as a man of two worlds, a Hebridean sea-king who was also in tune with contemporary European cultural trends. Ewen's descendants, Alexander and John, are also described as knights in many contemporary documents. Alexander appears as such in the Ragman Rolls of 1296,[57] and there are numerous references to his son, John, holding similar status in the later thirteenth and early fourteenth centuries. A manuscript recording Scottish nobles who swore fealty to Edward I in 1291–2 arranged them in order of status, and one of those mentioned in the ninth category of *armigeri*, young men of knightly class, was John of Argyll. English financial accounts indicate payments in 1314 to 'Sir John of Argyll, knight', and another similar document of 1313, which records payments to knights attending an English parliament on Scottish affairs, also mentions John.[58] It would seem that by

---

[53] On Matthew Paris see A. Gransden, *Historical Writing in England c. 550 to c. 1307* (London, 1974), pp. 360–1. It is worthwhile noting that Paris included details on heraldry in his text; he also painted armorial shields of English nobles in the margins of his chronicles: *ibid*, p. 362 and note 47.

[54] Thomson *et al.* (eds.), *Registrum Magni Sigilli Regum Scotorum*, ii, no. 3136; Duncan and Brown, 'Argyll and the Isles', appendix IV.

[55] On the term see M. Keen, *Chivalry* (New Haven and London, 1984), pp. 27–8; Duby, 'Lineage, nobility and knighthood', in *The Chivalrous Society*, pp. 75–7; J. Bumke, *The Concept of Knighthood in the Middle Ages*, trans. W. T. H. and E. Jackson (New York, 1982), p. 36; on its use see D. F. Fleming, '*Milites* as attestors to charters in England, 1101–1300', *Albion*, 22 (1990), pp. 185–7.

[56] Thomson and Innes (eds.), *Acts of the Parliament of Scotland*, i, p. 115. On the interchangeability of *miles* and *dominus* by the mid-thirteenth century see Duby, 'Lineage, nobility and knighthood', in *The Chivalrous Society*, pp. 75–7, and Fleming, '*Milites* as attestors', pp. 187, 191–3.

[57] *CDS*, ii, no. 791 and no. 823 (p. 195).

[58] 1291–2 document: *Edward I and the Throne of Scotland*, ed. E. L. G. Stones and

the early fourteenth century knighthood had become something of a norm, at least among the Mac Dougalls, and again it is striking how easily west-coast magnates adapted to the conventions current in European and Scottish society.

Some further illumination may be shed on the issue of the Mac Sorleys and the wider world by a consideration of the use of Latin charters in the western seaboard in our period. As Dauvit Broun has reminded us, it is wrong to see the Latin charter as anti-Gaelic; indeed, it was known and utilized throughout Gaeldom, and examples survive in surprising numbers. Moreover, the utilization of the Latin charter by Gaelic kings and nobles has been regarded as yet another facet of the growing international awareness or Europeanization that characterized the twelfth and thirteenth centuries. This being the case, the use of Latin charters by the descendants of Somerled provides yet another gauge by which we can measure their advance from the margins and their acculturation to the increasingly 'European' society in the thirteenth century.[59] Of course, as Michael Clanchy has pointed out, the use of the charter was itself dependent upon changing attitudes towards written records: 'laymen used documents among themselves as a matter of habit only when they became sufficiently familiar with literate modes to trust them'.[60] The use of Latin charters, then, implies changing attitudes towards literacy: certainly by the early thirteenth century the élite of the western seaboard seem to have been moving toward literate modes. As one illustration of this, *Hakon's Saga* relates how several Hebridean chieftains came to King Hakon in Bergen in 1224, 'and they had many letters concerning the needs of their land'.[61]

Beginning in the late twelfth century, the Mac Donald lords of Islay granted a series of charters to the abbey of Paisley. The texts of those charters are preserved in the *Register* of Paisley Abbey, a sixteenth-century compilation, and although they cannot be absolutely dated they can be dated relative to one another. It was probably sometime around 1200 that Ranald, the son of Somerled, granted eight oxen and two pence for one year from every house in his territory from which smoke issued, and thereafter one penny per year. The grant draws to a

G. Simpson, 2 vols. (Oxford, 1978), ii, p. 367 n. 4 and p. 368; 1312–1314 documents: *CDS*, iii, nos. 303, 355.
[59] See the important work of D. Broun, *The Charters of Gaelic Scotland and Ireland in the Early and Central Middle Ages*, Quiggin Pamphlets on the Sources of Mediaeval Gaelic History 2 (Cambridge, 1995).
[60] M. Clanchy, *From Memory to Written Record: England 1066–1307* (Oxford, 1993), p. 53.
[61] Anderson, *Early Sources*, ii, p. 455.

conclusion with a terrifying curse. Ranald ordered his friends and people to aid the monks,

> with the certain knowledge that, by St Columba, whosoever of my heirs molests them shall have my malediction, for if peradventure any evil should be done to them or theirs by my people, or by any others whom it is in my power to bring to account, they shall suffer the punishment of death.[62]

The curse of Ranald upon anyone who did injury to the monks of Paisley reminds us of the role that St Columba [Colum Cille] seems to have played as a formidable and vengeful protector of the Hebrideans, a role that was also illustrated by the dream of Alexander II before his death in 1249. As he lay dying, King Alexander dreamt that three figures appeared to him; that of St Columba bade the king turn back and abort his campaign in the Hebrides.[63] His subsequent death was linked to his refusal to obey the dream-men, and it would seem that St Columba, who always had a reputation as a vengeful and vindictive saint, had claimed another victim. Ranald's curse would certainly have conjured up these terrifying connotations, and so the document provides an interesting glimpse into a society that was moving towards new conventions but still hanging onto some traditional beliefs. Ranald's son, Donald, repeated his father's grant in similar terms (probably at the same time, since the witnesses to the two charters are identical) and repeated the curse that evil-doers would suffer the pain of death. But later charters by members of the same family are worded more conventionally, without any mention of the curse of St Columba; a charter of Alexander, the son of Angus Mór, was made 'for the welfare of my lord Alexander, illustrious king of Scots' (*pro salute domini mei Alexandri illustris regis Scotie*).[64]

It is also useful to consider the witnesses to these charters. The men who witnessed the charters of Ranald and Donald are identical and their names, at least, are suggestive of a Hebridean milieu; they bear names like Gillecolm Mac Gillemichel, and, in the case of Donald's charter, 'many others of my own men' (*multis aliis ex propriis hominibus meis*).[65] But when Angus Mór, the son of Donald, made his grant, the witnesses included men who, to judge by their names, came from a Scottish context, like Gilbert the son of Samuel and William of Strathgryfe; the witnesses to a charter of Alexander, the son of Angus Mór, included

---

[62] Innes (ed.), *Registrum Monasterii de Passelet*, p. 125.
[63] Anderson, *Early Sources*, ii, pp. 555–7. The episode is discussed further in McDonald, *Kingdom of the Isles*, pp. 101–2, 229–30 (with further references).
[64] Innes (ed.), *Registrum Monasterii de Passelet*, p. 128.
[65] *Ibid.*, p. 126. Gillecolm Mac Gillemichel turns up again as a witness to one of Ewen of Argyll's charters in 1240: Thomson *et al.* (eds.), *Registrum Magni Sigilli Regum Scotorum*, ii, no. 3136; Duncan and Brown, 'Argyll and the Isles', Appendix iv.

both Robert Bruce, the lord of Annandale, and his son, Robert Bruce, grandfather and father respectively of King Robert I.[66] Once again a definite transition is visible between about 1200 and the later thirteenth century; the changing composition of the witness lists to these charters reveals yet another way in which the Mac Sorleys came in from the margins in the thirteenth century, and by which the balance of old and new in the society of the western seaboard may be judged.

One notable authority has argued that the Hebridean chieftains, 'had not absorbed the sub-French culture of eastern and southern lands, nor could they share the Scots culture of east-country gentry, burghers and peasantry'.[67] It might be more accurate to state that the élite in the western seaboard had not absorbed the sub-French culture that characterized much of twelfth- and thirteenth-century Europe to the same degree, or as rapidly, as their counterparts in the eastern and southern regions of Scotland. But the political integration of the west into the Scottish kingdom between 1264 and 1293 was accompanied by an equally profound, though more subtle, transformation in society as the Hebridean chieftains adapted themselves to the conventions of European society. As Robin Frame has put it, 'the ... acquisition by Alexander III of the Western Isles seems to have been followed, not by assertive attempts at governmental incorporation, but by a gradual drawing of the noble kins of the region into the orbit of the Scottish court and aristocratic society'.[68] This process did not begin with the cession of the Western Isles to Scotland in 1266– indeed, in some respects it manifested itself in the first generation after Somerled himself – but it was certainly accelerated in the decades between the treaty of Perth and the first parliament of King John, and it was reflected in many diverse phenomena. Thus, the Hebridean chieftains utilized Latin charters; adopted patterns of naming and matrimony that reflected a Scottish/European influence; entered into feudal relationships with the Scottish monarchy; and even adopted the status and terminology of knighthood. The result of all of this was that what might be called a hybrid society emerged in the west, paralleling the rest of the thirteenth-century kingdom, which has been seen as possessing a 'hybrid kingship, hybrid institutions, hybrid law, a hybrid church, and an increasingly hybrid landowning class'.[69] Indeed, it might be argued that the processes whereby the Mac Sorleys were 'Europeanized' mirrored those whereby the Scottish kingdom itself had been transformed in the twelfth

[66] Innes (ed.), *Registrum Monasterii de Passelet*, pp. 127–9.
[67] Barrow, *Kingdom of the Scots*, p. 382.
[68] Frame, *Political Development of the British Isles*, p. 218.
[69] Grant, 'Scotland's "Celtic fringe" in the late Middle Ages', p. 119.

and thirteenth centuries: it was a transition from above, instigated by the Scottish kings in the east and the Mac Sorleys in the west; it was attained largely through peaceful means rather than by military conquest; and the balance between old and new in both east and west is certainly striking. Historians have come to regard the Lordship of the Isles in the fourteenth and fifteenth centuries as a hybrid Gaelic-feudal institution, but to do so may underemphasize the degree to which society in the western seaboard in the thirteenth century displayed some, at least, of the characteristics of such hybrid status, as the Mac Sorleys came in from the margins of the Scottish kingdom.

10 Nobility and identity in medieval Britain and Ireland: the de Vescy family, c. 1120–1314

Keith J. Stringer

As Rees Davies has re-emphasized, 'the length of the Matter of England needs to be balanced in some degree by the breadth of the Matter of Britain'.[1] But as its leading exponents also readily admit, 'British history' rarely lends itself to neat conceptual frameworks; and for the medievalist it is often unusually difficult to devise serviceable organizing principles. In the twelfth and thirteenth centuries our terms of reference seem to lie conveniently to hand in the apparently remorseless growth of the English state, in its deliberate cultivation of an intensified sense of English political and cultural individuality, and in the supposed 'unity' of baronial society in Britain and Ireland. Yet we must remind ourselves once again that, however passionately the Westminster-centred government believed otherwise, defining the contours of power and identity in these islands was not solely its prerogative.[2] This chapter is about the experience of belonging to a baronial family whose territories ultimately spread from England into Scotland, Wales and Ireland. It is concerned with how its members reacted to their varied surroundings and sought to defend and promote their interests; with their loyalties, priorities and values; and with the complexities and contradictions of their identity and self-image. Its main purpose, however, is to contribute to the discourse of 'British history' through an attempt, as Sir Frank Stenton once put it, 'to penetrate behind the abstraction to the individual'.[3]

It is best to begin with some basics.[4] The de Vescys ended in the

---

[1] R. R. Davies, *The Matter of Britain and the Matter of England. An Inaugural Lecture* (Oxford, 1996), p. 25.
[2] The indispensable studies are Davies, *Domination and Conquest* and Frame, *The Political Development of the British Isles*. A broader 'British history' agenda has recently been carried forward in *Uniting the Kingdom? The Making of British History*, ed. A. Grant and K. J. Stringer (London, 1995).
[3] *Preparatory to Anglo-Saxon England*, ed. D. M. Stenton (Oxford, 1970), p. 213.
[4] Basic information on the de Vescys is drawn without further reference from Sir Charles Clay's account in G. E. Cokayne, *The Complete Peerage*, revised by V. Gibbs *et al.* (London, 1910–59), xii, II, pp. 268–85, and Appendix B, pp. 7–11. Also valuable is W. P. Hedley, *Northumberland Families*, 2 vols. (Newcastle upon Tyne, 1968–70), i, pp. 198–202. Eustace fitz John, who for present purposes is treated as a 'de Vescy', is

legitimate male line on the death of William III de Vescy, former justiciar of Ireland, in 1297, though the family was continued in the bastard line by William de Vescy 'of Kildare' until his death without issue in 1314. By far its most important ancestor was Henry Beauclerk's industrious servant Eustace fitz John, an archetypal 'new man', who had founded the family fortunes by amassing in his own right widespread estates in Yorkshire, and by marrying as his first wife Beatrice de Vescy, heiress of the lordship of Alnwick in Northumberland. After Beatrice's death but in Eustace's lifetime, their son William took the de Vescy surname to symbolize the rise from modest origins to élite baronial status, and to forge anew a land-lineage bond that would be maintained and protected for over 150 years. Accordingly, the family name stood for an enviable durability compared with the rapid turnover of other magnate dynasties – and what was all the more impressive was that the line survived and even prospered despite at times a remarkable lack of dependence on, and deference to, the English crown.

The name of de Vescy, shouted as it was by the lord's knights as a rallying cry in battle,[5] also evoked courage and prowess, for this was a family that to a pronounced degree asserted its prestige and identity through warlike endeavour. That judgement may seem to be contradicted by the propaganda of the lord's seals, where the armed hand is nowhere to be seen. None is more beautiful than Eustace de Vescy's, the obverse of which displays an ornate device of ears of corn and pods of vetches, and a pair of two-legged creatures which may be wyverns (a warlord's emblem), but look more like peacocks. This delicate and inventive imagery, with its botanical motifs making a droll allusion to the family name, was enriched by driving an engraved gemstone finger-ring into the warm seal-wax to leave the impression of a galley under sail and what appear to be two dolphins at play.[6] Nevertheless, martial virtue was manifestly fundamental to the de Vescys' place in society and view of themselves. Their soldiering took them virtually the length and breadth of the British Isles, to Normandy, Brittany, Maine and

---

the only member of the family to have received extended discussion: P. Dalton, 'Eustace fitz John and the politics of Anglo-Norman England: the rise and survival of a twelfth-century royal servant', *Speculum*, 71 (1996), pp. 358–83.

[5] *Jordan Fantosme's Chronicle*, ed. and trans. R. C. Johnston (Oxford, 1981), line 1770.

[6] Fine examples are found on Scottish Record Office, Edinburgh, Melrose Abbey Charters, GD 55/168 and 168*. Eustace's elegant counterseal bears an antelope or a goat amid four vetch pods; the matrix was evidently an antique gemstone, possibly of Persian origin and worn around his neck in a locket. See Laing, *Descriptive Catalogue of Impressions from Ancient Scottish Seals*, p. 138 (with engraving at plate 6, no. 4), whence all subsequently published descriptions derive. A rent of a cap of peacock's feathers was owed to Eustace at Caythorpe, Lincolnshire: *Rotuli de Dominabus et Pueris et Puellis*, ed. J. H. Round, PRS, 35 (London, 1913), p. 10.

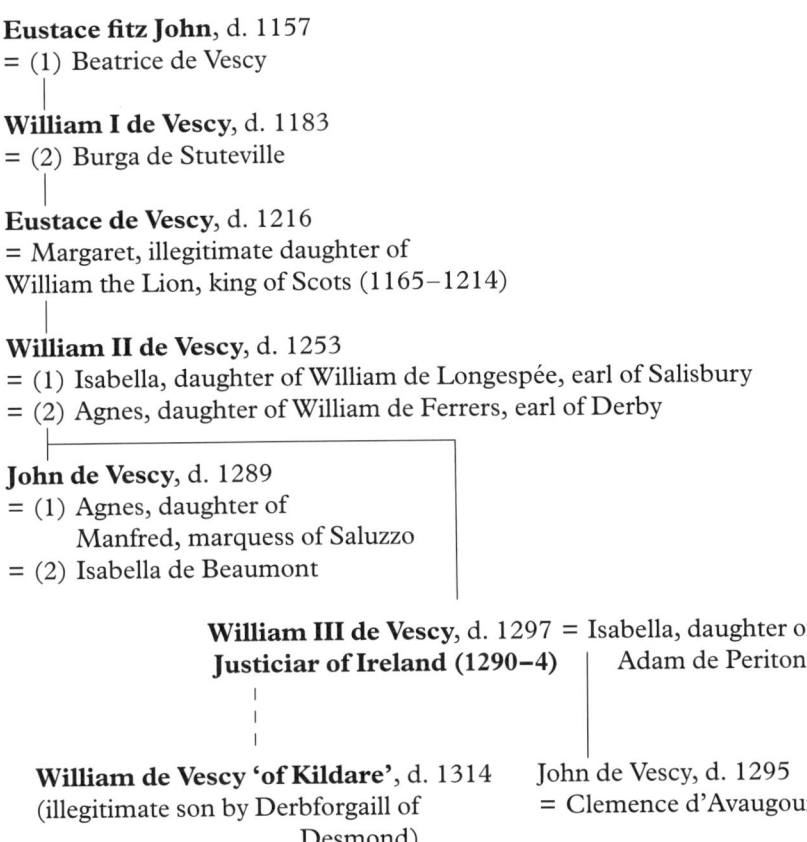

Fig. 10.1 Family table of the de Vescys (simplified)

Gascony, and as far afield as the Holy Land; their battle honours included the Standard (1138), Saintes (1242), Evesham (1265), the Isle of Man (1275) and Bannockburn (1314).[7] Eustace de Vescy was highly respected by contemporaries as a doughty warrior,[8] and others of his line were similarly hailed as paladins. Eustace fitz John was a battle-scarred veteran who had lost an eye; John de Vescy was wounded at Evesham. If such appearances on the casualty lists quickened the family's sense of bellicose pride, even more so did deaths on active

---

[7] William II de Vescy's presence at Saintes, Gascony, on 20 July 1242 can be inferred from *Cl. R.*, 1237–42, p. 504.
[8] Cf. Roger of Wendover, *Flores Historiarum*, ed. H. G. Hewlett, 3 vols., RS (London, 1886–9), ii, p. 194.

service. Eustace fitz John's brother Pain was killed by Welsh raiders in 1137; the Welsh also accounted for Eustace himself during King Henry II's campaign against north Wales in 1157. While inspecting the defences of Barnard Castle with Alexander II of Scotland in 1216, Eustace de Vescy raised his helmet for a proper reconnaissance, was hit in the forehead by a bolt from a crossbow, and died on the spot.[9] Bannockburn put paid to William 'of Kildare'. Although not killed in action, William II de Vescy was one of the many nobles who perished during Henry III's expedition to Gascony in 1253–4; his grandson, John de Vescy the younger, died of an illness aggravated by the rigours of winter warfare while serving with Edward I at Conway in 1295.

These then were sword-bearing lords who upheld the ideals of the chivalrous society perhaps more effectively than most. Their merit as men of blood affirmed their standing among their peers, and simultaneously validated their privileged role as leaders of society. In Wales and Ireland, and at times even in England, their local power itself depended on the regular use of their military arm. They sought additional fame in tourneying, and were quick to defend their rights and reputation by wager of battle. Indeed, perhaps nowhere was their martial culture more dramatically exhibited than during William the justiciar's spectacular quarrel with John fitz Thomas, the Geraldine baron of Offaly and one of the most influential members of the Anglo-Irish community. Accused by fitz Thomas of treason against the English crown, William threw down his glove, and in July 1294, on the eve of his forty-ninth birthday, he appeared before the king's court at Westminster as a fully armed knight replete with armoured warhorse. George Neilson described this episode as one of those 'reactionary symptoms' when 'trial by battle was ... on the high road to extinction', an opinion echoed by Maitland when he dismissed it as a 'picturesque dispute'.[10] It is a fair assumption that William would not have subscribed to such views. The affair did end in anti-climax when fitz Thomas denied him satisfaction by failing to appear. But what brought this 'chuvaler prus et sage' – Peter Langtoft's words[11] – in battle array into the precincts of Westminster palace was an acute sense of personal honour, reinforced by the chivalric ideology of noble society at large and of his own family in particular.

A powerful sense of identity was also shaped and sustained through consciousness of ancestry and family bonds, an awareness that was

---

[9] Stevenson (ed.), *Chronicon de Lanercost*, p. 19.
[10] G. Neilson, *Trial by Combat* (Glasgow, 1890), pp. 70, 72; Pollock and Maitland, *History of English Law*, ii, p. 536. For Eustace de Vescy's waging of the duel in a dispute about land, see *CDS*, i, nos. 330, 332.
[11] Wright (ed.), *Chronicle of Pierre de Langtoft*, ii, p. 230.

Nobility and identity

indeed carefully nourished by the monasteries with which the de Vescys were most closely associated.[12] Unfashionable though it is to stress the political significance of the kinship ties shared by the ringleaders of the baronial opposition to King John, among whom Eustace de Vescy prominently figured, they at least help to demonstrate how firmly the de Vescys embedded themselves within England's magnate class.[13] Strikingly, the extended family of Eustace's son, William II de Vescy, included at one time or another the earls of Chester and Huntingdon, Derby, Essex and Hereford, Gloucester and Hertford, Kent, Norfolk, Pembroke, Salisbury, Surrey, and Winchester.[14] On the other hand, however, the familial connections the de Vescys chose to cultivate and flaunt were by no means restricted to the English scene. Whether or not concern for family repute and blood lay at the root of Eustace's animosity to King John cannot be proved for certain, for the famous story whereby he artfully protected his wife's virtue against John's lustful advances may fall into the category of invented family tradition.[15] But there is no gainsaying the added lustre Margaret of Scotland, the lady in question, brought to the family's name, or the crucial long-term significance she had in determining the de Vescys' place in the wider 'British' arena of politics, patronage and social relationships. Margaret was the bastard child of King William the Lion by his liaison with a daughter of the Berwickshire laird Adam of Whitsome. Eustace was therefore a brother-in-law of Alexander II, who reportedly was desolated when Eustace was killed beside him at Barnard Castle.[16] William II de Vescy, by half-blood, was Alexander's nephew and a first cousin of Alexander III; William the justiciar, in his turn, is found in 1291–2 suppressing the fact of his grandmother's illegitimacy and claiming the vacant Scottish throne itself on the grounds that he was the nearest heir of Margaret the Maid of Norway. Difficult though it is for us to regard William's bid to rule Scotland as anything other than frivolous, the

---

[12] For the attention given to the family's history at Alnwick abbey, Malton priory and Watton priory, see C. H. Hartshorne, *Feudal and Military Antiquities of Northumberland and the Scottish Borders* (London, 1858), App., pp. iii–v, cxvi–cxvii; Dugdale, *Monasticon Anglicanum*, vi, II, pp. 956–7, 972–3.

[13] Cf. J. C. Holt, *Colonial England 1066–1215* (London, 1997), pp. 224–6.

[14] A charter of *c.* 1230 brings together this William, Countess Ela of Salisbury (his mother-in-law), William II de Longespée (his brother-in-law), and Richard Marshal, earl of Pembroke (uncle of his future second wife): *The Cartulary of Bradenstoke Priory*, ed. V. C. M. London, Wiltshire Record Society (Devizes, 1979), no. 303.

[15] The earliest known versions of the story were recorded in Edward I's reign: Howlett (ed.), *Chronicles of the Reigns of Stephen, Henry II, and Richard I*, ii, p. 521 (Furness abbey annals); and, at much greater length, *The Chronicle of Walter of Guisborough*, ed. H. Rothwell, Camden Society (London, 1957), pp. 152–3.

[16] Roger of Wendover, *Flores Historiarum*, ii, p. 194

persistence with which he pressed his case points unmistakably to pride in his Scottish royal ancestry and a firm grasp of its importance as a marker of family identity. An alliance of lesser but still defining significance was John de Vescy's marriage in 1279 or 1280 to Isabella de Beaumont, a great-granddaughter of Alphonso IX, king of Leon, and a granddaughter of John de Brienne, king of Jerusalem and emperor of Constantinople. This redoubtable Frenchwoman went on after her husband's death to serve in the household of Queen Isabella, wife of Edward II, and to fall foul of the Lords Ordainer, who in 1311 had her banished from court.[17] Of more immediate concern is her kinship with Edward I's first wife, Eleanor of Castile, which firmly secured John de Vescy's place at the very heart of English affairs. It was a measure of the influence she wielded that when she followed John to Gascony in 1288, Edward I gave her lodgings adjacent to the royal apartments at Bonnegarde, and then had them specially renovated in preparation for Christmas.[18]

More generally, if such marriages reflected and reinforced the family's position in political society, they were less significant in terms of territorial riches. After Eustace fitz John's success in grabbing the heiress of Alnwick, the family captured only one lady of equivalent fortune. This was William II de Vescy's second wife Agnes, a daughter of William de Ferrers, fifth earl of Derby, and his wife Sybil, sister of Walter Marshal, eighth earl of Pembroke. In 1246–7, shortly after her wedding, Agnes was officially recognized as a Marshal coheiress in right of her late mother; but initially her prospects were modest, for she had no fewer than six sisters, and her claims on the vast Marshal inheritance were further limited by those of several dowagers and Sybil Marshal's four sisters or their representatives. For the de Vescys, therefore, social and political considerations were often more important factors in their marriages than wealth.

None the less, land naturally held a focal place in the family's sense of itself and how it was perceived by others. For most of the twelfth century its ample territories were confined mainly to Northumberland and Yorkshire, and by far the bulk of them had been amassed by Eustace fitz John. The Scottish barony of Sprouston in Roxburghshire, a relatively small estate, came to the family through Margaret of Scotland in 1193.[19]

---

[17] J. C. Davies, *The Baronial Opposition to Edward II* (Cambridge, 1918), pp. 106, 370–1; M. Prestwich, 'Isabella de Vescy and the custody of Bamburgh castle', *Bulletin of the Institute of Historical Research*, 44 (1971), pp. 148–52.

[18] *Records of the Wardrobe and Household, 1286–1289*, ed. B. F. and C. R. Byerly (London, 1986), no. 1676.

[19] *Origines Parochiales Scotiae*, ed. C. Innes *et al.*, 2 vols. in 3, Bannatyne Club (Edinburgh, 1851–5), i, pp. 437–8, 440–1.

Thereafter there was no major shift in the landholding pattern until Agnes de Vescy began to make inroads into the Marshal patrimony, including its Welsh and Irish properties. Agnes's long widowhood from 1253 ensured, however, that none of her gains would be fully merged with the main family lands until as late as 1290, by which date the greatest of her assets was the liberty of Kildare, one of the four main subdivisions of the Marshal lordship of Leinster. Kildare then descended to her younger and only surviving son William the justiciar; and its extensive franchisal powers gave him the kind of authority denied to him in England but not, significantly, in Scotland, where his formal rights were in fact more completely 'royal'. According to an inquest of 1320 into the liberties and customs of Sprouston barony, it had been held 'royally (*regaliter*) by the same liberties with which lord Alexander [III], king of Scotland, recently held the other lands of his kingdom . . . and . . . the lord de Vescy could appoint in . . . Sprouston his own justiciar, chamberlain, chancellor, coroners and serjeants'.[20] If it seems hardly likely that Sprouston's regality rights were determined by its former status as an Anglian royal centre,[21] they were certainly a measure of the stature and respect the de Vescys commanded as the Scots king's close kin.

In terms of incomes, when the 'honour of William [I] de Vescy' was in Henry II's hands its value to the English crown for the exchequer year 1186–7 was set at £387 8s 2d, a figure that understates its true worth, for the lands were at farm rather than in custody. In 1254 the English patrimony was extended at £625 8s 10d a year, with three dower manors assigned to Agnes de Vescy excluded from the reckoning. Woefully sparse and uninformative though such statistics are, it seems that the yield of the English estates alone bore favourable comparison with those of important lordships like the honours of Chester, Cornwall, Huntingdon and Lancaster.[22] That would help to explain the hefty 1,300 – mark fine imposed on Eustace de Vescy when he came of age in 1190; while later it is impossible not to be impressed by John de Vescy's spending-power. To give a single example, he undertook in 1267 to pay Count Guy of Saint-Pol 3,700 marks to redeem his estates in England

---

[20] *RRS*, v, no. 172. By contrast with the de Vescys' judicial powers at Sprouston, the jurisdiction of the liberty court of Kildare did not extend to the four chief pleas of the crown: A. J. Otway-Ruthven, 'The medieval county of Kildare', *IHS*, 11 (1958–9), p. 190.

[21] I. M. Smith, 'Sprouston, Roxburghshire: an early Anglian centre of the eastern Tweed basin', *Proceedings of the Society of Antiquaries of Scotland*, 121 (1991), pp. 261–94.

[22] *Pipe Roll 1186–7: The Great Roll of the Pipe for the Thirty-Third Year of the Reign of Henry II*, PRS, 37 (London, 1915), pp. 12–13; *CDS*, i, no. 1954. Cf. K. J. Stringer, *Earl David of Huntingdon, 1152–1219: A Study in Anglo-Scottish History* (Edinburgh, 1985), p. 111; S. Painter, *Studies in the History of the English Feudal Barony* (Baltimore, 1943), pp. 170ff.

under the Dictum of Kenilworth, and accounted for all but 700 marks of that weighty sum within three years.[23] The focal points of the family lands included, or came to include, the major castles of Alnwick, Malton in the Vale of Pickering, Caerleon in Gwent and Kildare; there were lesser residences at Sprouston, Tughall in Northumberland, Newsholme in Yorkshire, Caythorpe in Lincolnshire and Eltham in Kent, not to mention townhouses in Pontefract, Lincoln and London.[24]

Their estates not only placed the de Vescys among the richest baronial families in the British Isles, but supported in addition numerous individual well-wishers who looked to them for leadership and – not least – religious communities which met their need for assistance in both this world and the next. This last aspect offers a particularly striking insight into family values and aspirations. While Eustace fitz John's brother Pain played an influential role in the success of Llanthony priory, the first Augustinian house in Wales,[25] far more remarkable and instructive is his own munificence in establishing a Premonstratensian abbey at Alnwick, a Gilbertine priory for both sexes at Watton, near Beverley and another – for canons only – at Malton. Watton and Malton, begun by 1150, were almost certainly the first Gilbertine plantations anywhere in England outside Lincolnshire; Alnwick, founded in 1147–8, was only the second English Premonstratensian abbey after Newhouse. In addition, at North Ferriby on the Humber, Eustace or William I de Vescy set up a small priory affiliated to the exotic canonical order of the Temple of the Lord in Jerusalem. A multiplicity of motives lay behind any magnate's support of reform monasticism, and important as good deeds were as a means of proclaiming a family's solidarity in terms of its spiritual well-being, Eustace's prominent involvement was scarcely based on religious considerations alone. Yet he nevertheless helped to set the fashion as a leading connoisseur of the new orders, surely the mark of lay piety of more than the conventional sort.[26] Moreover, receptiveness to religious innovation would become an increasingly conspicuous badge of family identity. William II de Vescy played a key role in introducing the Carmelites from Palestine to England by founding Hulne priory, 2 miles north-west of Alnwick, in or shortly

---

[23] *CDS*, i, nos. 213, 2456; cf. C. H. Knowles, 'The resettlement of England after the Barons' War, 1264–67', *TRHS*, 5th series, 32 (1982), p. 41.

[24] Alnwick, though heavily rebuilt in the fourteenth century and later, is the best preserved of the de Vescy castles, and the most thoroughly discussed: see D. J. C. King, *Castellarium Anglicanum: an Index and Bibliography of the Castles in England, Wales and the Islands*, 2 vols. (London, 1983), ii, p. 325.

[25] F. G. Cowley, *The Monastic Order in South Wales, 1066–1349* (Cardiff, 1977), p. 30.

[26] See especially Dalton, 'Eustace fitz John', pp. 374–9, supplemented by B. Golding, *Gilbert of Sempringham and the Gilbertine Order, c. 1130–c. 1300* (Oxford, 1995), pp. 215–17, 220–1.

before 1242.²⁷ Indeed, not only was Hulne probably the first English house of the Carmelite order, but William was then virtually its only benefactor of note in Western Europe as a whole. In 1286 John de Vescy undertook to endow a nunnery at Newcastle upon Tyne for the Poor Clares, who then had only one English convent to their name.²⁸ William the justiciar was an admirer of that outstanding advocate of the mendicant movement, Robert Grosseteste, whose holy life and good works he personally commended to Pope Honorius IV in 1286; he provided a new site in the Stonebow for the Carmelites of York in 1295, and had already helped to bring the order to Ireland by founding in *c*. 1290 St Mary's priory, Kildare. One or other of the de Vescys also has some claim to be regarded as the founder of the Franciscan friary at Kildare.²⁹

More obvious still is the profound influence exerted on the family's outlook and stature by the demands and benefits of English royal service. Eustace fitz John's empire-building as one of Henry I's chief agents in northern England has recently been highlighted, as has the almost equally meteoric career of his brother Pain, a rising star of Beauclerk's administration in western England.³⁰ None of Eustace's immediate successors enjoyed similar status as a royal officer, but in Edward I's reign the family came again to the forefront of public service. Controlling a vast bureaucratic, financial and military establishment as justiciar of Ireland (1290–4), William III de Vescy occupied the single most important and taxing position in contemporary English provincial governance. As Edward I's *alter ego* he presided over Irish parliaments; it was likewise within his power to intervene as a king-maker in Connacht during the Ua Conchobair succession dispute in 1293.³¹ Nor can it seriously be doubted from the storm of protest his regime provoked that William freely used his governorship to further his own interests as well as the crown's, however much his shortcomings were overdrawn by troublemakers bent on destroying him.³² His elder brother John, while holding no great office of state, enjoyed a long and distinguished career

---

[27] K. J. Egan, 'Medieval Carmelite houses, England and Wales', *Carmelus*, 16 (1969), pp. 145, 179–80. See also D. Knowles and J. K. S. St Joseph, *Monastic Sites from the Air* (Cambridge, 1952), pp. 256–7, for the substantial remains of the priory's buildings; other sites covered include Alnwick (at pp. 152–3) and Watton (at pp. 246–7).
[28] *Cal. Papal Letters*, i, p. 490.
[29] *Recueil de Lettres Anglo-Françaises (1265–1399)*, ed. F. J. Tanquerey (Paris, 1916), no. 53; Egan, 'Carmelite houses', pp. 225–6; Gwynn and Hadcock, *Medieval Religious Houses: Ireland*, pp. 252, 290.
[30] Dalton, 'Eustace fitz John', pp. 360–5; P. Dalton, *Conquest, Anarchy and Lordship: Yorkshire, 1066–1154* (Cambridge, 1994), pp. 96–9, 104–7; J. A. Green, *The Government of England under Henry I* (Cambridge, 1986), esp. pp. 250–3.
[31] *AC*, s.a. 1293.
[32] Cf. Otway-Ruthven, *History of Medieval Ireland*, p. 209: his 'activities produced a

in Edward I's service as a trusted senior counsellor (*familiaris et secretarius*).³³ Particularly well documented is the embassy that took him to Spain in 1282 to conclude the marriage contract between Edward I's eldest daughter Eleanor and Alphonso of Aragon. The surviving material includes a record of the actual words spoken by John when, as the absent Eleanor's proctor, he exchanged vows with Alphonso during the marriage ceremony at Huesca on 15 August; and still to be found in the Aragonese royal archives at Barcelona is the original notarial instrument, authenticated with his *signum*, in which he promised prompt payment of Eleanor's dowry.³⁴ Such weighty responsibilities placed John firmly at the hub of Edwardian diplomacy and policy-making, as was underlined when, on John's death, Edward I swiftly issued instructions to safeguard state secrets by having all the documents kept in John's private quarters at London secured and carefully sifted.³⁵ Crown service also brought him into close association with other prominent members of the king's inner council – most notably Anthony Bek, bishop of Durham, and Otto de Grandson, with whom he was frequently engaged on royal affairs in England, Wales, Ireland, the Low Countries, Savoy, Gascony and Spain.³⁶ Most of all, many are the indications of strong bonds of friendship between John and Edward I himself, none being more eloquent than the tributes paid by the king following John's death in 1289 at Montpellier in Provence. Edward attended John's obsequies on the return of his body to Gascony, ensured that masses were celebrated for his soul by the friars of Morlaàs, Orthez and Oloron-Sainte-Marie, and then in 1290 had his heart buried with the hearts of Eleanor of Castile and her son Alphonso at Blackfriars in London.³⁷

For similar glimpses of personal intimacy with an English king, we can look back to Eustace fitz John who, judged Aelred of Rievaulx, was Henry I's closest friend in noble society, and to Pain fitz John, the butt of a colourful tale by Walter Map about how King Henry's unpredict-

greater surviving volume of complaint than those of any other chief governor of the middle ages'.

[33] *CPR*, 1281–92, p. 11.

[34] P. Chaplais, *English Medieval Diplomatic Practice Part I: Documents and Interpretation*, 2 vols. (London, 1982), ii, pp. 471–8.

[35] *CPR*, 1281–92, p. 321.

[36] M. Prestwich, *Edward I* (London, 1988), pp. 84, 180, 199, 305, 321, 325; C. M. Fraser, *A History of Antony Bek, Bishop of Durham, 1283–1311* (Oxford, 1957), pp. 21, 24–5, 50–2; E. R. Clifford, *A Knight of Great Renown: The Life and Times of Othon de Grandson* (Chicago, 1961), pp. 50–2, 71, 84, 110; R. Flower, 'Manuscripts of Irish interest in the British Museum', *Analecta Hibernica*, 2 (1931), p. 332. John appointed both Bek and Grandson as executors of his will: *CPR*, 1281–92, pp. 322, 347, 356.

[37] Byerly and Byerly (eds.), *Records of the Wardrobe and Household*, nos. 1722, 2493, 2497, 2502; *Chronicles of the Reigns of Edward I and Edward II*, ed. W. Stubbs, 2 vols., RS (London, 1882–3), i, p. 99.

able drinking habits flummoxed his courtiers.³⁸ No evidence of an equivalent sort survives for William the justiciar; in fact the very nature of his office isolated him from court – a critical weakness that prevented him from defending himself in person when Edward I began to receive from Ireland complaints about his activities.³⁹ And William's humiliation – he was dismissed in disgrace in 1294 – reminds us of the possible pitfalls of English royal service. It also serves to introduce another key aspect of the family's priorities and values. Tactically it was a masterstroke by William's implacable enemy John fitz Thomas of Offaly to charge him with treason for, however paradoxical it may seem, the family identified itself almost as much by its opposition to the English crown as by its public service. During Stephen's reign, when in John of Salisbury's words 'the measure of right was force',⁴⁰ Eustace fitz John had the dubious distinction in 1138 of being the first of the king's victims to be summarily arrested at court under suspicion of treachery, and he openly allied himself with Stephen's enemies as soon as he could. This 'wicked traitor', as Roger of Howden remembered him, also paraded his contempt for Stephen's sovereignty by having coins struck in his own name at York.⁴¹ Eustace de Vescy, as one of King John's foremost opponents, was seemingly prepared to cast aside all convention by plotting regicide, and was publicly condemned in the county courts as a traitor in 1212; he was one of few magnates ever to be sent a special papal mandate not to conspire against the English crown, and became a member of the baronial committee of Twenty-Five charged with enforcing Magna Carta.⁴² John de Vescy, for all his subsequent prominence in Edward I's household and council, was a leader of the Montfortian cause, and gave ample proof of his commitment to it by mounting a rising against Henry III from Alnwick as late as 1267. The de Vescys were therefore by no means always at the service of the English monarchy, and their blemished past surely helps to explain Edward I's decision to dismiss William the justiciar once a charge of treason had

---

³⁸ Howlett (ed.), *Chronicles of the Reigns of Stephen, Henry II, and Richard I*, iii, p. 191; Walter Map, *De Nugis Curialium*, ed. and trans. M. R. James, C. N. L. Brooke and R. A. B. Mynors (Oxford, 1983), pp. 440–1.
³⁹ For a letter of 2 February 1293/4 in which the justiciar urged John Langton, chancellor of England, not to pay heed to the clerk Robert de Halywell, who had spoken against him to the king, see *Cal. Doc. Ire.*, 1285–1292, no. 1171.
⁴⁰ John of Salisbury, *Policraticus*, ed. and trans. C. J. Nederman (Cambridge, 1990), p. 119.
⁴¹ Roger of Howden, *Chronica*, i, p. 193; M. Blackburn, 'Coinage and currency', in *The Anarchy of King Stephen's Reign*, ed. E. King (Oxford, 1994), pp. 182–7.
⁴² J. C. Holt, *The Northerners: A Study in the Reign of King John*, new edn (Oxford, 1992), pp. 23, 81–2, 95; C. R. Cheney, *Pope Innocent III and England* (Stuttgart, 1976), p. 366.

been levelled against him. According to John fitz Thomas's sworn deposition, William had acted against both 'the lord our king and his state' by declaring that the people of Ireland, if so minded, could easily increase their power at Edward's expense; by insisting that Edward was 'the most perverse and dastardly knight of his kingdom'; and by asserting that he had been proved a coward during the Barons' Wars.[43] The emphasis fitz Thomas placed on the last of his allegations has puzzled historians.[44] His whole testimony may of course have been pure invention; but if so it remains the case that William himself had been a Montfortian, and no doubt the accusations were all the more damaging for being framed in terms bound to refresh Edward's memory of his previous unreliability.

So far we have looked at the most obvious defining aspects of the de Vescys' sense of themselves. All were more or less central to the *Weltanschauung* of contemporary baronial society, but they nevertheless had a particular importance for moulding the family's perception of its own identity. On closer inspection, however, it is difficult to see how study of its interests and outlook should be focused. At one level, an integrative 'British history' approach provides an admirable framework – the more so when fuller account is taken of how far Wales and Ireland figured in the family's experiences. As a war captain, for instance, John de Vescy followed in Eustace fitz John's footsteps to north Wales, where he served with distinction in Anglesey (1277) and Snowdonia (1283); he also supervised the building work at Builth, the first of Edward I's new Welsh castles, in 1284. Earlier, William II de Vescy had resolutely battled for his wife's rights in the former Marshal lordship of Caerleon in a 'private' war against Morgan ap Hywel (d. 1248).[45] In Ireland, there is no denying the vigour with which Agnes de Vescy herself set about restoring the territorial integrity of the 'shire' of Kildare, partitioned after the last Earl Marshal's death in 1245, and turning it into a formidable personal power base. By 1278, despite the claims of her surviving sisters and coparceners, she had secured the lion's share, with the right to control local government by appointing a steward, chancellor and treasurer.[46] Her successful power-building, which so impressed Archbishop Wickwane of York that he referred to her as

---

[43] *Cal. Doc. Ire.*, 1293–1301, no. 147; *Rotuli Parliamentorum*, 7 vols., Record Commission (London, 1783–1832), i, pp. 127, 132.
[44] Cf. G. J. Hand, *English Law in Ireland, 1290–1324* (Cambridge, 1967), p. 146, n. 1.
[45] J. E. Morris, *The Welsh Wars of Edward I* (Oxford, 1901), pp. 121, 134–5, 148, 187–92; *Cl. R.*, 1247–51, p. 136.
[46] *Cal. Doc. Ire.*, 1252–1284, nos. 896, 935, 1096, 1333, 1503. For helpful accounts of the complex story of the partition and descent of the Marshal lands in Ireland, see

'countess of Kildare',[47] was no doubt greatly assisted by the growing influence of her elder son John at Edward I's court; but it was William the justiciar who took it upon himself to complete the de Vescy campaign to impose effective mastery over Kildare – and who in the process quarrelled furiously with not only John fitz Thomas but, among others, the abbot of Clonard, the abbot of St Thomas's, Dublin, the bishop of Kildare and the burgesses of Castledermot. Following Agnes's example, he employed as his chief weapon the liberty court or *curia comitatus* at Kildare, whose jurisdiction was protected and extended as a means of asserting his superiority not just over his own estates but throughout the entire county, including the Geraldine territories in Offaly and Laois, and lands regarded by monastic proprietors as crosslands (*terre incroceate*) reserved to the king's direct jurisdiction. He summoned all freeholders in the county to his court, and repeatedly distrained those who defied its authority; he asserted his exclusive right to hear all manner of common pleas and almost all pleas of the crown; he defended his liberties by protesting against interference by royal officials; he demanded that his sheriff be allowed to take his tourn through the whole county; he insisted that his own peace as well as the king's be satisfied by felons; and he apparently had no scruples about using violence 'under the cloak of his jurisdiction'.[48] There was indeed nothing tentative about William's efforts to forge a mighty supremacy in Ireland; nor would the story be complete without stressing his attempts to build up a Gaelic clientage network by taking as his mistress Derbforgaill, daughter of Domnall Ruad Mac Carthaig, lord or 'king' of the Irish of Desmond (1262–1302).[49] Here seemingly was a magnate who, to borrow a phrase of Robin Frame, was confident of his ability 'to bestride the Gaelic, Anglo-Irish, and English worlds'.[50]

Nevertheless, the de Vescys' role on the broader 'British' stage involves considerable elements of complexity and ambiguity. It might be

Orpen, *Ireland under the Normans*, iii, ch. 26; and, more particularly, Otway-Ruthven, 'Medieval county of Kildare', pp. 181–99.

[47] *The Register of William Wickwane, Lord Archbishop of York, 1279–1285*, ed. W. Brown, Surtees Society (Durham and London, 1907), no. 624.

[48] Much of the evidence used in this section is conveniently calendared in *Cal. Doc. Ire.*, 1293–1301, nos. 22, 26, 42, 101, 106. Also indispensable is *Rotuli Parliamentorum Anglie Hactenus Inediti, MCCLXXIX–MCCCLXXIII*, ed. H. G. Richardson and G. O. Sayles, Camden Society (London, 1935), pp. 30–45; quotation at p. 39. The medieval county embraced modern Co. Kildare, much of the counties of Offaly and Laois, and part of county Wicklow. For the forcefulness of Agnes's judicial lordship, see Prestwich, *Edward I*, p. 263, and note 88, below (concerning Yorkshire).

[49] William 'of Kildare' is located as the justiciar's son by Derbforgaill, 'filia cujusdam regine [sic] Hibernie, nomine Dovenald Rochmaccarti', in a genealogy of the founders of Watton priory compiled by 1314: Dugdale, *Monasticon Anglicanum*, vi, II, p. 957.

[50] R. Frame, *English Lordship in Ireland, 1318–1361* (Oxford, 1982), p. 298.

claimed, for example, that in the thirteenth century the family's *European* experiences did as much to shape its identity and perceptions – an argument that John de Vescy's matrimonial adventures serve only to strengthen. Henry III and Edward I dangled in front of him a succession of potential continental brides, including a daughter of the viscount of Aosta and a sister of the count of La Marche and Angoulême. In the event, his first wife was the Savoyard, Agnes of Saluzzo, while his second marriage, to Isabella de Beaumont, was self-evidently another European alliance. Moreover, occasionally Western Christendom itself seemed to command the family's primary loyalty. John went on the Lord Edward's crusade in 1270–2, and in his will bequeathed 1,000 marks towards the Holy Land's defence.[51] His father, William II de Vescy, had apparently been a crusading companion of Earl Richard of Cornwall and, according to Carmelite tradition, he encountered among the hermits of Mount Carmel a Northumbrian convert, Ralph Fresborne, whom he brought back to England and established as first prior of Hulne. The precise details of this story may not be true.[52] Yet when John de Vescy is found referring to the 'brothers of the order of the Blessed Mary of Mount Carmel serving God ... in my forest of Alnwick', we are reminded not only of Robert Bartlett's striking phrase 'the Europeanization of Europe',[53] but that men like the de Vescys self-consciously viewed Latin Christendom in small-world terms. Politically, indeed, no more dramatic expression of this outlook was provided by the family than when Eustace de Vescy negotiated with the papal Curia early in 1215 through his clerk, John of Ferriby, who during a personal audience with Pope Innocent III urged him to curb King John's excesses by exercising his rights as overlord of England.[54]

---

[51] *Historical Papers and Letters from the Northern Registers*, ed. J. Raine, RS (London, 1873), no. 164. In 1276 John and William III de Vescy were granted safe-conducts to go on pilgrimage to Santiago de Compostela.

[52] The fourteenth-century Carmelite William of Coventry wrote that John de Vescy (sic) returned to Northumberland with a brother of Mount Carmel and endowed him at Hulne: *Medieval Carmelite Heritage: Early Reflections on the Nature of the Order*, ed. A. Staring (Rome, 1989), pp. 285–6. John Bale (*d.* 1563) identified the brother concerned as Ralph Fresborne, '*ex Anglia natus, in septentrionali insule regione*': J. Bale, *Illustrium Maioris Britanniae Scriptorum* (1548), fol. 103^v. I am most grateful to my colleague Dr Andrew Jotischky for his guidance here. Sceptical comment is provided in K. J. Egan, 'An essay toward a historiography of the origin of the Carmelite province in England', *Carmelus*, 19 (1972), pp. 67–100; but some historical basis for Ralph Fresborne's existence is suggested by the contemporary references in *A History of Northumberland*, 15 vols. (Newcastle upon Tyne, 1893–1940), xv, pp. 370–1, to members of the Frebern (Freborn) family, whose estates included Shipley, near Hulne. See also note 104, below.

[53] Hartshorne, *Feudal and Military Antiquities of Northumberland*, App., p. lxix; Bartlett, *Making of Europe*, ch. 11.

[54] *Diplomatic Documents, 1101–1272*, ed. P. Chaplais (London, 1964), no. 19.

But what of the day-to-day realities of the family's activities? In other words, the crucial next step is to address more rigorously the nuances of its identity in terms of its immediate environment and concerns. In 1279 John de Vescy's itinerary embraced Sprouston, Alnwick and London,[55] and there can be little doubt that, for all their prominence on a wider stage, the de Vescys felt most at home within this geographical context. From a 'British' perspective, it has after all to be underlined that while Kildare was the family's most substantial acquisition since Eustace fitz John's golden years of aggrandizement, the male line, in the person of William the justiciar, held it for only seven years. Furthermore, when William tried to insert himself as a newcomer into 'English' Ireland, in practice he rapidly found himself at sea in an unfamiliar world; while his effective rejection as an intruder by a powerful section of the Anglo-Irish community can only have emphasized his sense of estrangement and the need to retreat behind customary boundaries and identities. Indeed, the depth of his predicament was such that in 1294 John fitz Thomas and his Gaelic Irish allies plundered the town of Kildare and struck a crippling blow by burning all the court rolls kept in the castle; and his difficulties are further highlighted for us in an inquisition taken at Kildare in 1298, with its repeated references to property rendered worthless because of 'the war of the Irish'.[56] Most devastating of all, however, was fitz Thomas's determined assault on the very heart of William's being – his honour and good name. There was no better way of taking revenge on a fellow noble, or of proclaiming his 'otherness' and ostracizing him as an outsider, than by publicly shaming him. When, as we will see, William resigned the liberty of Kildare to Edward I, he probably had few regrets.

The family's 'British' outlook, even its own sense of Englishness, was also defined and limited by the concentrated nature of its main territories on the other side of the Irish Sea. It did not put down firm roots in Wales, for in c. 1269 Agnes de Vescy sold her rights in the castle and lordship of Caerleon to Earl Gilbert de Clare.[57] In England itself, lands were held at one time or another in at least eighteen different shires. The most southerly interests included Eltham manor in Kent, with which Edward I jointly enfeoffed John de Vescy and Isabella de Beaumont, and

---

[55] *Liber Sancte Marie de Melros*, ed. C. Innes, 2 vols., Bannatyne Club (Edinburgh, 1837), i, no. 346; *The Percy Chartulary*, ed. M. T. Martin, Surtees Society (Durham and London, 1911), no. 707; *Calendar of the Charter Rolls*, 6 vols. (London, 1903–27), ii, p. 218.

[56] *Calendar of the Justiciary Rolls . . . of Ireland*, ed. J. Mills *et al.* 3 vols. (Dublin, 1905–56), i, pp. 118, 189–90; *Cal. Doc. Ire.*, 1293–1301, no. 481.

[57] British Library, London [hereafter BL], Inventories of Mortimer Muniments, MS Additional 6041, fol. 78ʳ.

former Marshal estates in Dorset. Yet such gains as these – alongside which may be noted the castle and barony of Dunster in Somerset, held in custody by John de Vescy in 1282–9[58] – were never sufficient to redefine the twelfth-century orientation of the family's main English landholdings. That the North remained its chief centre of gravity and source of identity was indicated when Eustace de Vescy gave all his land at Saxlingham in Norfolk, the family's original English patrimony, in part-exchange for property in Cumberland and Yorkshire, and when in his land deals John de Vescy resorted to sales in Gloucestershire and Somerset.[59] Furthermore, the family's marriages often served to reaffirm their connections with Northumbrian society. Inheriting sons could explore broader horizons, and none did so more extensively than John himself, as has been seen. But alliances far from 'home' were not the rule, nor were they necessarily a matter of family policy;[60] and through successive marriages close links were forged with, among others, the Lacys and Stutevilles in Yorkshire and the Bertrams, Bolbecs and Muschamps in Northumberland.

A northern emphasis was demonstrated in an equally instructive fashion by the de Vescys' continued and vigorous involvement in local office-holding, whether as keepers of the castles of York and Scarborough or as justices of the forest north of the Trent. The force of their identification with the North was also clearly recognizable to others, as when Matthew Paris referred to William II de Vescy as 'one of the most noble barons of the northern parts of England'.[61] Above all, it was first and foremost as Northerners that the de Vescys were rewarded, cajoled or disciplined by the English crown. No king of England from Henry I to Edward I could afford to ignore the family's ability to influence the tempo of northern politics and the key role it played in determining whether or not the north was securely under the royal thumb. Eustace fitz John's rapid promotion reflected Henry I's need to incorporate what was then a semi-conquered province into the remainder of the kingdom;

---

[58] *Calendar of Inquisitions Post Mortem and other Analogous Documents ... Henry III – [Richard II]*, 16 vols. (London, 1904–74), ii, no. 723; *Inquisitions and Assessments Relating to Feudal Aids*, 6 vols. (London, 1899–1920), ii, pp. 6, 20; *Documents and Extracts Illustrating the History of the Honour of Dunster*, ed. H. C. Maxwell Lyte, Somerset Record Society (London, 1917–18), pp. xvii, xix, 51–2, 57, 65.

[59] *St Benet of Holme, 1020–1210: The Eleventh and Twelfth Century Sections of Cott. MS. Galba E.ii*, ed. J. R. West, Norfolk Record Society (Fakenham and London, 1932), no. 144; *CCR*, 1279–88, pp. 178, 186; *CCR*, 1288–96, p. 126.

[60] In the thirteenth century the minorities of William II (1216–26) and John (1253–64) meant that marriages twice passed out of family control: William was obliged to wed the daughter of his guardian Earl William of Salisbury; John's marriage to Agnes of Saluzzo was arranged by Peter of Savoy.

[61] Matthew Paris, *Chronica Majora*, v, p. 410.

and even in the more tightly integrated thirteenth-century English state, the crown needed little reminder that without the de Vescys' support its control of northern England was likely to falter. Their most fundamental duty was naturally to provide local leadership and defence in the event of a Scottish invasion. That was a task performed to perfection by William I de Vescy, of whom no more could have been asked when he shared command of the relief force that left Newcastle on the morning of 13 July 1174, and returned there in triumph at nightfall having surprised and captured William the Lion in front of Alnwick. His retinue added to King William's humiliation by taking nearly a hundred prisoners; church bells rang out across England;[62] and it was this stunning *coup de main* that above all established the de Vescys' military reputation and, not least, made their name as Northerners. Conversely, it was by drawing on their power as northern magnates that they played such a crucial and well-recognized role in the baronial opposition to Stephen and John; it was likewise their local hegemonies that made them such attractive allies to Scots kings in terms of their own ambitions towards the 'English' North. Thus whereas in 1173–4, when Alnwick castle stood firm, the Scottish invasions rapidly lost momentum, in 1138 and 1215 the family's backing for the Scots helped to bring Northumberland swiftly under Scottish control. And whereas in 1283 John de Vescy used his influence on Edward I's behalf to secure Anthony Bek's election as bishop of Durham, in 1141 Eustace fitz John had assisted David I of Scotland's former chancellor William Cumin to commandeer the bishopric.[63] Moreover, the family's influence south of the Tees was such that whenever it colluded with the Scots, Yorkshire itself became vulnerable. Even in 1264–5, when Alexander III did not exploit Henry III's difficulties, much of the blame for making the county effectively ungovernable was laid at John de Vescy's door.[64]

But if in terms of their military, political and territorial might the de Vescys paraded their identity primarily as Northerners, how would they have defined 'the North'? They were entitled to think broadly of a 'greater North' embracing even Lincolnshire, where they held in chief the important manor and soke of Caythorpe, near Grantham.[65] Much

---

[62] Johnston (ed.), *Jordan Fantosme's Chronicle*, lines 1888–9; Howlett (ed.), *Chronicles of the Reigns of Stephen, Henry II, and Richard I*, i, p. 185.
[63] Fraser, *History of Antony Bek*, p. 34; Dalton, 'Eustace fitz John', p. 371.
[64] See especially *Cl. R.*, 1268–72, pp. 148–9; *CCR*, 1272–9, p. 371.
[65] A vivid sense of Caythorpe's significance is supplied by BL, Cartulary of Malton Priory, MS Cotton Claudius D.xi, fol. 40^v: charter of William II de Vescy, 2 August 1251, addressed to 'all his stewards, bailiffs, serjeants and all his other ministers of the soke of Caythorpe'. On the other hand, Eustace de Vescy sacrificed part of his rent income at Caythorpe in exchange for land at Rugley, near Alnwick; while in 1290 William the justiciar leased out all the dower lands and rents held in Lincolnshire by his wife

more significant were their extensive Yorkshire holdings, which in crude financial terms were seen as their most valuable collection of English estates, at any rate in 1219.[66] Yet they were never as emphatically Yorkshire in their interests as were other magnates. That was one reason why no volume on the de Vescys ever appeared in William Farrer's and Sir Charles Clay's magnificent series, *Early Yorkshire Charters*. Another, as Clay himself stressed, lay in the sheer complexities of their place in the feudal map of Yorkshire.[67] Indeed, their scrambled assemblage of Yorkshire manors and knights' fees not only lacked geographical unity but consisted largely of property held by mesne tenure. There is, to be sure, unmistakable evidence that Eustace fitz John had wanted to impress by simultaneously developing Alnwick and Malton, or rather *New* Malton, as the twin 'capitals' of his northern lands. It was his vision and careful planning that equipped each with an important castle, a borough and an adjoining abbey or priory – the classic features of major headquarters estates.[68] Yet it can hardly be doubted that the family's territorial status in Yorkshire remained muddled and uncertain, exposed it to much jockeying for position, and in general left a good deal to be desired. In the East Riding all its chief demesne manors were held of more powerful neighbours – Langton of the Stutevilles, and Brind, Gribthorpe, Newsholme, Thornton and Wintringham of the Mortimers. In the North Riding its so-called 'honour' of Brompton (in Pickering Lythe wapentake) was a sub-tenancy under the Mowbrays, who also claimed superiority even over the 'honour' of Malton itself.[69]

While all this weakened the de Vescys' lordly authority and made it less of a force, that is far from saying that they did not routinely cut important figures among the Yorkshire élite. They regularly attended the county court and were often specially called on to arbitrate in local

---

Isabella, widow of Robert de Welle, albeit reserving the park at Aby: Martin (ed.), *Percy Chartulary*, no. 831; BL, Harley Charter 57.C.33.

[66] In 1219 the estimated annual values of the family's lands in Yorkshire, Northumberland and Lincolnshire were £135 8s 4d, £101 13s 4d, and £50 respectively: *The Book of Fees commonly called Testa de Nevill*, ed. H. C. Maxwell Lyte, 2 vols. in 3 (London, 1920–31), i, pp. 246–8, 250, 286.

[67] *Early Yorkshire Charters*, ed. W. Farrer, vols. i–iii (Edinburgh, 1914–16) and C. T. Clay, vols. iv–xii, Yorkshire Archaeological Society, Record Series, Extra Series (Wakefield, 1935–65) [hereafter *EYC*], x, p. ix. Both Farrer and Clay nevertheless did contemplate a de Vescy volume; and I have consulted with profit Farrer's preparatory notes (chiefly concerning Yorkshire): West Yorkshire Archives Service, Leeds, Yorkshire Archaeological Society, MS 869/20.

[68] See especially M. Beresford, *New Towns of the Middle Ages* (London, 1967), pp. 469–70, 517.

[69] *EYC*, iii, pp. 485–8; ix, pp. 177–9; *Victoria History of the Counties of England, Yorkshire: North Riding* (London, 1914–), i, p. 532; ii, p. 426. For the honorial court of Brompton, see *EYC*, xii, no. 52; Brynmor Jones Library, University of Hull, Constable-Maxwell Muniments, DDEV/50/1(j).

disputes;[70] they asserted their lordship through their own courts at Malton and Brompton; and they derived enhanced prestige in county society from their role as patrons of the Gilbertines at Malton and Watton. The canons of Malton were thus 'their' canons, on whose behalf, for instance, Eustace de Vescy – *'dilectus dominus et advocatus noster'* – wrote personally and forcefully to an ecclesiastical tribunal headed by the bishop of Durham when a judgement threatened to go against them.[71] Yet, as will be seen, relations between the de Vescys and the Gilbertines were by no means uniformly amicable; nor can it be doubted that both Malton and Watton also relied heavily on the goodwill of other influential laymen, not least the Lacys who – as successors and heirs of Eustace fitz John's second wife Agnes – adopted an overtly proprietorial attitude towards both priories.[72] And, most importantly, it can hardly be said that Yorkshire was fundamental to the family's interests and identity when in 1253 the manors of Malton, Brompton and Langton were allocated in dower to Agnes de Vescy, in whose hands they remained for the next thirty-seven years.[73]

In the final analysis, 'the North' meant to the de Vescys 'the *far* North' – perhaps one should say the 'real' North – for what shaped their assumptions and attitudes was above all their status as Borderers. Most lords of the northern march belonged to an identifiable and relatively close-knit group, with a strong sense of regional loyalty based on ties of residence, neighbourhood and mutual cooperation.[74] Yet what made the de Vescys special in this context was their outstanding position in English Border society. They lorded it in Northumberland in ways they could scarcely lord it in Yorkshire. The large and compact barony of Alnwick was far and away the most imposing in the county. It dominated the coastal lowlands along a 20-mile stretch from Amble Bay to Budle Bay, while its upland territories occupied much of the Cheviot foothills from Upper Coquetdale to Glendale.[75] Here indeed was 'a stately

---

[70] For examples concerning William II and John de Vescy, see *Abstracts of the Charters and other Documents contained in the Chartulary of the Cistercian Abbey of Fountains*, ed. W. T. Lancaster, 2 vols. (Leeds, 1915), ii, p. 462; Raine (ed.), *Historians of the Church of York and its Archbishops*, iii, p. 164; Fraser, *History of Antony Bek*, pp. 40, 137; *CPR, 1272–81*, p. 339.

[71] BL, MS Cott. Claud. D.xi, fols. 38^v, 39^r.

[72] Dugdale, *Monasticon Anglicanum*, vi, II, p. 956; *EYC*, ii, no. 1112; iii, no. 1889; Golding, *Gilbert of Sempringham*, p. 317. Agnes was sister and coheiress of William constable of Chester, and Watton priory (though not Malton) had been founded on her patrimony.

[73] *CDS*, i, no. 1954; *Calendar of Inquisitions Post Mortem*, ii, no. 723.

[74] For a recent exploration, see K. J. Stringer, 'Identities in thirteenth-century England: frontier society in the far North', in *Social and Political Identities in Western History*, ed. C. Bjørn, A. Grant and K. J. Stringer (Copenhagen, 1994), pp. 28–66.

[75] See *Book of Fees*, ii, pp. 1117–19, 1126–7; C. H. Hunter Blair, 'Baronys [sic] and

baronye', as its Tudor surveyors had no hesitation in reporting in 1569.[76] And whereas in Yorkshire the de Vescys were as a rule sub-tenants of other barons, in Northumberland they had the distinction of holding all but peripheral acquisitions directly of the English crown. Moreover, their local standing was such that neighbouring tenants-in-chief were often *their* vassals and duty bound to acknowledge their authority by paying suit to the *curia militum* at Alnwick. Thus, in the returns made for Northumberland in 1242–3, four barons were named among their tenantry: Hugh de Bolbec of Styford, Robert de Muschamp of Wooler, Gilbert de Umfraville of Prudhoe and Redesdale, and John le Viscount of Embleton.[77]

All-in-all this provided the de Vescys with rich opportunities to affirm their regional dominance, and time and again we are reminded of the centrality of Northumberland in their affairs and, more specifically, of Alnwick's role as the quintessential focus of their patrimony and lineage. These themes are reflected in the family's contribution to the economic dynamism of the region as the founders at Alnwick and Alnmouth of two of the county's earliest recorded markets and boroughs; and whereas Alnmouth remained little more than a tiny fishing port, Alnwick – which was not overshadowed by competitors as New Malton was by Scarborough – gradually established itself as the main commercial centre for north Northumberland and a major source of lordly revenue and prestige.[78] They are also amply confirmed by the family's entrepreneurship in the Northumberland land market, and by the unfolding pattern of its religious benefactions and associations. In both respects, the case of John de Vescy is especially telling. His extensive property dealings, supplemented in some measure by those of his brother William the justiciar, were designed almost exclusively to enhance the family's dignity and power as lords of Alnwick. John rounded off and enlarged Cawledge Park beside Alnwick; he and William made inroads into the baronies of Bywell, Mitford and Wooler; and they engrossed freeholds, mills and rents in the territories of Alnwick, Alnham, Alnmouth, Longhoughton and North Charlton, pre-

---

knights of Northumberland, A.D. 1166–1266', *Archaeologia Aeliana*, 4th series, 30 (1952), pp. 15, 17, with map facing p. 16.

[76] Hartshorne, *Feudal and Military Antiquities of Northumberland*, p. 164.

[77] Other crown tenants holding knights' fees of the barony in 1242–3 included Hugh de Morwick of West Chevington and Roger son of Ralph of Ditchburn. See *Book of Fees*, ii, pp. 1118–19; and, for the *curia militum* of Alnwick, Martin (ed.), *Percy Chartulary*, nos. 660, 679, 687.

[78] See especially E. Miller and J. Hatcher, *Medieval England: Towns, Commerce and Crafts, 1086–1348* (London, 1995), pp. 275, 277, 317. The de Vescys' surviving borough charters for Alnwick are printed in G. Tate, *History of the Borough, Castle, and Barony of Alnwick*, 2 vols. (Alnwick, 1866–9), ii, App., pp. i–ii.

dominantly by buying back assets alienated by their predecessors.[79] In similar vein, John gained Edward I's licence in 1279, for 'the laudable service he has given us', to impark his 300 acre moor at Chatton; he conveyed for life to Geoffrey Taylor 48 acres in the fields of Alnwick provided that 'if in due course I wish to consolidate the demesne ... I shall be permitted to take back what he holds'; and William extracted from Alnwick abbey the promise not to purchase anything in Ellington without his consent.[80] As for John's pious interests, the monastic houses he favoured included the Cluniac nunnery of Arthington, Yorkshire, and the Cistercian abbey of Rufford, Nottinghamshire;[81] yet it was as a Northumberland baron that he principally expressed his religious affections. He solicitously increased the endowments of the Carmelites at Hulne with, for example, 20 marks yearly out of his mills of Alnwick, and all the wild bees in his park and forest, whose honey and wax were earmarked for lighting the priory church. And although his projected foundation of a Franciscan nunnery at Newcastle remained unrealized, he ensured that Alnwick abbey continued to benefit from assorted gifts and favours. Furthermore, whereas John's heart was buried at Blackfriars, Abbot Alan of Alnwick went to the laborious lengths of having his body fetched from Gascony for burial at the abbey, doubtless in accordance with John's wishes.[82]

John de Vescy's pronounced sense of place as a Borderer may have been exceptional, even in the eyes of his own family; but if so, it was more a matter of increased emphasis than a totally new phenomenon. How else, for instance, can we explain how Alnwick abbey had already assumed the chief responsibility for enshrining the family's memory as its primary mausoleum? William I de Vescy maintained Eustace fitz John's patronage of Alnwick, Malton and Watton on a uniformly generous scale;[83] he also endowed the Gilbertine canons and nuns of North Ormsby priory, Lincolnshire, and the Cistercian monks of Rievaulx abbey and the Cistercian nuns of Keldholme priory, Yorkshire.

[79] Martin (ed.), *Percy Chartulary*, nos. 661–2, 683–4, 686–7, 689, 691, 695, 697, 701–3, 710–12, 790, 795; BL, Harl. Chr. 57.C.32.
[80] Martin (ed.), *Percy Chartulary*, nos. 665, 670; *CPR, 1272–81*, pp. 319–20; BL, Harl. Chr. 44.A.4.
[81] *The Chartulary of St John of Pontefract*, ed. R. Holmes, 2 vols., Yorkshire Archaeological Society, Record Series (Leeds, 1899–1902), i, no. 228(bis); ii, no. 266; *Rufford Charters*, ed. C. J. Holdsworth, 4 vols., Thoroton Society (Nottingham, 1972–81), ii, pp. 357–8. John's 'gift' to Rufford, however, looks more like a sale: cf. ibid., iii, p. 535.
[82] Hartshorne, *Feudal and Military Antiquities of Northumberland*, App., pp. v, lxix–lxxii, lxxiv–lxxvi; Tate, *History of ... Alnwick*, ii, App., pp. xiii–xiv.
[83] Tate, *History of ... Alnwick*, ii, p. ix; Hartshorne, *Feudal and Military Antiquities of Northumberland*, App., p. cxiii; BL, MS Cott. Claud. D.xi, fols. 36^r–7^v; Dugdale, *Monasticon Anglicanum*, vi, II, p. 971; *EYC*, ii, no. 1114; iii, nos. 1884, 1895.

But the fact remains that William and his wife Burga de Stuteville were buried near the entrance to Alnwick's chapter-house, he himself having converted as a Premonstratensian canon on his death-bed in 1183.[84] William II de Vescy was interred at Watton in 1253; yet not only did he bring the Carmelites to Hulne, but he was revered by the Alnwick canons as an open-handed benefactor, and saw to it that his first wife was buried in their church.[85] Unsurprisingly Malton priory also retained some claim on de Vescy loyalties. Indeed, its substantial cartulary (no other family foundation is similarly well served) contains no fewer than twenty-nine letters and charters issued by the thirteenth-century lords in its favour.[86] The vast bulk of these, however, are routine acts of confirmation, and 'grants' were sometimes made only for specified material counter-gifts. In October 1295 William the justiciar did give to Malton the advowson of Brompton church and leave his body to be buried in the priory[87] – yet it can be no coincidence that, as will later be made clear, he was already anticipating the loss of Alnwick barony to Anthony Bek. Finally, too important to be ignored are the sufferings of Malton and Watton at Agnes de Vescy's hands. In 1272 Watton invoked Henry III's protection when she scandalously abused her right to monastic hospitality; worse still, in 1283 the prior of Malton denounced Agnes and her servants for assaulting and imprisoning canons and lay brothers, denying him access to Malton market, impounding the priory's goods, and generally jeopardizing its very existence as a viable religious community.[88]

An anonymous northern commentator pithily made the crucial point

---

[84] *EYC*, ix, no. 13; xii, no. 68; *Cartularium Abbathiae de Rievalle*, ed. J. C. Atkinson, Surtees Society (Durham and London, 1889), nos. 190, 192, 237; Hartshorne, *Feudal and Military Antiquities of Northumberland*, App., p. iv. For William's support of Brinkburn priory and Durham priory's cell on Farne Island, both in Northumberland, see *The Chartulary of Brinkburn Priory*, ed. W. Page, Surtees Society (Durham and London, 1893), no. 165; J. Raine, *The History and Antiquities of North Durham* (London, 1852), App., no. 697.

[85] Dugdale, *Monasticon Anglicanum*, vi, II, p. 957; Hartshorne, *Feudal and Military Antiquities of Northumberland*, App., p. v. For William II's endowment of Alnwick abbey, see also Tate, *History of ... Alnwick*, ii, App., pp. x–xi; *Calendar of the Charter Rolls*, iii, p. 87. Unfortunately nothing is known of the burials of Eustace fitz John and Eustace de Vescy.

[86] BL, MS Cott. Claud. D.xi, fols. 37^v–40^v, 41^v, 50^{r-v}, 224^v, 238^r.

[87] Ibid., fol. 50^r; *CPR*, 1292–1301, p. 154. John de Vescy the younger, the justiciar's son, was interred at Malton priory in 1295: Dugdale, *Monasticon Anglicanum*, vi, II, p. 957.

[88] Golding, *Gilbert of Sempringham*, pp. 320–1; *CPR*, 1281–92, p. 76. Agnes's enmity towards Malton evidently arose primarily from the prior's claim to be exempt by royal charter from any obligation to answer in her court at Malton (BL, MS Cott. Claud. D.xi, fol. 32^v). Edward I determined the matter in her favour in 1284: *Select Cases in the Court of King's Bench, Edward I – Edward III*, ed. G. O. Sayles, 5 vols., Selden Society (London, 1936–58), i, no. 87.

Nobility and identity 221

for us when he likened Northumberland to 'a widow robbed of her children' after the family's departure from Alnwick in 1297.[89] But its strong attachment to the English Borders is by no means the end of the story. The complexities of noble identity in the far North were such that it was shaped in formative ways by a highly intricate network of cross-frontier linkages; and for 'British history' purposes the awkwardness here stems not so much from the existence of a sharply honed regional consciousness as from the juxtaposition of an English march and a separate sovereign polity. For now, however, it is sufficient to drive home that this Anglo-Scottish world was one in which the de Vescys habitually participated at the forefront. It would clearly overstate the case to say that after Eustace de Vescy's marriage to Margaret of Scotland in 1193 they dominated the Scottish east march as they did the English; but Sprouston, held in chief of the king of Scots, was nevertheless one of Roxburghshire's larger baronies.[90] Moreover, their 'royal' privileges as lords of Sprouston were by no means empty powers but were exercised routinely and successfully – in marked contrast to the problems William the justiciar experienced in asserting his supremacy over Kildare. Thus John de Vescy is found conveying land to be held 'in forest', with a penalty of £10 for any unauthorized felling of timber or hunting; and when he transferred to Melrose Abbey services due to himself, he did so 'saving to us and our heirs the pleas and escheats of the crown'.[91] The family also left its mark on local society by residing regularly at Sprouston, where Eustace de Vescy founded a chapel for his personal use; it secured the privilege of fraternity from the monks of Kelso abbey; and it numbered among its tenants the Avenels, Riddells and Stewarts – the last-named being one of the most powerful magnate dynasties in Scotland.[92] There is also mention of a Joan de Vescy who in the mid-thirteenth century held not only half the Roxburghshire barony of Wilton, but Strathmartine in Angus and land at Tarvit in Fife.[93] Even more strikingly, the rich Fifeshire barony of Crail was settled on John de

[89] *The Political Songs of England, from the Reign of John to that of Edward II*, ed. and trans. T. Wright, Camden Society (London, 1839), p. 173.
[90] Its members included Mow and Whitton, now in Morebattle parish, part of Lilliesleaf, and Appletreehall (in Hawick): Innes *et al.* (eds.), *Origines Parochiales Scotiae*, i, pp. 309–10, 409, 411, 419, 421, 423–5; *CDS*, ii, no. 1435; iii, no. 258.
[91] Innes (ed.), *Liber Sancte Marie de Melros*, i, nos. 346–7.
[92] Innes *et al.* (eds.), *Origines Parochiales Scotiae*, i, pp. 309–10, 409, 411, 421, 423, 437–8; R. C. Reid, 'The Scottish Avenels', *Transactions of the Dumfriesshire and Galloway Natural History and Antiquarian Society*, 3rd series, 37 (1960), p. 77.
[93] It is difficult to establish Joan's place in the de Vescy pedigree; her husband was Robert de Percehay of Crambe and Ryton, near Malton. See Barrow, *Anglo-Norman Era in Scottish History*, p. 190, supplemented by Tate, *History of . . . Alnwick*, i, p. 400; *CDS*, ii, no. 1435; Bodleian Library, Oxford [hereafter Bodl.], MS Dodsworth 95, fol. 85^r (a reference for which I am indebted to Dr G. G. Simpson).

Vescy's widow Isabella by King John Balliol, who recognized her as the heiress of Richard de Beaumont, to whom Crail had been granted by Alexander II.[94]

Yet the de Vescys' involvement in cross-Border society evidently entailed a good deal more than this. Before the norms and practices of that world were shattered by the outbreak of the Scottish wars of independence in 1296, a significant number of their English tenants or dependants had interests straddling the frontier, most notably the Umfravilles, who acquired the earldom of Angus through marriage in 1243. We might also mention, for example, the Muschamps, who had standing in Berwickshire under the earls of Dunbar;[95] Bernard of Ripley, who by c. 1230 was a landowner in Galloway at Kirkandrews, near Kirkcudbright;[96] Philip de la Ley, who recovered land in the sheriffdom court of Roxburgh in c. 1248, and apparently held half the barony of Minto;[97] or Ysolda, daughter of Guy the glass-worker of Alnwick, who in c. 1245 was moved to grant to the Cistercian nuns of Coldstream, Berwickshire, all her right in Shipley mill.[98] Yet again, many were those families normally resident in Scotland who as landholders south of the Tweed came within the orbit of the lords of Alnwick. In 1296, for instance, the sheriff of Northumberland confiscated the property of a dozen or so of their tenants who, as native-born Scots, adhered to King John Balliol – well-to-do or well-connected southern Scottish nobles such as Edmund Comyn, William Douglas and Richard Fraser, and less prominent figures like Henry Haliburton,

---

[94] *CDS*, ii, no. 1670; *Documents Illustrative of the History of Scotland, 1286–1306*, ed. J. Stevenson, 2 vols. (Edinburgh, 1870), ii, no. 409.

[95] *CDS*, i, nos. 1101, 1128; Innes (ed.), *Liber Sancte Marie de Melros*, i, nos. 232–7. It is also noteworthy that William de Alwenton, from Alwinton in the de Vescy lands of Upper Coquetdale, was a tenant of Robert de Muschamp (d. 1250) at Hassington, Berwickshire: *ibid.*, i, no. 330; ii, pp. 679–81.

[96] Barrow, *Anglo-Norman Era in Scottish History*, p. 192, which adds that Bernard's probable brother William was granted Dallas in Moray by William the Lion. Ripley, near Harrogate, was on the Trussebut fee; but the Galloway Bernard was almost certainly the Bernard of Ripley who, in a charter attested by Eustace de Vescy and William of Ripley, was appointed by Robert de Arturret to act in his place by rendering to Eustace the service of a thirteenth part of one knight's fee for 2 carucates of land at Sawdon, near Malton: Bodl., Yorkshire Charters 298.

[97] 'North country deeds', ed. W. Brown, in *Miscellanea*, ii, Surtees Society (Durham and London, 1916), pp. 124–5; cf. Innes (ed.), *Liber Sancte Marie de Melros*, i, no. 267. Philip was a tenant of the de Vescys at Budle and Spindleston, Northumberland, and of Durham bishopric in Yorkshire and County Durham; in 1302 his namesake and successor is found sharing Minto barony with Walter de Boredham, who took his name from Burradon in Upper Coquetdale: *Book of Fees*, ii, p. 1118; J. F. Hodgson, 'Eggleston abbey', *Yorkshire Archaeological Journal*, 18 (1905), pp. 161–3; 'North country deeds', pp. 112, 125–7.

[98] *Chartulary of the Cistercian Priory of Coldstream*, ed. C. Rogers, Grampian Club (London, 1879), no. 54; cf. Scottish Record Office, Yule Collection, GD 90/1/20.

lord of the small Berwickshire barony of Mordington, who forfeited his interest at Spindleston, near Bamburgh, specifically because he had 'burned churches and killed men in England when the king's Scottish enemies laid waste the county'.[99] In Yorkshire, even Earl Duncan of Fife (d. 1204) had held of the de Vescys at Plumpton, near Wetherby.[100]

A day's ride from Plumpton lay their tiny priory of North Ferriby, to which none other than William the Lion granted the land of Craigloun in Fife.[101] Nor can Christopher Brooke's suggestion be overlooked that in earlier days Eustace fitz John's discerning support of reform monasticism had been influenced by the cosmopolitan religious tastes of King David I.[102] Religious links, indeed, gave an important additional dimension to the family's thoroughgoing involvement in cross-Border society; and in this regard Scotland also owed something to fitz John and his successors. It can surely be no coincidence that one of the few attempts to extend the Gilbertine order beyond England was made by the Stewarts, who in the 1220s endeavoured, albeit unsuccessfully, to establish a double Gilbertine house at Dalmilling, near Ayr;[103] or that the first Scottish Carmelite house was founded in *c.* 1260 at Berwick upon Tweed – 26 miles north of Hulne, whose putative first prior, Ralph Fresborne, may himself have had strong Scottish connections.[104] It can be said even more confidently that the reception of the Premonstratensians into Scotland was facilitated by Eustace fitz John, for his foundation of Alnwick abbey in 1147–8 was followed in 1150–2 by the

[99] Stevenson (ed.), *Documents Illustrative of the History of Scotland*, ii, pp. 47–9; *CDS*, ii, nos. 736, 1131. Haliburton seems also to have been a tenant of Sprouston barony: Innes *et al.* (eds.), *Origines Parochiales Scotiae*, i, pp. 417, 422.
[100] *EYC*, xii, no. 53.   [101] *RRS*, ii, no. 551.
[102] C. N. L. Brooke, 'King David I of Scotland as a connoisseur of the religious orders', in *Mediaevalia Christiana, xie–xiiie Siècles: Hommage à Raymonde Foreville*, ed. C. E. Viola (Paris, 1989), p. 329.
[103] See Golding, *Gilbert of Sempringham*, pp. 252–4, and G. W. S. Barrow, 'The Gilbertine house at Dalmilling', *Collections of the Ayrshire Archaeological and Natural History Society*, 2nd series, 4 (1958), pp. 50–67, though neither account discusses the possible significance of the Stewarts' links with the de Vescys. The intended motherhouse for Dalmilling was apparently Sixhills priory, Lincolnshire; but when the project was abandoned in 1238, Walter son of Alan, steward of Scotland, appointed Prior William of Malton as his proctor charged with distributing the annual pension of 40 marks assigned for the Gilbertines' general use in compensation for relinquishing their Ayrshire endowments: *ibid.*, pp. 56, 65–6.
[104] R. Copsey, 'The Scottish Carmelite province and its provincials' in *The Land of Carmel: Essays in Honor of Joachim Smet*, ed. K. J. Egan and P. Chandler (Rome, 1991), p. 190 (for Berwick). A Ralph Frebern occurs as a tenant-in-chief of the Scots crown in Fife and Midlothian in the second half of the twelfth century (*RRS*, ii, no. 9); a Robert Frebern (Freborn) witnessed a charter concerning Sprouston soon after 1165, and also attested in Roxburghshire for the de Vescys' kinsman Philip de Valognes (*Liber S. Marie de Calchou*, ed. C. Innes, 2 vols., Bannatyne Club (Edinburgh, 1846), i, no. 216; Innes (ed.), *Liber Sancte Marie de Melros*, i, no. 150).

colonization of a daughter-house at Dryburgh in Lauderdale on the invitation of his friend Hugh de Morville, constable of Scotland.[105] It is appropriate to add that Abbot Geoffrey of Dryburgh was translated to Alnwick in 1209; that Alnwick became a property-owner in Scotland in its own right when it received a grant of fisheries on the Scottish side of the Tweed from William II de Vescy; and that, at least in the fourteenth century, Hulne priory possessed an altar cloth brocaded with the arms of the king of Scots.[106] It is likewise instructive to find that St Leonard's hospital, near Alnwick, was founded by Eustace de Vescy at the spot where Malcolm Canmore had been slain in 1093, specifically for the benefit of King Malcolm's soul. Nor does it surprise to discover that in c. 1217 Bishop Robert of Ross consecrated, at Margaret of Scotland's request, the cemetery attached to her private chapel at Tughall, or that in 1243 Bishop Gilbert of Galloway dedicated an altar in Malton priory.[107]

The range and intricacy of the web of cross-Border ties in which the family was enmeshed were indeed remarkable; and fundamental as was Eustace de Vescy's marriage to Margaret of Scotland, it should not be allowed to conceal the importance of other familial bonds. Philip de Valognes (d. 1215), who became chamberlain of Scotland in 1165 and lord of Ringwood, Roxburghshire, and of Benvie and Panmure, Angus, was a nephew of Eustace fitz John.[108] No doubt Philip's promotion in Scotland was itself assisted by his de Vescy attachments, and these were further strengthened when he inherited a tenancy in Alnwick barony and married his daughter Sybil to William I de Vescy's nephew, Robert de Stuteville (d. 1213).[109] William I's own daughter Matilda took as her second husband Adam of Carlisle (d. c. 1212), who became lord of

---

[105] H. M. Colvin, *The White Canons in England* (Oxford, 1951), p. 367. Fitz John appears in Hugh's company in *Early Scottish Charters prior to 1153*, ed. A. C. Lawrie (Glasgow, 1905), nos. 54, 123.

[106] Colvin, *White Canons in England*, p. 392; *Calendar of the Charter Rolls*, iii, p. 87; Hartshorne, *Feudal and Military Antiquities of Northumberland*, App., p. cviii. It was no doubt in respect of the Tweed fisheries that in 1296 Abbot Alan of Alnwick swore fealty to Edward I as overlord of Scotland: *CDS*, ii, p. 204.

[107] Hartshorne, *Feudal and Military Antiquities of Northumberland*, App., p. iv; *History of Northumberland*, i, p. 345; BL, MS Cott. Claud. D.xi, fol. 44ᵛ.

[108] Suggested in Hedley, *Northumberland Families*, ii, p. 33, and confirmed by charter evidence in W. T. Lancaster, *The Early History of Ripley and the Ingilby Family* (Leeds, 1918), p. 30. Philip's brother Roger accompanied him to Scotland, and gained the lordship of East Kilbride, Lanarkshire.

[109] *Rotuli de Oblatis et Finibus in Turri Londinensi Asservati, Tempore Regis Johannis*, ed. T. D. Hardy Record Commission (London, 1835), p. 425; *EYC*, ix, no. 54. Philip appears in William I de Vescy's following in both Northumberland and Yorkshire: Raine, *History and Antiquities of North Durham*, App., no. 697 (with Robert de Stuteville's grandmother and uncle); *EYC*, iii, no. 1896; York, Dean and Chapter Muniments, Magnum Registrum Album, part 2, fol. 54ʳ. Philip's grandson, Eustace

Kinmount in Annandale and was a progenitor of the family of Carlyle, Lord Carlyle.[110] Eustace de Vescy's appearance in the company of Alan of Galloway, constable of Scotland, becomes more understandable when it is realized that Alan's first wife was a daughter of Eustace fitz John's great-grandson Roger de Lacy, constable of Chester.[111] A later marriage tie linked the de Vescys and the Charterises, one of whom, Master Thomas Charteris, served as chancellor of Scotland (c. 1285–91).[112] Furthermore, a notable feature of the de Vescy entourage, at least in the later thirteenth century, was the part played there by men of Scots birth or descent like William Scot, John de Vescy's household retainer (*vallettus*), and the knight Philip Lindsay, son of a chamberlain of Alexander III, who served as tutor of John's nephew, and was reportedly so broken in mind and body by his charge's premature death in 1295 that only Saint Cuthbert's miraculous intervention restored him to health.[113] It is also the case that the answer to one of the thornier problems of Scottish family history, the origin of the Maitlands, lies with the de Vescys – or, more precisely, with Richard Maitland, steward of Alnwick, who took full advantage of the wider opportunities open to him and had established his seat at Thirlestane in Lauderdale by c. 1230.[114]

If the de Vescys' most deep-rooted sense of identity is to be found in their role as Borderers, that brings us more directly to some of the

de Stuteville (d. 1241), became lord of the baronies of Liddel Strength, Cumberland, and Cottingham, Yorkshire.

[110] Hedley, *Northumberland Families*, i, pp. 199, 201; Paul (ed.), *Scots Peerage*, ii, pp. 373–5. Adam's son and probable heir, Eudo of Carlisle, was regularly in attendance on his uncle Eustace de Vescy: see, e.g., Bodl., MS Dodsworth 7, fol. 319ʳ; *Calendar of the Laing Charters*, ed. J. Anderson (Edinburgh, 1899), no. 4; Innes (ed.), *Liber S. Marie de Calchou*, i, nos. 207–8, 210; Martin (ed.), *Percy Chartulary*, no. 831.

[111] Stringer, 'Periphery and core in thirteenth-century Scotland', p. 104. Alan's second wife, a niece of William the Lion, was a cousin of Margaret of Scotland, and his apparent sister Derbforgaill married Eustace de Vescy's cousin Nicholas de Stuteville (d. 1233): *EYC*, ix, pp. 20–1.

[112] In 1296 William Charteris, son of Henry Charteris and Agnes de Vescy (d. 1302) and a landowner in Roxburghshire and Banffshire, held Wooden, near Alnwick; in 1304 he was recognized as his mother's heir for Appletreehall in Sprouston barony: *CDS*, ii, nos. 736, 1435. The precise relationship of Agnes to the main de Vescy line is not known. By 1286 Mr Thomas Charteris had acquired rights in Wilton barony by agreement with Joan de Vescy, Agnes's possible sister: Bodl., MS Dodsworth 95, fol. 85ʳ, and *CDS*, ii, no. 1435, correcting D. E. R. Watt, *A Biographical Dictionary of Scottish Graduates to A.D. 1410* (Oxford, 1977), p. 85.

[113] Martin (ed.), *Percy Chartulary*, nos. 698, 704; Stevenson (ed.), *Chronicle of Lanercost*, p. 163. In 1240 Henry III warned William II de Vescy not to employ a friar who had absconded from Berwick: F. D. Logan, *Runaway Religious in Medieval England, c. 1240–1540* (Cambridge, 1996), p. 98.

[114] I intend to deal with the early history of the Maitland family on another occasion.

complexities of contemporary 'British' politics. From a 'British history' standpoint it would certainly be crass to suggest that these lords were backwoodsmen, or that their world as Border barons generally lacked an obvious regnal focus. As a normal course, their political nodal point was the English king's court, partly because influence in his household and administration opened up the main highway to personal advancement in the British Isles, partly because their successes in winning such influence naturally intensified their sense of belonging to the English political community. Nor is there any mistaking how profoundly the might of the English crown etched itself on their consciousness when family lands fell into the king's custody as a result of forfeiture or minorities. Even so, the nature of identities in the far North was evidently more complicated than the centralizing ideology and uniformist predisposition of the English government might lead us to suppose – at any rate until 1296, when the politically motivated killing of a Scotsman at Alnmouth encapsulated the sudden demise of long-established conventions of cooperation and coexistence between English and Scots.[115] We need to recognize that the easy trans-frontier rapport to which the de Vescys so notably contributed meant that there was less self-conscious identification with the English nation or state than might otherwise have been the case. Above all else, we need to reach beyond the traditional Westminster-centred view of the English polity to the crucial fact that thirteenth-century frontiersmen like the de Vescys also owed allegiance to the king of Scots. Accordingly, they were within the ambit of the power and authority of *two* states, and in an entirely different position from that of English lords who, even if their lands extended to Wales and Ireland, had a duty of obedience to a single ruler. Socially, the Anglo-Scottish Border was porous; it was quite otherwise in terms of governance, as was emphatically shown in 1290 by the fate of Richard Knout, sheriff of Northumberland, who was imprisoned in Roxburgh castle for a gross breach of Border custom when he presumed to survey Sprouston barony for assignment of Isabella de Vescy's dower.[116] For most of the twelfth and thirteenth centuries, English kings chose not to pursue provocative Scottish policies. That, indeed, was one reason why they

[115] The victim, William de Bolhope, who had lived in England until war broke out, was slain when he came (back?) to Alnmouth and refused to repudiate his Scottish allegiance. Edward I acquitted the two townsmen responsible on the grounds that William was a felon: *CDS*, iv, no. 1782. A contrasting incident concerns the resourceful Simon of Scotland, imprisoned in Alnwick castle in 1278 for stealing a horse. He killed the porter of the castle (and a companion) for his keys, fled to claim right of sanctuary in St Michael's church, and was allowed by the coroner to abjure the realm: *CDS*, ii, p. 42.

[116] G. W. S. Barrow, 'A kingdom in crisis: Scotland and the Maid of Norway', *SHR*, 69 (1990), pp. 131–2.

often employed the de Vescys in Anglo-Scottish diplomacy – to treat of peace, for example, or to escort the Scots king to the English court, resolve Border boundary disputes, or smooth over other potentially damaging disagreements.[117] Their reliance on such support reflected a ready awareness of the family's standing in Scottish society; but that was precisely why relations between the de Vescys and the English crown were bound to be politically ambiguous.

In particular, dual allegiance in the Borders sharpened and sustained that quality of 'Northernness' characterized, especially in King John's reign, by political protest against the pretensions of the southern-based English monarchy. In the bleak aftermath of the Barons' Wars, John de Vescy – whose rising at Alnwick in 1267 had benefited from 'unofficial' Scottish support – broadcast both his regional patriotism and his political independent-mindedness by promoting Alnwick Abbey as the northern centre of Simon de Montfort's cult. One of Simon's feet, salvaged from his dismembered remains on the Evesham battlefield, was brought by John to Alnwick, encased in a silver shrine in the shape of a shoe, and treasured by the canons until the Reformation, alongside a goblet of Thomas Becket. Credited with thaumaturgic powers, it encouraged the author of the *Opusculum de Simone*, which was added to the Melrose abbey chronicle in *c*. 1290, not only to venerate Earl Simon as a saint and political martyr but to compare him to Simon Peter.[118]

Broadly speaking, however, the far North became a critical arena in English politics only when Anglo-Scottish relations were overtly confrontational; and in such circumstances the de Vescys' reactions depended on their assessment of which sovereign was better able to safeguard their status and prospects. Accordingly, loyalty to the English crown was no reflex response; rather, its most characteristic aspect in a crisis was its conditional and fragile nature. Eustace fitz John's friendship with David I precipitated his arrest by King Stephen in 1138 and a rift with the English crown lasting sixteen years; even more sensationally,

[117] See, e.g., Roger of Howden, *Chronica*, iv, p. 89; *CPR*, 1232–47, p. 447 (peace-keeping); Howden, *Chronica*, iv, p. 140; *CDS*, i, nos. 450, 1257, 1349 (escort); *Foedera*, I, ii, p. 565 (frontier demarcation).

[118] Hartshorne, *Feudal and Military Antiquities of Northumberland*, p. 279; Anderson *et al.* (eds.), *Chronicle of Melrose*, pp. 133ff.; and see most recently C. Valente, 'Simon de Montfort, earl of Leicester, and the utility of sanctity in thirteenth-century England', *Journal of Medieval History*, 21 (1995), pp. 27–49. Besides the wardship of the Umfraville lands, Earl Simon's Northumberland interests had included Embleton barony, whose seat was 6 miles north of Alnwick, and a mesne tenancy under the de Vescys at Earle and Newton-by-the-Sea: J. R. Maddicott, *Simon de Montfort* (Cambridge, 1994), pp. 142–3; *History of Northumberland*, ii, pp. 16–18, 83–4. The anonymous author of the *Opusculum*, apparently a northern Franciscan, had an intimate knowledge of Simon's personality and religious practices, and it is tempting to regard John de Vescy as his chief informant.

in 1215–16 Eustace de Vescy played the Scottish card against King John by personally investing Alexander II with Northumberland, acknowledging his right to Cumberland and Westmorland, and encouraging the Yorkshire barons to place themselves under his lordship and protection.[119] No doubt both Eustaces were motivated more by the perceived failings and injustices of the English crown than by loyalty to the Scottish monarchy; but their allegiances were the more flexible because they could find a safe refuge and powerful political and military backing at the Scots king's court. *In extremis*, therefore, a choice of sovereigns was open to them, and their names became inseparably linked with phases of Scottish power-building that threatened to swallow up the Border counties as part of an extended Scottish state.[120] We are told, for example, that in 1212 the outlawed Eustace de Vescy 'chose rather to go into exile [in Scotland] than to suffer the king's displeasure or submit to his malice', and that in 1138 Eustace fitz John, who 'had long secretly favoured the king of Scotland, now with open treachery repudiated his natural lord ... and with his whole strength supported the Scots against the realm of England'.[121]

Nothing indeed reveals more starkly than do such episodes that the far North was by no means as politically insulated as was the rest of England. During the long years of Anglo-Scottish peace from 1217 to 1296 it is true that the Border baronage became much more of a political in-group. Socially, however, the de Vescys' Scottish ties continued to be important; and politically neither Henry III nor Edward I could automatically assume their unquestioning devotion. That was why the English government took all possible steps to prevent the family from strengthening its Scottish links through an independent marriage of the sort entered into by Eustace de Vescy.[122] And while the de Vescys' chequered political history also gave the English crown good reason to bind them more closely to itself through ties of royal service and reward,

[119] Holt, *Northerners*, pp. 131–2.
[120] For some recent comment, see K. J. Stringer, 'State-building in twelfth-century Britain: David I, king of Scots, and northern England', in *Government, Religion and Society in Northern England, 1000–1700*, ed. J. C. Appleby and P. Dalton (Stroud, 1997), pp. 40–62; Stringer, 'Periphery and core in thirteenth-century Scotland', pp. 88–92.
[121] *Scotichronicon*, v, p. 15; Howlett (ed.), *Chronicles of the Reigns of Stephen, Henry II, and Richard I*, iii, p. 158.
[122] *CDS*, i, nos. 701, 715; *CPR, 1247–58*, pp. 217, 237–8. The more revealing of the examples referenced here shows that in 1218 Henry III's government extracted a written undertaking from Margaret of Scotland to surrender the under-age William II de Vescy on its summons; she delivered him to England in 1219 only after she had been disseised of her English dower lands, and William was thereupon placed in the custody of Earl William of Salisbury, whose daughter he married as his first wife in 1226.

the fact remains that they never quite lived down their reputation for destabilizing the Border shires. Nor did the family cease to acknowledge its obligations to the king of Scots and regard his court as a source of possible favour. William II de Vescy's marriage in 1243 to Sybil Marshal's daughter Agnes – and a rich prize she proved to be – surely owed at least something to his Scottish connections, for Agnes's uncle Earl Gilbert Marshal had married in 1235 William's aunt Marjorie, the youngest sister of Alexander II. William had almost certainly attended the Scottish court for their wedding at Berwick; and it was indeed as one of the magnates of Scotland that he swore to uphold the peace between Alexander and Henry III when war threatened in 1244.[123] Similarly, while the family historians have stressed that John de Vescy's second wife Isabella was Eleanor of Castile's 'dear cousin', they have ignored the importance of her ties with Alexander III and his mother, the queen-dowager Marie de Coucy (d. 1284), whose marriage to Alexander II in 1239 had gravely alarmed Henry III on account of her strong French connections. Isabella was a daughter of Queen Eleanor's first cousin Louis de Brienne and his wife Agnes, daughter and eventual heiress of Ralph, *vicomte* of Beaumont-sur-Sarthe in Maine. But Isabella's maternal family had already produced a queen of Scots in the person of her great-aunt by blood, Ermengarde, wife of William the Lion and grandmother of Alexander III; the strength of its continuing links with Scotland had recently been demonstrated by Alexander II's grant of Crail to Richard de Beaumont (probably Queen Ermengarde's nephew); and last but by no means least, Marie de Coucy had married secondly in 1257 Isabella's uncle John de Brienne, butler of France (d. 1296).[124] It has to be admitted that, shortly after John de Vescy's marriage to Isabella in 1279 or 1280, he formally acknowledged she had been in Queen Eleanor's gift.[125] Nevertheless, it would perhaps be wrong to regard this alliance as exclusively an expression of Edwardian favour; and even if such caution seems misplaced, no doubt what made the match espe-

---

[123] *CDS*, i, no. 1655. Queen's College, Oxford, Antiquarian Notes attributed to Robert Glover, MS 166, fol. 28ʳ, shows that William was with Alexander II at Edinburgh on 10 August 1235, nine days after Gilbert Marshal's marriage to Marjorie at Berwick. Some other examples of William's presence at Alexander II's court are in Chalmers and Innes (eds.), *Liber S. Thome de Aberbrothoc*, i, no. 131; *Registrum Episcopatus Glasguensis*, ed. C. Innes, 2 vols., Bannatyne and Maitland Clubs (Edinburgh, 1843), i, no. 137; National Library of Scotland, Edinburgh, Anonymous 17th-century Transcripts, MS Advocates 34.6.24, p. 271.

[124] Cokayne, *Complete Peerage*, ii, p. 59 and n. b, with A. Duchesne, *Histoire Généalogique des Maisons de Guines, d'Ardres, de Gand et de Coucy* (Paris, 1631), p. 232.

[125] *CCR*, 1279–88, p. 67. See also J. C. Parsons, *Eleanor of Castile: Queen and Society in Thirteenth-Century England* (London, 1995), pp. 29, 178, 199–203, 214, for John's membership of Eleanor's circle.

cially attractive to John was its potential for promoting his standing at both royal courts.[126] In fact he had shown his commitment to Scotland as recently as 1275 by sharing command of the Scottish force responsible for restoring Alexander III's authority over the Isle of Man.[127]

When dealing with the de Vescys, therefore, it is the pluralistic nature of their aspirations and attachments that is so striking. Such was their ability to project and perceive different images of themselves that these varied not only from place to place but almost from decade to decade; and perhaps nowhere was their complexity communicated more vividly than through the nuances of the de Vescys' political identity. It cannot be stressed too strongly that the family grasped the opportunities for advancement largely by linking its fortunes to the expansion of the English state; and we have only to compare its position on the eve of Eustace fitz John's promotion by Henry Beauclerk with that held in the British Isles by William the justiciar under Edward I to see in its history pointed testimony to the mighty unifying force of an increasingly self-confident English polity. But however deeply and directly family identity was thereby shaped or modified, to speak of a monolithic 'English' consciousness, let alone a distinct 'British' outlook, would do far less than justice to the diversity and contradictions of the de Vescys' attitudes and experiences. Whereas William the justiciar saw himself in one situation as a member of Scotland's nobility and in another as intimately connected (through Derbforgaill of Desmond) with the native Irish, he spectacularly failed as a leader of the English community in Ireland to entrench himself among his Anglo-Irish neighbours – a paradox that serves only to remind us of the enigmas of the English metropolitan-colonial relationship, and that in Anglo-Ireland 'the formal pattern of English institutions [was] a thinnish coating over a very un-English set of political facts'.[128] The north of England was a less volatile arena, with more regular and coherent governmental traditions and structures, and

---

[126] The possibility of Scottish involvement may seem to be strengthened by the fact that relations between the Briennes and both Henry III and Edward I were notoriously frosty: Cokayne, *Complete Peerage*, v, pp. 169–70 (concerning the vain attempts of Isabella's close kinsmen, the Brienne counts of Eu, to recover their English estates). Marie de Coucy and John de Brienne had separated amicably in 1268, but Marie continued to spend time in both Scotland and France.

[127] Stevenson (ed.), *Chronicle of Lanercost*, pp. 97–8. Correspondence from both Eustace and John de Vescy was in the Scottish treasury in 1282: Thomson and Innes (eds.), *Acts of the Parliaments of Scotland*, i, pp. 98–9.

[128] R. Frame, 'Power and society in the lordship of Ireland, 1272–1377', *Past & Present*, 76 (1977), p. 5. See further R. Frame, '"Les Engleys nées en Irlande": the English political identity in medieval Ireland', *TRHS*, 6th series, 3 (1993), pp. 83–103. (Both reprinted in R. Frame, *Ireland and Britain 1170–1450* (London and Rio Grande, 1998), pp. 191–220; 131–50.)

this was unmistakably the de Vescys' natural habitat. Even so, their true home or *pays* within it was another far-flung marchland where the integrationist ideals of English governance took little account of local circumstances. We thus learn important lessons about the practical complications and anomalies that sustained varied senses of English self-identification even within England itself. We see how easily a leading baronial dynasty founded through English royal patronage could develop a localized culture, however freely and assertively its members also turned on the 'national', or even European, stage. We find that the de Vescys also adapted to frontier conditions in north Britain by basing their power on developing and preserving links with an independent Scottish polity; that from time to time their regional interests might take precedence over allegiance to the English crown; and that even 150 years after the Conquest of 1066 they did not shrink from participating in a drastic attempt to redraw the map of royal authority in northern England. It does no harm to be reminded in such ways of the rich tapestry of possibilities through which a family's identity might be displayed. Or, as it might otherwise be expressed, the 'state' provides an important mould for the casting of identity; but it often falls short of its own specifications, and its failures as well as its successes ought to be recognized.

Of course, the record of the de Vescys cannot necessarily be taken to represent some sort of typicality; indeed, such was the chameleon-like nature of their outlook, especially in the political domain, that it is difficult enough to capture salient characteristics that apply equally strongly to all the individuals concerned. Nevertheless, these lords could be loyal or disloyal, quick to be men of affairs or belligerent frontiersmen, fastened within the embrace of English governance or divorced from it; and it was only gradually that their options were largely superseded and eliminated. And perhaps after all, this is no more than should be expected of a family whose activities oblige us to shift our perspective from the atypical conditions of southern England to the complex and varied socio-political landscapes in the vastnesses beyond it.

Against this background, therefore, the de Vescys' collective history graphically demonstrates some of the strategic difficulties of conceptualizing 'British history' in ways that avoid, as Rees Davies has cautioned, imposing 'a specious uniformity ... in the name of a "new subject"'.[129] And yet, real though those difficulties are, it would certainly be wrong to close this account by giving the impression that an holistic, as opposed

---

[129] Davies, 'In praise of British history', p. 10.

to a comparative, 'British history' approach has little to commend it; for what is surely equally evident is that the notion of 'plural worlds' cannot be pressed too far at the expense of the notion of 'one world'. Thus, socially and politically, the family's experiences manifestly exemplify 'British' themes of divergence *and* convergence; the balance between them varied from period to period, but both can nearly always be found operating simultaneously. More particularly, what has become increasingly clear is that diverse circumstances acted *and* interacted to shape the de Vescys' fortunes and behaviour; that there are processes here whose full significance will be missed if we consider them only in 'English', 'Scottish' or 'Irish' terms; and that this applies to almost every major aspect of the family's history. But to re-emphasize and expand on these points it is also necessary to reconsider the role played in the articulation of identity by the ambitions and expectations of the English state. If these were not invariably central to the 'British' dimensions of the de Vescy story, such caveats must not be allowed to obscure the fundamental changes in which the British Isles were caught during Edward I's pivotal reign, when, for the first time, 'the day of a truly effective British monarchy, and thereby of a unitary British history, seemed imminent'.[130] And to drive home what that meant for the family, there is no better way of ending this chapter than by looking more closely at William the justiciar's career.

Without a 'British' treatment, William's promotion to the justiciarship of Ireland on 12 September 1290 would remain unexplained and rather perplexing. That he was an appointee from England (he had inherited Kildare only four months earlier) was not so unusual; yet after the reforms inaugurated at Edward I's behest by the previous justiciar, John of Sandford, it was arguably exceptional to replace a bureaucrat with a magnate, who was likely to be less effective in reinvigorating the Irish administration. Early in 1290, however, Edward had informed Sandford that Irish affairs would have to take second place to more urgent business,[131] and one of the king's current preoccupations was the relationship between England and the weakened Kingdom of Scots, which had lacked an effective ruler since Alexander III's death in 1286. A great deal was at stake, and William himself became a key player as Edward marshalled his resources for advancing English interests. That much was already suggested when, in or shortly before February 1290, William's son and heir, John de Vescy the younger, was betrothed to

[130] *Ibid.*, p. 23.
[131] *Documents Illustrative of English History in the Thirteenth and Fourteenth Centuries*, ed. H. Cole (London, 1844), p. 56.

Clemence d'Avaugour, another French relative of Eleanor of Castile and one of the damsels (*domicilla*) of her chamber.[132] Then, on 20 June 1290, William was appointed to the high-powered English embassy, given full authority and special mandate to undertake the critical task of resolving with the Guardians of Scotland outstanding issues concerning the dynastic union to be forged by the marriage of Edward I's heir, Edward of Caernarfon, to Alexander III's heiress, Margaret the Maid of Norway. These exceptionally delicate negotiations were safely carried forward; and as one of Edward's 'special proctors and envoys', William set his seal to the treaty agreed at Birgham (only 3 miles from Sprouston) on 18 July – two days after his son's marriage in Westminster Abbey to Clemence d'Avaugour, whose wedding apparel included a coronet graciously provided by Queen Eleanor.[133] Unquestionably, William had fully earned Edward's gratitude for his part in this diplomatic success, which might have paved the way for a joint English–Scottish monarchy; and his hand was further strengthened by the fact that Edward was already intent on adopting an interventionist role in Scottish government, a strategy that self-evidently maximized the king's dependence on the political support of influential lords in the Borders. It therefore seems inescapable that William's appointment as justiciar two months after Birgham was determined not so much by concern to address Ireland's problems as by the dynamics of Edward's Scottish policies.[134]

The Maid of Norway's death, about 26 September 1290, added a major new element of uncertainty to Anglo-Scottish relations, and it was early in June 1291 that William entered his claim to the Scots throne. Hardly a strong contender, he would withdraw during the hearings of the Great Cause shortly before the final judgement in John Balliol's

[132] *The Court and Household of Eleanor of Castile in 1290*, ed. J. C. Parsons (Toronto, 1977), pp. 46–8, and n. 174.
[133] Stevenson (ed.), *Documents Illustrative of the History of Scotland*, i, nos. 105, 108; Parsons (ed.), *Court and Household of Eleanor of Castile*, p. 48. M. Prestwich, 'Edward I and the Maid of Norway', *SHR* 69 (1990), p. 168, mistakenly omits William's name from the list of English plenipotentiaries, who also included Anthony Bek and Ralph Ireton, bishop of Carlisle. Edward I had earlier depended on William to soothe Scottish grievances jeopardizing his plans for a dynastic alliance by commissioning him, with others, on 16 February 1289 to punish those responsible for arresting at Doncaster Bishop Fraser of St Andrews (who had been on his way to Edward to discuss the Maid's marriage); and on 16 June 1290 to settle the protracted dispute between the Scots and the Bordeaux wine merchant John le Mazun: Stevenson (ed.), *Documents Illustrative of the History of Scotland*, i, nos. 53, 104.
[134] A parallel case was the appointment in June 1290 of Walter of Huntercombe as Edward I's keeper of the Isle of Man. Walter, of Styford and Wooler in Northumberland, was a tenant and close associate of the de Vescys: see, e.g. *Calendar of Inquisitions Post Mortem*, v, no. 403; Hartshorne, *Feudal and Military Antiquities of Northumberland*, App., pp. lxxi, lxxvi; Martin (ed.), *Percy Chartulary*, no. 688; BL, Harl. Chr. 57.C.36.

favour on 17 November 1292.[135] But it has recently been argued that his intervention was a vital service to Edward I, even in part engineered by him, for it helped to ensure that, confronted by multiple competitors, the Scots had to abandon their policy of defending Scottish independence by restricting Edward's role in the Great Cause to that of an arbiter.[136] There had to be a judicial decision, which meant that Edward, now fully committed to asserting his suzerainty over Scotland, would have to be recognized as lord superior so that he could exercise judgement.[137] Obligingly William (his son John acting for him) proceeded with eight other claimants, in June 1291, to take the momentous step of acknowledging Edward's overlordship of Scotland and his right to seisin of the kingdom and its castles.

We have clearly reached the point where William's new public identity as Edward I's chief minister in Ireland deeply influenced the role he took in politics as a 'Scottish' baron. Indeed, it is tempting to say that in 1291 William came second only to Edward himself as a force in the process of 'uniting' the British Isles. But it was in 1292 that complaints from the Anglo-Irish about William's conduct began to reach the English court, and as his enemies became more vocal in 1293–4, so Edward's relations with Balliol and the Scots became more contentious and confrontational. The appeals made from Ireland to Edward and his council in 1293 expressed much more than private grievances. According to William's accusers, he had refused to put the abbot of St Thomas's, Dublin, in seisin of his temporalities 'in contempt of the king's mandate'; as lord of Kildare, he had usurped the king's jurisdiction over ecclesiastical lands, proceeded with a plea of advowson against a royal writ of prohibition, directed his own prohibitions to the bishop of Kildare 'in lesion of the royal dignity', and claimed that his own peace was superior to the king's, to 'his manifest disinheritance'. It was further alleged that the sheriff of Kildare, with armed retainers bearing de Vescy banners, had invaded tenements belonging to the crown, impounded goods and livestock, and killed three men, 'to the king's detriment and prejudice'.[138]

[135] William's role in Anglo-Scottish politics, 1291–2, can be followed in detail in Stones and Simpson (eds.), *Edward I and the Throne of Scotland*, supplemented by A. A. M. Duncan, 'The process of Norham, 1291', *Thirteenth Century England*, 5 (Woodbridge, 1995), pp. 207–30. He had throughout to be represented by attorneys (including Walter of Huntercombe), presumably because he remained in Ireland.
[136] *Ibid.*, especially pp. 217–18.
[137] It might be added that in January 1291 Edward I had dispatched William's son John to urge the Scots spontaneously to accept his jurisdiction: Stones and Simpson (eds.), *Edward I and the Throne of Scotland*, ii, p. 4.
[138] The chief source drawn on in this section is Richardson and Sayles (eds.), *Rotuli Parliamentorum Anglie Hactenus Inediti*, pp. 30–45 (roll of sixteen petitions against

Justified or not, such serious charges were sufficient in themselves to have deeply concerned Edward I; and more alarming still was William's embroilment in bitter feuding that threatened to plunge Ireland into all-out war. Its origins lay in his strenuous efforts to curb the rising power of John fitz Thomas and bring his Offaly lands firmly within the liberty of Kildare;[139] but by 1293 what had begun as an essentially localized conflict had assumed near-catastrophic proportions. William had evidently exploited his alliance with Domnall Ruad Mac Carthaig, the father of his Irish mistress, by inciting him to wage war against fitz Thomas's kinsman Thomas fitz Maurice, head of the Desmond Geraldines. The repercussions of the feud were also felt in Connacht, where it interacted with and fuelled fitz Thomas's vendetta with Richard de Burgh, earl of Ulster; and in July 1293 Edward wrote urgently and angrily to William to restrain him from mobilizing against fitz Thomas the king's whole army of Ireland, a sure indication that William was acting independently in his own political interest.[140] Now Edward was not so imprudent as to risk an open breach with William, and the charges made against him by the Anglo-Irish in 1292-3 and later were quietly dropped. No royal pardon was forthcoming, however. Suspended from office in March 1294 and dismissed in the following June, William was also given to understand that investigation of his conduct could easily be renewed.[141]

By this stage in the discussion, the wider 'British' backdrop may appear to have become redundant; but it would be wrong to imagine that William's downfall can fully be explained without inspecting it. If we follow the lead of Irish historians, it seems important to bear in mind that John fitz Thomas had no peer in terms of his own unscrupulousness and ambition; and yet Edward I had shown a stronger commitment to

---

William heard in the Westminster parliament of Michaelmas 1293); quotations at pp. 40, 38, 44, 36, respectively. *Cal. Doc. Ire.*, 1293-1301, nos. 42 and 106 (roll of inquisitions subsequently taken in Ireland), supply a few extra details. For further comment, see Hand, *English Law in Ireland*, pp. 120, 122, 148; A. J. Otway-Ruthven, 'Anglo-Irish shire government in the thirteenth century', *IHS*, 5 (1946), pp. 7-8; Otway-Ruthven, 'Medieval county of Kildare', p. 191.

[139] See especially Richardson and Sayles (eds.), *Rotuli Parliamentorum Anglie Hactenus Inediti*, pp. 33-5 (fitz Thomas's complaint that in 1291 William had attempted to disinherit him by 'maintaining' one of the female claimants to the Geraldine lands who had impleaded him in the liberty court at Kildare).

[140] *Ibid.*, pp. 35-6, 41-2; *Cal. Doc. Ire.*, 1293-1301, no. 62. Instructive accounts of the complex ramifications of the de Vescy-fitz Thomas feud are available in Otway-Ruthven, *History of Ireland*, pp. 210-12, and by Lydon in *NHI*, ii, pp. 186-8. See also Frame, 'War and peace in the medieval lordship of Ireland', pp. 138-9. Hitherto, however, no historian seems to have explained or highlighted the role of members of the Mac Carthaig family, bitter enemies of the Geraldines, whose involvement was obviously a key reason for fitz Thomas's hostility towards the justiciar.

[141] *Rotuli Parliamentorum*, i, p. 134.

him than to a very senior royal servant. In Edward's eyes, of course, William had clearly overreached himself; nor could the crown risk alienating powerful members of the Anglo-Irish community when financial and military subventions were needed to meet the impending demands of a major war with France. What finally cost William the justiciarship, however, was the formal charge of treason made by fitz Thomas before the council in Dublin on 1 April 1294. When he lodged it – and when (if William should be believed) he had earlier represented the justiciar to Edward as having conspired against the crown[142] – fitz Thomas was no doubt fully aware of Edward's mounting problems with the Scots, whose view of the feudal relationship between England and Scotland was very different from his own. These may supply the likeliest explanation of why William had such difficulty in reassuring Edward of his fidelity, as was reflected in his decision to offer battle to fitz Thomas and thereby put himself at God's mercy rather than the king's. Certainly, that Irish and Scottish affairs occupied the same stage is vividly shown by the fact that William had first been hauled before Edward's council to answer accusations of flouting royal rights during the Westminster parliament (Michaelmas 1293) in which a resentful Balliol had himself been disciplined in person for attempting to uphold Scottish independence.[143] So in 1293–4, Edward's supremacy was being questioned both in Ireland and in Scotland – a potentially explosive combination. Viewed in this context, the king's anxieties about William's commitment to himself and his policies become all too apparent, especially when we remember that influential Scots well known to the de Vescys were by no means averse to meddling in the politics of Ireland and forging alliances there.[144] Another fundamental point, therefore, is that William's loss of the justiciarship was also at least partly determined by broader 'British' events; and since he had been unable to salvage his reputation, the knock-on effect was to leave his public integrity even as a northern English baron irredeemably tarnished.

Then in 1295–7 Irish, Scottish and English history merged with

---

[142] *Ibid.*, pp. 127, 132; *Cal. Doc. Ire.*, 1293–1301, no. 147.
[143] Barrow, *Robert Bruce* (3rd edn), p. 59; Prestwich, *Edward I*, pp. 371–2.
[144] By the famous Turnberry 'band' of 1286 the Stewarts and other Scottish magnates had bound themselves in a military pact with the earl of Ulster and Thomas de Clare of Thomond. It cannot escape notice that a prime target was almost certainly John fitz Thomas, an argument convincingly made in the important discussion in S. Duffy, 'Ireland and the Irish Sea region, 1014–1318' (Ph.D. thesis, University of Dublin, Trinity College, 1993), pp. 151–7. William himself was not a party to the 'band', nor can it be shown that he was a facilitator of it; but Dr Duffy has kindly pointed out to me that Thomas de Clare and Domnall Ruad Mac Carthaig were allies in 1283, and suggests that William may have been a member of the anti-fitz Thomas faction that emerged in the mid-1280s.

family history to determine the de Vescys' fate. On the death of William's only legitimate son John, in April 1295, the de Vescys were effectively doomed to extinction under feudal rules of inheritance. Apart from William 'of Kildare', his bastard by Derbforgaill of Desmond, William himself was now the only survivor of the direct line; he was nearly fifty and in failing health, and his lawful wife had been barren since 1269. These circumstances provide part of the background for the extensive reorganization of the de Vescy estates undertaken by William in 1295–7 to safeguard as far as possible his own and his family's position. The most straightforward arrangement was his grant to Edward I in February 1297 of the reversion of the castle, manor and county of Kildare, and of the barony of Sprouston. In return William was pardoned all his predecessors' unpaid debts at the exchequer and his own debts as justiciar of Ireland and justice of the forest north of the Trent; the crucial inducement, however, was arguably Edward's offer of immunity from punishment for any misdeeds committed in his service as a royal minister – a concession that takes us back to William's Irish misadventures and starkly underlines the weakness of his negotiating position *vis-à-vis* the English crown.[145] William's arrangements concerning his English lands were more complicated.[146] In 1295 the Yorkshire and Lincolnshire estates were entrusted to Anthony Bek, who regranted them to William and the heirs of his body, with remainder in tail to William 'of Kildare'. By this expedient, feudal rules were evaded and William did what he could to protect his name and blood by securing part of the inheritance for the bastard line. But what of the primary source of the de Vescys' power and identity, the castle and barony of Alnwick? In 1295 they were also committed to Bek, who entailed them on William with reversion to himself and his heirs in the event of William's death without lawful issue. There was no place for William's bastard in that agreement: just as Kildare fell to the crown when William died in July 1297, so Alnwick passed to Bek, and it remained in his clutches until he sold out to the Percys in 1309–10.

Over and above William's concern for his lineage, it is impossible not to be impressed by the increasingly pronounced imprint stamped on the de Vescys by the 'British' ambitions of Edward I. While it is not difficult to see why William sacrificed Kildare, Edward richly benefited the

---

[145] Martin (ed.), *Percy Chartulary*, no. 669; *CPR, 1292–1301*, pp. 238, 256. Perhaps significantly, there was a four-month gap between William's resignation of Kildare (18 February 1297) and Edward I's regrant by special grace for the term of his life (22 June 1297).

[146] Fraser, *History of Antony Bek*, p. 108, and J. M. W. Bean, 'The Percies' acquisition of Alnwick', *Archaeologia Aeliana*, 4th series, 32 (1954), pp. 310–11, provide brief summaries.

crown at the expense of the legitimate expectations of William's collaterals and their descendants. As for Bek, his rapacity was notorious, but it cannot be supposed that he took advantage of William's misfortunes entirely on his own initiative. Then the chief mainstay of Edward's power in northern England and his principal adviser on Scottish affairs, Bek was the obvious man to buttress the king's hegemony in the Borders, and had in fact already been granted Alexander III's liberty of Tynedale and honour of Penrith.[147] Conversely, William's relations with Edward had come under renewed strain in August 1295 when he and other magnates had resisted demands for military service in Gascony; on 3 September, indeed, Edward reacted sharply by ordering the exchequer to collect their debts, refuse them any favour and discipline them severely.[148] In practice, William still cut too influential a figure to be provoked beyond endurance, not least because the Scots were already preparing for war in alliance with the French. But once again Edward had been reminded of his uncertain loyalty, and in such critical circumstances the additional harm done to the family's standing at the English court was inevitably all the greater. On 5 October 1295 Edward appointed Bek and Earl Warenne as keepers of the northern counties with special responsibility for their military defence; on 16 October he ordered the confiscation of all property held in England by Scots.[149] And here the chronology of William's business with Bek assumes a crucial significance. Behind the final concords of 12 November 1295 and 20 January 1296 lie private undertakings of 19 and 29 October 1295, which reveal that they had already reached agreement on all essential points.[150] Other evidence indicates that they had begun to negotiate in earnest by 25 September.[151]

Finally, William 'of Kildare' was not entirely ignored, and that leads us back from Anglo-Scottish to Irish affairs. Under Gaelic Irish inheritance customs, he was entitled to regard himself as his father's successor to Kildare and, powerfully connected as he was to the family of Mac Carthaig of Desmond, he had a significant potential for adding to

---

[147] Fraser, *History of Antony Bek*, pp. 55–6, 89–90.
[148] *Book of Prests, 1294–5*, ed. E. B. Fryde (Oxford, 1962), p. xlviii; M. Prestwich, *War, Politics and Finance under Edward I* (London, 1972), pp. 76, 236.
[149] Fraser, *History of Antony Bek*, p. 66; *CDS*, ii, no. 718.
[150] BL, Harl. Chr. 57.C.34; Martin (ed.), *Percy Chartulary*, no. 791 (both dated at London, 19 October 1295); *ibid.*, no. 834 (dated at Stapleford, Leicestershire, 29 October 1295). The fines are Public Record Office, London, Common Pleas, Feet of Fines, CP25(1)/285/24/222, 224; 175/57/339.
[151] By letters patent issued at Brompton, 25 September 1295, William ordered his tenants at Eltham, Kent, to obey Bek as his feoffee (BL, Harl. Chr. 57.C.35). William's grant of Eltham to Bek for an annual reddendo of one sparrowhawk is recorded in two charters, both undated: BL, Harl. Chrs. 57.C.36–7.

Ireland's troubles. In 1295, however, he was offered an alternative establishment as a member of the English gentry; Edward I's take-over of Kildare as a royal shire in 1297 would be smoothly achieved; and the de Vescy feud with John fitz Thomas was at last put to rest. Moreover, Kildare gave Edward the leverage he needed to force fitz Thomas to reach a final compromise with the earl of Ulster in 1298, and so ended another great dispute that had escalated almost out of control. As the justiciar (John Wogan) wrote to Edward in the summer of 1297, Ireland was 'at peace according to its manner'.[152] Fitz Thomas was in fact a leader of the 3,000 strong Irish army mustered by Edward against Balliol in 1296,[153] and so we return to the Anglo-Scottish scene. It remains difficult to believe that the former justiciar gained much comfort from the results of his efforts to promote or protect his family's status and defend its identity; but only when set within 'British' parameters is the de Vescys' final lot fully intelligible. Here, as elsewhere, 'British history' has 'the advantage that it refreshes those parts of the past that "national" history does not reach'.[154]

[152] Quoted in Otway-Ruthven, *History of Ireland*, p. 213.
[153] J. F. Lydon, 'An Irish army in Scotland, 1296', *The Irish Sword*, 5 (1961–2), pp. 184–90. As Lydon comments (*ibid.*, p. 189): 'For the first time in this reign Irish soldiers had taken the field in large numbers in one of Edward's campaigns.'
[154] R. Frame, 'Aristocracies and the political configuration of the British Isles', in *The British Isles, 1100–1500: Comparisons, Contrasts and Connections*, ed. R. R. Davies, p. 150. (Reprinted in Frame, *Ireland and Britain 1170–1450*, pp. 151–70.) I am most grateful to Professor Robin Frame for commenting on an earlier version of this chapter.

Bibliography

PUBLISHED SOURCES

Abbo, *Le Siège de Paris par les Normands*, ed. H. Waquet (Paris, 1942)
Abstracts of the Charters and other Documents contained in the Chartulary of the Cistercian Abbey of Fountains, ed. W. T. Lancaster, 2 vols. (Leeds, 1915)
'Acallamh na Senórach', ed. W. Stokes, in *Irische Texte*, 4.1, ed. W. Stokes and E. Windisch (Leipzig, 1900)
Acta Sanctorum Quotquot Toto Orbe Coluntur, ed. J. Bolland et al. (Antwerp, Tongerloo, Paris, Brussels, 1643–in progress)
Acta Sanctorum Veteris et Majoris Scotiæ seu Hiberniæ, ed. J. Colgan (Louvain, 1645)
Acts of the Parliaments of Scotland, ed. T. Thomson and C. Innes, 12 vols. (Edinburgh, 1814–75)
Adam of Dryburgh, *De Tripartito Tabernaculo* in *MPL*, 198 (Paris, 1858), cols. 609–792
Adam Usk, *Chronicle*, ed. C. Given-Wilson (Oxford, 1997)
Adomnán, *Life of Columba*, ed. A. O. Anderson and M. O. Anderson (Oxford, 1991)
Adomnán of Iona, *Life of Columba*, ed. R. Sharpe (Harmondsworth, 1995)
Aelred of Rievaulx, *Genealogia Regum Anglorum*, in *MPL*, 195 (Paris, 1855), cols. 711–38
  Relatio de Standardo, in *Chronicles and Memorials of the Reigns of Stephen, Henry II and Richard I*, ed. R. Howlett, 4 vols., RS (London, 1884–9) iii, pp. 179–99
  De Sanctis Ecclesiae Haugustaldensis, ed. J. Raine, in *The Priory of Hexham*, 2 vols., Surtees Society 44, 46 (Durham and London, 1864–5)
Androw of Wyntoun's, The Orygynale Cronykil of Scotland, ed. D. Laing, Historians of Scotland, 3 vols. (Edinburgh, 1872–9)
The Anglo-Saxon Chronicle, trans. D. Whitelock, in *English Historical Documents I, c. 500–1042*, ed. D. Whitelock, 2nd edn (London, 1979), pp. 145–261
Annála Connacht, The Annals of Connacht (A.D. 1224–1544), ed. A. Martin Freeman (Dublin, 1944)
Annála Ríoghachta Éireann; Annals of the Kingdom of Ireland by the Four Masters from the Earliest Period to the year 1616, ed. and trans. J. O'Donovan, 7 vols. (Dublin, 1851 repr., New York, 1966)

Annála Uladh: Annals of Ulster, ed. W. M. Hennessy and B. MacCarthy, 4 vols. (Dublin, 1887–1901)
Annales Cambriae, ed. J. Williams ab Ithel, RS (London, 1860)
Annales Monastici, ed. H. R. Luard, 5 vols., RS (London, 1864–9)
The Annals of Fulda, ed. T. Reuter (Manchester and New York, 1992)
The Annals of Inisfallen (MS Rawlinson B 503), ed. and trans. S. Mac Airt (Dublin, 1951, repr. 1977)
The Annals of Loch Cé: A Chronicle of Irish Affairs, 1014–1690, ed. W. M. Hennessy, 2 vols., RS (London, 1871)
The Annals of St-Bertin, ed. J. N. Nelson (Manchester, 1991)
'The Annals of Tigernach', ed. W. Stokes, *Revue Celtique*, 16–18 (1895–7); (reprinted in 2 vols., Felinfach, 1993)
The Annals of Ulster (to A.D. 1131), ed. S. Mac Airt and G. Mac Niocaill (Dublin, 1983)
Armes Prydein, ed. Sir Ifor Williams, trans. R. Bromwich (Dublin, 1972)
The Asloan Manuscript: a Miscellany of Prose and Verse written by John Asloan, ed. W. A. Craigie, 2 vols., STS (Edinburgh & London, 1923)
Bernard of Clairvaux, *The Life and Death of St Malachy the Irishman*, ed. R. Meyer (Kalamazoo, 1978)
Bethu Phátraic: The Tripartite Life of Patrick, ed. K. Mulchrone (Dublin, 1939)
'The Birth of Brandub and of Aedan son of Gabran', ed. R. I. Best, in *Medieval Studies in Memory of Gertrude Schoepperle Loomis*, ed. P. Rajna et al. (Paris, New York, 1927), pp. 381–90
The Book of Fees commonly called Testa de Nevill, ed. H. C. Maxwell Lyte, 2 vols. in 3 (London, 1920–31)
The Book of Leinster, Formerly Lebar na Núachongbála, ed. R. I. Best, O. Bergin, M. A. O' Brien and A. O'Sullivan, 6 vols. (Dublin, 1954–83)
The Book of Obits and Martyrology of the Cathedral Church of Holy Trinity, ed. J. H. Todd (Dublin, 1844)
Book of Prests, 1294–5, ed. E. B. Fryde (Oxford, 1962)
Bristol Charters 1155–1373, ed. N. D. Hardinge, Bristol Record Society, vol. I (Bristol, 1930)
The Brut, or Chronicles of England, ed. F. W. D. Brie, 2 vols., EETS (London, 1906–8)
Brut y Tywysogyon or the Chronicle of the Princes. Peniarth MS. 20 Version, ed. and trans. T. Jones (Cardiff, 1952)
Brut y Tywysogyon or the Chronicle of the Princes. Red Book of Hergest Version, ed. and trans. T. Jones (Cardiff, 1955)
Das Buch vom Espurgatoire S. Patrice de Marie de France und seine Quellen, ed. K. Warnke, Bibliotheca Normannica, 9 (Halle, 1938)
Caithréim Thoirdhealbhaigh, ed. S. H. O'Grady, 2 vols., ITS (London, 1925)
Calendar of the Charter Rolls, 6 vols. (London, 1903–27)
'Calendar to Christ Church deeds', ed. M. J. McEnery, in *Report of the Deputy Keeper of the Public Records of Ireland*, 20 (1888)
Calendar of the Close Rolls (London, 1900–)
Calendar of Documents Relating to Ireland, ed. H. S. Sweetman, 5 vols. (London, 1875–86)

Calendar of Documents Relating to Scotland, ed. J. Bain *et al.*, 5 vols. (Edinburgh, 1881–1986)
Calendar of Entries in the Papal Registers Relating to Great Britain and Ireland: Papal Letters (London, 1893–)
Calendar of the Gormanstown Register, ed. J. Mills and M. J. McEnery (Dublin, 1916)
Calendar of Inquisitions Post Mortem and other Analogous Documents . . . Henry III – [Richard II], 16 vols. (London, 1904–74)
Calendar of the Justiciary Rolls . . . of Ireland, ed. J. Mills *et al.*, 3 vols. (Dublin, 1905–56)
Calendar of the Laing Charters, ed. J. Anderson (Edinburgh, 1899)
Calendar of the Patent Rolls Preserved in the Public Record Office 1216–1509, 54 vols. (London, 1891–1916)
Cartularium Abbathiae de Rievalle, ed. J. C. Atkinson, Surtees Society (Durham and London, 1889)
Cartularium Saxonicum, ed. W. de Gray Birch, 3 vols. (London, 1885–93)
The Cartulary of Bradenstoke Priory, ed. V. C. M. London, Wiltshire Record Society (Devizes, 1979)
Charters, Bulls, and other Documents relating to the Abbey of Inchaffray, ed. W. A. Lindsay *et al.*, Scottish History Society (Edinburgh, 1908)
Chartularies of St Mary's Abbey, Dublin, ed. J. T. Gilbert, 2 vols., RS (London 1884–6)
The Chartulary of Brinkburn Priory, ed. W. Page, Surtees Society (Durham and London, 1893)
Chartulary of the Cistercian Priory of Coldstream, ed. C. Rogers, Grampian Club (London, 1879)
The Chartulary of St John of Pontefract, ed. R. Holmes, 2 vols., Yorkshire Archaeological Society, Record Series (Leeds, 1899–1902)
Chrétien de Troyes, *Erc and Enide*, ed. C. W. Carroll (New York, 1987)
Chronica de Mailros, ed. J. Stevenson (Edinburgh, 1835)
Chronicle of Hugh Candidus, ed. W. T. Mellowes (London, 1949)
Chronicle of the Kings of Man and the Isles, ed. G. Broderick and B. Stowell (Edinburgh, 1973)
The Chronicle of Lanercost 1272–1346, trans. H. Maxwell (Glasgow, 1913)
The Chronicle of Melrose, ed. A. O. Anderson *et al.* (London, 1936)
The Chronicle of Pierre de Langtoft, ed. T. Wright, 2 vols., RS (London, 1866–8)
The Chronicle of Walter of Guisborough, ed. H. Rothwell, Camden Society (London, 1957)
Chronicles of the Picts, Chronicles of the Scots, and other early Memorials of Scottish History, ed. W. F. Skene (Edinburgh, 1867)
Chronicles of the Reigns of Stephen, Henry II, and Richard I, ed. R. Howlett, 4 vols., RS (London, 1884–9)
Chronicon Anglicanum, ed. J. Stevenson, RS (London, 1875)
Chronicon de Lanercost, ed. J. Stevenson (Edinburgh, 1839)
Chronicon Monasterii de Abingdon, ed. J. Stevenson, 2 vols., RS (London, 1858)
Chronicon Scotorum, ed. W. M. Hennessy, RS (London, 1866)
Close Rolls of the Reign of Henry III, 14 vols. (London, 1902–38)

The Codex Palatino-Vaticanus, No. 830, ed. and trans. B. McCarthy (Dublin, 1892)
Cogadh Gaedhel re Gallaibh, ed. J. Todd, RS (London, 1866)
Cormacán Eigeas, *The Circuit of Ireland*, ed. J. O'Donovan (Dublin, 1841)
Corpus Genealogiarum Hiberniae, ed. M. A. O'Brien (Dublin, 1962, repr. 1976)
Corpus Iuris Hibernici, ed. D. A. Binchy, 6 vols. (Dublin, 1978)
Councils and Ecclesiastical Documents relating to Great Britain and Ireland, ed. A. W. Haddan and W. Stubbs (Oxford, 1869–71: repr., 1964)
The Court and Household of Eleanor of Castile in 1290, ed. J. C. Parsons (Toronto, 1977)
Cronica Regum Mannie & Insularum, ed. G. Broderick, Manx Museum and National Trust (Douglas, 1991)
'Cronica de Wallia and other documents from Exeter Library MS. 3514', ed. T. Jones, *BBCS*, 12 (1946–8), pp. 27–44
'De maccaib Conaire', ed. L. Gwynn, *Ériu*, 6 (1912), pp. 144–53
'De shíl Chonaire Mór', ed. L. Gwynn, *Ériu*, 6 (1912), pp. 130–43
Decrees of the Ecumenical Councils, ed. N. P. Tanner (London, 1990), p. 202
Diplomatic Documents, 1101–1272, ed. P. Chaplais (London, 1964)
Documents and Extracts Illustrating the History of the Honour of Dunster, ed. H. C. Maxwell Lyte, Somerset Record Society (London, 1917–18)
Documents Illustrative of English History in the Thirteenth and Fourteenth Centuries, ed. H. Cole (London, 1844)
Documents Illustrative of the History of Scotland, 1286–1306, ed. J. Stevenson, 2 vols. (Edinburgh, 1870)
The Dublin Guild Merchant Roll, c. 1190–1265, ed. P. Connolly and G. Martin (Dublin, 1992)
Early Scottish Charters prior to 1153, ed. A. C. Lawrie (Glasgow, 1905)
Early Sources of Scottish History 500–1286, ed. A. O. Anderson, 2 vols. (Edinburgh, 1922; repr. Stamford, 1990)
Early Welsh Genealogical Tracts, ed. C. C. Bartram (Cardiff, 1966)
Early Yorkshire Charters, ed. W. Farrer, vols. i–iii (Edinburgh, 1914–16) and C. T. Clay, vols. iv–xii, Yorkshire Archaeological Society, Record Series, Extra Series (Wakefield, 1935–65)
Ecclesiastical Antiquities of Down, Connor, and Dromore: Consisting of a Taxation of those Dioceses compiled in the Year MCCCVI, ed. W. Reeves (Dublin, 1887)
Edward I and the Throne of Scotland, ed. E. L. G. Stones and G. Simpson, 2 vols. (Oxford, 1978)
Eiríks saga Rauda in *Eyrbyggja Saga*, ed. Einar Ól. Sweinsson and Matthías Pórdarson (Reykjavík, 1935)
English Benedictine Kalendars after A.D. 1100, ed. F. Wormald, 2 vols., Henry Bradshaw Society, 77, 81 (London, 1939–46)
English Kalendars before A. D. 1100, ed. F. Wormald, Henry Bradshaw Society, 72 (London, 1934; repr. Woodbridge, 1988)
Episcopal Acts and Cognate Documents relating to Welsh Dioceses 1066–1272, ed. J. Conway Davies, 2 vols. (Cardiff, 1946–8)
Félire Óengusso, ed. W. Stokes, Henry Bradshaw Society, 29 (London, 1905)
Fled Dúin na nGéd, ed. R. Lehmann (Dublin, 1964)

Florentii Wigorniensis Monachi Chronicon ex Chronicis, ed. B. Thorpe, 2 vols. (London, 1848–9)
Flores Historiarum, ed. H. R. Luard, 3 vols., RS (London, 1890)
Florilegium Insulae Sanctorum seu Vitae et Acta Sanctorum Hiberniae, ed. T. Messingham (Paris, 1624)
Foedera, Conventiones, Litterae et Cuiuscunque Generis Acta Publica, ed. T. Rymer, 4 vols. in 7 parts (London, 1816–69)
Fragmentary Annals of Ireland, ed. J. Radnor (Dublin, 1978)
'Gein Branduib maic Echach ocus Aedáin maic Gabráin inso sís', ed. K. Meyer ZCP, 2 (1899), pp. 134–5
Geoffrey of Durham, *Vita Bartholomaei Farnensis* in *Symeonis Monachi Opera Omnia*, ed. T. Arnold, 2 vols., RS (London, 1882–5), i, pp. 295–325
Giraldus Cambrensis [Gerald of Wales], *Expugnatio Hibernica: The Conquest of Ireland*, ed. A. B. Scott and F. X. Martin (Dublin, 1978)
De Invectionibus, 1. 2, ed. W. S. Davies, *Y Cymmrodor*, 30 (1920)
The Journey Through Wales and The Description of Wales, ed. and trans. L. Thorpe (Harmondsworth, 1978)
The History and Topography of Ireland, ed. J. J. O'Meara (Mountrath and Harmondsworth, 1982)
De Principis Instructione in *Giraldus Cambrensis, Opera*, ed. J. S. Brewer, J. F. Dimock and G. F. Warner, 8 vols., RS (London, 1861–91), vol. VIII
Giraldus Cambrensis, Opera, ed. J. S. Brewer, J. F. Dimock and G. F. Warner, 8 vols., RS (London, 1861–91)
'Giraldus Cambrensis in *Topographia Hibernie*', ed. J. J. O'Meara, *RIA Proc.*, 52 (1948–52) C, pp. 113–78
Guibert de Nogent, *De Vita Sua*, ed. G. Bourgin (Paris, 1907)
Gunnlaugs Saga Ormstungu, ed. P. G. Foote and trans. R. Quirk (London, 1953)
Hanes Gruffydd ap Cynan, ed. A. Jones (Manchester, 1910)
Die Heiligen Englands, ed. F. Liebermann (Hanover, 1889)
Highland Papers, ed. J. R. N. MacPhail, 4 vols. (Edinburgh, 1914–34)
Historia Ecclesiastica Gentis Scotorum, ed. D. Irving, 2 vols., Bannatyne Club (Edinburgh, 1829)
Historiae Dunhelmensis Scriptores Tres, ed. J. Raine, Surtees Society, 9 (London, Edinburgh, 1839)
Historians of the Church of York and its Archbishops, ed. J. Raine, 3 vols., RS (London, 1879–94)
Historic and Municipal Documents of Ireland, 1172–1320, ed. J. T. Gilbert, RS (London, 1870)
Historical Papers and Letters from the Northern Registers, ed. J. Raine, RS (1873)
History of Gruffydd ap Cynan (1054–1107), ed. and trans. A. Jones (Manchester, 1910)
Hrafns Saga Sveinbjarnarsonar, ed. G. P. Helgadóttir (Oxford, 1987)
Inquisitions and Assessments Relating to Feudal Aids, 6 vols. (London, 1899–1920)
The Irish Cartularies of Llanthony Prima and Secunda, ed. E. St John Brooks, Irish Manuscripts Commission (Dublin, 1953)
Johannis de Fordun, *Chronica Gentis Scotorum*, ed. W. F. Skene, Historians of Scotland, vol. i (Edinburgh, 1871)
John Barbour, *The Bruce*, ed. and trans. A. A. M. Duncan (Edinburgh, 1997)

John of Salisbury, *Policraticus*, ed. and trans. C. J. Nederman (Cambridge, 1990)
Jordan Fantosme's Chronicle, ed. and trans. R. C. Johnston (Oxford, 1981)
King Alfred's Orosius, ed. H. Sweet (London, 1883)
Lebor Bretnach: The Irish Version of the Historia Britonum ascribed to Nennius, ed. A. G. van Hamel (Dublin, 1932)
Lebor Gabála Éirenn, ed. and trans. R. A. S. Macalister, 5 vols. (London, 1938–56)
Lebor na Cert: the Book of Rights, ed. M. Dillon, ITS (London, 1962)
Lebor na hUidre: Book of the Dun Cow, ed. R. I. Best and O. Bergin (Dublin, 1929; repr. 1970)
Libellus de Admirandis Beati Cuthberti Virtutibus, ed. J. Raine, Surtees Society, 1 (London, Edinburgh, 1835)
Libellus de Ortu Sancti Cuthberti, ed. J. Raine, *Miscellanea Biographica*, Surtees Society, 8 (London, Edinburgh, 1838), pp. 63–87
Le Liber Censuum de l'église romaine, ed. P. Fabre and L. Duchesne (Paris, 1910)
Liber Eliensis, ed. E. O. Blake, Camden Society, vol. 92 (London, 1962)
Liber Landavensis: The Text of the Book of Llan Dâv, ed. J. G. Evans and J. Rhys (Oxford, 1893)
Liber Luciani de Laude Cestrie, ed. M. V. Taylor, Lancashire and Cheshire Record Society, 64 (Edinburgh and London, 1912)
Liber S. Marie de Calchou, ed. C. Innes, 2 vols., Bannatyne Club (Edinburgh, 1846)
Liber Sancte Marie de Melros, ed. C. Innes, 2 vols., Bannatyne Club (Edinburgh, 1837)
Liber S. Thome de Aberbrothoc Registrum Abbacie de Aberbrothoc, ed. P. Chalmers and C. Innes, 2 vols., Bannatyne Club (Edinburgh, 1848)
Magistri Adam Bremensis: Gesta Hammaburgensis Ecclesiae Pontificum (IV, 27), ed. R. Buchner, in *Ausgewählte Quellen zur Deutschen Geschichte des Mittelalters*, ix (Darmstadt, 1968)
'Mariani Scotti Chronicon', ed. G. Waitz, *MGH Scriptorum*, vol. V, ed. G. Pertz (Hanover, 1844) pp. 481–562
The Martyrology of Tallaght, ed. R. I. Best and H. J. Lawlor, Henry Bradshaw Society, 68 (London, 1931)
Matthew Paris, *Chronica Majora*, ed. H. R. Luard, 7 vols., RS (London, 1872–83)
A Mediaeval Prince of Wales. The Life of Gruffudd ap Cynan, ed. D. S. Evans (Felinfach, 1990)
Medieval Carmelite Heritage: Early Reflections on the Nature of the Order, ed. A. Staring (Rome, 1989)
Memoriale Fratris Walteri de Coventria: the Historical Collection of Walter of Coventry, ed. W. Stubbs, 2 vols., RS (London, 1872–3)
Memorials of Saint Dunstan, ed. W. Stubbs, RS (London, 1874)
The Metrical Chronicle of Robert of Gloucester, ed. W. A. Wright, 2 vols., RS (London, 1887)
The Metrical Dindshenchas, ed. E. Gwynn, 5 vols. (Dublin, 1903–35)
'A Middle-Irish poem on the birth of Áedán mac Gabráin and Brandub mac Echach', ed. M. A. O'Brien, *Ériu*, 16 (1952), pp. 157–70

Miscellaneous Irish Annals (AD 1114–1437), ed. S. Ó hInnse (Dublin, 1947)
'A new version of the Battle of Mag Rath', ed. and trans. C. Marstrander, *Ériu*, 5 (1911), pp. 226–47
'North country deeds', ed. W. Brown, in *Miscellanea*, ii, Surtees Society (Durham and London, 1916), pp. 107–30
Officia SS. Patricii, Columbae, Brigidae, ed. T. Messingham (Paris, 1620)
Orderic Vitalis, *Ecclesiastical History*, ed. M. Chibnall, 6 vols. (Oxford 1969–80)
The Original Chronicle of Andrew of Wyntoun, ed. F. J. Amours, 6 vols., STS (Edinburgh, 1903–14)
Origines Parochiales Scotiae, ed. C. Innes *et al.*, 2 vols. in 3, Bannatyne Club (Edinburgh, 1851–5)
The Patrician Texts in the Book of Armagh, ed. L. Bieler (Dublin, 1979)
'Eine Patricksvita in Gloucester', ed. L. Bieler, in *Festschrift Bernhard Bischoff zu seinem 65. Geburtstag*, ed. J. Autenrieth and F. Brunhölzl (Stuttgart, 1971), pp. 346–63, reprinted in Bieler, *Studies on the Life and Legend of St Patrick*, ed. R. Sharpe (London, 1986)
Patrologiae Cursus Completus. Series Latina, ed. J. P. Migne (Paris, 1841–64)
The Percy Chartulary, ed. M. T. Martin, Surtees Society (Durham and London, 1911)
Pipe Roll 1184–5: The Great Roll of the Pipe for the Thirty-First Year of the Reign of King Henry II, ed. J. H. Round, PRS, 34 (London, 1913)
Pipe Roll 1186–7: The Great Roll of the Pipe for the Thirty-Third Year of the Reign of King Henry II, PRS, 37 (London, 1915)
Pipe Roll 1201: The Great Roll of the Pipe for the Third Year of the Reign of King John, ed. D.M. Stenton, PRS, new series, 14 (London, 1936)
Pipe Roll 1202: The Great Roll of the Pipe for the Fourth Year of the Reign of King John, ed. D.M. Stenton, PRS, new series, 15 (London, 1937)
Pipe Roll 1203: The Great Roll of the Pipe for the Fifth Year of the Reign of King John, ed. D.M. Stenton, PRS, new series, 16 (London, 1938)
The Political Songs of England, from the Reign of John to that of Edward II, ed. and trans. T. Wright, Camden Society (London, 1839)
Pontificia Hibernica: Medieval Papal Chancery Documents concerning Ireland, 640–1261, ed. M. P. Sheehy, 2 vols. (Dublin, 1962–5)
Ralph of Coggeshall, *Chronicon Anglicanum*, ed. J. Stevenson, RS (London, 1875)
Ralph of Diceto, *Opera Historica*, ed. W. Stubbs, 2 vols., RS (London, 1876)
De Rebus Brittannis Collectanea, ed. T. Hearne, 6 vols. (London, 1774)
Records of the Wardrobe and Household, 1286–1289, ed. B. F. and C. R. Byerly (London, 1986)
Recueil de Lettres Anglo-Françaises (1265–1399), ed. F. J. Tanquerey (Paris, 1916)
Regesta Regum Scottorum, ii, *Acts of William I, King of Scots, 1165–1214*, ed. G. W. S. Barrow (Edinburgh, 1971)
Regesta Regum Scottorum, v, *The Acta of Robert I*, ed. A. A. M. Duncan (Edinburgh, 1988)
Reginonis Chronica, ed. R. Rau, in *Ausgewählte Quellen zur Deutschen Geschichte des Mittelalters*, VII, ii (*c*. 1960)

The Register of the Priory of St Bees, ed. J. Wilson, Surtees Society, 126 (Durham, London, 1915)
The Register of Richard de Swinfield, Bishop of Hereford (1283–1317), ed. W. Capes, Cantilupe Society and Canterbury and York Society, 6 (London, 1909)
The Register of William Wickwane, Lord Archbishop of York, 1279–1285, ed. W. Brown, Surtees Society (Durham and London, 1907)
Registrum Episcopatus Glasguensis, ed. C. Innes, 2 vols. (Edinburgh, 1843)
Registrum Magni Sigilli Regum Scotorum, ed. J. M. Thomson *et al.*, 11 vols. (Edinburgh, 1882–1914)
Registrum Monasterii de Passelet, ed. C. Innes (Edinburgh, 1832)
The Relics of Saint Cuthbert, ed. C. F. Battiscombe (Oxford, 1956)
Rhigyfarch, *Life of St David*, ed. and trans. J. W. James (Cardiff, 1967)
Robert of Shrewsbury, *Vita et Translatio Sanctae Wenefredae*, in Bolland (ed.), *Acta Sanctorum*, 1 Nov., pp. 708–31
Roger of Howden, *Chronica*, ed. W. Stubbs, 4 vols., RS (London, 1868–71)
 Gesta Regis Henrici Secundi Benedicti Abbatis, ed. W. Stubbs, 2 vols., RS (London, 1867)
Roger of Wendover, *Flores Historiarum*, ed. H. G. Hewlett, 3 vols., RS (London, 1886–9)
Rotuli Chartarum in Turri Londinensi Asservati, 1199–1216, ed. T. D. Hardy (London, 1837)
Rotuli de Dominabus et Pueris et Puellis, ed. J. H. Round, PRS, 35 (London, 1913)
Rotuli Litterarum Clausarum in Turri Londinensi Asservati, ed. T. D. Hardy, 2 vols. (London, 1833–4)
Rotuli de Oblatis et Finibus in Turri Londinensi Asservati, Tempore Regis Johannis, ed. T. D. Hardy, Record Commission (London, 1835)
Rotuli Parliamentorum, 7 vols., Record Commission (London, 1783–1832)
Rotuli Parliamentorum Anglie Hactenus Inediti, MCCLXXIX-MCCCLXXIII, ed. H. G. Richardson and G. O. Sayles, Camden Society (London, 1935)
Rufford Charters, ed. C. J. Holdsworth, 4 vols., Thoroton Society (Nottingham, 1972–81)
Sacrorum Conciliorum Nova et Amplissima Collectio, ed. G. D. Mansi, 31 vols. (Florence, 1759–98)
St Benet of Holme, 1020–1210: The Eleventh- and Twelfth-Century Sections of Cott. MS. Galba E.ii, ed. J. R. West, Norfolk Record Society (Fakenham and London, 1932)
St Bernard of Clairvaux's Life of St Malachy of Armagh, ed. H. J. Lawlor (London, 1920)
St Odo of Cluny: Being the Life of St Odo of Cluny by John of Salerno and the Life of St Gerald of Aurillac by St Odo, ed. G. Sitwell (London and New York, 1958)
Saltair na Rann, ed. W. Stokes (Oxford, 1883)
Sancti Bernardi Opera, ed. J. Leclercq, C. H. Talbot and H. M. Rochais (Rome, 1957–)
Sancti Dunstani Vita Auctore B in *Memorials of St Dunstan*, ed. W. Stubbs, RS (London, 1874), pp. 3–52

Scalacronica: a Chronicle of England and Scotland from A.D. MLXVI to A.D. MCCCLXII, ed. J. Stevenson, Maitland Club (Edinburgh, 1836)
Scalacronica: the Reigns of Edward I and Edward II and Edward III by Sir Thomas Gray of Heton, trans. Sir H. Maxwell, bart. (Glasgow, 1907)
Scotichronicon by Walter Bower in Latin and English, gen. ed. D. E. R. Watt, 9 vols. (Aberdeen/Edinburgh, 1987-98)
Scottish Annals from English Chroniclers, 500 to 1286, ed. A. O. Anderson (London, 1908)
Scottish Historical Documents, ed. G. Donaldson (Edinburgh, 1970)
Select Cases in the Court of King's Bench, Edward I-Edward III, ed. G. O. Sayles, 5 vols., Selden Society (London, 1936-58)
Series Episcoporum Ecclesiae Catholicae Occidentalis 6/1: Ecclesia Scoticana, ed. D. E. R. Watt (Stuttgart, 1991)
Silva Gadelica: A Collection of Tales in Irish, ed. S. H. O'Grady, 2 vols., ITS (London, 1892)
Sir Christopher Hatton's Book of Seals, eds. L. C. Loyd and D. M. Stenton, Northamptonshire Record Society, 15 (1950)
The Song of Dermot and the Earl, ed. G. H. Orpen (Dublin, 1892)
Táin Bó Cúalgne from the Book of Leinster, ed. C. O'Rahilly (Dublin, 1970)
The Text of the Bruts from the Red Book of Hergest, ed. J. Rhys and J. G. Evans (Oxford, 1890)
Thietmari Merseburgensis Episcopi Chronicon, ed. R. Holzmann, in *MGH Rerum Germanicarum Nova Series*, ix, 2nd edn (Berlin, 1955)
Translatio Sancte Helene, ed. P. Grosjean, *Analecta Bollandiana*, 58 (1940), pp. 199-203
Trias Thaumaturgæ seu Divorum Patricii, Columbæ et Brigidæ ... Acta, ed. J. Colgan (Louvain, 1647)
The Tripartite Life of St Patrick, ed. W. Stokes, 2 vols., RS (London, 1887)
De Tripartito Tabernaculo 2. 120, *MPL*, 198, cols. 609-792
Two Chartularies of the Priory of St Peter at Bath, ed. W. Hunt, Somerset Record Society (London, 1893)
'Two Middle-Irish poems', ed. and trans. K. Meyer, *ZCP*, 1 (1897)
Two of the Saxon Chronicles Parallel, ed. C. Plummer and J. Earle, 2 vols. (Oxford, 1892-9, repr. 1965)
Victoria History of the Counties of England, Yorkshire: North Riding (London, 1914-)
Vita Sancti Geraldi Auriliacensis comitis, in *MPL*, 133 (Paris, 1853)
Vita Sancti Kentigerni. Lives of St Ninian and St Kentigern, ed. A. P. Forbes, The Historians of Scotland, 5 (Edinburgh, 1874)
Vita Sancti Odonis abbatis Cluniacensis secundi, in *MPL*, 133 (Paris, 1853)
Vita Sanctorum Britanniae et Genealogiae, ed. A. Wade Evans (Cardiff, 1944)
Vita Wulfstani, ed. A. Campbell, Camden Society, vol. 40 (London, 1928)
Walafridus Strabo: Vita Sancti Blaithmaic Martyris, ed. E. Dümmler, in *M.G.H, Poetae Latini Aevi Carolini*, ii (1884, repr. 1978)
Walter Map, *De Nugis Curialium*, ed. and trans. M. R. James, C. N. L. Brooke and R. A. B. Mynors (Oxford, 1983)
William of Malmesbury, *De Antiquitate Glastonie Ecclesie. The Early History of Glastonbury*, ed. and trans. J. Scott (Woodbridge, 1981)

De Gestis Pontificum, ed. N. E. S. A. Hamilton, RS (London, 1870)
De Gestis Regum Anglorum Libri Quinque, ed. W. Stubbs, 2 vols., RS (London, 1887–89)
William of Newburgh, *Historia Rerum Anglicarum*, in *Chronicles and Memorials of the Reigns of Stephen, Henry II, and Richard I*, ed. R. Howlett, 4 vols., RS (London, 1884–9), i, pp. 1–408, ii, pp. 409–53
William Worcestre, *Itineraries*, ed. J. H. Harvey (Oxford, 1969)

SECONDARY SOURCES

Alcock, L., 'Was there an Irish Sea culture-province in the Dark Ages?', in *The Irish Sea Province in Archaeology and History*, ed. D. Moore (Cardiff, 1970), pp. 55–65
Anderson, M. O., *Kings and Kingship in Early Scotland* (Edinburgh 1973, repr. 1980)
  'Dalriada and the creation of the kingdom of the Scots', in *Ireland in Early Medieval Europe*, ed. D. Whitelock, R. McKitterick and D. Dumville (Cambridge, 1982), pp. 106–32
Arnold-Foster, F. E., *Studies in Church Dedications*, 3 vols. (London, 1899)
Attenborough, F. L., *The Laws of the English Kings* (New York, 1963)
Bale, J., *Illustrium Maioris Britanniae Scriptorum* (1548)
Bannerman, J., 'The king's poet and the inauguration of Alexander III', *SHR*, 68 (1989), pp. 120–49
  'MacDuff of Fife', in *Medieval Scotland: Crown, Lordship and Community*, ed. A. Grant and K. J. Stringer (Edinburgh, 1993), pp. 20–38
Barrow, G. W. S., *The Kingdom of the Scots: Government, Church and Society from the Eleventh to the Fourteenth Century* (London, 1973)
  Robert Bruce, 2nd edn (Edinburgh, 1976), 3rd edn (Edinburgh, 1988)
  The Anglo-Norman Era in Scottish History (Oxford, 1980)
  Kingship and Unity: Scotland 1000–1306 (London, 1981)
  David I of Scotland: the Balance of Old and New, Stenton Lecture 1984 (Reading, 1985) (reprinted in Barrow, *Scotland and its Neighbours in the Middle Ages* (London, 1992), pp. 45–66)
  'The Gilbertine house at Dalmilling', *Collections of the Ayrshire Archaeological and Natural History Society*, 2nd series, 4 (1958), pp. 50–67
  'The lost *Gàidhealtachd*', in *Gaelic and Scotland: Alba agus a' Ghàidhlig*, ed. W. Gilles (Edinburgh, 1989), pp. 67–88 (reprinted in Barrow, *Scotland and its Neighbours in the Middle Ages* (London, 1992), pp. 105–26)
  'A kingdom in crisis: Scotland and the Maid of Norway', *SHR*, 69 (1990), pp. 120–41
  'The army of Alexander III's Scotland', in *Scotland in the Reign of Alexander III 1249–1286*, ed. N. H. Reid (Edinburgh, 1990), pp. 132–47
Barry, T., 'Rural settlement in Ireland in the Middle Ages: an overview', in *Ruralia I, Pamatky archeologicke – Supplementum 5* (Prague, 1996)
Bartlett, R., *Gerald of Wales* (Oxford, 1982)
  The Making of Europe (Harmondsworth, 1993)
  'Rewriting saints' Lives: the case of Gerald of Wales', *Speculum*, 58 (1983), pp. 598–613

'Colonial aristocracies of the high Middle Ages', in *Medieval Frontier Societies*, ed. R. Bartlett and A. Mackay (Oxford, 1989), pp. 23–48

Bean, J. M. W., 'The Percies' acquisition of Alnwick', *Archaeologia Aeliana*, 4th series, 32 (1954), pp. 309–19

Benton, J. F., *Self and Society in Medieval France* (New York, 1970)

Beresford, M., *New Towns of the Middle Ages* (London, 1967)

Bethell, D., 'The making of a twelfth-century relic collection', in *Popular Belief and Practice*, ed. G. J. Cuming and D. Baker, Studies in Church History 8 (Cambridge, 1972), pp. 61–72

Blackburn, M., 'Coinage and currency', in *The Anarchy of King Stephen's Reign*, ed. E. King (Oxford, 1994), pp. 145–206

Blanchard, I., 'Lothian and beyond', in *Progress and Problems in Medieval England*, ed. R. H. Britnell and J. Hatcher (Cambridge, 1996), pp. 23–45

Bord, J., 'St Winefride's Well, Holywell, Clwyd', *Folklore*, 105 (1994), pp. 99–100

Bosworth, J., *King Alfred's Anglo-Saxon Version of the Compendious History of the World by Orosius* (London, 1859)

Bowen, E. G., *Saints, Seaways and Settlements in the Celtic Lands* (Cardiff, 1977)

Boyle, A., 'St Ninian and St Monenna', *Innes Review*, 18 (1967), pp. 147–51

'The Edinburgh synchronisms of Irish kings', *Celtica*, 9 (1971), pp. 169–79

'St Cadroe in Scotland', *Innes Review*, 31 (1980), pp. 3–6

Boyle, J., *Portrait of Canterbury* (London, 1974)

Bradshaw, B., 'Nationalism and historical scholarship in modern Ireland', *IHS*, 26 (1988–9), pp. 329–51

Bright's Old English Grammar and Reader, ed. F. G. Cassidy and R. N. Ringler, 3rd edn (New York, 1971)

Britnell, R. H., 'King John's early grants of markets and fairs', *EHR*, 94 (1979), pp. 90–6

'The proliferation of markets in England', *Econ. Hist. Rev.*, 2nd series, 34 (1981), pp. 209–21

Brooke, C., 'The archbishops of St Davids, Llandaff and Caerleon-on-Usk', in *Celt and Saxon: Studies in the Early British Border*, ed. N. K. Chadwick (Cambridge, 1963), pp. 258–322 (reprinted in his *The Church and the Welsh Border in the Central Middle Ages* (Woodbridge, 1986), pp. 16–49)

'King David I of Scotland as a connoisseur of the religious orders', in *Mediaevalia Christiana, xie-xiiie Siècles: Hommage à Raymonde Foreville*, ed. C. E. Viola (Paris, 1989), pp. 320–34

Broun [Brown], D., *The Charters of Gaelic Scotland and Ireland in the Early and Central Middle Ages*, Quiggin Pamphlets on the Sources of Mediaeval Gaelic History, 2 (Cambridge, 1995)

The Irish Identity of the Kingdom of the Scots in the 12th and 13th centuries (Woodbridge, forthcoming)

'The Scottish origin-legend before Fordun' (Ph.D. thesis, University of Edinburgh, 1988)

'The birth of Scottish history', *SHR*, 76 (1997), pp. 4–22

'Gaelic literacy in eastern Scotland, 1124–1249', in *Literacy in Medieval Celtic Societies*, ed. H. Pryce (Cambridge, 1998), pp. 183–201

'Defining Scotland and the Scots before the wars of independence', in *Image and Identity: the Making and Remaking of Scotland through the Ages*, ed. D. Broun, R. Finlay and M. Lynch (Edinburgh, 1998), pp. 4–17

'The seven kingdoms in *De situ Albanie*: a record of Pictish political geography or imaginary map of ancient Alba?', in *Alba: Celtic Scotland*, ed. E. J. Cowan and R. A. McDonald (East Linton, forthcoming)

Brown, E. A. R., 'The tyranny of a construct: feudalism and the historians of medieval Europe', *American Historical Review*, 79 (1974), pp. 1063–88

Brown, R. Allen, *The Normans and the Norman Conquest* (London, 1969)

Castles, Shire Archaeology (Aylesbury, 1985)

Bullough, D. A., 'What has Ingeld to do with Lindisfarne?', *Anglo-Saxon England*, 22 (1993), pp. 95–115

Bumke, J., *The Concept of Knighthood in the Middle Ages*, trans. W. T. H. and E. Jackson (New York, 1982)

Byrne, F. J., *Irish Kings and High-Kings* (London, 1973)

'Clann Ollaman Uaisle Emna', *Studia Hibernica*, 4 (1964), pp. 54–94

Cambridge, E., 'Archaeology and the cult of Oswald in pre-conquest Northumbria' in *Oswald: Northumbrian King to European Saint*, ed. C. Stancliffe and E. Cambridge (Stamford, 1995), pp. 128–63

Campbell, J., 'The debt of the early English church to Ireland', in *Irland und die Christenheit*, ed. P. Ní Chatháin and M. Richter (Stuttgart, 1987), pp. 332–46

Carey, J., *The Irish National Origin-Legend: Synthetic Pseudohistory*, Quiggin Pamphlets on the Sources of Mediaeval Gaelic History, 1 (Cambridge, 1994)

Carpenter, D. A., 'From King John to the first English duke: 1215–1337', in *The House of Lords, a Thousand Years of British Tradition*, ed. R. Smith and J. S. Moore (London, 1994)

Chaplais, P., *English Medieval Diplomatic Practice Part I: Documents and Interpretation*, 2 vols. (London, 1982)

Charles, B. G., *Old Norse Relations with Wales* (Cardiff, 1934)

Charles-Edwards, T., 'Language and society among the insular Celts AD 400–1000', in *The Celtic World*, ed. M. J. Green (London and New York, pbk. 1996), pp. 703–36

Cheney, C. R., *Pope Innocent III and England* (Stuttgart, 1976)

Clanchy, M., *From Memory to Written Record: England 1066–1307* (Oxford, 1993)

Clifford, E. R., *A Knight of Great Renown: The Life and Times of Othon de Grandson* (Chicago, 1961)

Cokayne, G. E., *The Complete Peerage*, revised by V. Gibbs *et al.* (London, 1910–59)

Colmcille, Fr. OCSO, *The Story of Mellifont* (Dublin, 1958)

'Abbatial succession of Mellifont, 1142–1539', *Co. Louth Archaeological Journal*, 15 (1961–64), pp. 23–38

Colvin, H. M., *The White Canons in England* (Oxford, 1951)

Conner, P. W., *Anglo-Saxon Exeter: A Tenth-Century Cultural History* (Woodbridge, 1993)

Cooper, T. M. (Lord Cooper of Culross), *Supra Crepidam* (London, 1951)

Coplestone-Crow, B., 'The dual nature of the Irish colonization of Dyfed in the Dark Ages', *Studia Celtica*, 16–17 (1981–2), pp. 107–19

Copsey, R., 'The Scottish Carmelite province and its provincials', in *The Land of Carmel: Essays in Honor of Joachim Smet*, ed. K. J. Egan and P. Chandler (Rome, 1991), pp. 189–203

Coss, P., *The Knight in Medieval England 1000–1400* (Stroud, 1993)

Cowan, E. J., 'Norwegian Sunset – Scottish Dawn: Hakon IV and Alexander III', in *Scotland in the Reign of Alexander III 1249–1286*, ed. N. H. Reid (Edinburgh, 1990), pp. 103–31

Cowan, I. B. and Easson, D. E., *Medieval Religious Houses: Scotland*, 2nd edn (London, 1976)

Cowley, F. G., *The Monastic Order in South Wales, 1066–1349* (Cardiff, 1977)

Crawford, B., 'The earldom of Caithness and the kingdom of Scotland, 1150–1266', in *Essays on the Nobility of Medieval Scotland*, ed. K. J. Stringer (Edinburgh, 1985), pp. 25–43

Crouch, D., *The Image of Aristocracy in Britain 1000–1300* (London, 1992)

Curtis, E., 'Murchertach O'Brien, high-king of Ireland, and his Norman son-in-law, Arnulf de Montgomery, circa 1100', *RSAI Jn.*, 51 (1921), pp. 116–34

'Two unpublished charters of John de Courcy, *princeps Ulidiae*', *Belfast Natural History and Philosophical Society Proceedings* (1928), pp. 2–10

Cuttler, S. H., *The Law of Treason and Treason Trials in Later Medieval France* (Cambridge, 1981)

Dalton, P., *Conquest, Anarchy and Lordship: Yorkshire, 1066–1154* (Cambridge, 1994)

'Eustace fitz John and the politics of Anglo-Norman England: the rise and survival of a twelfth-century royal servant', *Speculum*, 71 (1996), pp. 358–83

Davies, J. C., *The Baronial Opposition to Edward II* (Cambridge, 1918)

Davies, R. R., *Conquest, Coexistence and Change: Wales 1063–1415* (Oxford, 1987), published in paperback as *The Age of Conquest. Wales 1063–1415* (Oxford, 1991)

Domination and Conquest: the Experience of Ireland, Scotland and Wales, 1100–1300 (Cambridge, 1990)

The Matter of Britain and the Matter of England. An Inaugural Lecture (Oxford, 1996)

'Henry I and Wales', in *Studies in Medieval History presented to R.H.C. Davies*, ed. H. Mayr-Harting and R. I. Moore (London, 1985), pp. 132–47

'In praise of British history', in *The British Isles 1100–1500: Comparisons, Contrasts and Connections*, ed. R. R. Davies (Edinburgh, 1988), pp. 9–26

Davies, W., *An Early Welsh Microcosm: Studies in the Llandaff Charters* (London, 1978)

The Llandaff Charters (Aberystwyth, 1979)

Wales in the Early Middle Ages (Leicester, 1982)

Patterns of Power in Early Wales (Oxford, 1990)

Davis, R. H. C., *A History of Medieval Europe from Constantine to Saint Louis* (London, 1970)

Denton, J., *An Accompt of the County of Cumberland* (1610), ed. R. S. Ferguson (Kendal, 1887)

De Paor, L., 'The age of the Viking wars', in *The Course of Irish History*, ed. T. W. Moody and F. X. Martin (Cork, 1967), pp. 91–106

De Smedt, C., 'Documenta de sancta Wenefreda', *Analecta Bollandiana*, 6 (1887), pp. 305–52

Dickinson, W. C., *Scotland from the Earliest Times to 1603*, rev. and ed. A. A. M. Duncan (Oxford, 1977)

Dictionary of the Irish Language, Royal Irish Academy (Dublin, 1983)

Dillon, M., 'The Irish settlements in Wales', *Celtica*, 12 (1977), pp. 1–11

Dobbs, M. E., 'The history of the descendants of Ir', *ZCP*, 14 (1923), pp. 45–144

'References to Erc daughter of Loarn in Irish MSS', *Scottish Gaelic Studies*, 6 (1947), pp. 50–7

Doble, G. H., *Lives of the Welsh Saints* (Cardiff, 1971)

Dodds, M. H., 'The little book of the birth of St Cuthbert', *Archaeologia Aeliana*, 4th series, 6 (1929), pp. 52–94

Dolley, M., *The Hiberno-Norse Coins in the British Museum* (London, 1966)

Donaldson, G., *A Northern Commonwealth: Scotland and Norway* (Edinburgh, 1990)

Duby, G., 'Lineage, nobility and knighthood', in Duby, *The Chivalrous Society*, trans. C. Postan (London, 1977)

Duchesne, A., *Histoire Généalogique des Maisons de Guines, d'Ardres, de Gand et de Coucy* (Paris, 1631)

Duffy, S., 'Ireland and the Irish Sea region, 1014–1318' (Ph.D. thesis, University of Dublin, Trinity College, 1993)

'The Bruce brothers and the Irish Sea world, 1306–29', *Cambridge Medieval Celtic Studies*, 21 (1991), pp. 55–86

'Irishmen and Islesmen in the kingdoms of Dublin and Man, 1052–1171', *Ériu*, 43 (1992), pp. 93–133

'The first Ulster plantation: John de Courcy and the men of Cumbria', in *Colony and Frontier in Medieval Ireland: Essays presented to J. F. Lydon*, ed. T. Barry, R. Frame and K. Simms (London, 1995), pp. 1–27

'Ostmen, Irish and Welsh in the eleventh century', *Peritia*, 9 (1996), pp. 378–96

Dugdale, W., *Monasticon Anglicanum*, ed. J. Caley, H. Ellis, and B. Bandinel, 6 vols. in 8 (London, 1817–30; reprint [6 vols.] 1846)

Dumville, D., *Saint Patrick, A.D. 493–1993* (Woodbridge, 1993)

The Churches of North Britain in the First Viking-Age, Fifth Whithorn Lecture (Whithorn, 1997)

'Ireland and Britain in *Táin Bó Fraích*', *Études Celtiques*, 32 (1996), pp. 175–87

Duncan, A. A. M., *The Nation of Scots and the Declaration of Arbroath*, Historical Association Pamphlet no. 75 (London, 1970)

Scotland: The Making of the Kingdom (Edinburgh, 1975)

'The process of Norham, 1291', *Thirteenth Century England*, 5 (Woodbridge, 1995), pp. 207–30

Duncan, A. A. M. and Brown, A. L., 'Argyll and the Isles in the earlier Middle Ages', *Proceedings of the Society of Antiquaries of Scotland*, 90 (1956–57), pp. 204–5

Edwards, N., *The Archaeology of Early Medieval Ireland* (Philadelphia, 1990)

Egan, K. J., 'Medieval Carmelite houses, England and Wales', *Carmelus*, 16 (1969), pp. 142–226
'An essay toward a historiography of the origin of the Carmelite province in England', *Carmelus*, 19 (1972), pp. 67–100
Einarsson, B., '*De Normannorum Atrocitate*, or on the execution of royalty by the aquiline method', *Saga-Book*, 22, i (1986), pp. 79–82
'The blood-eagle once more: two notes', *Saga-Book*, 23, ii (1990), pp. 80–1
Farmer, D. L., 'Some price fluctuations in Angevin England', *Econ. Hist. Rev.*, 2nd series, 9 (1956), pp. 34–43
'Some grain price movements in thirteenth-century England', *Econ. Hist. Rev.*, 2nd series, 10 (1957–58), pp. 207–20
Fergusson, Sir James, *The Declaration of Arbroath* (Edinburgh, 1970)
Finberg, H. P. R., 'St Patrick at Glastonbury', in Finberg, *West Country Historical Studies* (Newton Abbot, 1969), pp. 70–88
Flanagan, D., 'The names of Downpatrick', *Dinnseanchas*, 4 (1971), pp. 89–112
'Transferred population or sept-names: Ulaid (*a quo* Ulster)', *Bulletin of the Ulster Place Name Society*, series 2, 1 (1978), pp. 40–3
Flanagan, M. T., *Irish Society, Anglo-Norman Settlers, Angevin Kingship. Interactions in Ireland in the Late Twelfth Century* (Oxford, 1989)
'Monastic charters from Irish kings of the twelfth and thirteenth centuries' (MA thesis, NUI Dublin, 1972)
'St Mary's abbey, Louth, and the introduction of the Arrouasian observance into Ireland', *Clogher Record*, 10 (1980), pp. 223–34
'*Historia Gruffud vab Kenan* and the origins of Balrothery, Co. Dublin', *Cambrian Medieval Celtic Studies*, 28 (1994), pp. 71–94
'Henry II, the Council of Cashel and the Irish bishops', *Peritia*, 10 (1996), pp. 184–211
'Irish and Anglo-Norman warfare in twelfth-century Ireland', in *A Military History of Ireland*, ed. T. Bartlett and K. Jeffery (Cambridge, 1996), pp. 52–75
Fleming, D. F., '*Milites* as attestors to charters in England, 1101–1300', *Albion*, 22, 2 (1990), pp. 185–98
Flower, R., 'Manuscripts of Irish interest in the British Museum', *Analecta Hibernica*, 2 (1931), pp. 292–340
Frame, R., *English Lordship in Ireland, 1318–1361* (Oxford, 1982)
The Political Development of the British Isles 1100–1400 (Oxford, 1990)
Ireland and Britain 1170–1450 (London and Rio Grande, 1998)
'Power and society in the lordship of Ireland, 1272–1377', *Past and Present*, 76 (1977), pp. 3–33. (Reprinted in Frame, *Ireland and Britain 1170–1450*, pp. 191–220)
'War and peace in the medieval lordship of Ireland', in *The English in Medieval Ireland*, ed. J. F. Lydon (Dublin, 1984), pp. 118–41. (Reprinted in Frame, *Ireland and Britain 1170–1450*, pp. 221–40.)
'Aristocracies and the political configuration of the British Isles', in *The British Isles, 1100–1500: Comparisons, Contrasts and Connections*, ed. R. R. Davies (Edinburgh, 1988), pp. 141–59. (Reprinted in Frame, *Ireland and Britain 1170–1450*, pp. 151–70)

'England and Ireland, 1171–1399', in *England and her Neighbours 1066–1453*, ed. M. Jones and M. Vale (London, 1989), pp. 139–56. (Reprinted in Frame, *Ireland and Britain 1170–1450*, pp. 15–30)

'"Les Engleys nées en Irlande": the English political identity in medieval Ireland', *T.R.H.S*, 6th series, 3 (1993), pp. 83–103. (Reprinted in Frame, *Ireland and Britain 1170–1450*, pp. 131–50.)

Frank, R., 'Viking atrocity and Skaldic verse: the rite of the blood-eagle', *EHR*, 99 (1984), pp. 332–43

'The blood-eagle again', *Saga-Book*, 22, v (1988)

'Ornithology and interpretation of Skaldic verse', *Saga-Book*, 23, ii (1990), pp. 81–3

Fraser, C. M., *A History of Antony Bek, Bishop of Durham, 1283–1311* (Oxford, 1957)

Freeman, A. M., 'Annals in Cotton MS Titus A. XXV', *Revue Celtique*, 41 (1924), pp. 301–30; 42 (1925), pp. 283–305; 43 (1926), pp. 358–84; 44 (1927), pp. 336–61

Fryde, N., *The Tyranny and Fall of Edward II* (Cambridge, 1979)

Gillingham, J., 'The beginnings of English imperialism', *Journal of Historical Sociology*, 5 (1992), pp. 392–409

'The English invasion of Ireland', in *Representing Ireland: Literature and the Origins of Conflict, 1534–1660*, ed. B. Bradshaw et al. (Cambridge, 1993), pp. 24–42

'Conquering the barbarians: War and chivalry in twelfth-century Britain', *Haskins Society Journal*, 4 (1993), pp. 67–84

'1066 and the introduction of chivalry into England', in *Law and Government in Medieval England and Normandy*, ed. G. Garnett and J. Hudson (Cambridge, 1994), pp. 31–55

'Henry II, Richard I and the Lord Rhys', *Peritia*, 10 (1996), pp. 224–36

Golding, B., *Gilbert of Sempringham and the Gilbertine Order, c. 1130–c.1300* (Oxford, 1995)

Goldstein, R. James, *The Matter of Scotland: Historical Narrative in Medieval Scotland* (Lincoln, NB, 1993)

Graham, R., 'Four alien priories in Monmouthshire', *Journal of the British Archaeological Society*, new series, 35 (1929), pp. 102–21

Gransden, A., *Historical Writing in England c. 550 to c. 1307* (London, 1974)

Grant, A., 'Crown and nobility in late medieval Britain', in *Scotland and England 1286–1815*, ed. R. A. Mason (Edinburgh, 1987), pp. 34–59

'Scotland's "Celtic Fringe" in the late Middle Ages: The Macdonald lords of the Isles and the kingdom of Scotland', in *The British Isles 1100–1500: Comparisons, Contrasts and Connections*, ed. R. R. Davies (Edinburgh, 1988), pp. 118–41

Grant, A., and Stringer, K. J. (eds.), *Uniting the Kingdom? The Making of British History* (London, 1995)

Grant, I. F. and Cheape, H., *Periods in Highland History* (London, 1987)

Green, J. A., *The Government of England under Henry I* (Cambridge, 1986)

Greenwell, W., and Hunter-Blair, C. H., *Catalogue of Seals in the Treasury of the Dean and Chapter of Durham*, 2 vols. (Newcastle upon Tyne, 1911–21)

Gregory, D., *History of the Western Highlands and Islands of Scotland from AD 1493 to AD 1625*, 2nd edn (London and Glasgow, 1881)
Grosjean, P., 'The alleged Irish origin of St Cuthbert', in *The Relics of Saint Cuthbert*, ed. C. F. Battiscombe (Oxford, 1956), pp. 144–54
Gwynn, A., *The Irish Church in the Eleventh and Twelfth Centuries* (Dublin, 1992)
  'The antiphonary of Armagh', *Journal of the Co. Louth Archaeological Society*, 9 (1945), pp. 1–12
  'Armagh and Louth in the 12th and 13th centuries', *Seanchas Ardmhacha*, 1 (1954–5), no. 1 (1954), pp. 1–11; 2 (1955), pp. 17–37
  'Tomaltach Ua Conchobair, coarb of Patrick (1181–1201)', *Seanchas Ardmhacha*, 8 (1975–7), pp. 231–74
  'Brian in Armagh, 1005', *Seanchas Ardmhacha*, 9 (1978–9), pp. 35–50
Gwynn, A. and Hadcock, R. N., *Medieval Religious Houses: Ireland* (London, 1970)
Hamlin, A., 'A recently discovered enclosure at Inch Abbey, Co. Down', *Ulster Journal of Archaeology*, 40 (1977), pp. 85–88
Hand, G. J., *English Law in Ireland, 1290–1324* (Cambridge, 1967)
Hart, C. [R.], *The Danelaw* (London, 1992)
Hartshorne, C. H., *Feudal and Military Antiquities of Northumberland and the Scottish Borders* (London, 1858)
Hayes-McCoy, G. A., *Scots Mercenary Forces in Ireland (1565–1603)* (Dublin and London, 1937)
Hechter, M., *Internal Colonialism: The Celtic Fringe in British National Development 1536–1966* (London, 1975)
Hedley, W. P., *Northumberland Families*, 2 vols. (Newcastle upon Tyne, 1968–70)
Heist, W. W., *Vitae Sanctorum Hiberniae e Codice olim Salmanticensi nunc Bruxellensi*, Subsidia Hagiographica, 25 (Brussels, 1965)
Hennig, J., 'The place of Irish saints in medieval English calendars', *Irish Ecclesiastical Record*, 5th series, 82 (1954), pp. 93–106
Herbert, M., *Iona, Kells and Derry: the History and Hagiography of the Monastic Familia of Columba* (Oxford, 1988, pbk. Dublin, 1996)
  'The preface to *Amra Coluim Cille*', in *Sages, Saints and Storytellers: Celtic Studies in Honour of Professor James Carney*, ed. D. Ó Corráin, L. Breathnach and K. McCone (Maynooth, 1989), pp. 67–75
  '*Fled Dúin na nGéd*: A reappraisal', *Cambridge Medieval Celtic Studies*, 18 (1989), pp. 75–87
  'Charter material from Kells', in *The Book of Kells: Proceedings of a Conference at Trintiy College, Dublin, 6–9 September 1992*, ed. F. O'Mahony (Aldershot, 1994), pp. 60–77
  'The Death of Muirchertach mac Erca: a twelfth-century tale', in *Celts and Vikings: Proceedings of the Fourth Symposium of Societas Celtologica Nordica*, ed. F. Josephson (Göteborg, 1997), pp. 27–39
A History of Northumberland, 15 vols. (Newcastle upon Tyne, 1893–1940)
Hodgson, J. F., 'Eggleston abbey', *Yorkshire Archaeological Journal*, 18 (1905), pp. 161–3
Hollister, C. W., *The Military Organization of Norman Britain* (Oxford, 1965)

Holm, P., 'Between apathy and antipathy: the Vikings in Irish and Scandinavian history', *Peritia*, 8 (1994), pp. 151–68
Holt, J. C., *The Northerners: A Study in the Reign of King John*, new edn (Oxford, 1992)
Colonial England 1066–1215 (London, 1997)
Hoste, A., 'A survey of the unedited work of Laurence of Durham with an edition of his letter to Aelred of Rievaulx', *Sacris Erudiri*, 11 (1960), pp. 249–65
Hudson, B. T., *Kings of Celtic Scotland* (Westport, CT, 1994)
Prophecy of Berchán (Westport, CT, 1996)
'The Family of Harold Godwinsson and the Irish Sea Province', *RSAI Jn.*, 109 (1979), pp. 92–100
'Knútr and Viking Dublin', *Scandinavian Studies*, 66 (1994), pp. 319–35
'William the Conqueror and Ireland', *IHS*, 29 (1994), pp. 145–58
'Economy and trade', in *A New History of the Isle of Man*, ed. S. Duffy, vol iii (forthcoming)
Hughes, K., 'British Museum MS. Cotton Vespasian A. XIV ("*Vitae Sanctorum Wallensium*"): its purpose and provenance', in *Studies in the Early British Church*, ed. N. K. Chadwick *et al.* (Cambridge, 1958), pp. 183–200
Hunter Blair, C. H., 'Baronys [sic] and knights of Northumberland, A.D. 1166–1266', *Archaeologia Aeliana*, 4th series, 30 (1952), pp. 1–56
Jackson, K. H., 'Common Gaelic: The evolution of the Goedelic languages', *Proceedings of the British Academy*, 37 (1951), pp. 71–97
Jaski, B., 'The Vikings and the kingship of Tara', *Peritia*, 9 (1995), pp. 310–53
Jolliffe, J. E. A., *Angevin Kingship*, 2nd edn (London, 1963)
Jones, S. R. H. 'Transaction costs, institutional change, and the emergence of a market economy in later Anglo-Saxon England', *Econ. Hist. Rev.*, 2nd series, 46 (1993), pp. 658–78
Kaeuper, R. W., *War, Justice and Public Order: England and France in the Late Middle Ages* (Oxford, 1988)
Keating, Geoffrey, *The History of Ireland. Foras Feasa ar Éirinn*, ed. D. Comyn and P. S. Dineen, 4 vols., ITS (London, 1902–14)
Keen, M., *Chivalry* (New Haven and London, 1984)
Kelleher, J. V., 'The pre-Norman Irish genealogies', *IHS*, 16 (1968–9), pp. 138–53
Kelly, F., *A Guide to Early Irish Law* (Dublin, 1988)
Kenney, J., *The Sources for the Early History of Ireland: Ecclesiastical*, ed. L. Bieler (Dublin, repr. 1979)
Ker, N. R., *Medieval Libraries of Great Britain*, 2nd edn (London, 1964)
Medieval Manuscripts in British Libraries (Lampeter, Oxford, 1983)
King, D. J. C., *Castellarium Anglicanum: An Index and Bibliography of the Castles in England, Wales and the Islands*, 2 vols. (London, 1983)
Kirby, D. P., *The Earliest English Kings* (London, 1991)
Knowles, C. H. 'The resettlement of England after the Barons' War, 1264–67', *TRHS*, 5th series, 32 (1982), pp. 25–41
Knowles, D. and St Joseph, J. K. S., *Monastic Sites from the Air* (Cambridge, 1952)

Laing, H., *Descriptive Catalogue of Impressions From Ancient Scottish Seals*, 2 vols. (Edinburgh, 1850)
Lancaster, W. T., *The Early History of Ripley and the Ingilby Family* (Leeds, 1918)
Latham, R. E., *Revised Medieval Latin Word-list from British and Irish Sources* (London, 1965)
Legge, D., 'La piere d'Escoce', *SHR*, 38 (1959), pp. 109–13
Lewis, C. P., 'Gruffudd ap Cynan and the Normans', in *Gruffudd ap Cynan. A Collaborative Biography*, ed. K. L. Maund (Woodbridge, 1996), pp. 61–77
Lewis, E. A., 'Industry and commerce in medieval Wales', *TRHS*, new series, 17 (1903), pp. 121–74
Lloyd, J. E., *A History of Wales from Earliest Times to the Edwardian Conquest* (London, 1911, 3rd edn, 1939)
Logan, F. D., *Runaway Religious in Medieval England, c. 1240–1540* (Cambridge, 1996)
Lopez, R. S. and Raymond, I. W., *Medieval Trade in the Mediterranean World* (New York, 1990)
Loyn, H. R., *The Vikings in Wales* (London, 1976)
Lucas, A. T. 'The plundering and burning of churches in Ireland: 7th to 16th century', in *North Munster Studies: Essays in Commemoration of Monsignor Michael Moloney*, ed. E. Rynne (Limerick, 1967), pp. 172–229
Lydon, J. F., 'An Irish army in Scotland, 1296', *The Irish Sword*, 5 (1961–2), pp. 184–90
Lyon, C. S. S., and Stewart, B. H. I. H., 'The Northumbrian Viking coins in the Cuerdale hoard' in *Anglo-Saxon Coins: Studies presented to F.M. Stenton*, ed. R. H. M. Dolley (London, 1961), pp. 96–121
Mac Cana, P., *Celtic Mythology* (London, 1970)
McCormick, F., 'Farming and food in medieval Lecale', in *Down: History and Society*, ed. L. Proudfoot (Dublin, 1997), pp. 33–46
McDonald, R. A., *The Kingdom of the Isles: Scotland's Western Seaboard, c. 1100–c. 1336* (East Linton, 1996)
  'Matrimonial politics and core-periphery interactions in twelfth- and early thirteenth-century Scotland', *Journal of Medieval History*, 21 (1995), pp. 227–47
  'Images of Hebridean lordship in the twelfth and early thirteenth centuries: the seal of Raonall Mac Sorley', *SHR*, 74 (1995), pp. 129–43
Mac Eoin, G. S., 'The date and authorship of Saltair na Rann', *ZCP*, 28 (1960–61), pp. 51–67
Mac Erlean, J., 'Synod of Ráith Bresail: boundaries of the dioceses of Ireland', *Archivium Hibernicum*, 3 (1914), pp. 1–33
McKerral, A., 'West Highland mercenaries in Ireland', *SHR*, 30 (1951), pp. 1–14
MacKinlay, J. M., *Ancient Church Dedications in Scotland*, 2 vols. (Edinburgh, 1910–14)
Mac Niocaill, G., *The Medieval Irish Annals* (Dublin, 1975)
  'Cartae Dunenses XII–XIII Céad', *Seanchas Ardmhacha*, 5 (1969–70), pp. 418–28
Macquarrie, A., '*Vita Sancti Servani*: the Life of St Serf', *Innes Review*, 44 (1993), pp. 122–52

MacQueen, H., 'Scots law under Alexander III', in *Scotland in the Reign of Alexander III, 1249–1286*, ed. N. H. Reid (Edinburgh, 1990), pp. 74–102
Maddicott, J. R., *Simon de Montfort* (Cambridge, 1994)
Mallory, J. P., and T. E. McNeill, *The Archaeology of Ulster from Colonization to Plantation* (1991)
Marshall, J. W. and Walsh, C., 'Illaunloughan: Life and death on a small early monastic site', *Archaeology Ireland*, 8, 4 (1994), pp. 25–8
Mason, J. F. A., 'Roger de Montgomery and his sons (1067–1102)', *TRHS*, 5th series, 13 (1963), pp. 1–28
Masschaele, J., 'Transportation costs in medieval England', *Econ. Hist. Rev.*, 2nd series, 46 (1993), pp. 266–79
Maund, K. L., *Ireland, Wales, and England in the Eleventh Century* (Woodbridge, 1991)
Megaw, B. R. S., 'The ship seals of the kings of Man', *Journal of the Manx Museum*, 6, 76 (1959–60)
Miller, E. and Hatcher, J., *Medieval England: Towns, Commerce and Crafts, 1086–1348* (London, 1995)
Miller, M., 'Matriliny by treaty: the Pictish foundation-legend', in *Ireland in Medieval Europe*, ed. D. Whitelock, R. McKitterick and D. Dumville (Cambridge, 1982), pp. 133–61
Miller, W. I., *Bloodtaking and Peacemaking. Feud, Law and Society in Saga Iceland* (Chicago, 1990)
Moore, D., 'Gruffudd ap Cynan and the medieval Welsh polity', in *Gruffudd ap Cynan. A Collaborative Biography*, ed. K. L. Maund (Woodbridge, 1996), pp. 23–31
Morris, J. E., *The Welsh Wars of Edward I* (Oxford, 1901)
Muhr, K., 'The location of the Ulster cycle: part 1: tóchustal Ulad', in *Ulidia*, ed. J. Mallory and G. Stockman (Belfast, 1994), pp. 149–58
Neilson, G., *Trial by Combat* (Glasgow, 1890)
Nelson, L. H., *The Normans in South Wales 1070–1171* (Austin, 1966)
A New History of Ireland, ix, *Maps, Genealogies, Lists*, ed. T. W. Moody, F. X. Martin, F. J. Byrne (Oxford, 1984)
A New History of Ireland, ii, *Medieval Ireland 1169–1534*, ed. A. Cosgrove (Oxford, 1987)
Nicholson, R., 'A sequel to Edward Bruce's invasion of Ireland', *SHR*, 42 (1963), pp. 30–40
Ó Cathasaigh, T., 'The Déisi and Dyfed', *Éigse*, 20 (1984), pp. 1–33
Ó Corráin, D., *Ireland before the Normans* (Dublin, 1972)
  'Prehistoric and early Christian Ireland', in *The Oxford Illustrated History of Ireland*, ed. R. F. Foster (Oxford, 1989), pp. 1–52
Ó Cróinín, D., *Early Medieval Ireland 400–1200* (London, 1995)
Ó Cuív, B., 'A poem composed for Cathal Croibhdhearg Ó Conchobhair', *Ériu*, 34 (1983), pp. 157–74
  'The Irish marginalia in *Codex Palatino-Vaticanus* no. 830', *Éigse*, 24 (1990), pp. 45–67
O'Keefe, T., 'Omey and the sands of time', *Archaeology Ireland*, 8, 2 (1994), pp. 14–17
O'Neill, T., *Merchants and Mariners in Medieval Ireland* (Dublin, 1987)

O'Rahilly, C., *Ireland and Wales. Their Historical and Literary Relations* (London, 1924)
O'Rahilly, T. F., *Early Irish History and Mythology* (Dublin, 1946)
Oram, R., 'A family business? Colonisation and settlement in twelfth- and thirteenth-century Galloway', *SHR*, 72 (1993), pp. 111–45
Ó Riain, P., 'St Abbán: The genesis of an Irish saint's Life', in *Proceedings of the Seventh International Congress of Celtic Studies*, ed. D. Ellis Evans et al. (Oxford, 1986), pp. 159–70
Ormont, H., 'Satire de Garnier de Rouen contre le poète Moriuht', *Annuaire bulletin de la Soc. de l'hist. de France*, 31 (1894), pp. 193–210
Orpen, G. H., *Ireland under the Normans 1169–1333*, 4 vols. (Oxford, 1911–20, repr. 1968)
Otway-Ruthven, A. J., *A History of Medieval Ireland* (London, 1968)
  'Anglo-Irish shire government in the thirteenth century', *IHS*, 5 (1946), pp. 1–28
  'Dower charter of John de Courcy's wife', *Ulster Journal of Archaeology*, 3rd series, 12 (1949), pp. 77–81
  'The medieval county of Kildare', *IHS*, 11 (1958–9), pp. 181–99
Page, R. I., *Chronicles of the Vikings: Records, Memorials and Myths* (London, 1995)
Painter, S., *Studies in the History of the English Feudal Barony* (Baltimore, 1943)
Parsons, J. C., *Eleanor of Castile: Queen and Society in Thirteenth-Century England* (London, 1995)
Paul, Sir James Balfour (ed.), *The Scots Peerage*, 9 vols. (Edinburgh, 1904–14)
Pinkerton, J. *Pinkerton's Lives of the Scottish Saints*, ed. Rev. W. M. Metcalfe, 2 vols. (Paisley, 1889)
Piper, A. J., 'The first generations of Durham monks and the cult of St Cuthbert', in *St Cuthbert, his Cult and Community to A.D. 1200*, ed. G. Bonner, D. Rollason and C. Stancliffe (Woodbridge, 1989), pp. 437–46
Plummer, C. and Earle, J., *Two of the Saxon Chronicles Parallel* (Oxford, 1892–96)
Pollock, F. and Maitland, F. W., *The History of English Law before the Time of Edward I*, 2 vols. (Cambridge, 1898)
Poole, A. L., *Domesday Book to Magna Carta 1087–1216*, 2nd edn (Oxford, 1955)
  'Live-stock prices in the twelfth century', *EHR*, 55 (1940), pp. 284–95
Powicke, M., *The Thirteenth Century 1216–1307* (Oxford, 1953, 2nd edn, 1962)
Prestwich, M., *War, Politics and Finance under Edward I* (London, 1972)
  Edward I (London, 1988)
  'Isabella de Vescy and the custody of Bamburgh castle', *Bulletin of the Institute of Historical Research*, 44 (1971), pp. 148–52
  'Edward I and the Maid of Norway', *SHR*, 69 (1990), pp. 157–74
Raine, J., *The History and Antiquities of North Durham* (London, 1852)
Reid, R. C., 'The Scottish Avenels', *Transactions of the Dumfriesshire and Galloway Natural History and Antiquarian Society*, 3rd series, 37 (1960), pp. 70–8
Reynolds, S., *Fiefs and Vassals: The Medieval Evidence Reinterpreted* (Oxford, 1994)

'Medieval *origines gentium* and the community of the realm', *History*, 68 (1983), pp. 375–90
Richards, M., 'Irish settlements in south-west Wales: a topographical approach', *RSAI Jn.*, 90 (1960), pp. 133–62
Richardson, H. G., 'Some Norman monastic foundations in Ireland', in *Medieval Studies presented to Aubrey Gwynn, S.J.*, ed. J. A. Watt, J. B. Morrall and F. X. Martin (Dublin, 1961), pp. 29–43
Ridyard, S. J., *The Royal Saints of Anglo-Saxon England: A Study of the West Saxon and East Anglian Cults* (Cambridge, 1988)
Rigg, A. G., *A History of Anglo-Latin Literature 1066–1422* (Cambridge, 1992)
Ritchie, R. L. G., *The Normans in Scotland* (Edinburgh, 1954)
Robertson, A. J., *Laws of the Kings of England from Edmund to Henry I* (Cambridge, 1925)
Robinson, J. A., 'St Brigid and Glastonbury', *RSAI Jn.*, 83 (1953), pp. 97–9
Rollason, D., 'Lists of saints' resting-places in Anglo-Saxon England', *Anglo-Saxon England*, 7 (1978), pp. 61–93
Round, J. H., *Feudal England* (London, 1895)
  'The conquest of Ireland' in Round, *The Commune of London and other Studies* (London, 1899), pp. 137–70
Rowlands, I. W., 'The making of the March: aspects of the Norman settlement of Dyfed', in *Proceedings of the Battle Conference* III, ed. R. A. Brown (Woodbridge, 1981)
Sawyer, P. H., *The Age of the Vikings*, 2nd edn (London, 1971)
  Kings and Vikings: Scandinavia and Europe AD 700–1100 (London and New York, 1982)
  'The wealth of England in the eleventh century', *TRHS*, 5th series, 15 (1965), pp. 145–64
Seaby, W. A., 'A St Patrick halfpenny of John de Courci', *British Numismatic Journal*, 29 (1958–59), pp. 87–90
Sellar, W. D. H. (ed.), *Moray: Province and People* (Edinburgh, 1993)
  'Celtic law and Scots law: survival and integration', *Scottish Studies*, 29 (1989), pp. 1–27
Sharpe, R., *Medieval Irish Saints' Lives* (Oxford, 1991)
  'Were the Irish annals known to a twelfth-century Northumbrian writer?', *Peritia*, 2 (1983), pp. 137–9
Sheehy, M. P., *When the Normans Came to Ireland* (Cork, 1975)
Simms, K., *From Kings to Warlords. The Changing Political Structure of Gaelic Ireland in the Later Middle Ages* (Woodbridge, 1987)
  'The O Hanlons, O Neills and Anglo-Normans in 13th Century Armagh', *Seanchas Ardmhacha*, 9 (1978), pp. 70–94
  'Gaelic warfare in the Middle Ages', in *A Military History of Ireland*, ed. T. Bartlett and K. Jeffery (Cambridge, 1996), pp. 99–116
Simpson, G. G., 'Why was John Balliol called "Toom Tabard"?', *SHR*, 47 (1968), pp. 196–9
Slover, C. H., 'William of Malmesbury's *Life of St Patrick*', *Modern Philology*, 24 (1926), pp. 5–20
Smith, I. M., 'Sprouston, Roxburghshire: an early Anglian centre of the eastern

Tweed basin', *Proceedings of the Society of Antiquaries of Scotland*, 121 (1991), pp. 261–94
Smyth, A. P., *Scandinavian Kings in the British Isles 850–880* (Oxford, 1977)
  Celtic Leinster: Towards an Historical Geography of Early Irish Civilisation (Dublin, 1982)
  Scandinavian York and Dublin: the History and Archaeology of Two Related Viking Kingdoms, 2 vols. (Dublin, repr. 1987)
  Warlords and Holy Men: Scotland A.D. 80–1000 (London, 1984)
  King Alfred the Great (Oxford, 1995)
Stefánsson, J., 'The Vikings in Spain from Arabic (Moorish) and Spanish sources', *Saga-Book of the Viking Club: Society for Northern Research*, 6 (1909), pp. 31–46
Stenton, D. M. (ed.), *Preparatory to Anglo-Saxon England* (Oxford, 1970)
Stenton, F. M., *Anglo-Saxon England* (Oxford, 2nd edn, repr. 1967)
Stevenson, J. M., and Wood, M., *Scottish Heraldic Seals*, 2 vols. (Glasgow, 1910)
Stokes, W., 'The Bodleian Amra Choluimb Chille', *Revue Celtique*, 20 (1899), pp. 30–55, 132–83, 248–87, 400–37
Strickland, M., *War and Chivalry: The Conduct and Perception of War in England and Normandy, 1066–1217* (Cambridge, 1996)
Stringer, K. J., *Earl David of Huntingdon, 1152–1219: A Study in Anglo-Scottish History* (Edinburgh, 1985)
  'Periphery and core in thirteenth-century Scotland: Alan son of Roland, lord of Galloway and constable of Scotland', in *Medieval Scotland: Crown, Lordship and Community*, ed. A. Grant and K. Stringer (Edinburgh, 1993), pp. 82–113
  'Identities in thirteenth-century England: frontier society in the far North', in *Social and Political Identities in Western History*, ed. C. Bjørn, A. Grant and K. J. Stringer (Copenhagen, 1994), pp. 28–66
  'State-building in twelfth-century Britain: David I, king of Scots, and northern England', in *Government, Religion and Society in Northern England, 1000–1700*, ed. J. C. Appleby and P. Dalton (Stroud, 1997), pp. 40–62
Suppe, F., 'The cultural significance of decapitation in high medieval Wales and the Marches', *BBCS*, 36 (1989), pp. 147–60
Szoverffy, J., 'The Anglo-Norman conquest of Ireland and Saint Patrick', *Reportorium Novum*, 2 (1958), pp. 6–16
Tate, G., *History of the Borough, Castle, and Barony of Alnwick*, 2 vols. (Alnwick, 1866–9)
Thomas, C., 'Irish settlements in post-Roman western Britain', *Journal of the Royal Institution of Cornwall*, 6 (1972), pp. 251–74
Thomas, I. G., 'The cult of saints' relics in medieval England' (Ph.D. thesis, University of London, 1975)
Thurneysen, R., 'Synchronismen der irischen Könige', *ZCP*, 19 (1931), pp. 81–99
Todd, J. M., 'St Bega: cult, fact and legend', *Transactions of the Cumberland and Westmorland Antiquarian and Archaeological Society*, 80 (1980), pp. 23–35
Tupling, G. H., 'The origins of markets and fairs in medieval Lancashire', *Transactions of the Lancashire and Cheshire Antiquarian Society*, 49 (1933), pp. 75–94

Tyson, D. B., 'Les manuscrits du Brut en prose française', in *Les Manuscrits Français de la bibliothèque Parker, Actes du Colloque 24–27 mars 1993*, ed. N. Wilkins (Cambridge, 1993), pp. 101–20

Ussher, James, *The Whole Works of the Most Reverend James Ussher, D.D.*, ed. C. R. Elrington and J. H. Todd, 17 vols. (Dublin 1847–64)

Valente, C., 'Simon de Montfort, earl of Leicester, and the utility of sanctity in thirteenth-century England', *Journal of Medieval History*, 21 (1995), pp. 27–49

Veitch, K., 'The Scottish material in *De domibus religiosis*: date and provenance', *Innes Review*, 47 (1996), pp. 14–23

Wallace, P. F., 'The economy and commerce of Viking age Dublin', in K. Düwel et al., *Untersuchungen zu Handel und Verkehr der vor- und frühgeschichtlichen Zeit in Mittel- und Nordeuropa IV* (Göttingen, 1987), pp. 200–45

Wallace-Hadrill, J. M., *Early Germanic Kingship in England and on the Continent* (Oxford, 1971)

The Vikings in Francia, Stenton Lecture (Reading, 1975)

Warren, W. L., 'The interpretation of twelfth-century Irish history', in *Historical Studies*, 7, ed. J. C. Beckett (New York, 1969), pp. 1–19

Watson, F., 'The enigmatic lion: Scotland, kingship, and national identity in the wars of independence', in *Image and Identity: the Making and Remaking of Scotland through the Ages*, ed. D. Broun, R. Finlay and M. Lynch (Edinburgh, 1998), pp. 18–37

Watt, D. E. R., *A Biographical Dictionary of Scottish Graduates to A.D. 1410* (Oxford, 1977)

Watt, J. A., *The Church and the Two Nations in Medieval Ireland* (Cambridge, 1970)

Webster, G., et al., 'A Saxon treasure hoard found at Chester', *Antiquities Journal*, 33 (1953), pp. 26–9

Wightman, W. E., *The Lacy Family in England and Normandy* (Oxford, 1966)

Index

Abbo of Fleury, 17, 29
Aberdeen, 65
Abergavenny, 120
Abernethy, 139 nn. 22, 23, 140 n. 24
Abernethy, Hugh, 124 and n. 54
Abingdon, 74 n. 25, 77
Abram of Cardigan, 56
Acallam na Senórach, 96
Adam, bishop of Caithness (d. 1222), 121
Adam, *judex* in Angus, 140 n. 24
Adam of Bremen, 19, 38
Adam of Carlisle, lord of Kinmount, 224
Adam of Drybugh, 81
Adam le Savonier, 106
Adam son of Ailsi, 70 n. 12
Adhemar of Chabannes, 11
Adomnán, abbot of Iona (d. 704), 16, 26, 36, 41, 68, 69, 83 and n. 49
Adrian IV, pope (d. 1159), 174
Áedán mac Gabráin, king of Dál Riata (d. 608), 89, 93
Aedh (Heth) son of Donald son of Malcolm mac Heth, 117
Ælfheah, archbishop of Canterbury (d. 1012), 19, 22, 23, 24 and n. 102
Ælla, king of Northumbria (d. 867), 18, 19
Aelred, abbot of Rivaulx, 54, 74, 208
  author of Life of St Ninian, 81 and n. 46, 82, 83, 84, 85
Æthelbald, king of Mercia (d. 755), 5, 26
Æthelflaed of Mercia, 45
Æthelraed, king of Wessex (d. 871), 9
Æthelraed the Unready, king of England (d. 1016), 4, 47, 50
Æthelstan, 46
Æthelswith, 6
Æthelwulf, king of Wessex (d. 858), 6, 7, 9
Affrica, daughter of Godred II, king of Man, wife of John de Courcy 154, 155, 171
Agnes, daughter of William de Ferrers, earl of Derby and Sybil Marshal, wife of William II de Vescy, *see* de Vescy, Agnes
Agnes, wife of Eustace de Vescy, 217
Agnes of Saluzzo, wife of John de Vescy, 212, 214 n. 60
Airgialla, 154 n. 2, 168, 170
Alan, abbot of Alnwick, 219
Alan, lord of Galloway, constable of Scotland, 179, 225
Alan of Garmoran, *see* Mac Ruairi, Alan
Alan son of Thomas of Galloway, 183
Alba, 89, 90 and n. 13, 91, 92, 93, 94, 95, 96, *see also* Scotland
Alba/Scotia, 95
Alcuin, 9 and n. 29 10, 28, 38
Alexander II, king of Scotland (d. 1249), 140, 142 n. 32, 147, 186, 189, 191
  connections with de Vescy family, 202, 203, 222, 228, 229 and n. 123
  treatment of political opponents, 121, 123, 124, 141, 192, 196
Alexander III, king of Scotland (d. 1286), 124, 129, 182, 191, 215, 232, 233, 238
  connections with de Vescy family, 203, 205, 225, 229
  dealings with western chieftains, 186, 190, 230
Alexander III, pope (d. 1181), 178
Alexander, son of Alexander III, king of Scotland, 184
Alexander Óg son of Angus Mór of Islay, 181, 196
Alexander son of Donald son of Ranald son of Somerled, 186
Alexander son of Ewen of Argyll, sheriff of Lorn ('Alexander Fitz John', 'Alex de Ergadia') 180, 181, 182, 183, 184, 187, 193, 194
Alfred, ealdoman, 16
Alfred, king of Wessex (d. 899), 4 n. 7, 6, 7, 16, 39

Index

dealings with Vikings, 9, 40, 72
Alfred, son of the king of the Mercians and West Saxons, 70
Alnham, 218
Alnmouth, 218, 226
Alnwick, 200, 204, 206 and n. 24, 209, 212, 213, 215–24, 227, 237
Alnwick, Premonstratensian abbey at, 206
Alnwick, Alan, abbot of, 224 n. 106
Alphonso of Aragon, 208
Alphonso, son of Eleanor of Castile, 208
Alphonso IX, king of Leon (d. 1230), 204
de Alwenton, William, 222 n. 95
Amble Bay, 217
America, 42, 55
Amlaím, abbot of Saul, 'bishop of Ulaid', 161, 162 and n. 34, 163
Amra Coluim Cille, 91
Anagassan (Co. Louth), 22, 27
Anarawd ap Einion ap Anarawd, 117 and n. 18
Andresey, 70
Anglesey, 43, 105, 106, 107, 210
   activities of Gruffudd ap Cynan on, 102, 104
   Roman garrison, 41, 62
Anglo-Normans, *see* English
Anglo-Saxon Chronicle, 4, 7, 8, 24, 27, 43, 45, 72
Anglo-Saxons, 7, 67, 68
Angus (Scotland), 221, 222, 224
Angus Mór son of Donald of Islay (Anegus filius Douenaldi), 181, 184, 186, 188, 193, 196
Angus Óg son of Angus Mór of Islay, 181, 186
Angus son of Somerled, 186
Annals of Connacht, 120, 121, 126
Annals of the Four Masters, 103, 107
Annals of Inisfallen, 56, 100, 101, 126, 127
Annals of Loch Cé, 118, 121, 127
Annals of St-Bertin, 7, 14, 30
Annals of St Vaast, 29
Annals of Tigernach, 43
Annals of Ulster, 8, 20, 21, 27, 30, 36, 69, 89, 93, 97, 101, 127, 161, 162, 178
Annandale, 225
Anselm, archbishop of Canterbury (d. 1109), 52, 101
Aosta, viscount of, 212
Appletreehall, 221 n. 90, 225 n. 112
Aquitaine, 40
Aragon, 208
Aran, 32
Arbroath Abbey, 142 n. 32
Arctic Circle, 39, 40

Ardbrackan, 34
Ardee, 120 n. 33
Ardfert, 32
Ardskeodnish, 190
Argyll, 152 n. 66 179, 180, 183, 184, 189
   bishopric of, 194
Arisaig, 181
Arklow, 61
Armagh, 36, 50, 83, 89 nn. 8 and 9, 130, 173, 176
   abbot of, 89
   primacy of within Irish church, 90, 91, 171, 172
   Viking attacks on, 21, 30, 33
Armes Prydein, 46
Arrouaisian observance (Augustinian), 170
Arthington, Cluniac nunnery at, 219
Arthur, 84
Arthur, son of Geoffrey of Brittany, 119
de Arturret, Robert, 222 n. 96
Askulv, king of Dublin (d. 1170), 120
Atlantic, 40, 42, 48, 64
Augustinian order, 165, 166, 170
d'Avaugour, Clemence, 233
Avenal family, 221
Avon, 62
Avranches, 35
Ayr, 58, 61, 223

Baginbun, 120 and n. 30
Balliol, John, *see* John, king of Scotland
Balmerino, 141 n. 30
Balrothery West (Co. Dublin), 105, 107
Baltic, 40, 65
Bamburgh, 68, 223
Banffshire, 225 n. 112
Bangor (Co. Down, Ireland), 16, 32, 36, 161, 164, 166, 168 n. 61, 170
   connections with St Malachy, 158, 159, 163, 165
Bangor (Wales), 79, 80, 122
Bannockburn, 181, 201, 202
Barcelona, 208
Barnard Castle, 202, 203
Barra, 181
Barrow, 40
Basingwerk, 54, 77
Bath, 68
Bayeux, 35
Bay of Biscay, 40, 53, 59
Bayonne, 64
de Beaumont, Isabella, wife of John de Vescy, 204, 212, 213, 222, 226, 229
de Beaumont, Richard, 222, 229
Beaumont-sur-Sarthe, Ralph, *vicomte* of, 229

Becket, Thomas, archbishop of Canterbury (d. 1170), 227
Beddington, Surrey, 13
Bede (d. 735), 26, 68, 69, 71, 72, 136 n. 7
Begerin, 32
Begu, 71, *see* St Bega
Bek, Anthony, bishop of Durham (d. 1311), 208, 215, 220, 233 n. 133, 237, 238
Belfast Lough, 63
Benderloch, 181
Benedictine order, 164, 166, 168, 175
Benvie, 224
Beorhtric, 5
Bergen, 64, 65, 195
Berkshire, 6
Bernard, bishop of St Davids (d. 1148), 78
Bernard of Clairvaux (d. 1153), 158, 159, 166
Bernard of Ripley, 222
Bertram family, 214
Berwickshire, 222, 223
Berwick upon Tweed, 223, 225 n. 111, 229
Beverley, 206
Birgham, 233
Bishop's Island, 32
Bisset, John, 123
Bisset, Walter, 123
Blackfriars, London, 208, 219
Black Parliament, 132
'Blood-eagling', 17, 18, 19
Bolbec family, 214
Bolbec, Hugh de, of Styford, 218
de Bolhope, 226 n. 115
Bonn, 11
Bonnegard, 204
Book of Armagh, 90
Book of Kells, 26
Book of Leinster, 168
Book of Llandaff, 78
Book of Rights, 50
Bordeaux, 34, 37 n. 145, 53
de Boredham, Walter, 222 n. 97
Boroughbridge, 130, 133 n. 93
Botí, 167
Bourges, 34
Bourgneuf Bay, 53
Bower, Walter, 136
Boyne, 8, 30, 32, 40
Brandub mac Echach, 93
de Braose, William, 120, 122
Brechin, 139 nn. 22, 23, 140 n. 24
Brechin, David, 133 n. 93
Brega (Meath), 21
Bretwalda, 5

Brian Bóruma, high-king of Ireland (d. 1014), 45, 46, 51, 90, 91, 92, 135
de Brienne, John, king of Jerusalem, emperor of Constantinople, 204
de Brienne, Louis, 229
Brihtwulf, king of Mercia (d. 852), 6
Brind, 216
Brinkburn, priory of, 220 n. 84
Bristol, 53, 57, 59, 60, 62, 63, 64
  connections with Ireland, 40, 45, 50, 51, 58, 61
  policies of King John and King Edward towards, 47–8, 60
Bristol Channel, 41, 100
Britain, British, 68, 87, 112, 129, 136, 150, 153, 179, 180, 192
  activities of Vikings in, 6, 7, 9
  Irish settlements in, 97, 98, 99
  Welsh perceptions of, 103, 108, 109, 147
Brithem, 139
British Isles, 35, 67, 114, 115, 133, 140
  activities of de Vescy family in, 199, 200, 206, 211, 213, 226, 230 239
  hagiography within, 79, 84, 86
  trade within, 40, 41, 46, 56, 57, 58, 65
Brittany, 22, 200
Brompton, 216, 217, 220, 238 n. 151
Bruce, Robert, *see* Robert I, king of Scotland
Bruce, Robert, earl of Carrick (d. 1304), 184, 197
Bruce, Robert, lord of Annandale (d. 1295), 197
Bruges, 55
Brut (English), 130, 131
Brut (Welsh), 100, 102, 117, 122. 129
Bruton, Robert, 155
Brytenwealda, 5
Buckinghamshire, 57
Budle, Northumberland, 222 n. 97
Budle Bay, 217
Builth, 48, 60, 210
de Burgh, Richard, earl of Ulster (d. 1326), 235, 236 n. 144, 239
Burgred, 6
Burton-on-Trent, 69, 74
Bywell, 218

Cadwallon ap Caradog, 117
Cadwallon ap Madog of Maelienydd (d. 1178), 120
Cadwallon son of Owain Cyfeiliog, 117
Cadwgan ap Bleddyn, 102
Caerleon, 111, 112, 206, 210, 213
Caher, 32
Cáin Adomnáin, 15, 29

Index

Cairbre, 107
Cairell, *judex* in Angus, 140 n. 24
Cairell, king of Ulaid, 160
Caithness, 121, 123, 124
Callann, 120 n. 33
Cambridge, 49
Cambuskenneth Abbey, 58
Campbell, Colin son of Neil, 188, 190
de Camville, Gerard, 119
Canons Ashby, Augustinian house of, 155
Canterbury, 14, 16, 70 n. 12, 78
Cardiff, 64
Cardigan, 48, 60, 129
Cardigan Castle, 107
Carhampton, 7 and n. 17, 9
Carlingford Lough, 54
Carlisle, 41, 54, 55, 58, 61, 83 n. 50, 142 n. 32
Carlyle family, 225
Carmarthen, 48, 60, 64
Carmelite order, 206, 207, 212
Carmen, 44
Carrickfergus, 170
Carrigogunnel (Co. Limerick), 127 n. 67
Cashel, 178
Castledermot, 211
Cathasach son of Fergusán, 160
Cawledge Park, 218
Caythorpe, 200 n. 6, 206, 215 and n. 65
Cedifor ap Griffi, 122
Célí Dé, 3, 30, 32, 139 nn. 21, 22, 140 n. 24
Cellach, superior of Iona and Kells 12
Cellach, archbishop of Armagh, 159
Cellachán, king of Munster, 23
Cenél Conaill, 168
Cenél nEógain, 49, 92, 93, 168, 178
Ceredigion, 48, 60
Charlemagne, 10, 22
Charles the Bald, emperor (d. 877) 14, 29, 34
Charteris family, 225
Charteris, Henry, 225 n. 112
Charteris, Master Thomas, chancellor of Scotland, 225
Charteris, William, 225 n. 112
Chartres, 37 n. 145
Chatton, 219
Chepstow, 78, 111
Cheshire, 45
Chester, 79, 80, 165, 175, 205
 decline of, 63
 role in Irish Sea trade, 39, 40, 41, 44, 45, 47, 48, 53, 58, 60, 64
 Roman garrison at, 43, 62
Chester (Lichfield), diocese of, 73

Chester and Huntingdon, earl of (John the Scot), 203
Chester-le-street (Lindisfarne), 2, 11
Cheviots, 217
Christian, bishop of Whithorn (d. 1186), 81 n. 46, 83 and n. 50
Christiana, daughter of Alan Mac Ruairi of Garmoran, 181, 188
Chronica Gentis Scottorum, 143, 144, 145, 146, 147
Chronicle of Melrose, *see Melrose Chronicle*
Cináed mac Ailpín, king of Alba (d. 858) 89–90
Cistercian order, 53, 54, 77, 82, 165, 168, 170
Citeaux, 53
de Clare, Gilbert, earl of Gloucester and Hereford (d. 1295), 131, 213
de Clare, Thomas, of Thomond, 236 n. 144
Cleggan, 32
Clogher, 22, 171
Cloghran, 105
Clonard, 211
Clondalkin, 32
Clonfert, 33
Clonmacnoise, 33, 36
Clonmore (Co. Carlow), 21
Clontarf, 51, 65, 91, 135
Cloyne, 32
Clyde, 83
Cnut the Great, king of Denmark and England (d. 1035), 42, 47, 48, 50
Codex de Hibernia, 74
Coibdenach, abbot of Killeigh, 23
Colbán, earl of Fife (d. 1270), 138
Coldstream, 222
Coll, 181
Cologne, 11
Colonsay, 181
Comgall, 16
Comyn, Alexander, earl of Buchan (d. 1290), 184
Comyn, Edmund, 222
Comyn, John (the Red) lord of Badenoch (d. 1303), 183, 184, 187
Comyn, John, (the Red) lord of Badenoch (d. 1306), 125, 132
Comyn, Robert, 125
Comyn, William, earl of Buchan (d. 1233), 137 n. 12
Congalach son of Echaid, 20, 22
Connacht, 30, 112, 125, 126, 127, 154 n. 2, 207, 235
Connor, 157 and n. 16, 158, 159
Conrad II, emperor (d. 1039), 42

Convention of Druim Cet, 91
Conway, 202
Copeland, 71
Copeland Island, 63
Coquetdale (Upper), 217, 222 n. 95
Cordoba, 8
Cork, 64, 130
Corkeran, 61
Cormac mac Airt, 42
Cormeilles, 78
Cormery, 16
Cornwall, Cornish,Cornishmen, 6, 8, 205
Cottingham, Yorkshire, 225 n. 109
de Coucy, Marie, queen of Scotland, wife of Alexander II, 229, 230 n. 126
Coupar Angus, 117, 141 n. 30
de Courcy, John (d. c. 1219), 76, 83, 187, 190
   dealings with church in Ulster, 154–79
Coutances, 35
Coventry, 165
Cowal, 189 n. 36
Craigloun, 223
Crail, 221, 222, 229
Crieff, 187 n. 25
Culross, 138 n. 17, 139 n. 21, 141 n. 30
Cumberland, Cumbria, 55, 71, 154, 155, 214, 228
Cumin, John, archbishop of Dublin (d. 1212), 166, 172 and n. 80
Cumin, William, 215
Cumméne Ailbe, abbot of Iona, 83 and n. 49
Cuscraid Mend Macha, son of Conchobar, king of Ulster, 168
Cyfeiliog, bishop of Archenfield, 22, 23
Cynan ap Iago, 104
Cynan ap Maredudd, 132

Dafydd ap Gruffudd (d. 1283), 122, 132
Dafydd ap Llywelyn (d. 1246), 122 and n. 42
Dafydd ab Owain, 106, 122, 129
Dál nAraide, 157
Dál Cais, 46
Dál Fiatach, 154, 157 and n. 12, 170
Dál Riata, 88, 89, 91 n. 21, 92, 95
Dalkey, 23, 54, 61
Dallas, 222 n. 96
Dalmilling, 223 n. 103
Danegeld, 3, 4 n. 7, 24
Danelaw, 3, 35
Danes, Danish, 42, 49
   impact of attacks by on church, 2–39
David I, king of Scotland (d. 1153), 61, 82, 143 n. 36, 147 n. 49, 215, 227

   importation of new customs by to Scotland, 54, 55, 191, 223
David, earl of Huntingdon (d. 1219), 139 n. 18
Declaration of Arbroath, 136, 151 n. 62
Dee, 40, 41, 44, 54, 61, 63, 135
Deer, 139 n. 21, 141 n. 30
Deheubarth, 98, 100, 103, 107, 122, 123
Denbighshire, 79
Denewulf, bishop of Winchester (d. 909), 13
De Ortu Sancti Cuthberti, 73, 75, 81
Derbforgaill daughter of Domnall Ruad Mac Carthaig, 211 and n. 49, 230, 237
Derbforgaill, wife of Nicholas de Stutueville, 225 n. 111
Derby, earls of (de Ferrers), 203
Derry, 32, 159
Desmond, 126, 127, 154 n. 2, 211
Devon, 4, 8
Diarmait, superior of Kells, 12, 17
Diarmait mac Máel na mBó, king of Leinster (d. 1072), 47, 51, 93
Dictum of Kenilworth, 206
Dicuil, 36
Dinefwr, 129
Ditchburn, Roger son of Ralph of, 218 n. 77
Dobí, 167
Domesday Book, 44, 47
Don, 135
Donaghmoyne (Co. Monaghan), 16
Donaghpatrick, 34, 160 n. 26
Donald mac William, 123
Donald son of Ranald son of Somerled, 181, 186, 188, 196
Doncaster, 233 n. 133
Donnchad ua Maíle Choluim, *see* Duncan I, king of Scotland
Donnchad, earl of Fife, *see* Duncan
Donnchad, son of Brian Bóruma, 46 and n. 32
Donnybrook, 60
Dorset, 214
Douglas, William, 222
Dover, 142 n. 32
Down, Downpatrick, 54, 76, 83,
   activities of John de Courcy in ecclesiastical politics of, 154–78
Drogheda, 40, 54, 60, 61, 62, 64
Dromore, 160
Dryburgh, 81, 224
Duan Albanach, 97 n. 47
Dublin, 39, 54, 99, 100, 105, 130, 171, 172 and n. 79, 178, 236

Index

interest of Irish kings in, 48, 49, 51, 93
policies towards of King John, 60, 61, 62
role in Irish Sea trade, 40, 41, 45, 53, 55, 56, 58, 59, 64
synod of (1186), 166
Viking connections with, 8, 14, 26, 31, 32, 42, 43, 44, 104, 106
Dublin Guild Merchant Roll, 105
Dugald, son of Somerled, of Argyll, 180, 182, 186
Dulane, 160 n. 26
Dumbarton, 8
Dún dá Lethglas, *see* Down
Dunbar, earls of, 222
Dunblane, 139 n. 23, 140 n. 24
Duncan I (Donnchad ua Maíle Choluim), king of Scotland (d. 1040), 138 n. 18, 185
Duncan II, king of Scotland (d. 1094), 56, 185
Duncan (Donnchad) I, earl of Fife (d. 1154), 137, 138
Duncan (Donnchad) II, earl of Fife (d. 1204), 138, 223
Duncan (Donnchad) III, earl of Fife (d. 1288), 124 and n. 54, 138
Duncan (Donnchad) IV, earl of Fife (d. 1353), 138
Duncan son of Donald earl of Mar, 188
Duncan son of Dugald of Argyll, 180, 182, 186
Duncan son of Ewen of Argyll, 186
Dundalk, 98
Dundee, 65
Dundrennan, 54, 82
Dundrum, 170
Dunkeld, 139 n. 23
Dunster, 214
Dunwich, 35
Durham, 182, 217, 220 n. 84, 222 n. 97
hagiographical tradition at, 68, 69, 73, 74 and n. 25, 82
Dyfed, 100
Dyle, 29

Eadmar, 85
Eadred, king of Wessex (d. 955), 14
Ealhburg, 14
East Anglia, 5
Éber, 145, 146 and n. 43, 147, 148, 149
Ecclesiastical History, 68, 71, 72
Ecgberht, king of Wessex (d. 839), 6
Echmilid (Malachy III), bishop of Down (d. 1204), 76,
connections with John de Courcy, 156, 162–72

Edgar, king of England (d. 975), 44, 46, 49
Edinburgh Castle, 143 n. 36, 229 n. 123
Edmund, king of East Anglia (d. 870), 17
Edward I, king of England (d. 1307), 113, 132, 133, 194
dealings with de Vescy family, 202, 204, 207–15, 226 n. 115, 230 and n. 126
dealings with William III de Vescy, justiciar of Ireland, 232–9
policies towards Irish Sea commerce, 48, 59, 60
wars of in Scotland and Wales, 116, 125, 132 n. 92, 144 n. 38, 153
Edward II (of Caernarfon), king of England (d. 1327), 116, 130. 131, 133 n. 93, 204, 233
Edward the Elder, king of Wessex (d. 924), 13, 22, 45, 46
Egypt, 145
Eigg, 181
Eilaf, 74
Einar, 18
Einion of Porth, 117
Eirik the Red, 42
Eleanor, daughter of Edward I, wife of Alphonso of Aragon, 208
Eleanor of Aquitaine, 59
Eleanor of Castile, queen of England, wife of Edward I, 204, 208, 229, 233
Eleutherius, 15
Elfael, 117
Elham, 35
Ella, countess of Salisbury, 203 n. 14
Ellington, 219
Elphin, 171
Eltham, 206, 213, 238 n. 151
Ely, 35
Emain Macha, 168
Embleton, 218, 227 n. 118
England, English, Anglo-Normans, 98, 99, 135 n. 3, 150, 155, 178 180, 182, 207, 208, 223, 226
chivalric conventions in, 114, 119
estates in of the de Vescy family, 205, 214, 215
impact of Viking attacks on, 2, 4, 8, 9, 10, 20, 21, 26, 27, 31, 33, 35, 36
involvement with Irish Sea trade, 39, 41, 43, 47, 48, 52, 54, 55, 58, 59, 65
intervention in Ireland and Wales, 103, 104, 106 109, 111, 112, 178, 213
relations with Scotland, 136, 153, 199, 236
saints' cults in, 67, 68, 70, 71, 72, 74, 76, 77, 78, 79, 81, 83, 86
English Channel, 39

Erc, 92
Érémon son of Míl Espáina, 146 n. 43
Ériu ard, inis na ríg, 94
Eriugena, 36
Ermengarde, queen of Scotland, wife of William I, 229
Erne, 32
Espec, Walter, 71
Essex, 6
Essex and Hereford, earls of (de Bohun), 203
Eudo of Carlisle, 225 n. 110
Eugenius, archbishop of Armagh, *see* Mac Gilla Uidir, Echdonn
Eugenius, bishop of Ardmore, 73
Eure, 23
Eustace fitz John (d. 1157), 200–2, 204, 206–10, 213–16, 219, 221, 223, 225, 227, 228, 230
Everard, abbot of Holm Cultram, 82, 83 and n. 49
Evesham, 120 n. 33, 131, 201
Evreux, 35
Ewen (Eugenius) son of Duncan (MacDougall), king of Argyll, 180, 182, 184, 186, 187, 193, 194, 196 n. 65
Exeter, 8, 52, 63, 74 n. 25
Eyrbyggja Saga, 55

Fahan, 32
Fair of Tailtiu, 91
Farne Island, 220 n. 84
Feidlimid, king of Munster, 26
Fergus, bishop of Druim Lethglaisse, 157 n. 13
Fergus of Galloway, 187
Fergus mac Ferchair, 145 n. 41, 146, 149
Fergus Mór, son of Erc, 89
Ferns, 54, 167 n. 54
de Ferrers William, earl of Derby (d. 1254), 204
Fianna, 96
Fife, 137, 221, 223 and n. 104
Fingal, 104, 106
Flanders, 53, 64, 65
Flann ua Sculu, 'bishop of Connere', 157
Flaxly, 54
Flemings, 55, 101
Fleury, 12, 13
Flintshire, 79
Florence, 64
Florence/John of Worcester, 24
Flotbald, bishop of Chartres, 23
Fomoire, 95
Forannán, abbot of Armagh, 23, 24, 33

Fordun, John of, 142 n. 34, 143, 144, 145, 146, 147, 148 n. 50
Forest of Arden, 70
Forfar, 123
Forth, 140, 152 n. 66
Fortriu, 89
France, French, 64, 102, 103, 133, 135 n. 3, 153, 236, 238
  nature of warfare in, 108, 114, 116, 119, 133
Francia, Frankish, 67, 114
  impact of Viking attacks on, 2, 3, 7–9, 12, 13, 15, 17, 20–8, 31, 34–6
Franciscans, 127
Fraser, Richard, 222
Fraser, William, bishop of St Andrews, 233 n. 133
Fresborne, Ralph, 212 and n. 52, 223 and n. 104
Frescobaldi, 64
Frey, 38
Furness, 53, 54, 76, 83

Gaedel Glas, 145, 146
Gáedil, *see* Gael
Gael, *Goídil*, 135, 152, 153
  shared identity of in Ireland and Scotland, 88–91, 96, 97
Galicia, 40
Gall, 107
Gallgoídil, 97
Galloglass, 183
Galloway, 59, 85, 179, 183, 222
  connections with Ireland, 40, 54, 96
  politics of, 117, 124, 141, 180
Galway, 98
Gascony, 59, 201, 202, 204, 208, 219, 238
Gaul, 41, 42
Gauzelin, 22
Gaveston, Piers, earl of Cornwall (d. 1312), 131
Geoffrey, abbot of Burton, 69, 70, 74, 84
Geoffrey, abbot of Dryburgh, 224
Geoffrey of Monmouth, 147
Geoffrey of York, Life of, 116
Gerald de Barri, *see* Gerald of Wales
Gerald of Wales (Gerald de Barri/Giraldus Cambrensis) (d. 1223), 50, 63, 103, 111, 114 n. 2, 119, 120 and n. 30, 154, 156 n. 10, 178
  author of Life of St David, 78
  condemns Irish, 116
  comments on Irish Sea trade, 44, 45, 54, 55, 58, 61
  comments of Irish–Welsh relations, 108, 109, 110, 128

Index

observations on John de Courcy, 154, 156, 164, 175, 176 n. 94
observations on the Welsh, 117, 118, 122, 132
Gerald of Windsor, 100
Gerald, Count of Aurillac, Life of, 11
Germany, 35, 90, 114
Gilbert, bishop of Galloway (d. 1253), 224
Gilbert (Gille Brigte), earl of Strathearn (d. 1223), 138
Gilbert, lord of Galloway, 117
Gilbert, monk of Louth, abbot of Basingwerk, 77
Gilbert son of Samuel, 196
Gilbertine order, 206, 217, 223
Gilla Coémáin, 94 n. 31
Gilla Domangairt Mac Cormaic, *see* Mac Cormaic, Gilla Domangairt
Gilla Meic Liac (Gelasius), abbot of Derry, archbishop of Armagh (d. 1174), 159
Gille-Aldanus, bishop of Whithorn (d. *c.* 1140), 81 n. 46
Gillebridge son of Somerled, 186
Gille Mícheil, earl of Fife (d. *c.* 1136), 137–8
Gilrodh, 124
Giraldus (Cambrensis), *see* Gerald of Wales
Glasgow, 83
Glastonbury, 14, 68, 74 n. 25, 75 and n. 26, 76
Glendale, 217
Glenluce Abbey, 59
Gloucester, 45, 79
Gloucester and Hertford (de Clare), earls of, 203
Gloucestershire, 214
Godfrey mac William, 123
Godred Crovan, king of the Isle of Man (d. 1095), 51
Goídil see Gael
Golden Gospels, 16
Goscelin, 85
Gothfrith, king of Dublin (d. 934), 21 30
Gothfrith Sytryggsson of Dublin, 34
de Grandson, Otto, 208
Graham, David, 125
Grantham, 215
'Great Army', 4, 5, 6, 9, 10, 18
Great Cause, 233, 234
Greece, 145
Greenland, 42, 64
Grey Abbey, 82, 83 and n. 51, 167 n. 55
Grey, Thomas, 143, 144, 147, 148, 149 n. 51 150
Greyfriars Kirk, 132
Gribthorpe, 216

Grosseteste, Robert, 207
Gruffudd ap Cynan (d. 1137), 40, 100, 102, 104, 105, 106
Gruffudd ap Madog (d. 1238), 122
Gruffudd son of Rhys ap Tewdwr (d. 1137), 100
Guardians (Scottish), 125, 233
Gúbretha Caratniad, 48
Guibert de Nogent, 114 n. 2
Guinevere, 84
Gunnlaug 'Serpent's tongue', 43, 49
Guthrum, 8
Gwent, 48, 60, 111, 206
Gwenwynwyn son of Owain Cyfeiliog (d. 1216), 117
Gwynedd, 99, 100, 104, 105, 106, 107, 122
Gwynllwg, 111
Gwytherin, 79, 80
Gytha, 50

Hackness, 71
Haddington, 123, 124
Hæsten, 7, 29
Hakon IV, king of Norway (d. 1263), 183, 195
Hakon's Saga, 195
Halfdan, 18, 20
Halfdan (son of Gothfrith, king of Dublin) Gothfrithsson (d. 926), 5, 21
Haliburton, Henry, 222
Hallkirk, 121
de Halywell, Robert, 209 n. 39
Harald, earl of Orkney and Caithness (d. 1206), 123
Harald son of Olaf 'the Black', king of Man (d. 1248), 193 n. 50
Harold Godwinsson, king of England (d. 1066), 50, 51, 52
Harris, 181
Harrogate, 222 n. 95
Hassington, Berwickshire, 222 n. 95
Hastings, 52
Hartlepool, 71
Hauksbók, 42
Haut-Limousin, 11
Hawick, 221 n. 90
Hebrides, 40, 96
  integration into Scottish kingdom, 180–6, 196, 197
  Viking influence in, 11, 36, 37, 52, 97
Heiu, 71
Henry I, king of England (d. 1135), 54, 79
  dealings with de Vescy family, 200, 207, 208, 214, 230
  relations with Ireland, 51, 52, 100, 101, 102

Henry II, king of England (d. 1189), 110, 177, 202, 205
  dealings with Irish, 126 n. 60, 155, 160 n. 24, 172, 178
  dealings with Welsh, 108, 111, 112, 120, 121
  Gerald of Wales's opinions of, 116 and n. 9, 119, 132
  trade policies in Irish Sea region, 52, 53, 57, 59, 60, 65
Henry III (the 'young king') (d. 1183), 110
Henry III, king of England (d. 1272), 143 n. 36, 220, 228, 229, 230 n. 126
  connections with John de Vescy, 209, 212, 215
  connections with William II de Vescy, 202, 225 n. 113, 228 n. 122
Henry V, king of England (d. 1422), 80
Henry of Almain, 131 and n. 83
Henry of London, archbishop of Dublin (d. 1228), 172 n. 81
Henry, *judex* in Fife and Fothriff, 140 n. 24
Hervy, bishop of Bangor (trs. 1109), 78
Hexham, 35, 82
Higbald, bishop of Lindisfarne (d. 802), 9, 10
Hincmar, archbishop of Rheims, 23, 25 and n. 105
Historia Brittonum, 147
Historia Gruffud vab Kenan, 104, 105
Historia Regum Britannie, 147
Holm Cultram, 54, 82, 83
Holyhead, 40, 41, 43
Holy Land, 201, 212
Holy Roman Empire, 43
Holyrood Chronicle, 117
Holy Trinity, church of, Downpatrick, 165 n. 45, 166, 169
Holywell, 79, 80
Honorius IV, pope (d. 1287), 207
Howth (Co. Dublin), 21, 61
Huesca, 208
Hulne, Carmelite priory at, 206, 207, 212 and n. 52, 219, 220, 223, 224
Humber, 114, 206
Huntercombe, Walter of, keeper of the Isle of Man, 233 n. 134, 234 n. 135
Huntingdon, 205
Hywel, 104
Hywel, 117
Hywel Sais ap Rhys, 122
Hywel son of Iorwerth ab Owain of Gwynllwg, 111

Iberia, Iberian, 8, 9
Ibn Adhari, 8
'Ibracense', 159, n. 20
Iceland, Icelandic, 18, 40, 43, 49, 54, 55, 63, 64
Illaunloughan, 32
Imino, 26
Immo, bishop of Noyon, 20 n. 84, 22
Inch, Inchcourcy (Inis Cúscraid), Cistercian house of, 54, 83 and n. 51, 156, 167 and n. 55, 168 and n. 61, 170, 173
Inchaffray, 138 n. 17
Inisboffin, 32, 37
Inis Cúscraid, Inis Causcraid, Inis Caumscraid, *see* Inch
Inisglora, 31
Iniskea North, 31
Inismurray, 31
Innocent II, pope, 63
Innocent III, pope, 173 and n. 82, 174, 176, 177, 212
Innocent IV, pope, 163
Instructions for Princes, 63
Iona, 83, 91, 160 n. 24
  Viking attacks on, 3, 11, 12 and n. 44, 16, 17, 33, 36, 37
Iorwerth ab Owain of Gwynllwg, 111
Ireland, Irish,
  activities of John de Courcy in, 154–78
  activities of de Vescy family in, 199, 207, 208, 209, 210, 236, 239
  contacts with Scotland, 87, 90, 91, 94, 96, 135–53, 182
  contacts with Wales, 98–113
  impact of Viking raids on, 2–38
  nature of political violence in, 115–21, 125–9, 134
  trading links with Britain, 39–67
  use of saints' cults from Britain, 68–70, 73, 76, 77, 79, 81, 83, 84
Ireton, Ralph, bishop of Carlisle, 233 n. 133
Irish Sea, 87, 179, 181, 182, 187, 188, 213
  economic life around, 42–66
  Irish–Welsh connections around, 97, 102, 110, 112, 113
  Viking influence in, 32, 96
Isabella, queen of England, wife of Edward II, 204
Isabella daughter of Donald earl of Mar, wife of Robert Bruce, 188
Islay, 96, 181
Isle of Anglesey *see* Anglesey
Isle of Man, Manx, *see also* Isles (Scottish, Western Isles) 174, 179, 187, 188, 190
  importance in Irish Sea trade, 40, 41, 48, 54, 63, 64

Index

Irish conquest of, 51, 93
Scottish conquest of, 181, 183, 201, 230
Viking influence on, 43, 52
Isle of Wight, 4
Isles (Scottish, Western Isles), kingdom of, lordship of, *see also* Man, 6, 52, 53–4, 55, 180, 185, 197, 198
Isodore, 151, 152
Isolde, 84
Itinerarium Kambrie, 117
Italy, Italian, 42
Ivar, king of Dublin (d. 873), 5, 8, 18, 36

Jews, 56
Joan, wife of Llywelyn ab Iorwerth, 120
Jocelin, abbot of Melrose, bishop of Glasgow, 81, 83
Jocelin of Furness, 84, 169
hagiographical work of, 76, 81, 82, 83 and n. 49
use of his Life of St Patrick by Armagh, 171, 172 and n. 78, 176
John, bishop of Caithness (d. 1202), 123
John, earl of Atholl (d. 1306), 132
John, earl of Orkney and Caithness (d. 1231), 121 and n. 36
John of Ferriby, 212
John fitz Thomas, baron of Offaly, earl of Kildare (d. 1316), 202, 209, 210, 211, 213, 235, 236 and n. 144, 239
John, king of England, lord of Ireland (d. 1216), 119, 127 n. 67, 130, 132, 174
dealings with de Vescy family, 203, 209, 212, 215, 227, 228
involvement in Irish Sea trade, 47, 56, 60, 61, 62, 65
policies in Ulster, 173, 176, 177
visits to Ireland, 109, 127, 128
John (Balliol), king of Scotland (abd. 1296, d. 1313), 144, 147
abdication, 144 n. 38
dealings with de Vescy family, 222, 233, 234, 239
dealings with Western Isles, 181, 184, 187, 193, 197
John of Salerno, 12,
John of Salerno, Cardinal *titulus* of the Coelian Mount, 175, 176
John of Salisbury, 209
John son of Alexander (Mac Dougall) of Argyll, 180, 181, 193, 194
Jura, 181

Keating, Geoffrey, 59
Keldholme, Cistercian priory, 219

Kells, 12 and n. 44, 18, 34, 160 and n. 24, 177
Kelso, 221
Kenilworth, 64
Kenneth mac Aht, 123
Kent, 5, 6, 7, 9, 14, 206, 213
Kent, earls of (de Burgh), 203
Kildare,
attacked by Vikings, 21
bishop of, 211, 234
Franciscan friary at, 207
St Mary's priory, Carmelite, at, 207
de Vescy involvement in, 205 and n. 20, 206, 210, 211 and n. 48, 213, 221, 231, 232–9
Killaloe, 127
Killeigh (Co. Offaly), 23
Killevy, 69
Kilskyre, 34
Kincora, 167 n. 54
Kinloss, 139 n. 21, 141 n. 30
Kinmount, 225
Kinninmonth, Master Alexander, 136 n. 6
Kintyre, 181, 182 n. 11, 189 n. 36
Kirkandrews, 222
Kirkcudbright, 81, 82, 222
Knapdale, 189 n. 36
Knout, Richard, sheriff of Northumberland, 226
Knoydart, 181
Knútsdrápa, 18, 19

Lachlan son of Alan of Garmoran, 181
Lachlan (Roland) son of Uhtred son of Fergus of Galloway, constable of Scotland, 192
Lacy family, 214, 217
de Lacy, Hugh I, lord of Meath (d. 1186), 110, 154, 156, 171, 177
de Lacy, Hugh II, earl of Ulster (d. 1242), 173, 174, 176, 177
de Lacy, Roger, constable of Chester, 225
de Lacy, Walter, lord of Meath (d. 1241), 173, 177
La Marche and Angoulême, count of, 212
Lambay, 32
Lancashire, 53
Lancaster, 60, 205
Langtoft, Peter, 131, 132, 202
Langton, 216, 217
Langton, John, chancellor of England, 209 n. 39
Laois, 211 and n. 48
Largs, 179, 180
Lateran Council, second (1139), 165
Lateran Council, third (1179), 63

Laudabiliter, 174, 175 n. 87
Lauderdale, 224, 225
Laurence of Durham, 74, 75, 82, 84
Lebor Gabála Érenn, 94, 149
Leicester, 35
Leinster, 44, 56, 154, 156, 177, 205
  involvement with Scotland, 93, 94
  involvement with Wales, 99, 111, 112
Le Mans, 14
Lennox, 138 n. 16
Leominster, 74 n. 25
Liddle Strength, Cumberland, 225 n. 109
Liffey, 8, 30, 32, 40, 41, 54, 61
Lilliesleaf, 221 n. 90
Limerick, 23, 60, 127, 130
Limousin, 11
Lincoln, 131, 206
Lincolnshire, 206, 215 and n. 65, 219, 237
Lindisfarne (Chester-le-street), 2, 9, 10, 11, 16 and n. 66, 21, 69
Lindsay, Philip, 225
Lindsey, 35
Lisbon, 8
Liseux, 35
de Lisle, Jourdain, 133
Lismore (Ireland), 32, 158
Lismore (Scotland), 181, 194
Liverpool, 61
Llandovery, 129
Llanthony, Augustinian priory (Wales), 206
Llywelyn ap Cadwallon, 117
Llywelyn ap Gruffudd (d. 1282), 122
Llywelyn ab Iorwerth (d. 1240), 106, 120, 122, 129
Loarn, 92
Lochawe, 189, 190
Loch Fyne, 189
Loch Leven, 139 n. 21
Loingsech, abbot of Dún Lethglaise (Down), 160
Loire, 11, 27, 29, 34, 41, 53
London, 6, 24, 50 56, 59, 206, 208, 213
de Longespée, William, earl of Salisbury (d. 1226), 203 n. 14, 214 n. 60, 228 n. 122
Longhoughton, 218
Lords Ordainer (England), 204
Lorn, 181, 182
Lothar, 14
Lothian, 81, 82
Lough Brickland (Co. Down), 20
Lough Derg, 77
Lough Neagh, 21, 32
Lough Ramor (Co. Cavan), 27
Louis VII, king of France (d. 1180), 110

Louis, abbot of St Denis, 22
Louis the Pious, emperor (d. 840) 14
Louth (Ireland), 21, 171
Louth (Lincolnshire), 77
Louvain, 29
Low Countries, 208
Lucca, 64
Lucian, 39–40, 63
Ludlow, 77
Luncarty, 69
Lusk, 32

Mabinogion, 39
Mac Carthaig, Cormac, 126, 159
Mac Carthaig, Diarmait, 73
Mac Carthaig, Diarmait, 126
Mac Carthaig, Domnall Got Cairprech, 126
Mac Carthaig, Domnall Ruad, king of Desmond, 211, 235, 236 n. 144 238
Mac Carthy's Book, 126, 127
Maccintsacairt, Farquhar, earl of Ross (d. 1251), 192
Maccintsacairt, William, 182 n 11
Mac Cormaic, Gilla Domangairt, abbot of Bangor, 'bishop of Ulaid', 161, 162, 163 and n. 39
Mac Cormaic, Óengus, abbot of Bangor, 163 n. 39
Mac Craith, Seaán, 118
Mac Diarmata, Cathal, 127
Mac Donald family, lords of Islay, 181, 184, 188, 195
Mac Dougall family, lords of Argyll, 180, 184, 187, 193, 195
Mac Duinn Sléibe family, kings of Ulaid, 157, 166, 170
Mac Duinn Sléibe, Áed, 170
Mac Duinn Sléibe, Cú Ulad, king of Ulaid, 157 n. 12, 162 n. 33
Mac Duinn Sléibe, Donn Sléibe, 162, 170
Mac Duinn Sléibe, Eochaid, 119, 170
Mac Duinn Sléibe, Magnus, king of Ulaid, 157 n. 12, 161, 162, 170
Mac Gilla Uidir, Echdonn (Eugenius), abbot of Bangor, archbishop of Armagh (d. 1216), 169 n. 68 176 and n. 96
Mac Gilchrist, Gillascop, 189
Mac Gillemichel, Gillecolm, 196 and n. 65
mac Heth, 182
Mac Lochlainn, Muirchertach, king of Cenél nEógain (d. 1166), 119, 158 n. 17 159, 160, 167, 168
Mac Murchada, Diarmait, king of Leinster (d. 1171), 61, 111, 120, 142 n. 33

Index

activities in Ireland, 48, 101, 120, 167 n. 54
appeal to English for help in Ireland, 52, 56, 58, 61, 103
Mac Ruairi family, lords of Garmoran, 181, 184
Mac Ruairi, Alan, lord of Garmoran (Alanus filius Rotherici), 181, 183, 184, 188
Mac Ruairi, Dugald, of Garmoran, 181, 188
Mac Ruairi, Ruairi son of Alan of Garmoran, 181, 190
Mac Sorley family, 180–98
Mac Sween, Dugald, 189 n. 36
Mac Turnin, 107
mac William family, 117, 123, 182
Madog, 117
Máel Brígte mac Tornáin, abbot of Armagh and Iona, 36, 38
Máel Brígte son of Cathasach, bishop and abbot of Dromore, 160
Máel Coluim Cenn Mór, king of Scotland, *see* Malcolm Canmore
Máel Coluim, earl of Fife, *see* Malcolm
Máel Coluim, *judex* in Angus, 140 n. 24
Maelgwn ab Owain, 105, 106, 107
Maelgwn son of Rhys ap Gruffudd (d. 1231), 107, 122
Máel Ísu mac in Cléirig Chuirr (Malachy II), bishop of Ulaid (d. 1175), 160, 161, 162, 163, 166
Máel Martain, abbot of Movilla, 161, 162, 163
Máel Muire, bishop of Down, 157
Máel Sechnaill I, king of Uí Néill (d. 862), 27
Máel Sechnaill II, high-king of Ireland (d. 1022), 45, 91
Magna Carta, 209
Magnus Barefoot, king of Norway (d. 1103), 52, 59, 65
Magnus Olafsson, king of Man (d. 1265), 121 n. 37, 187 and n. 50
Mag Rath, 95
Magyars, 28
Maine, 200, 229
Mainz, 11, 95
Maitland family, 225
Maitland, Richard, steward of Alnwick, 225
Malachy I, 'bishop of Ulaid', *see*, Ua Morgair, Máel Máedoc
Malachy II, 'bishop of Ulaid', *see* Máel Ísu mac in Cléirig Chuirr
Malachy III, bishop of Down, *see* Echmilid
Malcolm III 'Canmore' (Máel Coluim Cenn Mór), king of Scotland (d. 1093), 152, 191, 224
Malcolm IV, king of Scotland (d. 1165), 97, 191
Malcolm, earl of Atholl (d. 1187 x 1198), 117
Malcolm (Máel Coluim), earl of Fife (d. 1230), 138
Malcolm (Máel Coluim), earl of Fife (d. 1266), 138
Malcolm, earl of Lennox (d. *c.* 1303–5), 184
Malcolm mac Heth, 123, 187
Malise (Máel Ísu) I, earl of Strathearn (d. 1271), 138, 187
Malise (Máel Ísu) II, earl of Strathearn (d. 1313), 138, 184
Malise (Máel Ísu) III, earl of Strathearn (d. 1333), 138
Malise (Máel Ísu) IV, earl of Strathearn (d. 1353), 138
Malton (New Malton), 206, 216, 217, 218, 219, 220, 224
Man and the Isles, kingdom of, 63, *see also* Isle of Man, and Isles
Map, Walter, 208
Mar, earl (*mormaer*) of, 91, 135
March, Marchers, 98, 122
Maredudd ap Madog, 122
Margam, 54
Margaret, queen of Scotland, *see* St Margaret
Margaret daughter of Alexander III of Scotland, queen of Norway, 184
Margaret, the 'Maid of Norway', 184, 203, 23
Margaret of Scotland, daughter of William I, king of Scotland, wife of Eustace de Vescy, 203, 204, 221, 224, 228 n. 122
Marianus Scottus, 94, 95
Marjorie, sister of Alexander II, king of Scotland, wife of Gilbert Marshal, 229
de Marisco, Geoffrey, 121
Markland, 42
Marne, 29
Marshal family, 122, 210, 214
Marshal, Gilbert, earl of Pembroke (d. 1241), 229 and n. 123
Marshal, Richard, earl of Pembroke (d. 1234), 125, 127, 203 n. 14
Marshal, Sybil, wife of William de Ferrers, earl of Derby, 204, 229
Marshal, Walter, earl of Pembroke (d. 1245), 204
Marshal William I, earl of Pembroke (d. 1219) 58

Martyrology of Óengus, 167
Martyrology of Tallaght, 167
Matilda, queen of England, 54
Matilda daughter of William I de Vescy, wife of Adam of Carlisle, 224
de Mauleon, Savari, 130
Meath (Brega), 14
Mediterranean, 42, 64
Meilyr the soothsayer, 111
Mellifont Abbey (Cistercian), 161, 162 n. 34, 165, 168 n. 63
Melrose, 81, 82, 83, 140, 221, 227
Melrose Chronicle, 121, 123, 124, 141, 142
Menteith, 141
'Merchant's Island', 63
Mercia, Mercians, 5, 6, 43, 44
Merlin, 84, 104, 132 n. 92
Methven, 139 n. 23
Metz, 146 n. 46
Middleton Cheney, 154, 155 and n. 7, 173
Mide (Meath), 154, 156, 177
Milton Regis, 7
Minto, 222 and n. 97
Mitford, 218
MoBíu of Inis Cúscraid, 167
Moel-Y-Don Ferry, 43
Moidart, 181
de Montfort, Gui, 131 n. 83
de Montfort, Simon, earl of Leicester (d. 1265), 131, 132, 209, 210, 227
Montgomery, 48, 60
de Montgomery, Arnulf, 52, 100, 101, 102
de Montgomery, Roger, earl of Shrewsbury, 79
de Montmorency, Hervey, 110
Montpellier, 208
Monymusk, 139 nn. 22, 23
Morar, 181
Moray, 92, 93, 135, 140, 150, 179
Mordington, 223
Morebattle, 221 n. 90
Morgan ap Hywel, 210
Morgannwg, 111
Moriuht, 50
Morlaàs, 208
Mortimer family, 216
de Morville, Hugh, constable of Scotland, 224
Morvois, 15
de Morwick, Hugh, of West Chevington, 218 n. 77
Mount Carmel, *see* Carmelite order
Movilla, 161, 168 n. 61
Mow, 221 n. 90
Mowbray family, 216

Muirchertach mac Erca, 92
Muirchertach mac Neill ('Muirchertach of the Leather Cloaks), 49
Muirchertach, son of Toirrdelbach ua Briain, *see* Ua Briain, Muirchertach
Muirchú, 157 n. 13
Mull, 181
Munster, 135, 150
  connections with Scotland, 90, 91 and n. 21, 92
  connections with Wales, 99, 100, 112, 113
Murchad, son of Diarmait mac Máel na mBó, 47
Muschamp family, 214, 222
Muschamp, Robert de, of Wooler, 218, 222 n. 95
Muthill, 139 n. 23, 140 n. 24
Mynydd Carn, 100

Nantes, 4, 16, 21, 29
Neath, 54
Nehemias, bishop Connor (d. *a*. 1178), 160 n. 24
Nendrum, 168 and n. 64, 169, 170, 171, 175, 176
Nest, 103
Newcastle, 215, 219
Newcastle upon Tyne, house of Poor Clares at, 207
Newhouse, Premonstratensian house at, 206
New Malton, *see* Malton
Newry, 54, 160, 167
Newsholme, 206, 216
Niall of the Nine Hostages, 62
Njal's Saga, 51
Nogent, 15
Noirmoutier, 11
Nore, 40
Norfolk, 214
Norfolk, earls of (Bigod), 203
Normandy, 26, 35, 56, 65, 79, 110, 111, 200
Normans, 100, 101, 102, 104
North (Far North) of England, 214–30
Northampton, 155 n. 7
North Channel, 40
North Charlton, 218
North Ferriby, 206, 223
Northmen, Norse, Ostmen, Scandinavians, Vikings, 87, 96, 97, 100, 104, 106, 107
  attacks on Britain and Ireland, 1–38
  involvement in Irish Sea trade, 39, 43, 44, 49, 62, 63

Index

North Ormsby, Gilbertine priory of, 219
North Sea, 10
Northumberland, Northumbria,
  impact of Viking raids on, 2, 5, 9 and n. 29, 10, 11
  saints' cults in, 71, 81
  de Vescy influence in, 204, 206, 212 n. 52, 214–22, 228
Norway, 71, 180, 181, 184, 193
  involvement in Irish Sea trade, 39, 40, 43, 48, 52, 63, 64, 65
Nostell, 139 n. 21
Nottinghamshire, 219
Noyon, 22, 37 n. 145
Nuthurst, Warwickshire, 13

Ócán ua Cormacáin, 168
Ó Conchobhair Donn of Connacht, 128 n. 68
Odin, 18, 26, 38
Odo of Cluny, 11, 12
  Life of, 12
Óengus, 'bishop of Ulaid', see Ua Gormáin
Offa, 5, 6
Offaly, 211 and n. 48, 235
Olaf I, king of Man (d. 1153), 187
Olaf II 'the Black', king of Man (d. 1237), 193 n. 50
Olaf, king of Dublin (d. 873), 21
Olaf Gothfrithsson, king of Dublin (d. 941), 5, 21
Olaf Sigtryggsson, 50
Olaf son of Somerled, 186
Old Uppsala, 19, 38
Oloron-Sainte-Marie, 208
Omey Island, 32
Opusculum de Simone, 227
Orderic Vitalis, 52, 101, 147 n. 49
Ordinance of Kenilworth, 64
Original Chronicle, 147
Orkneyinga Saga, 18, 51
Orkneys, 26, 40, 43, 51, 64
Orleans, 16
Oronsay, 181
Orthez, 208
Osbert of Clare, 85, 86
Osney, 132
Ostmen, see Northmen
Othere, 39
Otto III, emperor (d. 1002), 90
Owain ap Caradog, 117
Owain ap Iorwerth of Caerleon, 120
Owain ap Madog (Owain Fychan) of Powys, 117
Owain son of Cadwgan ap Bleddyn (d. 1116), 102

Owain Gwynedd, son of Gruffudd ap Cynan (d. 1170), 104, 111, 121
Oxford, Oxfordshire, 57
Oxmantown, 106

Pain fitz John, 202, 206, 207, 208
Paisley, 68, 195
Palestine, 206, see also Holy Land
Panmure, 224
Paparo, John, Cardinal, 177
Paris, 20, 29, 30, 133 n. 93
Paris, Matthew, 122 n. 42, 129, 193, 214
Parthalón, 145, 147, 148, 149
'Patricius, abbot of Saballo', 169
Patrick, earl of Atholl (d. 1242), 123, 124
Patrick, earl of Dunbar (d. 1289), 184
Pembroke, Pembrokeshire, 100, 101
Pembroke, earls of (Marshal), 203
Penda, 5
Penrith, 238
Peter of Savoy, 214 n. 60
de Percehay, Robert, of Crambe and Ryton, 221 n. 93
Perche, count of, 131
Percy family, 237
Périgord, 11
Perth, Perthshire, 64, 65, 70, 179
Peterborough, 35
Phillip IV, king of France (d. 1314), 133 n. 93
Philip de la Ley, 222
Picardy, 144 n. 38
Pickering, Vale of, 206, 216
Picts, 89, 90
Pippin II of Aquitaine, 20, 27
Pîtres, 20, 27
Plumpton, 223
Poitiers, 12, 34
Poitou, 58
Polesworth, Warwickshire, 70
Pontefract, 206
Poor Clares, order of, 207
Portmagee Channel, 32
Powys, 107, 122
Premonstratensian order, 206
de Prendergast, Maurice, 48
Preston, 60
Provence, 208
Prudhoe, 218
de la Pumerai, Jollanus, 119

Quentovic, 28, 30, 37 n. 145

Ragman Rolls, 193
Ragnall Godredsson, lord/king of Man (d. 1229), 62, 190, 192 n. 49

Ragnhild, 104
Ráith Bressail, synod of (1111), 157, 158, 163, 168
Ralph, archbishop of Dublin, 172 n. 79
Ralph of Coggeshall, 108
Ralph of Diceto, 126 n. 60
Ramsey, 35
Ranald son of Somerled (Mac Sorley), 186, 192 and n. 49, 193, 195
Randolph, Thomas, lord of the Isle of Man, 190
Ranulph Higden, 53
Raphoe, 32
Rathlin, 31
Ráth Lugdach, 160 n. 26
Reading, 9, 74 n. 25
Redesdale, 218
'Reginald, bishop of Dalnard', 169
Reginald of Durham, 73, 81, 82
Reginald Olafsson, lord/king of Man (d. 1249), 121 n. 37
Regino of Prüm, 29
Rheims, 23
Rhigyfarch, 78
Rhine, 29
'Rhirid ab Owain', 'Richerid Macchanan', 105, 106
Rhodri ab Owain, 105, 107
Rhum, 181
Rhys ap Gruffudd (the Lord Rhys), of Deheubarth (d. 1197), 103, 107, 108, 111, 121
Rhys ap Maelgwyn, 132
Rhys ap Maredudd (d. 1292), 132
Rhys ap Tewdwr (d. 1093), 100, 101, 102
Riccardi, 64
Richard, earl of Cornwall, 212
Richard I, king of England (d. 1199), 60, 119, 177
Richard II, king of England (d. 1399), 128 n. 68
Richard fitz Gilbert, earl/lord of Pembroke/Strigoil, *see* Strongbow
Richard, monk of Shrewsbury, 80
Riddell family, 221
de Rienzo, Cola, 147 n. 49
Rievaulx, 82, 219
Ringwood, 224
Ripley, 222 n. 96
Robert (Bruce) I, king of Scotland, earl of Carrick (d. 1329), 125, 133 n. 93
  associations with Ireland, 132, 135, 150
  dealings with Western Isles, 180, 181, 188, 189, 190, 197
Robert, bishop of Ross, 224

Robert, earl of Strathearn (d. 1237 X 1244), 138
Robert of Gloucester, 131
Robert, prior of Shrewsbury, 79, 80
Robert fitz Harding, 52
Robert fitz Stephen, 58, 103, 104
Rochester, 130
Roger of Howden, 178, 209
Rome, Romans, 41, 42, 145 n. 41, 173 n. 82
Roscrea, 21
Ross, 138 n. 16
Rossynell, Bartholomew, 40–1
Rouen, 30, 35, 50, 56, 58
Roxburgh, Roxburghshire, 204, 221, 222, 224, 225 n. 112, 226
Ruairi son of Alan, *see* Mac Ruairi, Ruairi son of Alan
Ruairi son of Ranald son of Somerled, of Garmoran, 181, 182
Rufford, 219 and n. 81
Rugley, 215 n. 65
Rushen, 53, 54
Rusticus, 15

St Abbán, 77, 82
St Aidan, 68, 69, 71
St Alban, 67
St Albans, 193
St Amand, 67
St Andrew, house of, in Ards (Ulster), 173 n. 82
St Andrew, house of, in Stoke Courcy (Somerset), 173 n. 82
St Andrews (Scotland), 125, 139 nn. 21, 22
St Augustine, 26
St Augustine's church, Canterbury, 14
St Bees, Benedictine priory of, 71, 72, 74, 168, 169 n. 68
St Bega, 69, 70, 71 and n. 14, 72, 73, 74
  Life and Miracles of, 70, 82
St-Bertin, monastery of, 17
St Blathmac, 12 n. 44, 17
  Life of, 16
St Boniface, 26
St Brendan, 77
  'legend of', 146, 147, 149 n. 51
St Brigit, 21, 67, 74, 75, 76, 86, 164, 175
  Life of, 74, 75, 82
St Cadog, *Vita* of, 49
St Cathroe, Life of, 146 n. 46
St Columba *see* Colum Cille
St Colum Cille (Columba), 16, 17, 26, 91, 164, 175, 196
  cult of, 68, 69, 76
  Life of, 41, 68, 89 n. 8

Index

St Congal, 'legend of', 146 and n. 45, 147, 149 n. 51
St Cuthbert, 9, 11, 16, 26, 225
  cult of, 67, 72, 73, 74, 81, 82, 83
St David, 68, 103
  Life of, 78
St Davids (Wales), 40, 41, 54, 61, 78
St Denis, monastery of, 15
St Dogmaels, abbey of, 54
St Dubricius, 78
St Dunstan, 67
  Life of, 14, 85
St Edburga, 85
St Edith, 70
St Edmund, 67
St George's Channel, 40
St Giles, church of, 80
St Helen, 76, 83
St Hilda, 67, 71
St John, 67
St John, Augustinian hospital of, Downpatrick, 167
St John the Baptist, hospital of, Downpatrick, 156 n. 8
St John the Baptist, hospital of, Dublin, 156 n. 8
St Kentigern, 76, 84
  Life of, 81, 82
St Leonard's, hospital of, near Alnwick, 224
St MacDara's Island, 32
St Margaret of Scotland, 54, 143 n. 36 152, 191
St Martial, 11
St Martin of Tours, monastery of, 16
St Mary, 67
St Mary's Abbey, Dublin, 54
St Mary's, Laon, canons of, 47
St Mary's priory, Kildare, 207
St Mary's, York, 168
St Milburga, 68
St Mochoi, 169
St Modwenna, 69, 70, 73, 74
  Life of, 70, 75, 84
St Monenna (Moninna, Darerca), 69, 70
St Ninian, 70
  Life of, 81, 83, 84, 85
St Oswald, 35, 67, 71, 85
St Oudoceus, 78
St Patrick, 89, 90, 92
  cult of in England, 75, 76, 84
  John de Courcy and cult of, 164, 165 n. 45, 169, 171, 172, 175, 178
  Life of, 76, 83, 157 n. 13 169, 171, 172
  Viking attacks on shrine of, 21, 23, 26

St Patrick, church of, Downpatrick, 164, 166, 174 n. 87
St Patrick's Purgatory, 77, 82
St Paulinus, 10
St Peter, 67
St Philibert of Jumièges, *Vita* of, 41
St Philibert, monastery of, 11
St Radegund, 67
St Remigius, 23
St Sebastian, Life of, 18
St Teilo, 78
St Thomas of Canterbury, 67
St Thomas's, Dublin, abbot of, 211, 234
St Waltheof of Melrose, 76, 83 and n. 49
St Wenefreda, 79, 80, 82
St Werburghs, church of, Chester, 165, 175
St Wilfrid, 67
St Wulfstan, 39, 50
Saintes, 201
Saint Pol, Count Guy of, 205
Salisbury, earls of (de Longspée), 203
Saltair na Rann, 90
Sanday, 6
Sandford, John of, justiciar of Ireland, 232
Santiago de Compostela, 212 n. 51
Saul, Augustinian abbey of, 161, 162 and n. 34, 164, 168 n. 61
Savigny, Savigniac 53, 54
Savoy, 208
Sawdon, 222 n. 96
Sawtry, 77
Saxlingham, 214
Saxony, 37
Scalacronica, 143, 144, 146
Scarborough, 214, 218
Scattery, 32
Scone, 139 n. 21, 146
Scot, William, 225
Scota, 145
Scoti, 95, 135, 145, 146, 149, 150, 152
Scotia, 152, 189
Scotland, Scots, 6, 17
  absorption of Western Isles into, 180, 182, 184, 185, 191
  connections with Ireland, 87, 88, 93, 135–53
  involvement in Irish Sea trade, 40, 50, 53, 54, 55, 59, 65
  political violence in, 114, 116, 117, 123, 124, 125, 126, 128, 129
  saints' cults in, 67, 68, 69, 70, 74, 81, 83, 86
  de Vescy family connections with, 199, 205, 215, 221, 222, 223, 226, 230, 236, 238

'Scottish service', 189
Sedulius Scotus, 36
Séez, 79
Seine, 8, 22, 29, 30, 34
Severn, 40, 45, 54, 118
Seville, 28
Shannon, 32, 33
Shetlands, 40, 64
Shipley, 222
Shrewsbury, 64, 79, 80, 82
Shropshire, 68, 77
Sighvatr, 19
Sigurd, jarl of the Orkneys (d. 1014), 51
Simón Brecc, 146 and n. 45
Sitriuc mac Amlaím 'Silkenbeard', king of Dublin (d. 1042), 43, 51, 104, 168
Sixhills, priory of, Lincolnshire, 223 n. 103
Skellig Michael, 22, 32
Skipness, 189 n. 36
Skye, sheriff of, 182 n. 11
Slaney, 40, 41
Slave-raiding, 4, 10, 13, 21, 50
Slavs, 28
Snowdonia, 210
Sodor, 63
Solomon of Cardiff, 56
Solway Firth, 41, 54, 55
Somerled, 180, 182, 186, 197
Somerset, 57, 154, 214
Somme, 29
Song of Dermot and the Earl, 57, 61, 103, 108, 120
Spain, 27, 37, 208
Speratus, 28
Spindleston, Northumberland, 222 n. 97 223
Sprouston, 204, 205 and n. 20, 206, 213, 221, 223 n. 104 226, 233, 237
Standard, battle of the, 201
Stephen, king of England (d. 1154), 80, 119, 209, 215, 227
Stewart family, 68, 221, 223
Stewart, James, 182 n. 11, 184
Stewart, Walter, earl of Menteith (d. 1294 x 1296), 184 188, 189 n. 36
Stewart, Walter son of Alan, 223 n. 103
Stonebow, York, Carmelite house at, 207
Stracathro, 147 n. 49, 179
Strathclyde, 8
Strathearn, 137
Strathearn, earls of, *see* Malise
Strathmartine, 221
Strigoil, 111
Strongbow (Richard fitz Gilbert), earl/lord of Pembroke/Strigoil (d. 1176), 56, 100, 107, 111, 120, 154, 156

dealings with Henry II, 52, 110, 112, 177
Stuteville family, 214, 216
Stuteville, Burga de, wife of William I de Vescy, 220
de Stuteville, Eustace, 224 n. 109
Stuteville, Robert de, 224
Styford, 218
Suir, 40
Surrey, 13
Surrey, earls of (de Warenne), 203
Swanage, 8
Swords, 104, 105
Sybil, daughter of Philip de Valognes, wife of Robert de Stuteville, 224

Tadcaster, 71
Táin, 168
Tallaght, 32, 36
Tara, 92, 146
Tara Brooch, 16
Tarvit, 221
Taylor, Geoffrey, 219
Tecosca Cormaic, 42
Tees, 215
Tellas, 8
Temple of the Lord in Jerusalem, order of the, 206
Terryglass, 36
Thietmar of Merseburg, 23, 24, 26
Thirlestane, 225
Thomas, archbishop of Armagh, *see* Ua Conchabair, Tomaltach
Thomas fitz Maurice, 113, 235
Thomas of Galloway, 124
Thomas of Lancaster, 130
Thomond, 127, 128, 154 n. 2
Thor, 38
Thora, 55
Thorfinn son of Harald earl of Orkney and Caithness, 123
Thorney, 35
Thornton, 216
Thurles, 107
Thursby, 83 n. 49
Thurso, 123
Tickhill, Humphrey of, 176
Tiree, 181
Tír Eógain, 178
Tiron, 53, 54
Toirrdelbach ua Briain, 47, 51, 56
Tomaltach, archbishop of Armagh, *see* Ua Conchabair, Tomaltach
Tongland, 141
Topographia Brittanica, 116
Topography of Ireland, 116

Index

Tory Island, 31
Tours, 12, 13, 16, 17
Treaty of Perth (1266), 64, 181, 182, 185, 197
Treaty of Windsor (1175), 172
Trent, 70, 214, 237
Treshnish Isles, 181
Tripartite Life of Patrick, 89, 90, 169
Tristan, 84
Triumphs of Turlough, 118
Trondheim, 63, 64
Trussebut, 222 n. 95
Tughall, 206, 224
Tulane, 34
Turenne, 11
Turnberry 'band', 236 n. 144
Tweed, 81, 222, 224 and n. 106
Twynham, Augustinian house at, 76 n. 28
Tynedale, 238

Ua Bánáin, Máel Pátraic, 'bishop of Connor and Dál nAraide', 160 n. 24
Ua Brain, Murchad, 120
Ua Briain, Conchobar, 128
Ua Briain, Diarmait son of Muirchertach, 128
Ua Briain, Diarmait son of Toirrdelbach, 118
Ua Briain, Domnall Mór, 107, 111, 118
Ua Briain, Donnchad Cairprech, king of Thomond, 127, 128
Ua Briain, Ioan son of Conchobar, 128
Ua Briain, Muirchertach, king of Munster, high-king of Ireland (d. 1119), 47, 51, 52, 92 n. 23 100, 101, 102, 112
Ua Canannain, Ruaidrí, 118
Ua Cathasaig, Domnall, 160
Ua Cathasaig, Gilla Aodar, 160
Ua Cerbaill, Donnchad, king of Airgialla (d. 1168), 119, 166 n. 50, 170
Ua Cerbaill, Máel Ísu, bishop of Clogher (d. 1187), 171
Ua Cerbaill, Murchad, king of Airgialla (d. 1189), 171
Ua Conchobair family, 207
Ua Conchobair, Áed, king of Connacht (d. 1228), 120, 127 n. 62
Ua Conchobair, Áed, king of Connacht (d. 1274), 188
Ua Conchabair, Cathal Crobderg, king of Connacht (d. 1224), 103, 126, 127 and nn. 62, 63
Ua Conchabair, Cochobar Máenmaige, king of Connacht (d. 1189) 118
Ua Conchobair, Ruaidrí, high-king of Ireland (d. 1198), 56, 107, 110, 111, 119, 135, 171, 172 and n. 80
Ua Conchabair, Toirrdelbach, 127
Ua Conchabair, Tomaltach (Thomas), archbishop of Armagh (d. 1201), 76, 165, 169 n. 68, 171, 172 and n. 80, 176
Ua Connairche, Gilla Críst, bishop of Lismore, papal legate (d. 1186), 178
Ua Donnocáin, Donnchad, 127 n. 64
Ua Flainn, Cú Maige, 170
Ua Flaithbertach, Conchobar, 118
Ua Gormáin, Oéngus, abbot of Bangor,' bishop of Ulaid' (d. 1123), 158, 163, 166
Ua Máel Doraid, Flaithbertach, 118
Ua Máel Muaid, Ailbe (Albinus), bishop of Ferns (d. 1223), 77
Ua Morgair, Máel Máedoc (Malachy I, St Malachy), bishop of Ulaid, bishop of Armagh (d. 1148), 163
Life of, 158
reform policies of, 158, 159, 161, 162 and n. 33, 165, 166 and n. 50, 170
Ua Néill, Áed, king of Cenél nEógain (d. 1230), 126
Ua Ruairc, Cathal, 118
Ua Tuathail, Lorcán, archbishop of Dublin, papal legate (d. 1180), 165, 172
Uhtred, 117
Uí Cairell, 160, 161
Uí Cathasaig, 161
Uí Chennselaig, 93
Uí Néill dynasty, 3, 24, 27, 89 and n. 8, 90, 91, 92, 93, 95, 96
Uí Sínaich, 159
Uists, the, 181
Ulaid, 154, 156, 161, 168 and 61, 170, 177
Ulaid, bishop of, 158
Ulster, 76, 83, 96, 112, 154, 155, 173, 177, 190
Umfraville family, 222
Umfraville, Gilbert de, of Prudhoe and Redesdale, 218
Umfraville, Ingram, 133 n. 93
Urban III, pope (d. 1187), 176 n. 94
Urban, bishop of Llandaff (d. 1134), 78, 79
'Uroneca, bishop of Uvehe', 169
Usk, 111

Valentia, 32
de Valognes, Philip, chamberlain of Scotland, 223 n. 104, 224

de Valognes, Roger, lord of East Kilbride, 224 n. 108
de Vescy family, 199–238
de Vescy, Agnes, 204, 205, 210, 213, 217, 220, 229
de Vescy, Beatrice, 200
de Vescy, Eustace (d. 1216), 200, 201, 202, 205, 206, 215 n. 65, 221, 224
    opposition to King John, 203, 209, 212, 228
de Vescy, Isabella, see de Beaumont, Isabella
de Vescy, Joan, 221
de Vescy, John (d. 1289), 204, 205, 207, 209, 210, 211, 212 and nn. 51, 52, 213, 214 and n. 60, 218, 219, 229
    connections with Scotland, 183, 201, 215, 221, 222, 227
de Vescy, John (d. 1295), 202, 232, 234, 237
de Vescy, William I, son of Eustace fitz John and Beatrice de Vescy (d. 1183), 200, 205, 206, 215, 219, 220, 224
de Vescy, William II (d. 1253), 201 n. 7, 203, 204, 214 and n. 60, 229
    military campaigns of, 202, 210, 212
    religious interests, 206, 207, 220, 224
de Vescy, William III, justiciar of Ireland (d. 1297), 200, 203, 207, 211, 212 n. 51, 219, 220, 232, 233
    conflict with John fitz Thomas, 202, 209, 210, 213, 221, 230, 234, 235, 236
    estates of, 205, 218, 237, 238
de Vescy, William 'of Kildare' (d. 1314), 200, 202, 211 n. 49, 237, 238
Viking, see Northmen
le Viscount, John, of Embleton, 218
Viterbo, 131
Vivian, cardinal, 174 n. 87

Wærburh, 16
Wærferth, bishop of Worcester (d. 915), 13
Wala, bishop of Metz, 25 n. 105
Walafrid Strabo, 16
Wales, Welsh, 199, 202, 210
    connections with Ireland, 87, 93, 98–113
    involvement in Irish Sea trade, 40, 43, 45, 46, 53, 54, 58, 59, 64
    political violence in, 115, 116, 117–18, 120, 121–3, 125, 128, 129, 132
    saints' cults in, 49, 51, 67, 74, 77, 78, 79, 81, 82, 86
    Viking involvement in, 6, 23
Wallace, Malcolm, 125
Wallace, William, 132

Walter, earl of Menteith, see Stewart, Walter
Waltham, 68, 74 n. 25
Waltheof, earl, 132
Warden, 77
Warenne, earl, 238
Warin fitz Gerold, 155 n. 7
Warwickshire, 13
Waterford, 40, 41, 43, 58, 60, 100, 109, 111, 127, 130
Watton, Gilbertine priory at, 206, 217, 219, 220
Waverly, 77
Weland, 8
de Welle, Robert, 216 n. 65
Wessex, 2, 5, 6, 8, 93
Western Isles, see Isles, kingdom of
Westminster, 38, 202, 233, 236
Westmorland, 228
Wetherby, 223
Wexford, 40, 41, 43, 48, 58, 100
Whitby, 71 and n. 14
Whithorn, 35, 54, 81 and n. 46, 83 n. 50
Whitsome, Adam of, 203
Whitton, 221 n. 90
Wicklow, 61, 211 n. 48
Wickwane, archbishop of York, 210
Wiglaf, king of Mercia (d. 840), 6
William I, king of England (d. 1087), 44, 50, 51, 56, 130
William I ('the Lion'), king of Scotland (d. 1214), 142 n. 32, 191, 203, 222 n. 96, 223
    campaigns in Caithness, 123, 124
    invasion of England by, 110–11, 215
William II (Rufus), king of England (d. 1100), 41, 51, 55, 59, 61, 100
William fitz Osbern, earl of Hereford (d. 1071), 78
William of Coventry, 212 n. 52
William of Malmesbury, 76, 85, 86, 112, 114 n. 2
    comments on Irish Sea trade, 43, 46, 50, 52, 58
William of Newburgh, 58, 111
William of Strathgryfe, 196
William of Worcester, 40
Wilton, 221, 225 n. 111
Wiltshire, 55
Winchester, 8, 38, 165
Winchester, earls of (de Quincy), 203
Wintringham, 216
Wogan, John, justiciar of Ireland, 239
Wooden, 225 n. 112
Wooler, 218
Worcester, Worcestershire, 39, 57, 58, 79

Index

Wulfstan II, bishop of Worcester (d. 1095), *see* St Wulfstan
Wye, 118
Wyntoun, Andrew of, 147, 149 n. 51

York, 74 n. 25 168, 207, 209
  Viking influence at, 2, 3, 10, 18, 21, 36, 38, 43

York, archbishops of, 2
York, castle of, 214
York, Vale of, 3
Yorkshire, 83,
  de Vescy property in, 200, 204, 206, 214–19, 222 n. 97, 223, 228, 237
Ysolda daughter of Guy, 222